ALCOHOLISM
and
OTHER DRUG PROBLEMS

A successor to *Alcohol Problems and Alcoholism*

ALCOHOLISM
and
OTHER DRUG PROBLEMS

James E. Royce
and David Scratchley

THE FREE PRESS

THE FREE PRESS
A Division of Simon & Schuster Inc.
1230 Avenue of the Americas
New York, NY 10020

THE FREE PRESS and colophon are trademarks of Simon & Schuster Inc.

Designed by Michael Mendelsohn of MM Design 2000, Inc.

Manufactured in the United States of America

10   9   8   7   6   5   4   3

Library of Congress Cataloging-in-Publication Data

Royce, James E.
    Alcoholism and other drug problems / James E. Royce and David Scratchley.
        p.   cm.
    Rev. ed. of: Alcohol problems and alcoholism. 1989.
    Includes bibliographical references (p.   ) and index.
    ISBN 0-684-82314-4 (hc)
    1. Alcoholism.   2. Drug abuse.   I. Scratchley, David, 1959–.
II. Royce, James E.   Alcohol problems and alcoholism.   III. Title.
RC565.R68   1996   95–44546
362.29'2–dc20   CIP

Previous editions of this work were entitled *Alcohol Problems and Alcoholism*.

*To the many recovering and
recovered persons from whom
we have learned so much.*

Contents

Preface

THE PREDECESSOR to this book, *Alcohol Problems and Alcoholism,* has been expanded to include entirely new chapters on drugs other than alcohol, plus enrichment throughout with fuller treatment by both authors of the facts of cross-addiction and the polydrug culture. Chapter 19 on the spiritual has been rewritten. Other chapters have been updated and purged of older material to maintain usable size.

The new chapters are by David Scratchley, Ph.D., Adjunct Professor of Addiction Studies at Seattle University. He is a psychologist and addiction specialist with training and experience in neurosciences and pharmacology. Chapter 2 depicts the social and Chapter 5 the pharmacological aspects of commonly used legal and illegal drugs.

Rather than left scattered through the General Bibliography, much reference material has been grouped under *Sources* at the ends of chapters, for example the items on Prohibition at Chapter 3, on Prevention and College Programs at Chapter 12, and on Spiritual and Moral Aspects at Chapter 19.

A vast amount of literature exists on the use of alcohol and on alcoholism. Contributions come from a multitude of disciplines, from professionals and from laymen, from objective researchers and from fiery proselytizers. There seems not to be any general survey of the whole field that is suitable as a college textbook, or any integrated formulation that provides the general reader with an overall, balanced understanding. This book is an attempt to fill that double need.

Alcohol use is involved in many more problems than alcoholism. In recent years excessive use of alcohol is more often than not combined with the use of other drugs. Theories of the causes of alcoholism are varied and contradictory, treatments and the goals of treatment are controversial, prevention is still more of a hope than a reality. Vested interests, which range from the alcoholic beverage industry to those who would restore prohibition, try to influence what is thought and done. Research continually uncovers new facts. Amid such a clamor of voices, there is a need for a dispassionate survey and evaluation.

It would be more than naïve to imagine this will be easy. Bitter memories of prohibition, lingering moralistic do-goodism, libertarian resentment of any infringement on one's freedom to drink, alarm at the tragic death toll from alcohol-related accidents and the medical complications of alcoholism, the perennial popularity of drinking songs—all attest to the wide divergence of values placed on the use, excessive or otherwise, of alcoholic beverages. The joys of wine have been praised by poet and psalmist for thousands of years, yet we all feel uncomfortable when passing the skid-road derelict lying in a drunken stupor.

The concept of alcoholism as a disease is looked upon as progress by one group and escape by another. How do we reconcile the disease concept with that of moral responsibility? How are we to discourage premature drinking among youth without putting a premium on drinking as a sign of maturity? These and a dozen other questions challenge our collective wisdom.

One of the most exciting developments has been the recognition by professionals that standard academic courses have not given them expertise in this specialized field; and likewise by recovered alcoholics that the experience of recovery is not enough: Special training and professionally supervised experience are necessary to prepare either to perform effectively in what is being called the "new profession" of alcoholism workers. This book is intended for both groups and is based on experience in working with both.

My interests in the field began in 1942, through discussions with Father Ed Dowling, S.J., a close friend of Bill W. (whose definitive Fifth Step he took) and Dr. Bob, the co-founders of Alcoholics Anonymous. This led to some forty years of counseling alcoholics and their spouses at Seattle University, and to starting in 1950 the oldest college course on alcoholism in the country offered as part of the regular undergraduate curriculum. I am neither a recovered alcoholic nor a prohibitionist, but a teacher with no treatment to sell and no special cause to plead. Always interdisciplinary in approach, the course has, over the years, gained a reputation for broad balance, representing all viewpoints. My hope is that this book can make a real contribution in clarifying concepts and balancing attitudes toward our nation's number-one public health problem.

The subject matter of this book is an exciting field, both because it is gratifying to see alcoholics getting well and because research is bringing us closer to understanding the true nature of addiction. Optimism on both counts, however, is tempered with the reality that we are a long way from 100 percent successful in either venture and, especially, in our efforts at prevention. Naturally, not all has been quite serene, as Jay Lewis (1987)* reminisced in reviewing his fifteen years of writing *The Alcoholism Report*. But, being an optimist, I prefer to focus on the positive, on gains, and can only hope that this present effort contributes to further progress and unity in the field.

Now Professor Emeritus and no longer director, I remain active—and grateful to my many friends and colleagues.

JAMES E. ROYCE, S.J.
Seattle University

---

*For easy reading, only a brief identification of sources is in the text. Full information will be found in the General Bibliography. If there is more than one book or article by the same author published in the same year, they are listed as 1987a, 1987b, and so on.

Acknowledgments

JOAN K. JACKSON, Ph.D., has provided invaluable service as collaborator, contributing to every aspect of the book—especially the bibliographical. James W. Smith, M.D.; Nola Moore, M.D.; and S.E.C. Turvey, M.D., are foremost among the many physicians to whom we are indebted. Of the many others, our former colleagues at Seattle University and our many students of over forty-three years of teaching in the field must be mentioned.

Thanks are due to the following for permission to quote from copyrighted materials:

AA World Services, Inc.

American Journal of Psychiatry

Annals of Internal Medicine

Hazelden Publications, Inc.

Journal of Studies on Alcohol

National Council on Alcoholism and Drug Dependence, Inc.

Dr. Ann P. Streissguth, of the Pregnancy and Health project at the University of Washington (for the photographs of FAS Children)

PART ONE

ALCOHOL
and
OTHER DRUGS

CHAPTER 1

Alcohol and Alcohol Problems

MOST ARE AWARE that drugs are a major factor in our biggest social problems: violence, crime, poverty, AIDS, family disintegration—but many do not think of alcohol as a drug at all, only as a social beverage. We shall see that alcohol causes immense problems, of which alcoholism is only one. (The other drugs are dealt with in Chapters 2 and 5.)

The facts about alcohol are distorted by our emotionally charged attitudes toward drinking, drunkenness, and alcoholism. Those attitudes are the result of many factors: family situation, sociocultural experience, biological differences, prohibition, differing religious beliefs, and political, economic, and personal feelings unique to each individual. Obvious as they may seem, we must spell out some distinctions that are ignored in most arguments on the subject.

Drinking. Abstinence from alcohol is the opposite of drinking. Technically anyone who drinks alcoholic beverages, however rarely and moderately, is a drinker. About 60 percent of Americans over eighteen drink at least occasionally (down from 71 percent a dozen years ago); most are neither drunkards nor alcoholics. In fact, about 11 percent of drinkers consume 68 percent of our beverage alcohol, whereas many of those technically classed as drinkers have only a New Year's toast or the like. Less than half of American "drinkers" use alcohol more than once a month.

Drunkenness. Temperance is the opposite of drunkenness. In Chapter 3 we shall see how the prohibitionists created untold confusion by assuming that everyone who drinks is a drunkard. Actually, anybody can get drunk on a given occasion; they might not even be a drinker in the usual sense of the term. To the naïve guest at a wedding reception or the person honored at a retirement banquet, the champagne seems much like ginger ale; a subsequent arrest for driving while intoxicated is not presumptive of alcoholism. However, intoxication even by nonalcoholics is a major source of both civil and criminal problems: battered spouses and children, rape, fights, homicides, unwanted pregnancies, poor health, suicides, lawsuits, family disruptions, job loss, and a sizable share of accidents—not only traffic but also home, boat, small plane, and industrial. The degree of intoxication need not be that required to be legally drunk, as we shall see in Chapter 4, Section B.

Alcoholism. Alcoholism is the state of a person whose excessive use of alcohol creates serious life problems. An alcoholic may never get drunk, as in the Delta type (maintenance drinker) common in France and described in Chapter 6. They may not even drink, as in the case of the 2 million or so recovered alcoholics who still identify themselves as such (Chapter 8).

Alcoholics

In most minds, the word alcoholic conjures up an image of a skid-road bum. Yet only about 3 percent of alcoholics are on skid road. (Incidentally, Skid Road is the original term, named for Yesler Way in Seattle, where logs were skidded down to Yesler's mill; skid row is a later version, by analogy with Cannery Row.)

What kinds of people are alcoholics? Alcoholics may be young or old, male or female, black or white, banker or bum, genius or mentally retarded. A large body of research data has accumulated on this subject, and there have been intensive educational efforts to make these facts known to the public. Yet the old stereotypes persist and must be dealt with before any meaningful discussion of alcoholism can occur.

Skid Road? It is essential to eradicate right now the stereotype of the alcoholic as a skid-road, old, male, weak-willed, inferior derelict. If 3 percent of alcoholics are on skid road, the other 97 percent of American alcoholics have jobs, homes, and families. About 45 percent of alcoholics are in professional and managerial positions, 25 percent are white-collar workers, and 30 percent are manual laborers. Over half have attended college; only 13 percent have not finished high school. No suggestion of skid road there. Physicians, brokers, attorneys, judges, dentists, and clergymen all have a high incidence of alcohol problems.

Instead of being inferior, the average intelligence of alcoholics is slightly above that of comparable groups—for example, compared with other employees in their company. Alcoholics also appear to be superior in talent and sensitivity. Hence it is not mere emotional loyalty that prompts a spouse or foreman to assert that their alcoholic is "the finest" when not drinking. That is important, because both alcoholic and spouse tend to deny the problem by saying that the person is too intelligent to be an alcoholic.

Weak Will? Anyone with experience in the field can testify that when an alcoholic needs a drink there is no one on earth with a stronger will: They will get a drink come hell, high water, or prohibition. The notion of weak-willed moral depravity rather than a compulsive disorder stems from the days before alcoholism was accepted as a disease by the World Health Organization and important national professional associations.

Mentally Ill? The notion that a typical alcoholic is a person who drinks to escape from some inner conflict raises a complex question that is addressed in Chapters 7 and 8. Suffice it to say here that research now shows that about 80 percent of alcoholics are normal personalities who began drinking for the same reasons as anybody else: custom, sociability, relaxation, or just to feel good.

Male? The ratio of men to women alcoholics is often still reported as four or five to one. That is probably due to the double standard in our society regarding women and drunkenness. Women alcoholics are often better able to hide their drinking at home (though in the business world they may be more exposed than men) and, in any case, are not as likely to be counted by the fact-gatherers. Even when they die of alcoholism, the diagnosis is written as a total liver failure or something similar, because the doctor is a gentleman and it's not ladylike to be an alcoholic. Hence the statistics are questionable. If the truth were known, the ratio of male to female alcoholics in this country is probably fifty-fifty, an opinion shared by such national authorities as M. Block, L. Cloud, R. G. Bell, R. Fox, M. Mann, M. Nellis, and M. Chafetz. (Since English just does not have a suitable pronoun for the clumsy he/she or her/his, our use of pronouns in this book is not taken as sexist but is simply due to the inadequacy of our language.)

Old? One does not have to drink heavily for thirty or forty years in order to develop alcoholism. More than a million American teenagers have serious alcohol problems. There are full-blown alcoholics who are eight or nine years old. A visitor at open AA meetings will frequently hear, "I was an alcoholic at the time I took my first drink." Although this evidence is subjective, it is in accord with scientific findings that up to 60 percent of alcoholics are such from the onset of drinking.

Alcohol as a Drug

We reject the phrase "alcohol and drugs" because it implies that alcohol is not a drug. We insist on "alcohol and other drugs." Is alcohol really a drug? Yes, in every sense of the word. Alcohol can produce all the classic signs of addiction: changes in tolerance (the need of more alcohol to get the same effect), cellular adaptation or tissue change, and withdrawal. Chemically very similar to ether and chloroform, alcohol is a sedative, a hypnotic, a tranquilizer, a narcotic, and sometimes a hallucinogenic. For centuries it was our only anesthetic, although for practical reasons a very poor one. If it were not dangerously addictive, it would be hailed as the world's greatest tranquilizer. It is most like the barbiturates, except for three important differences:

1. *Stimulant or depressant?* Both. Alcohol is perhaps the only common drug that gives a lift or stimulates before acting as a sedative or depressant. Some of the latter results from the depression of inhibitory centers in the brain. But the initial effect of alcohol on tissue is to irritate or agitate or stimulate, as well as to provide quick caloric energy. Some research evidence indicates that this is more true for alcoholics than for others, perhaps right from the beginning of their drinking careers; and it is this initial stimulation that many beginning alcoholics seem to look for rather than the later sedative effect. (See Chapter 4, Section B.)

2. *Selective addiction.* The reason why alcohol is often not thought of as a drug is that, in contrast to other drugs, it becomes addictive to only one in ten of its users. Most people drink moderately all their lives, with perhaps an occasional drunk. Why only some drinkers become addicted to alcohol is not known for certain; we shall examine this question when we deal with causality. The fact that alcohol seems safe for most people makes it harder to accept that it is a dangerous drug for a minority of 10 million to 12 million, making alcohol by far the biggest problem drug in America. The important thing here is that people differ in their reaction to alcohol.

3. *Socially acceptable.* One is tempted to call alcoholism a respectable addiction. Millions of people casually invite friends in for a drink who would be horrified at hearing "Come over tonight and we'll shoot a little heroin, or drop a few barbs." Even when there is misuse, we pass it off lightly or with minor embarrassment, perhaps with the remark that everybody has a few too many once in a while. How often do we think of drunkenness as a drug overdose? Do we think alcoholic beverages should be in childproof bottles? Serving drinks is a mark of hospitality, and failure to do so smacks of puritanical repressiveness. As a result of such attitudes, even when a friend is in serious trouble with alcohol there is a tendency to minimize or excuse the behavior rather than face the issue of debilitating and even terminal illness. Society feeds the denial of the alcoholic by implying that heroin and cocaine may be dangerous, but not alcohol. Until MADD (Mothers Against Drunk Driving) influenced public opinion, manslaughter by a drinking driver was almost a socially accepted form of homicide.

Definition of Alcoholism

There are nearly as many definitions of alcoholism as there are those who write or lecture on the subject. Why bother to define? There are many reasons. The alcoholism worker must have a definition that will stand up in court under cross-examination, whether alcoholism is being used as a defense or as grounds for involuntary commitment. The counselor must be able to proffer a definition that will induce the client to accept treatment and that will be neither so loose nor so rigid that clients can say in their denial, "That doesn't apply to me!" (In this vein, an alcoholic is said to define alcoholism as a disease that others get.) If insurance companies are going to pay health benefits for treatment, they are going to demand a strict definition of the object of their dollars. Physicians need solid criteria for making a diagnosis. Some of the fallacies occurring in the controversy about conditioning alcoholics to drink socially stem from dubious definitions of who is an alcoholic. Industrial alcoholism programs need to be precise in order to protect the rights of both labor and management. Defining alcoholism as a disease has moved it from the criminal justice system and the jail drunk tank to the health care system and treatment centers. It is crucial to any prevention campaign.

Problems in Definition

A good definition must be coterminous with what is being defined. A definition of alcoholism as "a horrible disease that affects the whole person" is unacceptable, because it is so broad it can apply to cancer or schizophrenia. Conversely, to define alcoholism in terms of one type of alcoholic is likewise unsatisfactory, because it misses many other types of alcoholics. Alcoholics cannot be defined as those who get drunk every time they drink, nor as those with a prolonged history of drinking, nor as those who crave alcohol, nor as those with any other single symptom.

A common fallacy is to define alcoholism by the amount or the beverage consumed. "He only drinks beer" ignores the fact that the same alcohol is present in the most expensive liquor and in the cheapest beer or wine. At an upper-class hospital for alcoholics 15 percent of the patients have never drunk anything but beer. People in Australia, New Zealand, and other countries with an incidence of alcoholism as high as that in America drink beer ("grog") as their primary source of alcohol. Yet our laws and our advertising still imply a difference.

The amount of alcohol drunk combined with the frequency of drinking (quantity/frequency index) is also a misleading way to define alcoholism. Because of individual differences some alcoholics might actually drink less than some nonalcoholics. Average consumption per week or month means nothing. An Italian might spread out fourteen ounces of absolute alcohol per week as wine and not be alcoholic, while an American alcoholic might consume the same amount of absolute alcohol in the form of a quart of 86 proof whiskey each Saturday night with total intoxication. More important than how much one drinks is the question of how one drinks. Moreover, alcoholics either lie about the amount they drink or just don't remember.

Some define an alcoholic as one who cannot predict what will happen after one drink. But one can think of many alcoholics who can predict exactly what will happen. (True, most alcoholics cannot predict consistently or accurately.)

Some define alcoholism as drinking alcoholic beverages in excess of customary dietary usage or social use of the community. This confuses average with normal. In a "dry" Southern town one beer on a hot day would exceed custom, but that is hardly alcoholism. In a north Alaska village, where every adult male gets drunk every weekend, the mere fact that this is customary usage does not preclude the presence of alcoholism.

A Working Definition

We define alcoholism as *a chronic primary illness or disorder characterized by some loss of control over drinking, with habituation or addiction to the drug alcohol, or causing interference in any major life function, for example: health, job, family, friends, legal, or spiritual.*

1. *Some* loss of control is involved, but it need not be total. Most alcoholics can take one or two drinks under certain circumstances without getting drunk, but that does not prove they are not alcoholic. Sooner or later they are in trouble again. Total loss of control is usually seen only in late-stage, deteriorated alcoholics. Loss of consistent control is sufficient for diagnosis. The loss can be over how much they drink, or over when they drink, or both. One may not get drunk, but drinking more than one intends or drinking at inappropriate times would indicate alcoholism.

2. *Dependence or need* can be either psychological or physiological. Psychological dependence or need is *habituation* (discussed in Chapters 4 and 7). As the poster slogan says, "If you have to drink to be social, that's not social drinking." Discomfort if deprived of alcohol and inability to quit on one's own are symptoms, even if no physical need is apparent. Physiological dependence or need is *addiction*, with its familiar signs of increased tolerance initially, cellular adaption, and withdrawal symptoms. One physically needs a drink to function. *DSM-III-R* distinguished abuse from alcoholism largely by using the notion of dependence.

    The tendency in America is to focus on addiction and to dismiss habituation as "only" psychological need. Yet in every respect except the physical dangers of withdrawal, psychological dependence can be more devastating. To appreciate this one has only to look at the way compulsive gambling can destroy a family. Cocaine causes no physical withdrawal, yet it fulfills all the other parts of the definition; nobody would deny it is very addictive. And marijuana users are coming to treatment centers in increasing numbers, saying that they want to quit and can't—obviously addiction.

3. *Interference with normal functioning.* The interference must be notable or habitual, to exclude the case of the turned ankle from one drink. This is the least subjective criterion and closest to an operational or behavioral definition. It can be quantified for research purposes, which is why it is the major factor in *DSM-IV,* **303.90** (American Psychiatric Association, 1994). For example, anybody can be arrested for drunk driving

once, but three DUIs (Driving Under the Influence) in the same year suggest alcoholism. Likewise if drinking is involved in more than one fight where there is serious injury or a lethal weapon is used. Social disruption and health damage may be very different measures, but both are valid.

This last element complements the earlier parts of the definition, because the fact that one continues to drink after he has been told his health or marriage or job is endangered would indicate dependence and some loss of control; otherwise why continue? "Chronic" means enduring, something that can be arrested but not cured. The complex physical, psychosocial, and spiritual nature of this illness will be explored in Chapters 7 and 8. At least it seems that continuing to drink in spite of such unwanted consequences is sick behavior.

Our definition seems quite congruent with that developed by a joint Committee of the National Council on Alcoholism and Drug Dependence and the American Society of Addiction Medicine (NCADD/ASAM Joint Committee, 1992), which, like that in *DSM-IV,* is more a clinically useful description than a strict definition. Leaving detailed symptoms to Chapter 6, let us round out our definition by noting three common errors in diagnosis:

1. Joe can drink anybody under the table. He is not safe, but rather in serious danger. Increased tolerance, the ability to function with higher than average amounts of alcohol in the bloodstream, is the first sign of physical addiction.
2. Cutting down or quitting drink for a period of time (going on the water wagon) is not proof that one has it under control. Most do not realize that this is a classic symptom of alcoholism. The true social drinker does not need to play games of control.
3. The assertion, "I can take it or leave it alone," especially when made often or with vehemence, is usually indicative of denial and betrays the alcoholic. The social drinker doesn't feel compelled to say such things. This subtle self-deception is so characteristic that we have long defined an alcoholic as "one who says I can quit any time I want to."

Primary Versus Secondary Alcoholism

The terms primary and secondary have acquired ambiguous and even contrary or reversed meanings. Some old medical literature even uses the term "acute alcoholism" to refer to any severe intoxication. In this book we shall use primary when the alcoholism is the basic pathology, regardless of cause ("essential alcoholism"), and secondary to refer to alcoholism as a symptom of some other disorder ("reactive alcoholism"). Remove the alcohol, and you will find anything: normal people, neurotics, sociopaths, mentally retarded, psychotics. Any psychopathology may then be either the cause of the alcoholism or the effect of the alcoholic drinking on the brain.

Alcoholic Versus Problem Drinker

Scientific researchers like W. Madsen, D. Cahalan, and S. Bacon rightly insist that to gather meaningful and comparable data one must have an operational, quantifiable definition that guarantees consistency as to which cases are counted as alcoholics and which are not. But clinicians and field workers often find it advantageous to ignore such precision and not to allow themselves to get trapped into games of labeling or arguments about whether a client is or is not an alcoholic. There is a general tendency to use the term *alcoholic* when loss of control and dependence are stressed, and *problem drinker* when the emphasis is on consequences. There is no standard or sacrosanct terminology here. One could argue the pros and cons of even dropping the term *alcoholic* entirely:

Con. In view of the great progress that has been made in the last few decades to eliminate the social stigma attached to alcoholism, it would seem a strategic mistake to reverse the trend. Dropping the term would cause the alcoholism movement, after having espoused the term, to lose face before the medical profession, the courts, and the insurance companies. There would be a loss in continuity of research. It might feed the denial system of some alcoholics, encouraging them to delude themselves into attempts at social drinking. It would take the focus off alcohol as our major drug: The alcoholic beverage industry would be delighted to have NCADD change its name to "National Council on Chemical Dependency." A major loss would be the sense of identity that people feel within the fellowship of Alcoholics Anonymous.

Pro. Yet dropping the term would have its advantages. In spite of progress, alcoholism is still odious in the minds of many. Some wish to name it Jellinek's disease, as we now call leprosy Hansen's disease. The stereotype of the skid-road derelict or the "fallen woman" prostitute and the suggestion of insanity still cling to the word, making early detection more difficult and fostering a defeatism or sense of hopelessness not warranted by current success rates in rehabilitation.

For alcoholics in the denial stage the term raises their defenses, and many an initial interview goes smoother if there is no attempt to hang the label "alcoholic" on a new client but just an effort to explore calmly together whether drink is causing some problems. If the client later wishes to label himself, perhaps in an AA meeting, the victory was well worth the tactic. (AA members working in the field too often take for granted the ease with which the word is used among them now and forget how defensive they were in the denial phase, or how painful it was the first time to say "I am an alcoholic.")

Dropping the term might make it easier to sell a program to industry and might lessen the denial or defensiveness of the spouse and family by making them less self-conscious. Alcohol education would be easier and more positive, with less scare tactics centered around alcoholism. Traffic problems and court referrals might be handled more easily if alcoholism were brought into the picture under a different name.

The change might even stimulate a fresh, innovative approach to research. Alcoholism is not a single disease entity like TB or malaria, and cross-cultural differences further confuse the issue. Data might be more objectively gathered from emergency hospitals and police stations if not contaminated by subjective perceptions of alcoholism, as in one study where the physician missed the diagnosis half the time if the patient was well-dressed and not unkempt. Last and perhaps most important, the connotations of the term alcoholic prevent many women from being properly diagnosed, which not only yields misleading statistics but keeps those women from getting the help they need.

What to do? As in many aspects of this field, there is no clear answer. We reject outright the term *substance abuse,* because it suggests behavioral choice rather than compulsive disease. This is not just "political correctness" but avoids putting those recovering from a disease in the same category with child abusers or sexual abusers. Both *DSM-IV* and the title of the National Institute on Alcohol Abuse and Alcoholism (NIAAA) distinguish between abuse and alcoholism. *Chemical dependency* is better, but like "substance" it detracts from the fact that alcohol is our biggest drug problem. We prefer *alcohol and other drug addiction.*

Extent of Alcohol Problems

(For fuller discussion of this topic see Royce, *Alcohol Problems and Alcoholism*, Chapter 2 and references therein.)

Alcohol causes more significant problems than all other drugs combined. Alcohol kills over five times more people each year than all illegal drugs together (*JAMA*, 1993, 270: 2207–12). We now know that a great number of deaths once attributed to accidents and to physical illnesses such as heart or liver failure, acute pancreatitis, internal hemorrhaging, and the like should really be counted as alcohol deaths. And there is clear evidence that alcohol contributes to the causality of cancer. Yet even reasonably well-informed people do not realize the extent to which alcohol use and misuse pervade every aspect of American life: social, economic, political, medical, legal, historical, moral, and emotional. Smoking is now considered our number-one cause of death, but smoking rarely causes one to cross the highway center line to wipe out a carload of innocent people, or a man to beat up his wife. So alcohol can still be ranked as our number one *public* health problem drug.

Estimating Is Difficult. Lengthy treatises—to some more boring than the statistics themselves—have been written about the problems involved in trying to compile accurate figures on alcoholism. Vagueness of definition and a lack of standard criteria for alcoholism are complicated by our society's emotional attitudes toward the misuse of alcohol and consequent tendencies to gloss over it. Some apparent increases in the estimates of the numbers of alcoholics are no doubt merely a reflection of better methods of case finding and reporting, along with the new willingness to face alcohol problems openly and without disguise, especially among women.

Estimates of the extent of alcohol abuse based on arrests and court convictions can be misleadingly low. Arresting officers will often settle for lesser charges, such as reckless driving, because there is a better chance of proving the charge in court. More severe penalties tend to predispose a jury toward acquittal. In 1984 three groups of Midwest pathologists claimed that their autopsies showed 91 percent of auto deaths were alcohol-related.

Often neglected in such discussions are the figures from the National Safety Council and other sources on the role of alcohol in death and injury other than by automobile. Other types of alcohol-related accidents should not be ignored: home, boat, fire, drownings, suicides, and a high percentage of fatal crashes in airplanes other than commercial or military. Thus one-third of industrial and home accidents, 25 percent of ski accidents, 19 percent of bicycle accidents, and an estimated 75 percent of boat and small plane deaths and injuries occur after drinking. Commercial pilots are rigidly monitored, but the Federal Aviation Administration (FAA) has no effective means of checking private planes. People who are used to boats and are around them all the time don't fall off and drown in the wee hours because they have been drinking milk all Saturday night. Not drunk nor an alcoholic, the man who has a few beers before climbing the ladder to paint his house may dull his sense of balance just enough to cause a broken neck, but it will not be reported as alcohol-related.

Rates on per capita consumption of alcohol do not necessarily reveal rates of alcoholism. Orthodox Jews, Greeks, and wine-drinking southern Italians have low rates of alcoholism (not zero, as is mistakenly thought) but relatively high rates of alcohol consumption. Some Scandinavian and other northern countries have high rates of alcoholism without overall per capita consumption of alcohol ranking equally high. High consumption rates for convention and vacation cities do not necessarily mean high alcoholism rates for the local citizens.

Another irritation is that statistics on rates of alcoholism among adults do not use a uniform age base. Some figures are based on all people over twenty-one, others on those over twenty, and some on those over eighteen or even fifteen—making comparisons difficult. Lastly, since research takes time to compile and this is a rapidly changing field, the latest figures are bound to be obsolete before the ink is dry.

Methods of Estimating. One method of estimating the percentage of alcoholics in a given population was the formula developed by E. M. Jellinek

(Haggard and Jellinek, 1942) based on deaths from cirrhosis of the liver. Jellinek (1959) himself repudiated the formula. Polling physicians, social workers, and clergymen regarding the prevalence of alcoholism in their clientele may not be very reliable, but it is useful to uncover those who do not get counted in data from agencies explicitly designated as serving alcoholics. Sociological surveys of drinking practices and alcohol problems, using methods like those of Cahalan, Room, and associates, are perhaps the most realistic approach. Community surveys, especially longitudinal studies that follow a group over a long period of time (e.g., Fillmore, 1988; Vaillant, 1983), are the most expensive but the best source of data when properly designed and administered. Even here, getting a representative cross-section for one's sample and standardizing criteria for comparison with other groups present nearly insurmountable problems, while adequate followup may require dogged (and expensive) detective work.

With all the above cautions in mind, we shall summarize the literature to substantiate our assertion that alcohol is a large factor in American life and a major cause of problems. For the reasons given, very few statistics here are more than estimates, but the expertise of social scientists is such that they are on guard against pitfalls and skilled in acquiring the most accurate data possible. It is better to lean toward the conservative side, lest we lose credibility. We must resist the temptation to inflate figures in order to impress either the public or legislators, though this becomes a crucial issue when funds are being allotted. Youngsters especially may not believe us on *anything* if they catch us in even *one* exaggerated statement.

Number of Alcoholics

In 1993 NCADD put the figure at 12.1 million. Using our working definition but applying it conservatively, one can say as a rule of thumb that alcoholics constitute 4 percent of the general population. In an adult population where at least three-fourths are drinkers, about 6 percent of the total group are probably alcoholic. In groups where practically all are drinkers, as in certain professions or types of work, the alcoholism rate may run about 8 percent, or one in twelve. If we include alcohol abusers as well as alcoholics, the best estimate is 10.5 percent of working Americans.

Those percentages vary markedly by locality and ethnic background, so the chances of developing alcoholism if you drink are not always one in twelve. They may be 1 percent for some and 90 percent for others. These are averages, which can be very misleading when applied to individuals, just as the concept of average temperature is meaningless if we talk about a man with his head in the refrigerator and his feet in the stove.

Among Americans, Eskimos and then other Native Americans seem to rank highest, followed by blacks, Irish, Poles, and those of Scandinavian origin. But again, generalizations are unwarranted. For example, upper-class blacks have less per capita alcoholism than whites at the same socioeconomic level. Jews have much more alcoholism than previously thought (see Blaine, 1981), although they still have the lowest rate of alcoholism in spite of a high rate of use.

Comparisons between countries in per capita incidence of alcoholism suffer to an even larger extent from all the research difficulties presented earlier in this chapter. Definitions, methods, samples, and survey objectives differ so widely that one despairs of any valid rankings. International figures and comparisons are difficult at best (Helzer and Canino, 1992). The United States and France top all lists, followed, usually in varied order, by Chile, England-Wales, Ireland, some Sandinavian countries, Canada, and Australia. It is a mistake to lump all of Italy together; rates among wine-drinking southern Italians have traditionally been reported as low, whereas industrialized northern Italy shows high rates now. The Irish in America have a higher incidence than the Irish in Ireland. Russia and Poland have very high rates; it was difficult to get accurate figures from behind the Iron Curtain, but the Kremlin's strong crackdown on alcohol in 1985 did reveal a widespread and severe problem. There has been a sharp rise in alcoholism in Japan in the last decade or so, especially in Tokyo. China has more than a billion people scattered over a vast area: to generalize about the Chinese seems vapid, as there must be wide differences in their use of and reaction to alcohol. Whereas the problems may be leveling off in some industrialized nations, the World Health Organization (WHO) says they are increasing in the developing countries.

Other Victims, Other Problems

Alcohol causes more than alcoholism. If each alcoholic affects the lives of four or five others—spouse, children, employer, employee, innocent victim of accident, or other—then our 12.1 million alcoholics have an impact on 40 to 50 million others for a total of about 60 million citizens. The president of a state association of judges stated that "90 to 95 percent of all the cases that come before my bench—civil, criminal and family—involve alcohol." Alcohol may not be the sole cause, but is a part-cause in much juvenile delinquency, illegitimate pregnancy, truancy, and fights. Numerous reports indicate that about 73 percent of felonies are alcohol-related. A survey of the literature shows that in about 67 percent of child-beating cases, 41 percent of forcible rape cases, 80 percent of wife-battering, 72 percent of stabbings, and 83 percent of homicides, either the attacker or the victim or both had been drinking. Hard to research, incest is now coming out in the open; one report estimates as high as 90 percent of incest may be alcohol-related. Alcohol accentuates depression, and reports indicate a range of 30 to 80 percent of suicides as alcohol-related (Murphy, 1992). As high as 45 percent of our social welfare aid in categories like Aid to Dependent Children, and 60 percent of "mental cruelty" divorce cases, have been estimated as associated with alcohol and other drugs, which is the primary complaint in one-third of all broken marriages (see Parker and Rebhun, 1995; Pernanen, 1991).

Traffic. Automobile crashes in the United States kill nearly as many people each year as the total of 46,483 American soldiers killed in the entire dozen years of the Vietnam War. (Why no protest parades about that?) Including the drinking pedestrian, alcohol is involved in about 46 percent of those fatalities. Not all of the drinking drivers are alcoholics; some of them were not even legally drunk. Short of death, the cost from traffic crashes in broken bones, permanent disabilities, hospital bills, and auto repairs is staggering—a total of $46 billion in a 1992 NHTSA estimate.

Cost. Money may not be the most important value, but it is a useful measure to help grasp the size of alcohol problems (see Berry and Boland, 1977; Cook, 1984; Fein, 1984; Grant and Ritson, 1983). We complain about the high cost of life's necessities, yet we Americans spend $71.9 billion (more than $197 million a day, $8.2 million an hour) on taxable alcoholic beverages, plus an untold amount on bootleg liquor (about 24 million gallons) and home brew. And $60 billion more goes to pick up the pieces: health care, motor vehicle accident losses, fire losses, losses caused by violent crime, social programs responding to the problems created by alcoholism, and loss to business and industry. Total losses to the nation from alcohol problems and alcoholism were estimated at $116.7 billion in 1982 by Research Triangle Institute, $120 billion in 1983 by the U.S. General Accounting Office, $142 billion in 1986 by the University of California at Berkeley School of Health, 136 billion in 1990 by NIAAA, and $148 billion in 1993 by MADD.

About 29.2 percent of our liquor bill goes to federal and local taxes, more than $10 billion a year. Obviously this is not enough to pay for the loss, even if the whole alcohol tax went into programs instead of only the one-twentieth that actually does. Yet treatment and rehabilitation could turn a large number of alcoholics from tax liabilities into taxpayers; one Seattle treatment center claims that the recovered alcoholics it returned to society as wage earners paid more than $100,000 in taxes in one year. A cost/benefit study by NIAAA shows that for every dollar spent in treatment there would be three dollars in benefits returned to the nation. Yet in some states a public welfare recipient gets more from the state if he continues drinking than is paid to a rehabilitation center if he tries to stop. Families seem to get even less help than alcoholics.

The Immeasurables. We cannot measure in dollars the value of lost human lives, wrecked families, deteriorated personalities, suicides, reduced quality of life, and human misery. We cannot ever know the impact of all this deep inside a spouse or child. Statistics ignore individuals: Even one alcoholic in your family is one too many. We talk of "victimless crimes," but here we are all victims, and especially the alcoholic.

This also answers the question, "Is it any of your business if I drink?" If you pay taxes and insurance premiums, it is indeed your business. As our number-one *public* health problem, alcohol misuse adds enormously to the cost of living for all of us. In addition, the life of everyone who gets into a car is threatened by drinking drivers. Alcohol impinges on almost every aspect of our lives.

Sources

Full identification of sources cited in the text will be found in the General Bibliography. Listing there does not mean full agreement; the reader must decide on particular points. The principal scholarly journals are listed at the beginning of the General Bibliography. Much material in this relatively new field, of varying quality, is to be found in semipopular pamphlets and books, many of them in paperback, produced by the publishers listed in the Appendix. No attempt is made to list the many biographies and autobiographies of recovered persons, though these are especially useful for those who are not alcoholics themselves.

Penny B. Page (1986) compiled *Alcohol Use and Alcoholism: A Guide to the Literature.* Kaye M. Fillmore (1988) has produced *Alcohol Use Across the Life Course: A Critical Review of 70 Years of International Longitudinal Research.* Other important sources are SALIS (Substance Abuse Librarians—see Appendix); the Classified Abstract Archives of Alcohol Literature (CAAAL), initiated at Yale and continued by the Rutgers Center of Alcohol Studies in New Brunswick, NJ; and the bibliographical search service provided by the National Clearinghouse for Alcohol and Drug Information (NCADI) in Rockville, MD. In Canada, the Addiction Research Foundation (ARF) in Toronto has done extensive bibliographical work.

Computer search can be accessed via ETOH at NCADI, or *Medline,* or *Psychinfo,* or the Project Cork database at Dartmouth Medical School, or Drug Information Services (DIS) at the University of Minnesota College of Pharmacy. This last and many databases are available through BRS Information Technologies at 800-468-0908. Since items on this topic are widely scattered in other scientific, medical, and social science journals, consult *Index Medicus* (including the "Medical Reviews" section, which often cites valuable review articles) and the annual or volume index of the journals.

EXTENT OF ALCOHOL PROBLEMS

In view of all the difficulties mentioned in the chapter, plus the inevitable lag between fact gathering and publishing, it is obviously impossible to give current figures. In addition to the sources cited that are listed in the General Bibliography (e.g., the Berry and Boland study), the following are useful founts of statistical information: *The Bottom Line,* the Center for Science in the Public Interest (Washington, DC); DISCUS (Distilled Spirits Council of the U.S., Washington, DC); the Gallup polls; NCADD; National Highway Traffic Safety Administration (NHTSA, U.S. Department of Transportation, Washington, DC); NCADI and NIAAA *Special Population Issues;* Research Triangle Institute (Research Triangle Park, NC 27709), U.S. General Accounting Office; U.S. Public Health Service; Dr. Robin Room and Dr. Don Cahalan at the University of California at Berkeley; and the *Wall Street Journal.*

CHAPTER 2

Drugs Other than Alcohol

C LEARLY, drugs other than alcohol are misused in the United States (frequently in conjunction with alcohol). A brief overview reveals the scope of the problem and its alarming impact on society (Kelly, Foltin, and Fischman, 1990). It is estimated that three-fourths of all foster children in this country are from families with drug- or alcohol-dependent parents. A quarter of all deaths in the United States involve alcohol, tobacco, and/or other drugs. Of the more than 1 million prisoners in the United States, over half are incarcerated for drug offenses. Fifty percent of all workplace fatalities involve drug and alcohol abuse (Lehman and Simpson, 1990). Add to the figures from Chapter 1 on alcohol a 1987 NIDA estimate of $80 billion in losses from the misuse of illegal drugs, on which Americans spent a staggering $140 billion in 1988, more than $60 billion on cocaine alone. One physician who had called marijuana and cocaine "harmless recreational drugs" in 1977 publicly retracted in 1987, saying they are "viciously addictive" and physically very damaging.

With those shocking statistics, few people would deny that America's drug problem is out of control. How to manage this drug problem, however, is at the center of a vigorous public policy debate. Society is divided on the issue. Some call for more emphasis on treatment. Others attack the current methods of treating chemical dependency as ineffective or too costly. Still others argue that legalizing drugs is the best way to gain control over their use. The use of psychoactive substances has historically been a target of regulation by many governments, and public concern over the use of drugs is nothing new in the United States or in other countries. Movements to control the use of drugs like cocaine and the opiates have occurred repeatedly over the last hundred years.

In many instances, the decision to regulate a drug reflects a society's response to the impact of the drug on its values and the health of its members. This decision also reflects the attitudes and customs of the culture. Often the decision to regulate a drug can be seen as creating a double standard. In the United States, for example, many laws have been created to control drugs like heroin and cocaine. The authors of those laws frequently cite the dangers the drugs present to society. Yet, despite the devastating consequences of tobacco use, efforts to pass laws related to the control of tobacco use frequently encounter stiff opposition. An important means of understanding drugs, including alcohol, is to examine the culture, values, and history of the people who use them.

We have already had occasion to mention the difficulties inherent in the first World Health Organization (WHO) definition of alcoholism as drinking that exceeds the customary dietary usage of a community. Any norm based on custom rather than on a drug and its effect on the organism is bound to be troublesome, since customs differ so widely among cultures. Moreover, guilt feelings will vary widely, depending on divergent moral values. The problems might be similar in different countries, but how they are perceived is an important factor affecting what is done about them. Attitudes are reflected in our language: "weed" in the slums becomes "grass" in upper suburbia. Drugs other than alcohol differ in toxicity, pharmacology, withdrawal times, and speed of addiction, but the difference between alcoholics and other addicts is often mostly sociocultural: "hippie" versus "straight."

Opiates

For more than six thousand years, the opium poppy (*Papaver somniferum*) has been harvested for the potent opiates contained in its seed pod. In its year-long life cycle, this annual grows 3½ to 4 feet tall and produces flowers with large flimsy petals in colors of purple, red, pink, or white. As the petals drop off, a seed pod matures. Harvesters move through the fields slicing the pods prior to maturation to release a milky, opiate-laced resin. Overnight, the sap dries to form a ruddy resin. This resin, called opium, contains approximately 10 percent morphine and 0.5 percent codeine, along with a mixture of proteins, sugars, and oils.

The use of the crude opium extract for medicinal and recreational purposes has an ancient history. Indigenous to Asia Minor, the plant found its way into use by a number of Mediterranean cultures. The harvesting of opium by scraping seed pods and collecting extrudate has been found documented on Assyrian cuneiform tablets prepared sometime around 700 B.C. Hippocrates (born circa 400 B.C.) was known to use opium medicinally, and Galen, another early Greek physician (born circa A.D. 140), noted the sale of opium cakes and sweets in Greece (Scott, 1969). As the Roman empire increased in scope and influence, the medicinal use of opiates waned. Opiates were neglected by Western medicine for the next thousand years. To the East, however, opiates had more than a thousand years of use in Arabic cultures, which scientifically characterized opium and its medical usages. Traveling with Muslim explorers and traders, opium poppy seeds were sold and planted throughout India and China.

Arabic physicians were responsible for rekindling interest in opium within Europe when they established the School of Salerno in Sicily during the twelfth century. The renewed interest in the medicinal use of opium suffered a setback with the emergence of the plague. It was not until 1525 that Paracelsus, a noted European physician, introduced a "miracle drug" called laudanum, a mixture of opiates and alcohol! Laudanum drinking caught on, and soon a variety of new opium-containing mixtures were being used throughout Europe.

Opium smoking, a favored means of administering the drug, originated in China. Although opium had been used in China since sometime around A.D. 1000, for hundreds of years users there had eaten it, and acceptance of opium was limited. In contrast, tobacco smoking, which was introduced to China much later than opium, caught on quickly—so quickly, in fact, that by 1644 tobacco smoking was forbidden in China. As those restrictions reduced the availability of tobacco, the practice of smoking was modified to incorporate opium in place of tobacco. Smoking opium, which produces a rapid delivery of opium into the bloodstream with pronounced effects, quickly gained popularity. Early in the eighteenth century China enacted laws to prohibit the nonmedicinal use of opium, which made the smuggling of opium a profitable industry. Supplied by the British through a complicated pipeline, Chinese merchants continued to smuggle opium into China. By 1839, tensions between the Chinese and British over the supply of opium led to the "Opium Wars" (Scott, 1969).

The use of opiates also took hold in the United States. Opium smoking was brought to the United States in the mid-nineteenth century by Chinese laborers. Opiate addiction was already a problem by the time the Chinese arrived, however, because of expanding use in patent medicines. Morphine presented another problem.

Although *morphine* had been isolated in 1806, the full impact of morphine wasn't appreciated until the hypodermic syringe was perfected in 1853. The hypodermic syringe revolutionized drug delivery by allowing the direct administration of morphine into the blood. The utility of morphine and the hypodermic syringe were quickly tested on battlefields around the world, including those of the United States Civil War. Many soldiers returning from combat found themselves addicted. So common was morphine addiction in returning veterans that soon morphine addiction came to be known as the "Soldier's Disease."

Following the epidemic of addiction that resulted from the battlefield use of hypodermically injected morphine, the Bayer Laboratories marketed a substitute for codeine and morphine called *heroin,* which the company claimed was nonaddicting. When used in low doses to produce effects comparable to codeine, heroin's liability for abuse and addiction was minimal. Heroin, however, was in reality two to three times more potent than morphine. Produced by adding acetyl groups to morphine, heroin is significantly more fat-soluble than morphine, which allows it to enter the brain faster, where it is converted back into morphine. The ease with which heroin reaches its targeted tissue sites in the brain makes it more desirable to addicts, who value drugs that provide a rapid onset of action.

By the turn of the century, patent medicines containing alcohol and opiates were commonplace in America, and so was addiction. Addiction to opiates was especially recognized as an increasingly serious problem. Legislation designed to regulate patent medicines was introduced in the Pure Food and Drug Act of 1906. The Harrison Act of 1914 did not block the sale of addictive drugs but did require those drugs to be obtained from registered physicians and the transaction to be recorded. In 1915 it was made illegal to obtain opiates from any other source than a registered physician. By the 1920s doctors were prohibited from prescribing opiates to addicts to treat addiction.

Despite efforts to control the addictive use of heroin and other opiates, it is currently estimated that more than 1.8 million Americans have used heroin at some point in their lives. It is also estimated that more than 300,000 Americans currently use heroin. The heroin used in the United States is produced in Southwest Asia (Afghanistan, Pakistan, and Iran), Southeast Asia (Thailand and Laos), and Mexico. The purity of heroin has steadily increased. In the 1970s and 1980s, most heroin was a mixture of 4–6 percent pure heroin and 94–96 percent cutting agents or filler. In 1990 a "bag" of heroin contained over 36 percent pure heroin (Kaa, 1994). Interestingly, the price of heroin per bag has not increased greatly in the last twenty years. As a result, today's heroin user is getting many times the amount of drug per unit as did the users of twenty years ago.

With the failure of laws designed to eradicate the use of heroin by addicts, other options were explored. In 1964 a study was conducted in New York City to test the efficacy of a long-acting synthetic opiate called *Methadone* (Dolophine). Unlike heroin, which provides four to six hours of relief from the symptoms of physical withdrawal, Methadone is a longer-acting drug that results in a more gradual withdrawal. That is especially important to heroin addicts, who spend most of their time high on heroin or withdrawing from heroin and searching for more. Addicts receiving methadone have more time to engage in normal activities, like holding a job.

The value of methadone depends on one's goal. If the goal of methadone treatment is complete abstinence from opiates, many people receiving methadone will not make the goal. In this sense, methadone maintenance is not a "cure" for addiction. If, on the other hand, the goal of methadone maintenance is to increase productivity and decrease criminal activity, many methadone users will achieve the goal. In addition to methadone maintenance programs, heroin addicts can also seek treatment in therapeutic communities, where the addict undergoes detoxification and then receives counseling and support, or in supportive 12-Step groups like Narcotics Anonymous, which is patterned after Alcoholics Anonymous.

Stimulants

The South American coca plant is the source of the potent behavioral stimulant and local anesthetic *cocaine*. For centuries, the leaves of coca plants have been chewed by natives of Bolivia, Peru, and Colombia for their stimulant, mood-enhancing properties (Weil, 1995). The active ingredient in the leaves is cocaine. Cocaine is isolated from the leaves by mashing them in an organic solution like kerosene. This produces a paste, which can be dried and purified into a white powder to be snorted, or the paste itself can be smoked.

The use of cocaine eventually made its way to Europe and America in the latter half of the nineteenth century. Europeans and Americans quickly came to appreciate the mood-altering characteristics of the drug, which was found in everything from patent medicines to wine and in an innovative new beverage called Coca-Cola (today, Coca-Cola contains no cocaine). Even physicians were taken with the restorative qualities of the drug. For a time, Sigmund Freud actively promoted the use of the drug for treating depression and the symptoms of opiate withdrawal, but he later saw its potential for addiction and rejected it.

As the use of cocaine increased in the United States during the last years of the nineteenth century, fears about the dangers associated with the use of the drug took hold. Stories of its use by criminals and crazed "dope fiends" were melded together with the fact that cocaine was often used by impoverished whites or blacks in the ghettos. Soon many states passed laws designed to control its use. In 1914 cocaine was grouped with the opiates as a narcotic under the Harrison Act, which taxed the sale and importation of narcotics (Musto, 1991).

From the 1920s until the end of World War II, cocaine use waxed and waned in the lower-class neighborhoods and ghettos. Cocaine was always expensive. As a result, the use of cheap and abundant amphetamine, as well as marijuana and heroin, overshadowed cocaine use with most drug addicts until the end of the 1960s.

Amphetamine was originally developed in the 1920s as a synthetic alternative to the naturally occurring substance ephedrine, used for centuries by the Chinese to dilate bronchial passages. Amphetamine was first used as an alternative to ephedrine in treating asthma. In the 1930s it was discovered to be a stimulant. With that discovery, amphetamine was used to treat narcolepsy, a condition in which individuals involuntarily fall asleep. The stimulant characteristics of amphetamine caught the eye of military commanders, who were interested in any drug that might keep soldiers awake. Amphetamines were heavily used during World War II by all sides.

The nonmedical use of amphetamine flourished after the war. Amphetamine was used in pill form, via inhalers, and intravenously. One of the most popular means of getting amphetamine was by dismantling over-the-counter inhalers, which contained amphetamine as a treatment for asthma. Other forms of amphetamine, like methamphetamine, also became popular. By the mid-1960s, widespread abuse of amphetamine had become a national problem.

Efforts to restrict the use of amphetamine in the late 1960s led to renewed interest in cocaine. By the early 1970s, cocaine had escaped the ghetto and had gained entry into middle- and upper-class society. Wealthy young users made cocaine into a status symbol. At that time the widespread belief was that cocaine could be used recreationally with little harm or risk of dependence. By the 1980s that belief was recognized to have been false. The image of cocaine as a carefree drug of the wealthy was replaced with the image of cocaine as a killer.

This new reputation was bolstered by the spread of a new form of cocaine, *crack*. The perception that cocaine use did not result in dependence may have resulted from the fact that most cocaine was taken by inhalation and in small amounts because of its expense. Crack was cheap and offered users more drug for their money. Crack is a derivative of cocaine freebasing, which had appeared in the 1970s as a means of cleansing cocaine of its impurities by the use of organic solvents like ether. The purified cocaine could then be vaporized and inhaled, resulting in a more intense high than if the cocaine had been snorted as a powder. Although cocaine freebasing produced an intense high, the complexity of producing the freebase limited its appeal. Crack was produced with a simpler, cheaper procedure.

The method of smoking crack in a crack pipe produces a high in a matter of seconds. A ten-dollar chunk of crack is all a user needs to get high. Cocaine is no longer a drug of the rich; now anybody can use it. Crack-smoking ripped through American ghettos in the late 1980s, and it continues to keep its grip today. Although portrayed in the media as an epidemic striking all parts of American society, in reality the epidemic of crack use strikes more heavily in certain geographic areas and socioeconomic classes. Lower-class urban neighborhoods in midsize to large cities appear to be most heavily hit by the crack epidemic. For the population as a whole, the use of cocaine is continuing to decline.

As for amphetamines, their use also continues to decline. Methamphetamine, in the form of "crank" or in the crystalline form known as "ice," continues to be a problem in some groups. Crank and ice, like crack, can be smoked by the user. Ice has been described as being as addicting as crack, but predictions of "ice" epidemics for the most part have failed to materialize. That might change as efforts to control the use of crack intensify.

Nicotine and Smoking

Tobacco has been entwined in American culture from the start. Early American settlers not only smoked, chewed, and snorted tobacco regularly but exported it as well. Tobacco use followed the first European explorers beyond the borders of North and South America, where *Nicotiana tobacum* and *rustica* grew indigenously, to Europe and beyond. Today tobacco use continues to hold a deadly grasp on an international market, where exports of American tobacco products sometimes increase as much as 20 percent in a single year. Meanwhile, in the United States the toll from tobacco use has been increasing as the health consequences in smokers who began their habits twenty to thirty years ago have become apparent.

Early explorers reported seeing Native Americans smoking tobacco, but cigarette smoking appeared only in the middle of the nineteenth century. Cigarette smoking rapidly gained popularity, and by 1885 the rate of consumption of cigarettes was over 1 billion a year in the United States. Smokers may be seeking to satisfy a craving for nicotine when they light up, but they get a lot more than just nicotine with every drag. Cigarette smoke contains at least three thousand substances, many of which are known to be harmful to biological tissue. With every inhaled puff of smoke, the smoker is exposed to tars, carbon monoxide, hydrogen cyanide, nitrous oxide, and nicotine, to name just a few.

Along with "crack" cocaine, *nicotine* is our most addictive drug. The reason is that both are absorbed directly from the lining of the lungs into the bloodstream and carried immediately to the brain, where the instant reinforcement sets the stage for craving.

The health consequences of tobacco dependence are horrifying. Deaths from smoking in the United States alone reach nearly 400,000 per year. Smokers have ten times the risk of lung cancer, several times the risk of cancers of the mouth, throat, esophagus, pancreas, kidney, bladder, and cervix, and twice the risk of coronary heart disease. They also have a much higher risk of poorly healing peptic ulcers and chronic obstructive lung disease. Not surprisingly, tobacco smoking remains the single most important cause of preventable death in developed countries.

Marijuana

For thousands of years, in Asia and the Middle East, *Cannabis sativa* has been used for its psychoactive and medicinal characteristics. Also known as the hemp plant, it originally had been grown in tropical and temperate areas of the world for the more practical reason that hemp fibers are excellent for making rope. Cannabis was probably imported to South and Central America by the Spanish in the mid-sixteenth century for that purpose. Cannabis plants were cultivated and allowed to grow wild in the United States for centuries and came to be known as a weed (Abel, 1980).

The cannabis plant is the source of marijuana and hashish. Marijuana is a mixture of the ground leaves and stems of the plant. Resin from the bud of Cannabis sativa plants is the source of the powerful psychoactive drug called hashish. Cannabis plants contain hundreds of chemicals. Those unique to the cannabis plant are called cannabinoids. Many cannabinoids are thought to have psychoactive properties. The cannabinoid delta-9-tetrahydrocannabinol (THC) is the essential psychoactive ingredient in marijuana. Marijuana's psychological action is mildly sedating, euphoria-producing, and hallucinogenic.

In Europe, hashish smoking had attracted some attention in the mid-1800s, but outside artistic and literary circles few people knew or cared about its use. In the United States, hemp smoking began in the mid-nineteenth century and gradually increased in the years between the turn of the century and the 1920s. Public suspicion about the effects of marijuana smoking was on the rise during the same period. Marijuana use increasingly became linked to crime in the late 1920s and early 1930s. By the mid 1930s, several states had enacted regulations to control the use of marijuana.

A central figure in the move to regulate marijuana use was Harry Anslinger, the head of the Federal Bureau of Narcotics. Marijuana in his day was rumored to cause crazed violence and wild, disinhibited behavior. Those allegations were unfounded exaggerations having to do more with the lifestyle of the smokers than the marijuana they were smoking. In 1937 the Marihuana Tax Act was passed. It taxed growers, distributors, and purchasers of the drug.

Regulatory efforts continued in the 1940s and 1950s. Marijuana continued to be used, but its use was primarily restricted to ghettos and minority subcultures. In the 1960s marijuana caught the eye of middle- and upper-class youth. By the 1970s widespread use of marijuana could be found among youth from all levels of society. Marijuana use, however, was not limited to the young in the 1970s; people of all ages experimented with the drug, and in many states efforts were made to decriminalize its use.

According to data from the annual survey of drug use among high school students, the peak year of use in the United States was 1979. Use continues to be high in the United States today, although it has been gradually declining since the 1980s. No longer is the most powerful marijuana imported; marijuana grown in the United States today contains significantly more THC than the most powerful imported marijuana of fifteen years ago.

Hallucinogenic Drugs

Since ancient times, a wide variety of plants and other natural products possessing hallucinogenic properties have been smoked or ingested to alter perception. Despite the natural origin of many hallucinogenic drugs, perhaps the best known of the hallucinogenic drugs is *LSD*, which ironically is synthetic, not natural, in origin. LSD, however, is related to ergot compounds, which are produced by the ergot fungus, the source of numerous poisonings in the Middle Ages. The fungus, which can grow on grains, will cause horrific convulsions, burning sensations, and sometimes gangrene in the limbs of those who eat it.

Synthesized in 1938, LSD fortunately packs none of the toxic, physical complications of the ergot fungus. In 1943 the drug's inventor, Dr. Albert Hofmann, noted the perception-altering effects of low doses of LSD (Hofmann, 1970 [1994]). Reports of the psychoactive effects of LSD attracted the interest of researchers and eventually of psychiatrists, who felt it reduced barriers to therapy. The military was also interested in the actions of LSD and its utility in interrogations, an application that was eventually dropped. LSD's popularity picked up in the 1960s. The drug's rise in popularity was assisted by the advocacy of Timothy Leary, a proponent of using hallucinogenics as a means of enhancing a particular brand of spiritual discovery. The use of LSD peaked in the 1960s and began to fade in the 1970s.

The 1960s saw the introduction of other hallucinogenic compounds to the drug scene in the United States as well. *Psilocybin,* from the Psilocybe mushroom, and *mescaline,* from the Peyote cactus, both became popular in the 1960s, again with the strong advocacy of Timothy Leary.

The use of mescaline is especially controversial, because ingesting mescaline containing "buttons" from the Peyote cactus is part of many Native American religious ceremonies. That continues to be a source of friction between the federal government and Native Americans. Many Native Americans believe that the sacramental use of peyote is protected religious activity. The federal government, for many years, agreed. However, the sacramental use of peyote in the Native American Church has come under scrutiny at both the federal and state levels. Today, the activity is no longer protected under the Constitution as an expression of religious freedom.

In the mid-1980s a burst of new interest in hallucinogenic drugs in the form of *"designer drugs"* occurred. Most designer drugs were derivatives of amphetamine. By modifying the chemical structure of amphetamine, these drugs took on a character similar to mescaline, hence the term "designer drugs." The fact that the new drugs were chemical analogs of existing drugs meant that many of them were not covered by existing laws. Drugs like Ecstasy or "XTC" (MDMA) became fashionable and remain popular (Cuomo, Dyment, and Gammino, 1994). Some psychiatrists reported that the MDMA induced positive mood states and supported its use in therapy. The Drug Enforcement Administration (DEA) disagreed. In 1988 the DEA restricted the use of Ecstasy by classifying it as a Schedule I drug (a category used to describe drugs considered to have high potential for abuse and no current medical use in treatment; see Chapter 5 for additional information on Schedule I and II classifications).

Efforts to create new drugs that, because of the novelty of their chemical structures, could escape legal descriptions and regulation continued in the mid-1980s. Congress moved to close that loophole by passing the Analogs Act of 1986, which allowed the DEA to ban drugs with actions that were "substantially similar" to those of an already banned drug.

Sedatives and Hypnotics

Drugs capable of producing an alcohol-like sedation have always been popular. Since the early 1800s several classes of drugs have been produced and prescribed for the purpose of sedation and, at high doses, to induce sleep. Drugs like paraldehyde, chloral hydrate, and bromides were employed to induce a calm, sleeplike state. Those drugs lost popularity by the turn of the century. One reason was the discovery of a new class of *sedative-hypnotic* drugs called the barbiturates. The first barbiturate introduced was Veronal, in 1903. Soon other types of barbiturates were under investigation. Luminal (phenobarbital) was marketed in 1912 and is still used today for certain medical conditions like epilepsy. Shorter-acting barbiturates, like Amytal and Nembutal, were introduced in the 1920s. Since their introduction, thousands of barbiturate analogs have been produced.

The popularity of barbiturates was always balanced against the risks inherent in taking them. Problems of tolerance, dependency, and overdose plagued their use. Many efforts were made to find substitutes offering the same level of efficacy as the barbiturates but with fewer side effects. Doriden (glutethimide) was popular in the 1950s. Although Doriden was thought to be safer than the barbiturates, it has since been found to produce both tolerance and dependency, which are signs of addiction.

Despite safety issues, barbiturates and barbituratelike drugs remained popular as "sleeping" pills until the late 1950s. In 1960 a new drug, Librium (chlordiazepoxide) exploded on the scene. Librium and an earlier drug, Miltown (meprobamate), were members of a new type of drugs known as anxiolytics, drugs designed to reduce anxiety. Both drugs continue to be popular today. The most popular class of anxiolytics is the *benzodiazepines*. In addition to Librium, members of this class include such popular drugs as Valium, Dalmane, Xanax, and Halcion. Millions of prescriptions for benzodiazepines are written in the United States each year.

Although designed to reduce anxiety, benzodiazepines and other related drugs share many of the characteristic actions of earlier drugs like barbiturates. At moderate doses they produce sedation, and at high doses sleep. They tend to lessen the risk overdose and are *less* likely to produce dependency (Miller and Gold, 1990). Debate continues over the addiction potential of the benzodiazepines and over the characteristics of physical withdrawal from these drugs (Lader, 1994). Most overdoses associated with the benzodiazepines occur when the drugs are mixed with alcohol, as explained in Chapter 4 under "Potentiation."

Inhalants

Children and adolescents inhale gasoline fumes, aerosol sprays, model airplane glue, and other chemicals to get high. These cause serious and permanent damage to the brain, lungs, liver, and other internal organs.

A 1995 Texas survey indicated such behavior is on the increase, with 28 percent of seventh graders reporting use of inhalants. Many began when they were ten years of age or younger. Young inhalant abusers tend to use heavily. They have a high rate of dropping out of school before high school graduation, and their proclivity for other addictions later on is a real danger.

Sources

Abel, E. L., *Marijuana, the First Twelve Thousand Years.* Plenum Press, New York, 1980.

Austin, G. A., *Perspectives on the History of Psychoactive Substance Use.* NIDA Research Issues no. 24. Washington, DC: U.S. Department of Health, Education, and Welfare, 1978.

Courtwright, D. T., *Dark Paradise: Opiate Addiction in America Before 1940.* Harvard University Press, Cambridge, 1982.

Cuomo, M. J.; P. G. Dyment; and V. M. Gammino, "Increasing Use of Ecstasy (MDMA) and Other Hallucinogens on a College Campus," *Journal of American College Health,* 1994, 42(6): 271–74.

Hafen, B. Q., *Addictive Behavior: Drug and Alcohol Abuse.* Norton, Chicago, 1985.

Hanson, Bill (ed.), *Life with Heroin: Voices from the Inner City.* Lexington Books, Lexington, MA, 1985.

Herrington, R., et al. (eds), *Alcohol and Drug Abuse Handbook.* Warren Green, St. Louis, 1987.

Hofmann, A., "Notes and Documents Concerning the Discovery of LSD," *Agents and Actions,* 1994, 43(3–4): 79–81 [classic article, originally published in 1970].

Kaa, E., "Impurities, Adulterants, and Diluents of Illicit Heroin," *Forensic Science International,* 1994, 64(2–3): 171–79.

Kelly, T. H.; R. W. Foltin; and M. W. Fischman, *Effects of Alcohol on Human Behavior: Effects on the Workplace.* NIDA Research Monograph no. 100. Washington, DC: U.S. Department of Health and Human Services, 1990.

Lader, M., "Anxiolytic Drugs: Dependence, Addiction, and Abuse," *European Neuropsychopharmacology,* 1994 4(2): 85–91.

Lehman, W. E., and D. D. Simpson, *Patterns of Drug Use in a Large Metropolitan Work Force.* NIDA Research Monograph no. 100. Washington, DC: U.S. Department of Health and Human Services, 1990.

Miller, N. S., and M. S. Gold, "Benzodiazepines: Reconsidered," *Advances in Alcohol and Substance Abuse,* 1990 (3–4): 67–84.

Musto, D. F., "Opium, Cocaine and Marijuana," *Scientific American,* 1991, 265(1): 40–47.

Rippey, J. N., *Drug Abuse in America: A Historical Perspective.* Behavioral Health Resources Press, Alexandria, VA, 1995.

———, *Treatment of the Pregnant Addict.* Behavioral Health Resources Press, Alexandria, VA, 1995.

Scott, J. M., *The White Poppy: A History of Opium,* Heinemann, London, 1969.

Seymour, R. B., and D. E. Smith, *The Physician's Guide to Psychoactive Drugs.* Haworth, New York, 1987.

Siegel, Larry (ed.), *AIDS and Substance Abuse.* Vol. 7, no. 2 of *Advances in Alcohol and Substance Abuse,* 1988.

Washton, Arnold, *Willpower's Not Enough: Understanding and Overcoming Addiction and Obsessive Behavior.* Harper/Lippincott, Philadelphia, 1989.

Weil, A., "Letter from Andes: The New Politics of Coca," *The New Yorker,* May 15, 1995, pp. 70–80.

Weiss, Roger D., and S. M. Mirin, *Cocaine,* 2d ed. American Psychiatric Association, Washington, DC, 1994.

CHAPTER 3

Sociocultural Aspects

I F ALCOHOL OR ANY DRUG is a chemical substance introduced into a living organism, one might well ask why we should consider social, cultural, and historical factors instead of just the biochemistry and pharmacology of alcohol. The reasons are many.

Obviously there would be no alcoholism if there were no drinking of alcoholic beverages. Since most drinkers do not become alcoholics, alcohol consumption cannot be the sole or sufficient cause of alcoholism. But drinking is a necessary and important cause, and drinking is largely a matter of social custom, determined greatly by attitudes prevalent in the culture. History helps us understand both drinking customs and social attitudes toward drinking, drunkenness, and alcoholism. Attitudes are especially important, because alcoholics usually come from a background of confused and ambivalent attitudes about drinking. That was the conclusion of research done decades ago by Ullman (1953) and is confirmed by the stories of alcoholics heard at AA meetings and elsewhere. Jackson and Connor (1953b) found that alcoholics come from homes where the two parents tended to disagree quite markedly in their attitudes toward the use of alcohol. Cultures that have clear-cut, consistent attitudes about drinking and do not condone drunkenness usually have low rates of alcoholism, while those that don't know what to think or how they feel about alcohol tend to have higher rates. Orthodox Jews use wine in rituals and at meals, but to be "drunk like a Gentile" (*shikker vie ein goy* in Yiddish) is an absolute disgrace. Greeks and southern Italians drink wine daily at lunch and dinner, yet drunkenness is despised. Wine with meals is simply taken for granted. Conversely, in Paris there is more drinking outside of mealtime, more hard liquor (brandy) is consumed, far more social significance is attached to drinking, and drunkenness is more tolerated. Societies that push drinks and even boast about drunkenness have higher rates of alcoholism.

But, you say, alcohol is alcohol. True, but people are different. In Chapter 7, under "Psychological Factors," we shall see that expectancy, what people think alcohol will do for them, can change its effects. That varies with culture. In counseling alcoholics one cannot ignore the attitudes both client and therapist bring to the situation from their own backgrounds. A black or a Native American is less likely to be helped by one who does not understand that person's culture. The origins of an alcoholic's drinking problems are enmeshed in social, religious, economic, legal, and health systems that must be understood even to make a proper diagnosis. Denial and rationalizations can be penetrated and dealt with only if the counselor knows their language and social setting.

No rehabilitation effort will have lasting success if recovered alcoholics are not prepared in a very realistic and practical way to go back and live in their own environment with its specific drinking practices and values. Funding for treatment depends on understanding the impact of alcoholism on all our lives as a public health problem rather than as a difference of moral opinion. And no prevention campaign has a chance of success if it is conceived in a vacuum that ignores the attitudes of society, especially a society where both use and misuse of alcohol are accepted by custom and even reinforced by peer pressure.

Because America has been populated by peoples from different racial and national origins, with peculiar histories of use and misuse of alcohol, we probably have the most confused and ambivalent attitudes toward alcohol of all the nations in the world (Anderson, 1967). No wonder we have problems. The "drys" think it is a sin to have even one drink, while the civil libertarians will defend one's right to drink oneself to death.

Drinking alcohol is considered sophisticated and a mark of hospitality, even among people who look down on those addicted to other drugs. Youngsters are not impressed when parents view with alarm their marijuana use while holding a double martini. Contrast our picture of the skid-road bum with the "gentleman of distinction" liquor advertisements: Is alcohol a mark of moral depravity or of mature refinement? Is it an appetizer? We know that alcoholics are notoriously undernourished. Is it a sign of manliness or weakness? If it proves one a tough he-man, why does the salesman need a few belts before he goes after that big sale; or a boy need a couple of beers before he asks that pretty girl for a dance? Is alcohol "the root of all evil" or is it "good for what ails you"? Is whiskey good for a cold and brandy for shock, or are the American Medical Association and the Red Cross correct in rejecting all internal medical uses of alcohol, especially in an emergency, including snakebite? We boast about somebody flying high at a party, yet despise him in the gutter.

Alcohol in Various Cultures

Alcohol is the product of a natural process called fermentatioin, the action of yeast upon sugar. It can be made from almost any fruit or grain, and was probably discovered accidentally by primitive man when he tasted some rotting fruit, just as birds sometimes exhibit inebriation from eating overripe berries. Archaeology indicates that those natural products have been a part of human life since before recorded history. Isis, goddess of Egypt, was promoting beer in 30,000 B.C. A tablet in Babylonia from 6000 B.C. shows beer used in ceremony, and by 4000 B.C. Babylonia had sixteen kinds of beer. There is evidence from the very earliest writings: a brewery in 3700 B.C. And alcohol has meant trouble almost from the beginning: a temperance tract in ancient

Egypt, prohibition in Mesopotamia and among the ancient Greeks, Noah passed out from too much wine, ancient Chinese proverbs about beer and its abuse. The Code of Hammurabi, circa 1900 B.C., punished only two crimes by burning to death: incest and alcohol abuse.

Women seem to differ between cultures more than men in use of alcohol. A fascinating and little-known aspect of this history was the abusive drinking by women as related by Marian Sandmaier in *The Invisible Alcoholics* (1992, or *Alcohol Health and Research World,* Summer 1980, pp. 41–51). The Dionysian orgies involved not only drunkenness but savage brutality on the part of women. She recounts the role of women and drinking from those ancient times, through the era immortalized by the London painter William Hogarth in his 1751 *Gin Lane,* in colonial America, and the frequenting of "speakeasies" by women during Prohibition in the 1920s.

Beer and wine are the result of fermentation. Beer (a generic name that includes lager, ale, porter, and stout) is ordinarily made from malted grain flavored with hops. It usually contains about 4 percent (rarely more than 8 percent) alcohol. Wines are made from grapes or other fruit and are either dry (table) or sweet (dessert, fortified). Either may be red or white. Dry wines contain 12 to 14 percent alcohol, while sweet wines contain 18 to 20 percent and are made by adding alcohol before all the sugar has been fermented (for details see Ford, 1983).

Spirits or hard liquor (Scotch, bourbon, and rye or blended whiskey, gin, vodka, rum, brandy) are the result of distillation, a method of concentrating the alcohol by evaporating it and then condensing the vapor. That yields a beverage of 40 percent to 50 percent alcohol (80 to 100 proof). The Chinese may have invented the distillation process before 2000 B.C., and the Arabs, from whom our word *alcohol* comes, had improved it by 1700 B.C. About A.D. 1000 the Italians began to make brandy (*grappa*) out of wine, but distilled liquor did not become common in western Europe until about A.D. 1500.

Alcohol has been made by almost every people, and from almost anything. Mead was fermented from honey in Britain long before the Romans came. In Abyssinia there was a strong beer called *bouza* from which our word *booze* may have originated. Columbus found the Caribbean Indians drinking beer from fermented maize, and the Incas of Peru were making wine and beer before the arrival of Pizarro. But there was no distillation in this hemisphere before the white man came, and except for the areas mentioned, especially in the northern and northwestern areas of North America, the Native Americans seem to have had no contact with alcohol. The importance of this fact will be clear when we discuss causality in Chapter 7.

More important than its widespread use are the attitudes people develop toward alcohol. Once it has become part of a culture, it seems never to be eradicated. China is said by one author to have tried prohibition seventeen times, and another says forty-one times. England went through prohibition six times. Russia, Finland, and Iceland have all tried prohibition and repealed it. Bootlegging and home brewing had frustrated Russia's latest attempt by 1988. The Hindu, Buddhist, and other ancient traditions also prohibit alcohol, with mixed success. Mohammed strictly prohibited alcohol among his followers, perhaps because the date wine they made was very strong and because of wine's important symbolic role in Christian worship. But reports from predominantly Muslim countries indicate a certain amount of alcohol consumption, some of it in unusual forms such as shaving lotion, and other psychoactive drugs are common. One tribe of Muslims gave us our English word assassin: They were known as *hashashin* because they killed Christians with some enthusiasm while under the influence of hashish, the active ingredient in marijuana.

Among some South Pacific island peoples there was an absolute taboo against alcohol; we can surmise that the motivation included fear of getting lost at sea, as when they migrated to Hawaii with no modern navigational aids. Even small amounts of alcohol can dull one's sense of direction, as many a lost hiker or hunter has learned. *Kava* (*'awa* in Hawaii, *Yaqona* in Fiji) is a nonalcoholic intoxicating beverage made from the pounded root of the pepper tree throughout Polynesia and in some parts of Melanesia and Micronesia. Anthropologists differ in their interpretation of the kava culture, but the tragic fact is that what used to be a highly disciplined, ritualized structure important in Pacific society was destroyed when the white man brought liquor and chaos to the islands. Among many primitives, the use of alcohol seems to have been in the control of the group, not of the individual. In some tribes, the women took away all the knives and clubs before drinking began. Conversely, the Chinese are regarded as never getting hostile from drink; they take on a characteristic flush and perhaps become a bit boisterous and sleepy. The WHO film *To Your Health* says, "Alcohol means many things to many people."

Coming back to our Western Judeo-Christian tradition, we note that although drunkenness is condemned in both Old and New Testaments, nowhere in the Bible is total abstinence mandated. Drinking is often mentioned; the wines of Israel are praised. In medieval European monasteries liqueurs were developed: the Benedictines produced Benedictine, and the Carthusians made Chartreuse. Winemaking became a fine art, and the monk Dom Perignon is said to have invented champagne. Drunkenness was a sin, but church leaders were not total abstainers. Popes and cardinals drank, as did Luther, Calvin, Knox, and even Wesley, founder of the Methodists.

Although beer and wine contain the same intoxicating ethanol as distilled spirits, it seems that misuse and prohibitionistic reactions intensified when hard liquor became more widespread in Europe after A.D. 1500. History is full of ironies, and what we see here is a series of cyclic events redolent of our own more recent history: Abuse led to high tax and eventual prohibition, which occasioned graft and corruption, which led to repeal, followed by abuse and then prohibition again. In 1606 England shifted public drunkenness from ecclesiastical to civil law: Instead of a sin it became a crime. Since the high sheriff was busy pursuing felons, the town constable became involved with "handling drunks" as one of his main functions.

For all its intermittent disfavor with the law, alcohol had become an accepted part of most societies. Contrary to our stereotypes, it seems that in ancient times it was the rich who were the drunkards; the poor and slaves were allowed to drink only at festivals. Drinking has always been a part of the ritualistic ceremonies of almost all civilized peoples. Men pledged their loyalty and sealed a contract in wine. Eventually that mode of pledge was integrated into celebration of betrothals, marriages, births, baptisms, and wakes at death. Red wine was (erroneously) thought of as analogous to blood, and spirits were called *aquavit,* water of life, which became *üsque beath* in Celtic, then *usquebaugh* or whiskey. The effects of alcohol added zest to social entertaining and relief from stress and boredom. Wine or beer became a part of the meal in most European countries. Since alcohol can be made anywhere and out of almost anything, it has pervaded every stratum of life. Even in prison, where it is forbidden, convicts not only obtain it in a variety of forms (48-ounce bottles of Listerine disappear very fast in some prisons) but also hoard raisins and prunes (hence "pruno") and ferment them into wine, and even fashion ingenious distilling apparatus to manufacture moonshine behind the walls.

Can alcohol be eliminated? Symbolic of the problem is the action of one prison warden who heard that the inmates were fermenting apples and oranges into wine, so he substituted prunes! But the United States engaged for a century in a gigantic and less amusing attempt, to which we must now turn.

Alcohol in America

1620–1725—No Fuss. In the early American colonies the use of beer and wine with meals was simply transported across the Atlantic as a way of life, with no special significance. Drunkenness was not tolerated, but even the Puritans drank. More beer than water was brought over on the Mayflower (it didn't spoil). Beer was served in the dining hall at Harvard and at dinner in the Protestant seminaries. A midmorning break for beer or hard cider included women and children.

1725–1825—Excessive and Harmful Drinking. In the previous century 90 percent of the beverage alcohol consumed in America was in the form of beer, 5 percent as wine, and 5 percent as spirits or hard liquor. During this second century a dramatic shift occurred: 90 percent of the alcohol was consumed as distilled spirits, with only 5 percent as beer and 5 percent as wine. The reasons were varied. The harsh climate of the Eastern Seaboard was not conducive to viniculture. The British taxed French wine heavily. Beer was bulky to transport in an era before railroads and highway truckers; a barrel of whiskey contained as much ethanol as a wagonload of beer. (Another irony:

Table 1. Percentage of Beverage Alcohol Consumed in the United States

	Beer	Wine	Spirits
1630	90	5	5
1825	5	5	90
1970	50	10	40
1978	45	15	40
1995*	54	17	29

* Estimates.

Bourbon whiskey was invented by a Kentucky Baptist minister.) Whiskey became so negotiable that it was used for money when the Continental currency failed in 1780. A 1791 excise tax on it so encroached upon the lives of Pennsylvania farmers that George Washington had to send troops to quell the Whiskey Rebellion.

The shift toward hard liquor meant a substantial increase in intemperate drinking. Another factor was a total ignorance of addiction, at least as applied to alcohol. The American doctor Benjamin Rush in 1785 (see M. Keller, 1986) and the British doctor Thomas Trotter in 1804 had both recognized the danger of alcohol addiction, but they were not heard because of lack of good mass communication media and widespread illiteracy—to say nothing of popular denial. Thomas Jefferson, as third president, observed that "one-third of the people in these United States are killing themselves with whiskey." Diaries from the period record 30 gallons of punch being served to a party of eighty people and John Hancock serving two hundred guests with 136 punch bowls plus three hundred bottles of wine and brandy. The ship's log of the frigate *U.S.S. Constitution* showed hundreds of gallons of rum being loaded on at each port. No doubt the lack of social controls in this free and rapidly expanding frontier country made excess much easier than in the structured society of the early colonies, with their small, cohesive villages.

Added to that evidence is a most important fact: Excessive drinking was not only tolerated but admired. The image of the pioneer frontiersman as a hard-fighting, hard-drinking tough guy became the paragon of manliness. This persists to the present day, with obvious implications for prevention strategies.

A similar American attitude that persists from the same period is that serving drinks, even insisting that guests accept them, is a mark of hospitality. Before jet travel, it was indeed a warming welcome when one came in off the road or trail tired, wet, cold, and aching. From that developed a further insidious feeling: If one did not push drinks, one was likely to be considered inhospitable or downright stingy. No American wants to be thought of as either.

Later, another twist added to those pro-drinking attitudes: a backlash to the total abstinence movement. It is only partly in jest that we speculate as to how many Catholics may have drunk themselves into alcoholism trying to prove they were not Methodists or Baptists . . . but that does lead to our next period, the prelude to Prohibition.

1825–1919—Temperance to Abstinence. As early as 1789, in Litchfield, Connecticut, a movement to oppose the widespread intemperance began to stir. It grew out of a genuine concern for the future of the young nation whose democratic form of government depended on people's keeping their wits intact. Even more, it bespoke the Anabaptist, Puritan theology common in the colonies, especially in the Presbyterian and Congregationalist Churches of New England. The Calvinist clergyman Lyman Beecher (1775–1863) spearheaded the movement, beginning in 1812, with a strong stand for temperance that did not oppose wine and beer but only spirits. By 1825, however, he began advocating total abstinence from all alcoholic beverages, confusing use with abuse. The Temperance Society had become an Abstinence Society by 1836. It lost half its members, but not its momentum. The Good Templars, the Anti-Saloon League, the National Prohibition Party, and other groups were formed, especially the Woman's Christian Temperance Union (WCTU) in 1874, which completely distorted the issue, because the T stood not for temperance but for abstinence, creating confusion in the American mind to this day. Ironically, the "Temperance" movement wiped out the notion of temperate drinking: You were either a total abstainer or a drunkard.

Over those decades of increasingly strident propaganda, the focus shifted from the *abuse* of alcohol or the person misusing it to the substance itself: Alcohol became "demon rum" and was to be extirpated from the country. Only the Washingtonian Movement, and later the Salvation Army, showed concern for the *person* affected. To most he was a moral reprobate, a depraved person of weak will who could "reform" if only he willed it. To avoid any such connotations we now never say "reformed alcoholic" but prefer "recovered," which affirms that the person is not bad but rather recovering from a chronic illness. (This terminology has been accepted by the Associated Press/United Press International *Style Book*.) Likewise, to avoid criminal implications we say "relapsed" and not "recidivist."

It is hard for us today to grasp how profoundly this controversy pervaded every facet of American life for a century. Prohibition of alcohol by law became a major issue in every political campaign. By December 1917, 95 percent of the land in the United States and two-thirds of its population were legally dry. Without high-speed printing and only one-fourth the population, the prohibitionists in 1890 were spewing out 4 tons of paper a day. By 1914 there were 50,000 lecturers traveling the country. The legend of Carry Nation smashing saloon windows with a hatchet seems exaggerated to us, but it typifies the intense zeal of the prohibitionists and seems to be historical fact, though there is now some question as to her sanity.

The emotional bitterness was matched by conceptual confusion. People failed to distinguish between use and abuse. Temperance was confused with total abstinence, so many a moderate drinker who abhorred drunkenness found himself unwittingly in the camp of its defenders. The two factions polarized the positions and created artificial dichotomies we are still trying to live down. Thus the Lutherans, Episcopalians, Greek Orthodox, Roman Catholics, and Jews who advocated temperance were accused of condoning drunkenness because they did not support total abstinence.

1920–33—Prohibition. The total abstinence or so-called temperance movement culminated in the passage of the Eighteenth Amendment to the U.S. Constitution on January 16, 1920, and its implementation by the Volstead Act (named for Representative Andrew Volstead) on October 20 of that year. It prohibited the manufacture, sale, or transportation of any intoxicating beverage except for medicinal or sacramental purposes. Thus began a massive struggle between a whole people and its law enforcement authorities, the effects of which not only echo in our language (speakeasy, hijack, bootlegger, moonshine) but can be found in our attitudes toward law and authority to this day.

It is often said that Prohibition did not fail; it was never tried. In the sense that it never had the wholehearted support of the people, that is true. At the height of Prohibition, for example, speakeasies (false storefronts behind which liquor was served) known to the police in New York City alone totaled 32,000. In 1933, the last year of Prohibition, about 10,000 full-blown alcoholics were admitted to hospitals in New York City (Keller, 1975a). Bathtub gin and rotgut whiskey were more than phrases, and if you could get hold of a bottle of good Canadian rye you were the prince of your neighborhood block. Real Scotch became "the real McCoy," because Captain Billy McCoy had a fast ship that was able to outrun the U.S. Revenue Service boats charged with enforcing the law. A sad twist is that the rumrunners and those who drank were the heroes, and the U.S. federal agents (revenuers) were the bad guys. It is usually admitted that more women drank in bars than ever before, since going to a speakeasy or nightclub became the smart thing to do. Women also drank more at home, as male drinking shifted from the corner saloon to the home. Adolescents, subject to the same laws as anyone else, often were not only the customers but the bootleggers, as the senior author can attest firsthand.

It is true that statistics show a drop in per capita consumption, but the facts cited above make one wonder how accurate they could be. The law-abiding citizens who did decrease their drinking were probably those less prone to alcohol problems anyway. People who really need a drink can always get it, and Prohibition days were no exception. Drinking out of defiance or surreptitiously is more open to abuse than relaxed, uncomplicated drinking, if for no other reason than the need to finish the bottle and dispose of the evidence.

1934—Repeal. In 1929 President Hoover's Wickersham Commission reported that "law enforcement had failed." Pressures for repeal resulted in a redefinition of "intoxicating beverage" to exclude beer with 3.2 percent alcohol in 1933, and finally, on December 6, 1934, the Twenty-first Amendment repealed the Eighteenth, and the "noble experiment" came to an end.

Many factors contributed to repeal. Disillusionment was a factor: Prohibition had been oversold by promises that if passed it would end poverty, wife abuse, all social ills. The Great Depression led many to hope that restoring the alcoholic beverage industry would stimulate the economy by providing jobs in agriculture and viniculture, manufacture, transportation, and sales. Needless to say, the industry concurred and pressed for repeal. Some women's groups opposed the WCTU. Poor enforcement and widespread corruption were another incentive: A "godfather" or big-city boss like Al Capone considered law authorities simply pawns who could be bought for a price. Congress was ambivalent. It enacted the Volstead Act to please the Drys, but underfunded enforcement to please the Wets. Other factors leading to repeal were the gigantic increase in moonshining, congestion in the courts with violations cases, and the illegal conversion of denatured industrial alcohol ("dehorning"). But probably the crucial factor was the infringement on the personal freedom of people whose cultures had sanctioned normal use of alcohol for centuries. It was "an attempt to impose the will of the few on the thirst of the many." Imagine the revolt if tomorrow morning's paper announced that coffee is now forbidden!

The confusion and warped attitudes engendered by this long and bitter struggle have not disappeared. National prohibition is dead, but the movement is still with us under different names. Drinking and drunkenness are still equated by some, with moralistic implications contrary to the concept of alcoholism as a disease. The fifty states have varied and even conflicting laws. A few counties in local-option states are legally dry. Attitudes toward law and authority still suffer as an aftermath. The cocktail party, a social event with drinking as its primary focus, is a post-Prohibition phenomenon.

An illustration that should discourage any simpleminded thinking is the percentage of drinkers in supposedly dry denominations: 61 percent of Methodists and 48 percent of Baptists drink (Mulford, 1964), 53 percent of some fundamentalist sects, and a percentage of Mormons that can only be guessed at from the alcohol tax revenue in Utah and other evidence. Now the serious complication is that Mulford and others report a higher than average rate of alcoholics and problem drinkers among these "dry" group members who drink. It is not certain whether the reason is guilt, lack of consistent drinking norms, or something else, but the fact seems clear (Clark and Midanik, 1982, p. 32).

1935–Present. Since repeal, a new vision of the problem of excessive drinking has been slowly evolving. In 1935, Dr. Bob and Bill W., two "hopeless" alcoholics, discovered they could stay sober by helping others and following a program of twelve steps, which they extracted from their experience: The fellowship of Alcoholics Anonymous was born. The founders were careful to avoid affiliation with anything that smacked of Prohibition, focusing on the person rather than on the substance, alcohol. Not espousing any particular theory, in general the fellowship tended to think of alcoholism as an illness instead of a sin. They avoided moralizing and opened the way for acceptance of alcoholism as a disease.

Coincidentally, in the same year, 1935, Charles Shadel founded Shadel Hospital in Seattle, which was to become the first member of the American Hospital Association devoted exclusively to the treatment of alcoholism. Walter Voegtlin, M.D., longtime chief of staff, conducted pioneering research on the liver and on heredity, which turned out to be decades ahead of the field. Shadel used an aversion conditioning technique quite different from the approach of AA, but they had in common a focus on alcoholic drinking as the primary problem and on stopping it as the first line of attack. Both looked upon alcoholism as a pathology in its own right rather than merely the symptom of some other problem.

Also in 1935, again quite independently of the above events, Mark Keller and Norman Jolliffe at Bellevue Hospital in New York embarked upon a major research project to explore alcoholism from a medical-scientific rather than a moralistic view. Through a series of events they involved Dr. Howard Haggard of Yale and Dr. E. M. Jellinek, a biometrician doing research on schizophrenia, and in 1940 founded the multidisciplinary Yale Center of Alcohol Studies under Jellinek and the *Quarterly Journal of Studies on Alcohol* (*QJSA*) under Keller. In 1962 both were moved to Rutgers, the State University of New Jersey, and in 1975 the *Quarterly Journal* became a monthly (*JSA*). Meanwhile, a landmark date was the publication in 1960 of Jellinek's book, *The Disease Concept of Alcoholism*.

The Scandinavian countries (Sweden, Norway, Denmark, Finland) had been among the first to acknowledge alcoholism as a serious national problem and to initiate scientific research. Switzerland, Canada, and England got involved early, and by 1968 in Washington, DC, the Twenty-eighth International Congress on Alcoholism attracted more than two thousand persons— the largest group up to that date ever assembled on alcoholism. Antabuse (disulfiram, see Chapter 15) was discovered in 1947, and in 1949 Dr. Ruth Fox went to Copenhagen to study its use and brought it back to the United States.

Except for AA, the account so far has largely been the story of professionals. What of the general public? In April 1944 Fox had introduced to Jellinek a talented and articulate recovered alcoholic, Mrs. Marty Mann. Within a year she had founded the National Council on Alcoholism, a volunteer group dedicated to eradicating the stigma of alcoholism and educating the general public to its ultimate conquest through treatment and prevention. Like Alcoholics Anonymous, the council avoided the prohibition issue and concentrated on alcohol misuse and the problems arising therefrom. NCADD now has local and state affiliate councils scattered throughout the fifty states. Highly important was the development by the NCA of the National Nurses Society on Addiction (NNSA, followed by DANA, NCCDN, and CANSA), the American Society of Addiction Medicine (ASAM, formerly AMSA, then AMSAODD), the Research Society on Alcoholism (RSA), and the Association for Medical Education in Substance Abuse (AMERSA). The Association of Labor–Management Administrators and Consultants on Alcoholism (ALMACA, now EAPA) started in 1961, also as a component of the NCA. The existence of the NCA allowed many members of AA to help enact important national and state legislation, which they would have been forbidden to do by AA tradition, since they were acting as members not of AA but of the NCA or its state affiliates. Later Harold Hughes started the Society of Americans for Recovery (SOAR) as a public advocacy group.

Many states had meanwhile developed alcoholism programs, usually as part of their public health department or (later) of their social welfare department. But Senator Millard Tydings of Maryland could state that "the problem of alcoholism had been sadly neglected by the federal government" (*Congressional Record,* June 7, 1967, S7846), and not until 1970 did Senator Harold Hughes, who had been elected governor when the people of Iowa knew he was a recovered alcoholic, was able to facilitate passage of the Comprehensive Alcohol Abuse and Alcoholism Prevention, Treatment and Rehabilitation Act (PL 91-616). The Hughes Act established the National Institute on Alcohol Abuse and Alcoholism (NIAAA) in 1971; authorized financial assistance to states, communities, organizations, institutions, and individuals; funded research, education, training, and a variety of treatment and rehabilitation programs; withdrew federal funds from hospitals that refused to treat alcoholics; and required a comprehensive program for military and civilian federal employees with alcoholism.

Have Public Attitudes Changed? Very slowly! Ignorance, apathy, and downright hostility still pervade all levels, from the medical and other top professions down to the local tavern. Rehabilitation experts in several parts of the country asked people whether they would rather be blind, crippled, etc., and found that alcoholism ranked as "most undesirable" among twenty-one disabilities listed. Witness the emotional reactions to recent federal disability regulations that protect alcoholics from discrimination. It was not until October 12, 1984, that *JAMA* devoted an issue to alcoholism, which it did again on September 19, 1986. Alcoholism in 1976 still got only 90 cents per victim in private support, in contrast to $197.52 per victim for muscular dystrophy, $180 per victim for hemophilia, $171.62 per victim for cystic fibrosis, and $87.37 per victim for cancer. At least this is better than the 40 cents per victim alcoholism received in 1967, and it is doing slightly better today.

Progress is being made. In 1974 the Internal Revenue Service ruled that not only is treatment for alcoholism a deductible medical expense, but even transportation to and from an Alcoholics Anonymous meeting or clubhouse could qualify. In 1980 the IRS Form 1040 listed alcoholism as a disease. Sections 503 and 504 of the Federal Rehabilitation Act of 1973, which forbid discrimination, were in 1977 and 1978 explicitly made to include alcoholism and other drug addictions. Many states have passed laws that all insurance companies (which had been using poor recovery rates of late-stage, skid-road alcoholics as an excuse to avoid coverage) must include alcoholism treatment in their group policies. ASAM now has thousands of physician members certified by passing an examination as addiction specialists, and AMERSA offers career chairs in medical schools. Another important development has been the model Uniform Alcoholism and Intoxication Treatment Act (commonly referred to as the Uniform Act, discussed in Chapter 20), which has now been enacted by two-thirds of the states, making the alcoholic not a criminal but a sick person.

Per capita consumption of alcohol in the United States increased after repeal, but the percentage of available income spent on alcohol decreased. The 90 percent of alcohol consumed as spirits early in the last century has declined to about 29 percent now, with 54 percent as beer and 17 percent as wine. In the Pacific Coast states the proportion consumed as wine is higher. Since the figures represent largely table wine consumed with meals, they are probably a mark of moderation and not necessarily of an increase in the cheap fortified wine of the skid-road "wino." However, we must not forget that there are true alcoholics who have never drunk anything but beer or dry wine.

More important for prevention is the first glimmer of a change in our attitudes about pushing drinks and tolerating drunkenness, spurred in part by recent court decisions that people can be held liable for damages inflicted by a customer or guest to whom they served drinks. The reversal of public attitudes about smoking, unpredictable some decades ago, is paving the way for a similar shift in regard to drinking. The use of hard liquor reached a twenty-one-year low in 1994, and overall alcohol consumption is still going down, as is other drug use among youth, except for crack cocaine and marijuana. Use of those two drugs by young people is on the rise, the latter especially alarming because today's marijuana is many times more powerful than that of a decade ago.

Sources

HISTORY

A 1990 work is Jean Charles Sournia, *A History of Alcoholism*. The history of alcohol use and abuse has been dealt with effectively by Mark Keller, especially in "Problems with Alcohol: An Historical Perspective" (1976a) and "Alcohol in Health and Disease: Some Historical Perspectives" (1966). Bacon's "Concepts" (1976) surveys the ways of looking at alcohol and alcoholism and the kinds of actions people have taken. Other works include M. E. Lender and J. K. Martin, *Drinking in America* (1983); Gregory A. Austin, *Alcohol in Western Society from Antiquity to 1800* (1985); Bennett and Ames, *The American Experience with Alcohol* (1985). Part I of Ewing and Rouse, *Drinking: Alcohol in American Society* (1977), and Chapter 3 of Fort, *Alcohol: Our Biggest Drug Problem* (1973), also give surveys of the history of drinking, as does Fleming, *Alcohol: The Delightful Poison* (1975). Daniel J. Anderson, *A History of Our Confused Attitudes Toward Beverage Alcohol* (1967), is an important Hazelden booklet.

SOCIOCULTURAL ASPECTS

Everett, Waddell, and Heath, *Cross-Cultural Approaches to the Study of Alcohol: An Interdisciplinary Perspective* (1976), is an excellent presentation of sociocultural aspects and their implications. Dwight B. Heath writes from the anthropological perspective, always with exhaustive bibliographies (see General Bibliography). Babor (1986) edited *Alcohol and Culture: Comparative Perspectives from Europe and America*. The NCALI staff gave us "Ethnicity and Alcohol: Resource Listing," and NCADI has published several lists of references on sociocultural aspects of alcohol use and alcoholism. Mac Marshall (1979) has edited an excellent collection of both general and specific articles entitled *Beliefs, Behaviors, and Alcoholic Beverages: A Cross-cultural Survey*. Older but still valuable sources include Craig MacAndrew, *Drunken Comportment* (1969), and William Madsen, *The American Alcoholic* (1973). Some deal with a specific cultural upbringing pattern of drinking and the likelihood of becoming an alcoholic—for example, C. R. Snyder, *Alcohol and the Jews: A Cultural Study of Drinking and Sobriety* (1958) and articles such as those by Bacon (1973), Keller (1970), and Negrete (1973). Chapter 11 of this book and the references cited there deal with the effect on drinking behavior of having been raised within a particular group.

PROHIBITION

Prohibition and the "temperance" movement had far-reaching and profound effects on our society, only one of which was its importance in shaping our attitudes toward the use of alcohol. Here is a sampling from the voluminous literature.

Asbury, Herbert, *The Great Illusion: An Informal History of Prohibition*. Doubleday, New York, 1950.
Barker, John Marshall, *The Saloon Problem and Social Reform*. Arno Press, New York, 1970.
Bennett, Linda A., and G. M. Ames (eds.), *The American Experience with Alcohol*. Plenum, New York, 1985.

Billings, John S., et al., *The Liquor Problem*. Houghton-Mifflin, Boston, 1903.

Cherrington, Ernest, *The Evolution of Prohibition in the United States of America*. American Issue Press, Westerville, OH, 1920.

Chidsey, D. B., *On and Off the Wagon: A Sober Analysis of the Temperance Movement from the Pilgrims Through Prohibition*. Cowles, New York, 1969.

Clark, Norman H., *Deliver Us from Evil: An Interpretation of American Prohibition*. Norton, New York, 1976.

Coffey, Thomas M., *The Long Thirst: Prohibition in America*. Norton, New York, 1975.

Dobyns, Fletcher, *The Amazing Story of Repeal*. Willett-Clark, New York, 1940.

Furnas, J. C., *The Life and Times of the Late Demon Rum*. Putnam, New York, 1965.

Gusfield, Joseph R., *Symbolic Crusade: Status Politics and the American Temperance Movement*. University of Illinois Press, Urbana, 1963.

Hofstadter, R., *Age of Reform: From Bryan to F.D.R.* Alfred A. Knopf, New York, 1960.

Houghland, James G., Jr., and Samuel A. Mueller, "Organizational 'Goal Submergence': The Methodist Church and the Failure of the Temperance Movement," *Sociology and Social Research*, 1974, 58:408–16.

Johnston, Henry Alan, *What Rights Are Left*. Macmillan, New York, 1930.

Kobler, J., *Ardent Spirits: The Rise and Fall of Prohibition*. Putnam, New York, 1973.

Lee, H., *How Dry We Were: Prohibition Revisited*. Prentice-Hall, Englewood Cliffs, NJ, 1963.

Lender, Mark E., *Dictionary of American Temperance Biography: From Temperance Reform to Alcohol Research, the 1600s to the 1980s,* Greenwood Press, Westport, CT, 1984.

Mertz, Charles, *The Dry Decade*. Doubleday, New York, 1931.

Odegard, Peter H., *Pressure Politics: The Story of the Anti-Saloon League*. Columbia University Press, New York, 1966.

Rorabaugh, W. J., *The Alcoholic Republic: An American Tradition*. Oxford University Press, New York, 1979.

Rumbarger, John J., *Profits, Power and Prohibition*. State University of New York Press, Albany, 1988.

Sinclair, Andrew. *Prohibition: The Era of Excess*. Little, Brown, Boston, 1962.

Sorensen, Andrew A., *Alcoholic Priests: A Sociological Study*. Seabury, New York, 1976. Chapter 1.

Taylor, R. L., *Vessel of Wrath: The Life and Times of Carry Nation*. New American Library, New York, 1966.

Tyrrell, I. R., *Sobering Up: From Temperance to Prohibition in Antebellum America, 1800–1860*. Greenwood Press, Westport, CT, 1979.

Udell, Gilman G., *Liquor Laws,* U.S. Government Printing Office, Washington, DC, 1968.

Whealon, John F., "Church's Reply to the Alcoholic Plea," *The Blue Book: Proceedings, 28th National Clergy Conference on Alcoholism*. National Catholic Council on Alcoholism, 1976, pp. 1–7.

Winkler, Allan M., "Lyman Beecher and the Temperance Crusade," *QJSA*, 1972, 33:939–57.

CHAPTER 4

Alcohol: Physiology and Pharmacology

S O FAR WE HAVE DELINEATED what we are talking about, and the extent of the problems. At this point psychologists might be expected to launch into an analysis of why people become addicts. Indeed we shall; but good psychology starts with the fact that a human being is an organism—one indeed distinguished from other animals by powers of thought and choice—and alcohol and other drugs are chemicals introduced into that living organism. The physiology of addiction is essential to any understanding of addiction or even drinking behavior (Blum and Payne, 1991; Goodwin, 1994; N. S. Miller and Mark Gold, 1991).

A large portion of the myths and misinformation still heard in the local tavern and even in alcohol education are in this area. "I drank a fifth of whiskey that evening and was cold sober when I drove home" and "You can't get drunk on beer; just avoid the hard liquor" are typical myths contrary to the facts of biochemistry. One need not be a biochemist, but one must know the basic facts in order to deal effectively with the behavior and to penetrate the patient's denial and rationalizations. Moreover, patients even in early recovery find this information helpful: "I see now that cocaine messed up my brain chemistry and that's why I act funny" or, "I understand now that nicotine made my brain cells demand it."

This chapter is divided into three parts: (A) what the body does with alcohol; (B) what alcohol does to behavior, especially driving; (C) what alcohol does to the body. The next chapter will deal with the other drugs.

A.   What the Body Does with Alcohol

Alcohol is a colorless, flammable, volatile liquid with a burning taste. (It is nearly odorless, so what is smelled on the breath is more likely other components of the beverage, or acetaldehyde.) Since alcohol absorbs water readily from the atmosphere, it is practically impossible to obtain in pure form. It is an excellent solvent and is widely used in many products, such as paint and perfume. Fermentation takes place easily in a warm place when yeast, a microscopic plant either placed manually or dropped from the air where it exists naturally, acts upon crushed fruits or grains that contain sugar or starches readily convertible into sugar (see Ford, 1983). Tiny amounts of alcohol are produced naturally within the human body by certain enzyme systems and are disposed of in various ways.

Beverage alcohol is ethyl alcohol, called *ethanol* in chemistry and popularly abbreviated as ETOH. The formula is usually written C_2H_5OH. It is the same alcohol found in all intoxicating beverages, from the most expensive Scotch or liqueur to the cheapest wine or beer. The main difference is not chemical but physical: the sheer volume of fluid taken in along with the ethanol. It is true that there are minor chemical differences due to other substances in the drink, especially in wine. But the main ingredient besides water is ethyl alcohol.

Congeners. The other substances in alcohol beverages are called congeners, a term sometimes restricted to other alcohols and sometimes applied to many small-molecule compounds that may be present, depending on the fermented materials and the sanitary conditions of the process. All alcohols are intoxicating. Ethanol (two-carbon alcohol) is much less toxic than the others, because the body breaks it down into harmless substances—carbon dioxide and water. Methyl (wood) alcohol, or methanol, breaks down into formic acid and formaldehyde, which has a special affinity for the optic nerve and may cause blindness. Methyl (one-carbon), propyl (three-carbon), butyl (four-carbon), and amyl (five-carbon, fusel oil) alcohols occur in trace amounts in many drinks. Although ethanol is the principal intoxicant, other alcohols are present in real-life drinking, which make it different from the ethanol experiments in a laboratory—a fact that some researchers forget.

Proof is twice the percent of ethanol: 100-proof liquor is 50 percent ethanol (in Canada and Britain 100 proof is 57 percent) and 86-proof whiskey is 43 percent ethanol. Wine and beer are usually expressed in straight percentages of alcohol, as described at the beginning of Chapter 3.

Ingestion

We have already noted that amount consumed is less a criterion of alcoholism than is how it affects one's behavior, dependency, and control. We speak here simply of drinking. "A drink" is not a scientific term. People do not drink absolute alcohol, but for ease of discussion consumption rates are usually reduced to quantities of absolute alcohol, since this is the important factor rather than quantity of beverage. The following are some common drinks with nearly equivalent amounts of alcohol (about 12.5 grams or nearly a half-ounce): One 12-ounce bottle of beer, a 3½-ounce glass of dry 13 percent wine or a 2½-ounce glass of 18 percent sweet wine, 1 ounce of 86-proof liquor. From this it is obvious that proposed labeling of only bottles that contain over 24 percent alcohol would send a false message that beer and wine are not intoxicating.

Rate of Ingestion. In addition to the amount of ethanol ingested, the length of time over which consumption takes place is important. Sipping at the rate of one small drink an hour may allow the liver to prevent the blood level of alcohol from rising notably. A dare to "chug-a-lug" a pint of 100-proof whiskey all at once killed a thirteen-year-old boy in our city.

So much for drinking. How does intoxication or drunkenness occur? Here the difference between ingestion and absorption is important. A law officer cannot arrest you for DWI (DUI) merely because he observed you taking a drink; the alcohol must first enter the bloodstream. Likewise, in the Shadel aversion conditioning, which we shall discuss in Chapter 15, any ingested alcohol is immediately vomited, and none is absorbed.

Absorption

Alcohol is one of the few substances, along with water and some salts, that does not go through the usual digestive process even when taken into the digestive organs. Rather, it is absorbed directly and unchanged into the blood through the lining of the mouth and esophagus in tiny amounts, more through the stomach, and 70 to 80 percent through the upper or small intestine. Within a few minutes after ingestion the alcohol begins to be circulated throughout the body, including the brain. This shows the importance of that first drink, which the recovered alcoholic seeks to avoid, since it almost immediately affects one's ability to judge or control whether one should have a second drink.

Blood Level

The result of absorption is blood alcohol level (BAL), or blood alcohol content (BAC). Think of pouring so many ounces of alcohol into so many pints of blood and measuring the strength or percentage of the resultant solution. This depends on many factors, so it is foolish to judge blood level, and therefore degree of intoxication, solely by the amount one drinks. If Mary has had three drinks and is obviously drunk, we cannot conclude that Jane, with the same three drinks, is therefore equally drunk.

Body Size. Even two people drinking the same amount over the same time will achieve different levels of blood alcohol. The larger person has more pints of blood into which the alcohol is diluted, so a 250-pound man will have a lower BAC than a 100-pound boy drinking the same amount. In addition, two people of the same weight will have slightly different blood levels, depending on the proportion of body weight that is fat as opposed to bone and muscle; alcohol does not dissolve as readily in fat, which results in a higher concentration in the blood. But why do two people of equal weight and build, drinking equal amounts over the same time, still have different blood alcohol levels?

Rate of Absorption. Differences in the rate at which the ingested alcohol is absorbed through the lining of the digestive tract into the bloodstream are one important reason for different BACs. These in turn depend on many factors, varying so widely between individuals, and between different occasions for the same individual, that comparisons are useless and misleading. Here are some of those factors:

1. Strength, or percentage of alcohol in the beverage. Beer contains so much more water that it is absorbed more slowly than stronger drinks. Blood level rises more slowly, to a lower maximum, and with a faster decline in BAC as compared to spirits, with wine in between. But too high a concentration of alcohol seems to sear the mucosa and retard absorption. The most rapid rate is, by no coincidence, that of the martini (about 35 percent).
2. Other chemicals in the drink, especially in beer and wine.
3. The amount and kind of food in the stomach. If the alcohol is soaked up with large amounts of food, it will not be absorbed as quickly as from an empty stomach.
4. The condition of the tissue of stomach and bowel linings, whether healthy or not. Important here also is the pylorus, or pyloric valve, which opens to empty the contents of the stomach into the small intestine, where absorption is more rapid than from the stomach. The pylorus may go into spasm and cause the person to vomit, or may open suddenly and "dump" the alcohol quickly into the rapidly absorbing intestine.
5. Carbonation, either natural, as in champagne, or added, as in a Scotch-and-soda highball. The "tiny bubbles" speed absorption by opening the pyloric valve into the small intestine, and they may also facilitate penetration of the gastrointestinal walls.

Other factors cause different reactions to the same amount of alcohol:

6. Nervous or emotional state. Fear, anger, stress, and fatigue can influence the condition of the stomach and bowel, usually speeding the process of absorption but sometimes slowing it. Such states may also reduce tolerance in the central nervous system.
7. Altitude can also make a difference, as mountain climbers and aviators know. Rarified air means less oxygen for the brain, which alcohol further diminishes.
8. High or low blood sugar level. Low level of glycogen stored in very thin persons.
9. Individual differences in body chemistry and drinking history. No two people are exactly alike biochemically, nor have they had the same life experiences with alcohol. Each body reacts differently, so again no comparisons are justified even if all the above conditions were equal—which they never are.

Metabolism and Excretion

All the alcohol absorbed into the bloodstream (a) is pumped by the heart to every cell and tissue of the body, with effects on both (b) short-term behavior and (c) long-range health. Intoxication results when the alcohol being circulated through the brain reaches a level that interferes with the normal functioning of nerve cells. The precise mechanism is still in dispute, although research is making it better understood as we learn how alcohol interacts with some neurotransmitters and certain receptor sites.

What determines blood alcohol level? The rate of ingestion and absorption into the bloodstream varies with a dozen factors, as we have seen. In contrast, the rate at which it leaves the blood is fixed. Nothing can hasten the process, practically speaking. So the difference between the rate of absorption and the rate at which alcohol is gotten rid of gives us the residual blood alcohol level. If one takes in more alcohol than the body can dispose of, alcohol blood level rises. Only time will lower it after ingestion ceases.

Excretion

Some (5 to 10 percent?) of the alcohol circulating is passed out of the blood stream *unmetabolized* in the breath, perspiration, and urine. The amount varies slightly with higher BAC, but that is irrelevant, because regardless of how much comes out this way or at what speed (rate), it is always a fixed proportion (ratio), for example, about 1:2100 alcohol concentration in the breath to alcohol concentration in the blood, in the case of alveolar air from deep in the lungs.

Since this alcohol is unchanged, the Breathalyzer or other device is measuring true blood alcohol, not some product of metabolism. Because of the fixed ratio, it is thus a fair measure of intoxication, in spite of differences in amount consumed or rate of absorption. It tells the concentration of alcohol affecting the brain at the moment, regardless of how much was consumed or over how long. It is noninvasive, obviating the need to draw a blood sample. We shall see in section B that two factors that can complicate this picture are individual differences in tolerance and whether the blood alcohol level is rising or falling.

Metabolism

Most of the alcohol (90 to 95 percent, depending on the BAC) is eliminated by being *metabolized* (oxidized, changed, detoxified, burned, broken down) into other substances, which are eventually eliminated from the body in the usual ways. Most of the metabolic activity takes place in the liver. Since it happens at a fixed rate, only part of the alcohol being pumped through the liver is metabolized at a time, while the rest continues to circulate. Chemically, the process of metabolism is as follows:

Ethanol   + Oxygen → Acetaldehyde →   Acetate   – → Carbon Dioxide + Water
(C_2H_5OH) (O_2) (C_2H_4O) $(C_2H_4O_2)$ (CO_2) (H_2O)

which simply says that ethanol is oxidized first into acetaldehyde, which breaks down into some acetate, a salt or ester of acetic acid, and eventually into carbon dioxide and water.

All this metabolism is controlled by enzymes (biological catalysts that facilitate the process). Thus ethanol is broken down into acetaldehyde by alcohol dehydrogenase (ADH), and acetaldehyde is broken down to acetate by aldehyde dehydrogenase (ALDH). Both processes involve other enzymes, and also the coenzyme NAD (nicotinamide adenine dinucleotide) and its reduced form, NADH. The reader need not understand all the chemistry involved but should recognize the role of enzymes and know that they are important for research, since they are clues to what is happening and in what amounts.

The liver has at least one alternate metabolic pathway for the elimination of alcohol. It is the MEOS (microsomal ethanol oxidizing system). Research suggests that there may be important differences between the MEOS of alcoholics and nonalcoholics. Other differences may be a greater use of the enzyme catalase instead of ADH, or an alternate form of ADH.

The enzyme action at the acetaldehyde stage can be blocked by the drugs Antabuse (disulfiram, tetraethylthiuramdisulfide) and Temposil, preventing the acetaldehyde from breaking down further. If alcohol is taken while these drugs are in the system, the blocking causes a buildup that results in acute acetaldehyde poisoning, or "Antabuse reaction." We shall discuss this in Chapter 15, and only note the process here.

Rate of Metabolism. Overestimating how fast the liver burns up alcohol can send dangerously impaired drivers out on the highway. Ranging from less than ⅓ ounce to about ½ ounce, it is usually stated as ⅓ ounce per hour. Although a highly tolerant liver might burn up to a maximum of 12.5 grams or .535 ounce, Becker and colleagues (1974, p. 13) say that a "normal" liver can metabolize about 7 grams or 10 ml. (0.3 ounce) of ethanol per hour (the specific gravity of ethanol being .789).

Seven grams is about the amount of ethanol in ¾ ounce of 86-proof whiskey (=0.32 ounce ETOH). Unfortunately, some writer carelessly transcribed this to ¾ ounce of *alcohol* instead of ¾ ounce of *whiskey,* and the error was copied from one book to another, including some otherwise standard works. Thus "one drink an hour" can be very misleading. No human liver can metabolize ¾ ounce of alcohol in an hour. The ⅓ ounce that is the most the average liver can handle is less than the 0.43 to 0.48 ounces ETOH contained in the common drinks we listed under "ingestion." It is the amount contained in 8.8 ounces of beer, 2.6 ounces of dry wine, or ⅔ ounce of 100-proof liquor. Thus one "drink" an hour could be more than the liver can burn up, while the residual ethanol builds up in the bloodstream.

Another way of expressing this rate of metabolism is that a healthy liver can reduce the BAL about .015 percent each hour (Wallgren and Barry, 1970). This is useful because it is usually true regardless of body size, since the size of the liver is proportionate. If the average person has a BAL of 0.25 percent at 2 A.M. and goes to sleep, by 8 A.M. it is still 0.16 when it is time to start work, and at noon it is 0.10, which means that person is still legally drunk.

The rate at which the liver metabolizes alcohol may differ slightly between individuals, depending on the size and health of the liver. It may differ very slightly with the kind of alcoholic beverage. But by and large the rate is fixed by nature, except that chronic use can increase it somewhat. Research is still trying to discover a way of speeding up the process, and every partygoer would like to be able to eliminate the toxic effects once the party is over. Exercise, oxygen, cold showers, and black coffee are among the means tried, to no avail. If you give a gallon of black coffee to a drunk, you do not get a sober person but only an alert drunk. Fructose, or pure fruit sugar, was once claimed by some to accelerate metabolism of alcohol. Later research showed that, besides being impractical, it has harmful side effects such as depletion of ATP in the liver, plus toxic levels of uric and lactic acids (Iber, 1977; Levy et al., 1977; *Nutritional Review*, 1978, 36:14–15).

There is a faster metabolism rate at higher blood levels, but obviously to raise the alcohol level in order to speed the metabolism rate is to get nowhere fast. And stimulating a drinker with coffee may send him out on the highway instead of letting him sleep it off.

Hangover

The sobering-up process is dependent primarily on the ability of the liver to burn up the alcohol in the blood, so there is little one can do except wait for that to happen. The morning-after misery we call hangover has been the subject of many myths as to both cause and cure. The headache, nausea, and fatigue have been ascribed to such causes as drinking more than one type of beverage in an evening, but they are simply the result of drinking too much alcohol in any form. Hangover can be prevented only by not drinking or by drinking moderately, for example very slowly, with food in the stomach and under relaxed social conditions.

Hangover is an unpleasant experience but rarely dangerous medically, although it does impair driving skills even if one feels okay. The precise cause is uncertain but may include edema of the cranium plus allergy to the congeners. No satisfactory treatment is known. The numerous folk remedies—stale beer, tomato juice, raw egg, hot sauce, and so on—have no scientific validity. Coffee may help but can harm a stomach already irritated by alcohol. Aspirin can be quite harmful to the stomach lining. None of these remedies speeds up the sobering-up process; they merely relieve some of the uncomfortable symptoms—and, in the case of the beer, signal the vicious cycle of addiction.

Medical treatment of withdrawal in chronic alcoholism is an entirely different and more serious matter, to be dealt with in Chapter 15. Meanwhile, the search for *amethyst* or magic pill goes on: a pill one can take before the party so as to enjoy alcohol without suffering its harmful effects, a pill to sober up quickly afterward, a pill so the recovered alcoholic can drink socially, and a pill for instant cure of the hangover. All of these seem to be founded only in man's hope and run contrary to what we know of the biochemistry. In any case, they betray a questionable value assigned to alcohol. Worse, they have ethical and legal ramifications if one takes a pill that allows one to go out on the highway impaired, to become entrapped by the addictive properties of alcohol, or even to reach a lethal level of ETOH without feeling it.

B.   Alcohol and Behavior; Driving

We now turn to how alcohol affects behavior, especially when driving a motor vehicle because of its large place in American life and the high death and accident rates it engenders. If we were as concerned about safe drivers as we are about safe cars, there would be far fewer deaths on our highways.

We have seen that if ingestion and absorption of alcoholic beverages are faster than the rate at which the liver can metabolize the alcohol, blood alcohol level (BAC) rises. Until detoxified in the liver or eliminated through excretion, all the alcohol is being circulated through all organs of the body. But we shall focus on its effect on neural tissue, especially the brain, of both alcoholics and nonalcoholics.

Stimulant or Depressant?

At a cocktail party, after a few drinks the noise level goes up and the conversation is more animated. The obvious conclusion is that alcohol is a stimulant. Some of the observed effect is pseudostimulation, the result of the depressing action of alcohol on those brain centers that mediate inhibitions, judgment, and control. Knocking out the brakes is a depressant action on the braking system, but the net result might be more action by the car.

For years this was widely accepted as the total explanation, although Mark Keller (1966) reviewed a long history of experimentation showing that alcohol is a stimulant for a brief period before it is a depressant. Kraeplin said this as early as 1892. It is now recognized that the first action of alcohol on neural tissue is to irritate, agitate, or stimulate. Low doses of ETOH increase norepinephrine (noradrenalin), although higher doses inhibit its secretion. In addition, the calories present in alcohol supply quick energy—"candy is dandy, but liquor is quicker" has some biochemical basis. All this has been known for some time (Wallgren and Barry, 1970) and confirmed by more recent research, such as that of Yedy Israel on the hypermetabolic state in alcoholics (Isselbacher, 1977, p. 612; Marlatt, 1987; Marlatt and Gordon, 1985, pp. 144–46; and especially Lewis and Lockmuller, 1990). It will be relevant when we discuss the theory that all alcoholics drink to sedate inner stress from emotional conflict.

The question is not simple, since some brain cells and neurohormones are inhibitory and some are excitatory, and alcohol may facilitate nerve transmission in some cells while depressing it in others, even though it is bathing the whole brain. The "onion" or "layers" notion of brain functions is only schematic at best, but it may well be that alcohol depresses the more delicate areas of the cerebral cortex before depressing the centers for vital functions located in the old, or lower, brain. Suffice it to say that although the long-range effect of alcohol, even on alcoholics, is to depress nerve action to the point of coma and even death, its immediate effect is to stimulate.

It is important that alcoholics seem to get more of an initial lift from alcohol than nonalcoholics do (Goodwin, 1978a, p. 129). There is some evidence that this is true right from the beginning of their drinking careers, but research on that point is difficult, since it depends on retrospective reports that are highly subjective as well as distorted by time. The initial lift is congruent with the mounting evidence that alcoholics differ physiologically from nonalcoholics from the onset of drinking. Research on mice shows that some are stimulated by alcohol and some get depressed. Instead of sedation (nobody hosts a social hour where barbiturates are passed around instead of cocktails), it may be that the alcoholic is looking for that "glow," or extra lift, rather than for tension reduction (Cappell and Herman, 1972; Keehn, 1970).

Another reason why the alcoholic may function better after drinking a little alcohol is that he has developed a physical dependence and now needs alcohol to bring functions up to normal. And for everyone there is the possibility that a drink may quell anxiety and allow abilities to reach maximum operation, which does not mean that alcohol actually adds to our abilities. Research has shown that artists and writers who were alcoholic produced great works in spite of being alcoholic, not because of it (*Writer's Digest*, October 1978, 58: 25–33; *Drug Abuse and Alcoholism Review*, 1980, 3[3/4]:17; Vaillant, 1983, p. 215; Newlove, 1981). *The* ARF *Journal* says that drink gives the writer "obfuscation, not inspiration" (October 1981, p. 7).

Effects on Behavior

Many psychologists earn their living measuring human behaviors, and a review of the literature yields Figure 1, which depicts the effects of alcohol on driving and every other measurable behavior; the horizontal line represents increased levels of BAC from zero to coma and death. With variation due to individual differences, what it tells us is that alcohol initially improves behavioir slightly for a brief time, then decreases performance. Alcoholics (dotted line) with zero alcohol often start below normal, improve more than others, and continue improved for as long as they stay within their individually acquired tolerance [ ]. But as the blood level rises, the quality and quantity of performance for all drop below the initial norm, a fact easily observed as we watch a very drunk person attempt the simplest tasks and eventually pass out.

The role of alcohol in traffic accidents has been researched for decades (e.g., Borkenstein et al., 1964), with many experiments using cab or truck drivers or racing drivers, all of whom were drinkers, so they were not novices at either experience. Objective ratings according to standard criteria by driving instructors and licensing inspectors consistently showed the results charted here: Performance improved only slightly and temporarily, then quickly deteriorated. Similar results are obtained when any other human task or function is measured. Visual acuity, for example, was shown experimentally to improve with BAC below 0.02 percent (which many people could hardly feel), but to decrease at blood levels above that, even within a low legal limit of 0.08 percent (Tong et al., 1974).

Judgment. Most important is the dashed line on the graph that depicts estimated performance as rated by the persons themselves during the same period. Because alcohol interferes with judgment centers in the brain, our ability to judge how well we are doing is impaired equally to or worse than actual performance. "I always drive better after a couple of drinks" is not borne out by objective ratings; we only *think* we are driving better. As the great physi-

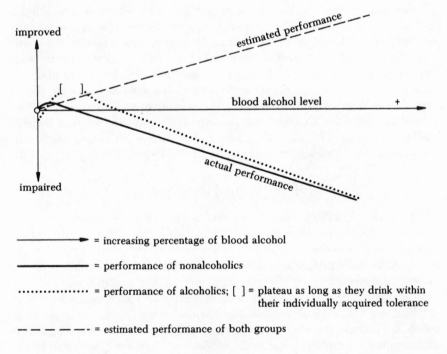

Figure 1

cian Sir William Osler put it, "Alcohol does not make us do things better; it just makes us less ashamed of doing them badly." The drivers in the experiments cited above varied more on their estimate of their own performance, but generally were surprised at how poorly they had done—particularly those who began the experiment convinced that they could drink and drive. Interesting and sometimes amusing confirmation of this discrepancy between estimated and actual performance has been garnered in other experiments. One college professor gave an objective test to his class, then repeated it a week later after giving each a bottle of beer. Asked whether the first test was easier or harder than the second, they all insisted they had done better on the second when actually they had made 17 percent more errors. Better yet, you might tape-record a party and play it back the next morning. In the cold gray dawn what you hear is that laughter got louder as the jokes got worse; we thought we were funnier (estimated performance up) but the quality of humor went down.

Obviously the situation is much more serious where driving is involved, since a person may insist on driving home when he is unable to judge how badly impaired he may be and consequently pose a threat to the lives of others. For this reason, otherwise excellent slogans are really not effective: "If you drink, don't drive" and the like. Much as one may accept their logic while sober, one cannot judge their applicability when most needed. Coffee or other stimulants at this point may increase the danger, as the person may feel alert enough to drive while blood alcohol has not gone down.

Driving. It is said that alcohol attacks judgment before skill, and then attacks the most recently learned skill. Driving is a skill learned much later in life than walking and talking. There are many specific ways in which driving is affected by alcohol, never fully appreciated by the driver because judgment is first dulled. Reaction time is slowed an extra fraction of a second in switching from accelerator to brake. With alcohol things seem to happen too fast, and one does not plan ahead as good driving demands. Deep muscle sense, a feel for the car's position and movement, on which racing drivers rely a great deal ("driving by the seat of one's pants"), is impaired. Depth or space perception of relative position to another car is less accurate, as are estimates of relative speed. Narrowing of the visual field ("tunnel vision"), blurred or double vision, and poorer discrimination between hues and between lights of different intensities have been reported. Night vision and resistance to glare (ability to readjust after exposure to bright lights) are notably impaired.

Poor motor coordination, faulty judgment, and lowered inhibitions are further complicated by a most important factor: emotional mood and personality change. Under the influence of alcohol, some people become very aggressive and impatient when they get behind the wheel, careless of others' rights and much more willing to take risks. Drowsiness and shortened attention span are dangers, as is a decreased ability to react to an unfamiliar situation; many alcoholics can drive home from their favorite bar or tavern while quite inebriated as long as they know what to expect, but don't make it when something occurs that requires a new reaction.

Apparently the initial stimulation does not last long enough to enhance driving, except perhaps for a high-tolerant alcoholic—and then only at low levels for a short time. Figures that suggest fewer accidents after one drink than after none are probably sampling errors tied to general personality characteristics of moderate drinkers versus nondrinkers.

Other Behavior. The drinking situation and the drinker's mood, attitudes, and previous experience with alcohol will all contribute to his or her reactions to drinking. Alcohol has little effect on the sense of touch but dulls sensitivity to pain. Sometimes the result is that fractures go unattended until too late to set them properly. It is a dangerous anesthetic, however, because there is too narrow a margin between the level of anesthesia and the level that could cause death. Even low doses of alcohol reduce sensitivity to taste and odors, which can mean failure to be alerted to danger. Critical or self-monitoring functions are dulled by even slight amounts of alcohol, decreasing the ability to profit from psychotherapy. In business negotiations a few drinks may lower your opponent's shrewdness, but they will not enhance your own ability to think sharply. Worse, the relaxed feeling may make you unaware of your lowered potential. Alcohol may dull one's sense of values because the drinker is too anesthetized to feel loss or emotional pain. This loss in value system is one reason why alcoholism is said to be also a spiritual illness.

Tolerance

Before we can discuss the relation between behavior and specific levels of blood alcohol, there are two important complicating factors to be noted: tolerance and potentiation.*

Tolerance here means the ability of brain cells to function in the presence of alcohol. It may be either initial or acquired. *Initial,* or innate, tolerance is that with which a person is born, be it high or low. It is not rate of metabolism, which may also vary initially and is often confused with tolerance in discussions of whether there are individual or racial differences. The precise relation of either of these to alcoholism is by no means clear. Thus, poor tolerance may be a protection against alcoholism rather than making one more vulnerable.

Acquired tolerance, or tissue adaptation, means that cellular changes have occurred as a result of drinking, which make the same amount of alcohol have less effect on the central nervous system. In other words, more alco-

* Lack of standard terminology causes different authors to use terms in different ways. Keller (1977) prefers to restrict the word *tolerance* to initial tolerance, and to use *adaptation* for aquired tolerance. Biologists sometimes use the terms *adaptation* or *habituation* for acquired physical tolerance. We use *habituation* in its psychological meaning.

Figure 2

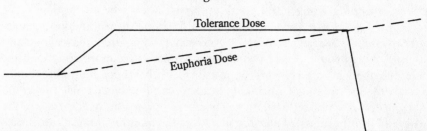

hol is now required to get the same effect as previously. It also means that eventually when deprived of alcohol the brain does not function so well, causing symptoms of withdrawal that are alleviated (temporarily) by alcohol. Probably about 20 percent of tolerance is metabolic (MEOS, different ADH, etc.), and 80 percent is pharmacodynamic compensation or adaptation in brain biochemistry, which leads to physical dependence. Changes in the brain cell membrane receptor sites for certain neurotransmitters, such as depletion of membrane enkephalins, are probably key factors. Loss of tolerance in later-stage alcoholism is due to death of brain cells and to oversensitivity of receptor sites.

Changes in Tolerance. It is commonly accepted that changes in tolerance are a sign of addiction. Different types of alcoholism, however, prevent us from generalizing too much here. Many alcoholics increase their initial tolerance in the early stages of their drinking, maintain that plateau through most of their alcoholic careers, and eventually experience a notable drop in tolerance, perhaps below their initial level. That drop seems irreversible. This would explain why some "experienced" drinkers cannot handle even a single small drink, even after a long period of sobriety. Their tolerance level has dropped below their euphoria level; that is, they get drunk (or sick) before they get happy, as shown in Figure 2. They can even die if they try to drink the amounts they used to handle before tolerance dropped. Many middle-stage alcoholics, on the other hand, typically have a high tolerance level. In this case, it is a symptom of alcoholism rather than a sign that they are immune. A high BAC upon admission to treatment, with ability still to function, is thus one useful diagnostic sign, although we never make a diagnosis on just one symptom.

In addition to the increase in physical tolerance, alcoholics usually develop some behavioral skills in masking the effects of alcohol: They learn not to slur their words, to walk straight, and so on. In any case, alcoholics do not develop physical tolerance to the extent that those who use heroin do. Moreover, both behavior and tolerance become unpredictable when alcohol is used with other drugs.

Since the use of alcohol in combination with other drugs is widespread, especially among women and youth, we must always be aware that *cross-addiction* and *cross-tolerance* are common. It should be routine for the alcoholism intake interviewer to ask, "And what other drugs have you been taking?" Many young people coming into AA have used more drugs than the older members have even heard of. It used to be that a good anesthesiologist was always careful to get a drinking history, since tolerance to alcohol could mean need for a greater amount of the anesthetic for an operation and the dosage had to be adjusted accordingly. Now the anesthesia must allow for a history of other drugs as well. Note that cross-tolerance or cross-addiction can be present even though one has not used the other drug; a Valium addict is practically an alcoholic without ever having had a drink. Many a recovered alcoholic has relapsed when the dentist gave Percodan, not realizing its similarity to alcohol. But the high tolerance of an alcoholic can be masked by a synergistic vulnerability, which we must now examine.

Potentiation or Synergism

If the person already has some sedative drug in the bloodstream, less will be required to achieve the effect, because of a phenomenon called potentiation or synergism. Some use synergism to refer to the *adding* effect of two drugs being present in the blood at the same time, and potentiation to refer to a *multiplying* effect. Terminology is not standard, and we shall speak of potentiation with an emphasis on the multiplier aspect.

Hollywood Death. To "slip someone a Mickey Finn" or knockout drops in former days meant to put a barbiturate pill in his or her drink. The effect of the two was not what would be expected from the mere addition of the two, but drastically more. The two drugs potentiate each other in the system; that is, they not only add but multiply their effects. One-half plus one-half here does not equal a full dose, but many times that. To be more scientific, one-fifth of the lethal dose of alcohol when combined with one-twentieth of the lethal dose of a barbiturate can be a fatal dose (Seixas, 1975, p. 87). This is obviously more than simple addition, which would yield only about one-quarter of a lethal dose. Here we have the explanation of the so-called Hollywood death, or apparent suicide, which is really an accidental death due to taking sleeping pills after drinking. One may not even be drunk, but immediately upon taking the pill one may become so disoriented that he or she loses all track of what is taken, or how many. Short of death, polydrug use is more likely to cause permanent brain damage.

Many Drugs

Alcohol potentiates with many drugs, including tranquilizers such as Valium, Librium, and Xanax; sedatives like the barbiturates and other sleeping pills;

marijuana; Demerol (a common problem for doctors, nurses, and dentists); opiates like morphine and heroin; and such "innocent" prescription drugs as blood thinners or the antihistamines one takes for allergies and hay fever. Even nonprescription drugs such as Midol can potentiate with alcohol. The only safe rule is never to drink alcohol when one is taking any other drug. If one can't stop drinking in this situation, that is a sign of alcoholism. Cocaine and amphetamines (speed, diet pills) interact with alcohol in a different way, with bizarre reactions and a tendency to think one's behavior is normal because the depressant effect of alcohol is not felt. Thus begins a vicious circle of uppers and downers, with gross self-deception because the person thinks that the cocaine keeps one from getting drunk and the alcohol keeps one from getting too high on cocaine—wrong on both scores (see Smith and Wesson, 1985). Cocaine makes one alert enough to start the car, but drowsiness from the alcohol can soon cause an accident. Caffeine and nicotine with alcohol also confuse the central nervous system, with unpredictable results.

Marijuana potentiates with alcohol, but in a peculiar way. Doses of alcohol and tetrahydrocannabinol (THC, the active ingredient in marijuana) that by themselves produce no significant change in perception or behavior have been shown experimentally in combination to cause distortions of sensory perception, time sense, and reaction time, which make driving hazardous (Franks et al., 1975). In one study 17 percent of fatal auto accidents involved marijuana, which the Breathalyzer does not show. But the marijuana tends to delay the peak effects of the BAC, with the result that the person may leave the party feeling neither intoxicated nor stoned and later become a serious menace on the highway. Marijuana smokers may be more impaired a half-hour after they have "come down" and feel they are unaffected. This impairment can last for a long time; THC also has a long half-life, because it stores in the fat cells and can remain in the body for six months to a year (see Mann, 1985). Marijuana is useful in chemotherapy for cancer patients because it blocks the vomit center in the medulla, but the same effect can be fatal if it allows the drinker to overdose on alcohol.

Withdrawal

Polydrug use creates serious problems in the hospital emergency room, where the attending physician may fear to use any medication because the patient might already have something similar in the blood. Sometimes they can only watch vital signs and hope for the best until nature detoxifies the patient. Since the liver does not eliminate all substances at the same time but tends to do selective burning whereby it metabolizes all of one substance before beginning another, in polyaddiction the result is a second withdrawal after the patient has successfully come through one withdrawal. A minimum of ten days may be necessary for the detoxification of polydrug cases. We know of one patient who was still toxic after thirty-two days, and another who required three months for complete withdrawal. Ignorance of these facts can lead to mistaking withdrawal symptoms at ten to fourteen days for signs of an underlying psychosis.

Withdrawal from alcohol, especially delirium tremens, can be very dangerous. In contrast, death from heroin withdrawal is extremely rare. Most heroin deaths (other than AIDS or hepatitis from dirty needles and the like) are probably from a synergistic "overdose" similar to the Hollywood death described above, in that they are due to the potentiating effect of combining heroin and alcohol in the bloodstream at the same time (Brecher, 1972, pp. 101–14). Prognosis in the polydrug misuser is unreliable. Many are combining methadone and alcohol, or cocaine and alcohol.

Effects of Blood Levels

Section A of this chapter contains a list of factors that can produce different blood levels even from the same amount of alcohol. To those individual differences in body chemistry and learned behavior can be added the facts of potentiation and synergism, and especially tolerance differences between individuals and in the same individual with varying BAC levels (Gross, 1977). Also, the same BAC level seems to affect behavior more when blood alcohol level is rising than when it is falling. The obvious conclusion is that one can hardly predict the consequences even when one knows the amount and kind of alcoholic beverage consumed, drinking time, and body weight. Yet those are usually the only factors included in popular charts or handy gadgets that purport to indicate levels of blood alcohol and whether it is safe to drive.

Taken with all these cautions, Table 2 gives a general idea of the effects of different blood levels. Of many ways of recording blood alcohol, we use the two most common. Although testing devices often give figures in milligrams (mg.) of alcohol per 100 cc. (or 100 ml.) of blood, the more understandable is a simple percentage. Thus a reading of 500 mg. equals 0.5 percent blood alcohol. Note that this is not 5 percent, but one-half of 1 percent—a tiny fraction of the concentration of alcohol used as an antiseptic.

For most individuals, judgment and self-control are affected first, at the lowest concentrations of alcohol in the blood. Moving up Table 2, sensory perception and coordinated muscular activity may be slightly impaired at a BAC as low as 0.035 percent, and notably at 0.1 percent. At 0.3 percent most people would appear quite drunk, with staggering gait and slurred speech. At about 0.4 percent, consciousness goes. If blood alcohol passes the 500 mg. or 0.5 percent level, brain centers controlling heart and breathing are sufficiently depressed to cause death from respiratory failure. Unless alcohol is potentiated by other drugs (e.g., marijuana, as explained above), this is rare for two reasons: pyloric spasm or plain nausea causes the person to vomit the alcohol before all of it passes into the small intestine for full absorption, or one passes out in coma before drinking enough to cause death. However, it can happen, as in the case of the boy who drank the pint of whiskey on a dare and did not

Table 2 Some Blood Alcohol Concentrations (BAC), with Effects Not Corrected for
Individual Differences (see text)

mg./100 cc.	Percentage	Effects
500 mg.	= 0.5%	Death (varies from 0.3% in young to 0.8% in alcoholics with very high tolerance)
400	= 0.4%	Coma, unconsciousness (not "blackout")
300	= 0.3%	Visibly drunk
100	= 0.10%	Present law in 37 states for DUI (DWI)
80	= 0.08%	DUI in Austria, Britain, Canada, France, Italy, Switzerland, and eleven U.S. states
50	= 0.05%	DUI in Japan, Netherlands, Norway, AMA 1985 recommendation
35	= 0.035%	All drivers on six subtests showed some impairment
30	= 0.03%	DUI in Belgium, Czechoslovakia
20	= 0.02%	Sweden
> 0	> 0%	Finland: any detectable alcohol in bloodstream

quite reach the 0.5 percent level. Conversely, some alcoholics develop such tolerance that they can still walk at 0.7 or 0.8 percent, a level that would kill most people. But lethal dose-tolerance increase does not parallel behavioral tolerance, as in heroin; the gap narrows so that the behavioral tolerance gets dangerously close to the lethal dose, as shown in Figure 3, which is why it is not used as an anesthetic.

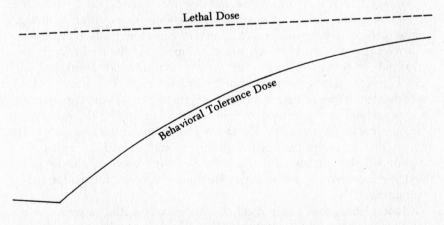

Figure 3

Impaired Driving

All driving skills are affected to the point that at 0.10 percent one is legally impaired, or under the influence (DUI), or driving while intoxicated (DWI), however the statute is worded. At the 1985 Delegate Assembly of NCA, "drunk" driving was dropped in favor of "drinking and driving," because a severely impaired driver will still say "I wasn't drunk." At the old level of 0.15 percent one is twenty-five times more likely to have an accident than with no alcohol, and at 0.10 percent one is still seven times more likely. Those are averages, skewed by the fact that alcoholics with high tolerance drive better than others at these levels, which are therefore even more dangerous for the inexperienced or less tolerant. In some states 0.10 percent is now not merely presumptive evidence but automatic proof of DUI. Even below 0.05 percent, one is no longer presumed legally "safe" in some states. In many states there is no legal presumption between 0.05 and 0.10 percent either for or against impaired driving, and other evidence is used.

Are the legal limits too severe? No (see Hunt and Witt, 1994). Based on a mountain of scientific evidence, the American Medical Association on June 21, 1985, recommended a minimum BAC at just half the common statute for DUI: 0.05 percent, with which NCADD concurred in its April 20, 1986, policy statement on drinking and driving. The FAA stated a 0.04 percent level for pilots (*Alcoholism Report,* April 16, 1985). This has been thoroughly researched in the Scandinavian countries, in England and Canada, and in many of our states, using university laboratories and other facilities. In a study of six thousand people, 10 percent were intoxicated at 50 mg. or 0.05 percent, and one-third before they reached 100 mg. or 0.10 percent (Crancer, 1969). In one study, 20.6 percent of accidents occurred with a BAC below 0.05 percent in the driver. Much research puts the start of impairment at 0.02 to 0.03 percent. So one does not have to be legally drunk, much less an alcoholic, to kill somebody with an automobile.

The research was so impressive that long ago Canada, the United Kingdom, France, Italy, Austria, Switzerland, and some states lowered the legal limit to 0.08 percent, hence the film title *Point Zero Eight,* which depicts racing drivers impaired at this level. Norway, Japan, and the Netherlands lowered it to 0.05 percent; Belgium, East Germany, and Czechoslovakia to 0.03 percent; and Sweden to 0.2 percent or 20 mg. An example of the kind of evidence that led to those changes was an experiment in which experienced drivers took alcohol and were subjected to a battery of tests of driving skill; at 0.035 percent or 35 mg. every one showed some impairment on each of the six tests (this is one-third the legal limit in most states). Such evidence caused Finland to change its law so that any measurable amount of alcohol in the blood is presumptive of impairment. See under "Alcohol and Traffic Laws" in Chapter 20.

Blood alcohol tests can protect the innocent as well. If a person is observed lying unconscious with the smell of liquor on the breath, a BAC test might show that blood alcohol is far too low to account for the coma and thus help diagnose a diabetic coma, heart attack, head injury, or any of a dozen possible causes other than alcohol. Likewise, if someone is driving after a single beer and is arrested for a traffic violation by an officer who smells the beer on the breath, a test will exculpate that individual from a drunk driving charge.

How Many Drinks?

With trepidation one approaches the question, How many drinks will it take to reach a given level of blood alcohol? "A drink" can mean anything from a 1-ounce jigger (which may be extinct) of 86-proof liquor to a massive highball glass containing three or more ounces of 100 proof. A physician told of one little old lady whom he hospitalized with severe liver damage who claimed she just had "two drinks" each evening; in spite of long experience with alcoholics it took him fifteen days to ferret out the fact that each "drink" was a pint of gin and some vermouth, so her two martinis totaled more than a quart. One friend says, "Just let mine run until it gets good and cold." Moreover, we often lie or just forget how much we have actually had. Even if size and strength of drink is controlled, we have pointed out so many variable factors and individual differences that the reader should be most wary of jumping to conclusions.

Using the "drinks" given at the beginning of this chapter, we shall consider a drink to be one bottle of beer, 3½ ounces of dry wine, or 1 ounce of 86-proof liquor—not to be confused with the amount of alcohol the liver can metabolize in an hour, which is slightly less than this but must be subtracted from the amount consumed over a given time.

Thus understood, one can estimate that an average 160-pound person would need to drink, within one hour, four or five drinks to attain a BAC of 100 mg. or 0.10 percent, the legal limit in most states. A 240-pound muscleman might require up to six drinks, and a 100-pound girl only two or three. The 160-pound man would reach the legal limit in the jurisdictions that set it at 50 mg. or 0.05 percent by consuming two or three drinks; at this level one is twice as liable to have an accident as with no alcohol and is above the 0.035 percent level in the driving experiment where all six subtests showed some impairment.

C.   Alcohol and Health: Long-range Effects
Nutrition

Some people quibble about whether alcohol should be classed as a food. Certainly it is a poor one. But since it can supply up to 70 percent of the body's caloric needs and is a ready source of energy, it meets a common meaning of the term food. Pure alcohol yields 7.1 calories per gram or more than 200 calories to the ounce. Wine and especially beer have some additional calories from the content of the original material that survives fermentation. Alcohol serves as a substitute source of energy, which allows the body to store other foods as fat, so it is fattening in an indirect but positive way. Moreover, the body can manufacture fat from acetate, one of the products of alcohol metabolism.

Alcohol is the classic example of "empty calories," because it contains no vitamins, minerals, or proteins. Even the small amount of vitamins and trace minerals in wine and beer cannot redeem their poor nutritional value. Many alcoholics suffer from some degree of avitaminosis (lack of vitamins) for three reasons: (1) Much of their intake is alcoholic beverages instead of a balanced diet, for which they often have little appetite; (2) alcohol causes poor absorption of vitamins from the gastrointestinal tract; and (3) alcohol interferes with the liver's ability to utilize the vitamins and other nutrients in whatever foods are eaten. Hence, even fat alcoholics are usually suffering from some degree of malnutrition. The "wine sores" on the skin of skid-road alcoholics, due to the substitution of cheap wine for a balanced diet, can occur in wealthy alcoholics also.

The truth of the preceding paragraph makes it tempting to blame malnutrition for all physical pathology in alcoholics, and even alcoholism itself. That is simplistic, and the answer is not to place multivitamin pills in all bars or add vitamin B_1 to beer—if for no other reason than that alcohol interferes with their assimilation and use.

Alcohol: A Direct Cause

In addition to its short-term effects on driving and other behaviors, alcohol is a prime cause of chronic damage to nearly every organ in the body—for six months to three years and often irreversibly (see Lieber, 1992). Death in alcoholics is due to the following causes in order of frequency: cardiovascular (heart attacks and strokes), cancer, suicide, accidents, cirrhosis of the liver.

In 1938 an article appeared claiming that the so-called wet brain was an unscientific scare story spread by the Woman's Christian Temperance Union to promote prohibition, and that alcohol itself did not cause damage to the brain, liver, and other organs. That was repeated for the next two decades even in the scientific literature, until research by J. Beard and D. Knott in Memphis, by Charles Lieber in New York, and at outstanding medical research centers such as Harvard, Cornell, and Stanford began to show that along with avitaminosis and other nutritional factors, alcohol itself can cause, both directly and indirectly, organic damage in well-nourished experimental animals and human beings. C. B. Courville's 1955 book *The Effects of Alcohol on the Nervous System of Man* has been superseded by more recent works by Ernest Noble, James Rankin, A. E. Bennett, H. Kalant, Yedy Israel, Frank Seixas, Henri Begleiter, and a host of scientists, making the conclusion irrefutable (Parvez et al., 1985). Perhaps the world's leading authority on alcohol and the liver, Lieber (1976), is quite clear that adequate diet does not prevent alcohol from doing widespread damage in the body. Of special interest is the research of James W. Smith and others, showing lowered intelligence and brain damage in alcoholics with middle or upper socioeconomic backgrounds to be equal to that in impoverished and presumably less well-nourished alcoholics.

Research is only now uncovering the specific mechanisms whereby alcohol causes physical damage, and much remains to be discovered. Although alcohol in high doses is a depressant in its ultimate effect, its initial effect on tissue is to irritate. For example, its role as a carcinogen in the upper digestive tract and elsewhere may be partly due to its property as an irritant. Not only is ETOH toxic, but the acetaldehyde into which it breaks down is extremely so. And the hydrogen given off in metabolizing both causes fatty liver, high blood lipids, high ammonia levels, and hypoglycemia.

We can only briefly enumerate the principal organic pathologies and refer the reader to more detailed medical treatises. But it should be kept in mind that the following does not apply only to alcoholics, and much of it not even to drunkenness. Even moderate social drinking can produce many of the phenomena to be presented here, to a lesser degree of course.

Hormones

Hormones are the chemical messengers that control and coordinate the functions of all tissues and organs. Current research indicates that alcohol disturbs the complex interactions of the endocrine glands that secrete hormones (Gordon and Lieber, 1992; NIAAA, 1994). By interfering with hormone actions, alcohol can alter blood sugar levels and exacerbate or cause diabetes, interfere with calcium metabolism and bone structure with increased risk of osteoporosis, and impair both male and female reproductive functions.

Liver

Although the action of alcohol on the brain produces the most common and serious behavioral consequences, the liver is the site of most illness and mortality among alcoholics (Hall, 1985). An enlarged, fatty liver is the first stage, due to accumulation of excess fat. This is reversible; it disappears with cessation of alcohol intake. However, Lieber says that some deaths may be due to just fatty liver. If fatty infiltration continues, necrosis or death of hepatic (liver) cells, irritation, and swelling that causes blockage result in inflammation of the liver called alcoholic hepatitis, not to be confused with infectious hepatitis or serum hepatitis—all of them having jaundice as a symptom. Although there is a high mortality rate, alcoholic hepatitis may still be reversible. But the next stage is not: cirrhosis. This is scar tissue in the liver, fibrous, hard material that like any scar is nonfunctional and will never be normal again. Increased scarring crowds and kills the liver cells, and the dead cells create acids that kill off still more cells. Cirrhosis is the fifth leading cause of death among alcoholics, and the third leading cause of death in males aged 25–65.

In assessing liver damage we must distinguish anatomy (structure) from physiology (function). Nature has lots of reserve and tends to compensate, so tests of liver function will sometimes show nothing when up to 70 percent of liver cells may be sick. But 80 percent damage could mean death. An old alcoholic with "just one more drunk left" might be in between the 70 and the 80 percent, though his friends don't know the exact explanation of his death after a binge. An alcoholic living on the 10 percent margin could die if the doctor allows drinking to be resumed when liver function tests are normal. A 1983 British study reported "no correlation" between liver damage and tests of liver function. Even the SGPT test shows *rate* of liver cell necrosis, not *extent*. Use of the radioisotope technitium 99 or snipping a bit of tissue in a biopsy may tell a different story, as in the experiment on a group of British medical students who drank only up to 0.1 percent (legal) BAC every night for two weeks. A biopsy on every one of them showed structural change.

The liver is the body's chemical laboratory, with an incredible array of functions. It *manufactures* bile, glycogen, albumin, globulin, prothrombin, and other substances for fighting infection, blood clotting (hence alcoholics show more bruises and bleeding), and general health. In vulnerable persons, drinking can trigger a painful gouty arthritis due to excessive uric acid. The liver controls the levels of cholesterol, fatty acids, and triglycerides, which harm both the liver and the cardiovascular system.

Since alcohol interferes with the proper conversion of sugar, it is obviously hard on diabetics. High blood sugar (hyperglycemia) and low blood sugar (hypoglycemia) can both be due to a sick liver. We must distinguish hepatic, or alcoholic, hypoglycemia from true hypoglycemia, which is relatively rare. Hypoglycemia is *not* a cause of alcoholism but a complication for which the worst remedy is a candy bar. This shoots blood sugar up, exciting the pancreas to secrete more insulin and thus dropping blood sugar even lower, as well as stressing the pancreas. What is needed is a balanced, low-carbohydrate, high-protein diet that levels off the blood sugar and prevents these gross fluctuations. Caffeine aggravates the instability. (However, hypoglycemia in an unconscious alcoholic patient may cause brain damage from low glucose levels; here intravenous glucose is indicated and can do no harm.)

These interactions are very complex and occur with great differences between individuals. Given the damage that alcohol does to the liver, pancreas, and adrenal glands, some abnormalities of sugar metabolism are to be expected in newly recovering alcoholics (Ryan, 1983–84). In a field prone to faddism, it is not surprising that hypoglycemia was seized upon in a simplistic way. Tests of blood sugar done on those shortly out of detox or on skid-road alcoholics should not be taken seriously—just as Milam's research (see Chapter 8) pointed out the wisdom of postponing psychological tests for three months or more until nature has had time to heal.

Another important function of the liver is that it *detoxifies* many substances in the blood, from alcohol and other psychoactive drugs to excess female hormones in the male. Alcohol creates a vicious cycle of lessening the liver's ability to metabolize it, which in turn allows more alcohol to accumulate and do more damage to the liver. A sick liver fails to eliminate the residue of dead red blood cells, with resulting yellow color in skin and whites of the eyes so characteristic of liver disease. The liver is thus an important part of the body's defenses.

Immune System. The liver is a very important part of the body's autoimmune system. Because a damaged liver makes less globulin and is otherwise less efficient, and alcohol interferes with the function of white blood cells, heavy drinkers are less able to fight off pneumonia and other infections (NIAAA, 1992). Tuberculosis has been practically wiped out in America, except among vagrant alcoholics whose immune systems do not readily handle the TB bacillus we are all exposed to, or whose life-style is conducive to reactivating a latent case while others stay cured. Alcohol seems to exacerbate skin diseases like psoriasis and acne rosacea, which often clear up when drinking stops.

Is alcohol good for a cold? It may make you feel the discomfort less, but it impedes the body's ability to fight off viruses and bacteria. Alcohol also interferes with the effectiveness of most medicines, including antibiotics and antihistamines. "I drink lots of alcohol and that kills the bugs" not only contradicts the two statements just made but also contains another fallacy: A solution of alcohol strong enough to be antibiotic is a hundred times stronger than the lethal dose of blood alcohol; it would kill you long before it killed anything else. "Red wine kills viruses" was once a front-page headline, but careful reading of the story revealed that grape juice was even more effective, as the active ingredient was some agent in the red skin of the grape and not the alcohol that characterizes wine.

AIDS (Acquired Immune Deficiency Syndrome) is a special problem here, for three reasons: Both alcohol and other drugs harm the body's immune system, thus adding to the AIDS damage and making the person even more vulnerable to the effects of the human immunodeficiency virus (HIV). Marijuana also deactivates white blood cells for twelve to twenty-four hours, and both it and alcohol affect T-cells. Second, alcohol and other drugs including cocaine lower one's inhibitions and caution, making sexual promiscuity with infected partners more likely (Edlin et al., 1994). They also make one less aware of the body's natural warning signals, postponing help. Third, intravenous drug users often have a ritual of sharing needles, which leads directly to HIV infection. For those reasons, issuing clean needles is hardly an adequate solution, nor is "safe sex" advice—plus the fact that the HIV carrier may show no symptoms. Using bleach to clean shared needles is of some help. AIDS is posing new dilemmas for treatment centers, but it is also causing some addicts to alter their life-styles in the light of the severe health risks. It does not seem to be a serious danger for staff who have had proper instruction on how to deal with patients that have the syndrome or at least test positive for the virus. (See "AIDS," 1988; AMSAODD/NCA, 1987, 1988; Siegel, 1988; Strange and Stimson, 1990.)

Cardiovascular System

Before discussing the heart and blood, we must point to a major impact of liver disease on blood circulation. Almost all blood circulating through the digestive tract passes through the liver on its way back to the heart; both hepatic inflammation and cirrhosis cause obstruction of that flow, with resulting back pressure in the portal vein. From this may develop varicose swelling in abdominal veins, internal bleeding, hemorrhoids (piles), and esophageal varices (swollen veins at the base of the esophagus, just above the stomach, due to back pressure). With high acidity and lowered clotting power to increase the danger, rupture of an esophageal varix is an extremely high mortality risk and is often precipitated by the alcoholic's vomiting or "dry heaves."

Heart. Richard J. Bing of Huntington Memorial Hospital introduced the 1978 AMSA panel of specialists on alcoholic cardiomyopathy by stating that research has shown both the fact that alcohol causes direct damage to the heart and the biochemical explanation of how it does so. Once in question, there is now no doubt that in addition to causing fatty infiltration, alcohol causes heart damage even when malnutrition or lipids are not a factor. Likewise, even moderate amounts of alcohol can stress the myocardium, or heart muscle, and can cause arrythmia. Even one drink has been shown to diminish myocardial contractility (Schuckit, 1978, p. 77). High blood pressure often drops to normal when drinking stops. Binge drinking followed by strenuous exercise can be fatal even in young people. The 1973 work of R. G. Pennington and M. H. Knisely on blood sludging has not been accepted by all authorities in the field, but there is enough other evidence to yield a consensus that alcohol, especially prolonged heavy drinking, is a significant cause of congestive heart failure, enlarged heart, elevated diastolic blood pressure, peripheral edema (swelling), and myocarditis (Burch and Giles, 1971; J. W. Smith, 1986a).

Do drinkers live longer? An old myth known as the French paradox and perpetuated by many physicians prescribed wine as beneficial to the heart, especially in the elderly. But as early as 1965 an AMA committee reported that although alcohol dilates arterioles in the skin (hence the "whiskey nose"), it has no beneficial effect on the coronary arteries (Webb and Degerli, 1965). More recently, some researchers found that moderate drinkers live longer than total abstainers or heavy drinkers. As every freshman in statistics knows, correlation does not mean causality. Probably there is a population sampling fallacy here: It is not necessarily true that moderate drinkers live longer because they drink, but because their personality and life-style may make them less prone to heart attack and stroke than total abstainers. So moderate use might be the consequence of good health rather than its cause (see Criqui and Ringel, 1994). Moderate drinkers in one study were also very light smokers, and in another ate a better diet, smoked less, and differed in other characteristics. And the total of shorter-lived abstainers is raised because many recovered, abstaining alcoholics already have damaged hearts from their drinking days.

In any case, the one drink a day associated with longevity is quite foreign to the problem drinkers who would love to use this to bolster their rationalizations. Habit-forming and open to self-prescription, alcohol is too easily abused for the physician to encourage its use. "Harm reduction" and "moderation management" programs rarely mention the danger of progression into alcoholism or the large body of scientific evidence that less-than-heavy drinking can cause high blood pressure, stroke, and other organic diseases discussed in this chapter. Ashley and Rankin (1980) found that even moderate drinking led to heart disease, and *JAMA* (May 2, 1986) says that the chance of hemorrhagic stroke doubles for light drinkers and triples for heavy drinkers. In fact, the same AMA committee reported that there is no acceptable use of alcohol as a medication—even for snakebite. And we do know that life expectancy for alcoholics is twelve to sixteen years shorter than for nonalcoholics.

Claims of high-density lipoproteins (HDL) or "good cholesterol" from alcohol have been made. But Lieber (1984) says that HDL_2, the important factor, is not increased except by heavy drinking and sees no benefits to the heart from alcohol-induced HDL_3. In any case, the use of alcohol to increase HDL creates worse health hazards and is not recommended even by the researchers who claim such an effect for alcohol.

Blood. "Red wine builds red blood" is another myth that modern science has disproved. The hematopoietic (blood-building) system is slowed down by alcohol, including that in both red and white wine, decreasing the production of red blood cells primarily, but also platelets and white cells. That interferes with clotting, fighting infection, and, in extreme cases, with the supply of oxygen to the brain. Some research indicates that red grape juice contains the beneficial agent, not the alcohol in wine. Alcohol causes an anemia which is not helped by vitamin B_{12} or iron; the latter can damage the liver by depositing excess iron.

Brain and Nervous System

The brain is by far the most important organ through which alcohol affects behavior (NIAAA, 1990). Nerve action requires energy from oxidizing glucose, with the aid of the coenzyme Adenosine Tri-Phosphate (ATP). Alcohol interferes with the supply of oxygen and glucose to the brain, decreasing the use of oxygen by the brain cells as much as 30 percent at 0.3 percent BAC, and 60 to 80 percent at 0.5 percent BAC. Even at blood levels of 0.1 percent to 0.2 percent, alcohol notably diminishes the ATP action.

Moreover, alcohol interferes with the production and functioning of a host of neurotransmitters and neuromodulators in the brain whose role and even existence research is still discovering, going by such names as endorphins, enkephalins, biogenic amines, neurohormones, catecholamines, neuroactive peptides, etc., and including dopamine, serotonin, acetylcholine, norepinephrine, GABA (gamma-amino-butyric acid, the brain's major inhibitory neurotransmitter), and tetrahydroisoquinolines (TIQ's or THIQ's) such as salsolinol. Neurotransmitters such as dopamine are opiatelike substances naturally produced in the brain in tiny amounts. They may be nature's tranquilizers, with which alcohol interacts in complex ways because they use the same receptor sites—the places on a nerve cell membrane surface that are stimulated by a specific chemical, much as a key fits a lock.

Much is still to be learned (Alling et al., 1994), but science makes it clear that addiction is largely a matter of altered brain chemistry, by which even psychosocial and spiritual therapies seem to work. The clue to cross-addiction and to the similarity with other compulsive behaviors may be a common reward or pleasure center in the medial forebrain bundle, which mediates euphoria. More than thirty of those substances are now known, and researchers estimate that there may be over twice that number, many of them interacting in complex ways. Certain of them act as blockers at the receptor sites, some are inhibitors and some facilitators—good reasons to avoid simplistic thinking or hasty generalizations such as were once made about TIQ, which some now claim is an artifact of the method used to "discover" it.

The results of all this interference may be divided into three phases: *immediate* effects on behavior and mental functioning due to alcohol's presence in the blood, as discussed in Section B above; *temporary* effects after alcohol has been eliminated; and *permanent* brain damage.

Temporary Effects

The second phase includes withdrawal phenomena; rebound effects like interference with sleep patterns, which may last some days or weeks; and residual toxicity in the brain marked by cognitive deficits, which may last long after blood alcohol has reached zero. Some are speaking now of "ninety-day detox" for this latter reason, and there is a rule of thumb allowing one month for every year of drinking, which is not scientifically precise but has some foundation in fact. Electroencephalographic (brain wave, EEG) changes last for six months to a year after sobriety (F. Seixas, 1977, p. 64). Injured brain cells take up to two years to return to normal, and even five to ten years according to more recent research at the University of Pittsburgh and at Johns Hopkins University (e.g., De Soto et al., 1985).

Alcohol diminishes the body's defenses against auditory nerve damage due to loud sound, which may explain why "the morning after" brings pain from sudden noises. Drinking bouts often leave the person anxious and depressed, which is ironic in view of the fact that many people drink in a futile attempt to combat anxiety and depression. Vaillant (1983, p. 78) lists five lines of evidence that alcohol *causes* depression.

Sleep disturbances may be due in part to nature's compensating for the depressing effect of alcohol by sending up extra volleys of nerve impulses through the reticular activating system (RAS), which continue after the alcohol has worn off. Thus it is a common experience to be drowsy in the evening after drinking, but to wake up earlier than usual as the compensation occurs. Other causes of insomnia can be the action of alcohol on biogenic amines like serotonin and norepinephrine, drug withdrawal, and the clinical depression that is often a concomitant of alcoholism (J. W. Smith, 1986b).

Blackouts are losses of memory, not to be confused with passing out. Anybody who drinks enough alcohol may become unconscious, but in a blackout people remain conscious and may continue with conversation or activities, only to discover later that they cannot remember parts or all of what went on. The period of amnesia may cover a few minutes or hours, a lost weekend, or much more. It can range from mere fuzziness as to where one parked the car to forgetting serious matters. The person may be astonished later when confronted with such tangible evidence as signed traffic citations, receipts, or checks. Such reminders, as well as therapeutic means of recall such as hypnosis, do not restore memory of the events, because rather than inability to recall there seems to be failure to record, probably in the mamillary body memory-storage center in the brain. It is usually associated with a rising BAC (Goodwin, 1977), possibly due to oxygen deprivation. Blackouts are not to be confused with fainting (syncope) or with seizure states.

Hallucinations may be visual, auditory, or mixed. We have never known an alcoholic who saw pink elephants, but imaginary dogs and cats running in and out of the room, little red bugs crawling all over the body, and imaginary voices are common. The old distinction that ascribed visual hallucinations to alcohol and auditory ones to schizophrenia or other psychosis seems invalid (Becker et al., 1974, p. 40). More important is the distinction between alcoholic hallucinosis and delirium tremens.

Hallucinosis in the first thirty-six hours of withdrawal may involve mild disorientation in time, but generally the patient is not disoriented, memory is fairly good, sensorium remains clear (patient is fairly alert and may be easily startled), and the patient may be able to converse intelligently with insight into the fact that he is hallucinating. It may appear in the history only if the patient is asked about nightmares and vivid daydreams. It is not serious.

Delirium tremens (DTs) is a most severe withdrawal state, with a high mortality rate from cardiovascular collapse if not well handled. It usually peaks after about three days of abstinence but can occur several days thereafter. It is marked by severe tremors, agitation and fast pulse, anxiety, paranoia, and profound disorientation with no insight. Profuse sweating, hypothermia, fever, diarrhea, vomiting, and short breath may also accompany the delirium. The distinction must be carefully made and emergency medication given.

Seizures, convulsions of the grand mal (epileptic) type, rarely occur during delirium tremens. These "rum fits" tend to occur during the first forty-eight hours of withdrawal after prolonged heavy drinking but may occur later, and especially after withdrawal from barbiturates or tranquilizers. They are usually not dangerous but can be. Alcoholic seizures are presumed not to be a symptom of epilepsy if clearly related to withdrawal and if neurological signs are normal. Alcohol does lower the seizure threshold in borderline epileptics, and a history of this should be investigated. *Status epilepticus* occurs in 3 percent of alcohol withdrawal seizures, with no agreement as to specific cause. It is a continuous series of seizures without regaining consciousness and is very serious.

Peripheral neuropathy (formerly called neuritis) usually begins with pain in the calf muscles and with tingling or burning sensations or numbness in the feet and lower extremities, and eventually in the hand and arms. It weakens muscles, producing a drop-foot gait; poor balance may lead to walking with legs spread. It can be due to many causes but is often found in malnourished alcoholics. Symptoms disappear with abstinence from alcohol, a good diet, and B vitamins, especially B_1 (thiamine). Antabuse is not recommended for these alcoholics.

Permanent Brain Damage

The third phase is interwoven with the normal loss of brain cells we all suffer, estimated over a lifetime at about 10 percent of the billions we are born with, which results in little loss of function before senility because nature can compensate to some extent by developing shunt, or alternate, pathways. Alcohol speeds up this aging process, and it has long been known that alcoholics have permanent brain damage (Tarter and Van Thiel, 1985). Dead nerve cells (gray matter) never regenerate, so such damage is irreversible. This has even been found in 85 percent of moderate drinkers. The electron microscope has revealed details of cell damage. Gross brain shrinkage is observed by postmortem examinations, by pneumoencephalogram (X-ray of skull after replacing cerebrospinal fluid with air), by computerized brain scan (CAT), by changes in brain-wave patterns (EEG), and by psychological tests of mental function designed to measure brain damage. One medical school professor is reported to have refused to accept cadavers of transients picked up by police because the brains were so deteriorated as not to be representative of the human brain he wanted his pupils to study.

It was once thought that malnutrition, specifically avitaminosis, caused all this. It is now conceded that alcohol itself also causes brain damage (Seixas, 1973), although the precise mechanisms are still being researched. Noble points out that young brains are particularly vulnerable, so this is not a mere matter of aging. Actually, a lot of damage explained away as just aging is due to alcohol. Sludging, a decrease in brain protein synthesis (Carlen et al., 1978), interference with RNA, damage to nerve call membranes, fluid pressure leading to atrophy, and other mechanisms may play a part in alcohol brain damage. Magnesium loss is a big factor in brain malfunction, according to Dr. Gustava Steindelenberg of the Karolinska Institute in Sweden. The Wernicke-Korsakoff syndrome is known to be due in great part to vitamin B_1 deficiency, but Victor et al. (1989) and others have shown that at least cerebellar degeneration is due to alcohol rather than just to avitaminosis; studies by Tewari and Noble (e.g., 1971) seem to point to this in the cerebral regions also. Needless to say, the numerous head injuries sustained by alcoholics contribute to the total picture of cerebral deficit.

The Wernicke-Korsakoff syndrome (NIAAA, *Alcohol and Health*, VI, 1987, pp. 106–12; *Alcohol and Health*, IV, 1981, Chapter III) is a result of brain damage. Symptoms of Wernicke's disease are first confusion and excitement, then double vision from palsy of the third or sixth cranial nerve, then sleepiness and stupor, with perhaps hypothermia. Korsakoff's psychosis is often found in patients clearing from the Wernicke syndrome. Peripheral neuropathy is common. Illogic, hallucinosis, disorientation, and severe memory deficit for recent events occur. The memory loss, coupled with poor judgment of appropriateness or plausibility, leads some patients to make up improbable stories: confabulation. Others confabulate stories far beyond the need to fill a memory gap. Not all exhibit confabulation, but all have severe lack of verbal recall along with emotional disturbances resembling psychosis. The syndrome is often reversible with thiamine treatment in the Wernicke phase, but in the Korsakoff phase it often shows only partial and poor recovery rates. The symptoms occur in other patients but are most common in chronic, undernourished alcoholics.

Other Systems

Genitourinary Tract. Does alcohol enhance sex? There are many myths that associate drinking with virility. Yet long ago Shakespeare (*Macbeth*, Act II, Scene 3) noted that drink both provokes and unprovokes lechery: "It provokes the desire, but it takes away the performance." In spite of the fact that drink lowers inhibitions and control by good judgment, alcoholics are known to be poor sex performers. We now know the reasons (Smith, Lemere, and Dunn, 1974; Van Thiel et al., 1975, 1976): (1) Alcohol causes inflammation of the prostate gland (prostatitis), which interfers with erection and climax; (2) it causes sedation and eventual atrophy of the testicles, causing decreased sperm output and lower male hormones in the blood (Gordon et al., 1976); (3) a toxic liver may produce up to five times the amount of liver enzyme that normally breaks down testosterone; and lastly (4) the adrenal glands in both men and women secrete both male and female hormones into the bloodstream, but in men a healthy liver detoxifies the female hormones. In an alcoholic man the adrenals may be putting out more female hormones than his sick liver can detoxify, with a resultant buildup that causes feminine characteristics, such as enlarged breasts and more hair (which may explain the lower rate of baldness some claim for alcoholics). For these four reasons one is usually not alcoholic because he is impotent, but impotent because he is alcoholic. See Abel (1985), Powell (1984), and the bibliography by O'Farrell and Weyand (1983) for other aspects.

In most women, sexual drive is decreased by alcohol, although inhibitions may initially be lowered by small amounts, and alcoholic women seem to have a higher incidence of menstrual irregularities (Schuckit, 1971). Alcohol decreases vaginal lubrication, making intercourse unpleasant for both partners. In one study, 98 percent of alcoholic patients and their spouses were "sexually dysfunctional" (*NIAAA Information Service*, April 1983). In both sexes alcohol causes problems with urination.

Digestive System. Alcohol iritates the lining of the gastrointestinal organs, especially the stomach, and complicates the problem of acidity. The result is gastritis and heartburn, and eventually ulcers or hiatal hernia. Hemorrhage from a perforated ulcer, or just seepage through the stomach lining, can be massive and even fatal. We have already mentioned death from ruptured esophageal varices. Death can also occur from choking on one's own vomit (aspiration), or from inhaling bits of vomit down the windpipe to cause lung abscess or aspiration pneumonia.

Sudduth has theorized (1977, 1989; Nolan, 1989) that drinking causes enterotoxemia (inflamed stomach and bowels) by increasing bacterial toxin absorption. More alcohol then sedates the irritation from these bacterial neurotoxins, in turn causing more toxin absorption and more discomfort, calling for more sedation. This may provide a physiological explanation for the vicious circle of alcohol addiction. He also points out that (along with malnutrition) alcohol causes liver damage via endotoxins from gastrointestinal bacteria rather than directly, as carbon tetrachloride does; the evidence is that this cannot happen in a germ-free animal where enterotoxemia is impossible.

The *pancreas* is a major organ of the body because of its secretion of digestive enzymes and insulin, which converts blood sugar. Alcohol causes inflammation, or pancreatitis, and pancreatic cirrhosis, sometimes resulting in alcoholic diabetes. Acute pancreatitis is extremely painful and has a high mortality rate. but after an attack subsides pain may not recur, which does not mean that the damage is gone.

Electrolytes and Fluid Balance. Many of the trace mineral ions important for body functioning are dissipated or lost because of the action of alcohol on the kidneys. Magnesium, zinc, phosphate, and potassium levels are among those that can be affected. Calcium loss aggravates osteoporosis and makes bones weaker, especially in older people. In addition, when the BAC level is rising, alcohol inhibits the antidiuretic hormone from the pituitary gland in the brain, causing frequent urination and flushing out of body electrolytes. This action reverses as blood alcohol goes down, causing retention of body fluids and bloating. That fluid retention also causes salt to accumulate and increase the workload on the heart and contributes to high blood pressure, headaches, and *ascites* (bloating of the abdomen in people with liver or heart disease).

Other Disorders

In addition to fractures and other injuries, the disorders associated with excessive use of alcohol range from dermatitis to weakening of body muscles (myopathy and myositis), from subdural hematoma to necrosis of the femoral head requiring surgical replacement. One surgeon reports that every male patient over fifty on whom he has done a hip replacement was a heavy drinker.

Hypothermia, or loss of body heat, is an important effect of alcohol. We talk of feeling a glow, but actually the warmth felt in the face and extremities happens because heat is being dissipated at an abnormal rate. Many deaths of hunters and hikers listed as due to exposure are really due to rapid loss of body heat because they were drinking. Patients in detoxification units must be kept warm to prevent death from hypothermia. Although Lieber and others have challenged the notion that alcohol precipitates shock through adrenal failure, its use in emergencies is prohibited by the Red Cross Manual for good reasons. To explode another myth, the St. Bernard dogs who rescued people in the Swiss Alps had cold tea and not brandy in the keg tied around their necks.

Cancer. "Alcohol is indisputably involved in the causation of cancer" according to the HEW-NIAAA *Third Special Report to Congress on Alcohol and Health* (1978, pp. 47–51). An impressive amount of evidence suggests that it may be at least a contributing factor or part cause in many cases (*Alcohol Health and Research World,* special issue on "Alcohol and Cancer," Spring 1986; Tuyns, 1978; Whelan, 1978). The high incidence of cancer in the mouth, esophagus, and stomach among those who drink hard liquor points to its irritant quality before it gets diluted in the bloodstream. It also seems to be carcinogenic in lower concentrations in all parts of the body, and especially in the pancreas and liver. Tobacco complicates the issue, and the two may be mutually reinforcing; a 1987 report that moderate drinkers had 30 to 50 percent higher incidence of breast cancer may have been contaminated by smoking.

Fetal Alcohol Effects

In ancient Carthage and Sparta it was the custom for newlyweds to drink no wine, lest a defective child be born. Aristotle reported the custom and agreed with the reason. In 1748 a British physician noted that when gin became cheap more mothers gave birth to babies that were physically defective or mentally retarded. Similar observations were made by the Liverpool physician William C. Sullivan in 1899 and 1900, and in a 1923 British scientific journal by A. L McElroy. During the long and bitter fight over Prohibition, those facts were brushed aside as WCTU scare tactics. Even more enlightened alcohol publications in the 1940s through the 1960s repudiated them. In 1968 Lemoine investigated the children of alcoholics in France, with results that supported the British findings (Lemoine et al., 1968). Controlled studies began to be made elsewhere. Medical reports confirmed that the fetus does indeed take in alcohol through the placenta from the mother's blood. Infants are born intoxicated and show distinct signs of withdrawal (much of what was called colic may have been just this). But more permanent and irreversible damage to the newborn child was identified in 1973 after Dr. Christy Ulleland in Seattle noted a fairly consistent pattern of symptoms now known as the *fetal alcohol syndrome* (FAS).

Short of the full-blown syndrome, recent research shows that much of what has been called dyslexia, learning disability, and minimal brain damage (MBD) or attention deficit hyperactivity disorder (ADHD), are really fetal alcohol effects (FSE) or alcohol-related birth defects (ARBD) (see "Sources" at end of chapter). Although the basic syndrome is through fetal environment and not heredity, some of these symptoms *may* be associated with genetic alcoholism, with Tourette's syndrome, or with post-traumatic stress disorder (PTSD).

Babies whose mothers were known to be imbibing alcohol during pregnancy are statistically more likely to exhibit some or all of the following symptoms: short length and underweight, which do not catch up to normal later; small head, small brain, and mental deficiency; heart defects, poor coordination, abnormal creases on the palms; joint and limb irregularities, such as hip dislocation and odd fingers or toes; and hyperactivity later in childhood. But along with the irreversible mental retardation and underweight, the most characteristic sign is the peculiar face, as seen in the accompanying illustrations: short palpebral fissures (narrow eye socket), epicanthal folds (skin over the inner corner of the eyes), low nasal bridge with short upturned nose, narrow upper lip with little or no philtrum, giving the mouth a fishlike shape, and often a receding chin, protruding forehead, and deformed ears. Winsome, "elfinlike" children of this description are often mentally retarded, says Ann Streissguth (1976a and b; 1994; Streissguth et al., 1978; Streissguth and LaDue, 1985), perhaps the leading researcher in the field.

After some healthy scientific skepticism, it is now recognized that maternal blood alcohol is the specific cause. Many animal studies show these results with good controls: no smoking, no other drugs, no nutritional deficiency. But wide studies on human mothers also controlled for these varibles, including socioeconomic and other environmental factors, nutrition, and smoking. Many alcoholic mothers do smoke heavily, and nicotine may combine with alcohol here. But FAS still occurs in the progeny of drinking

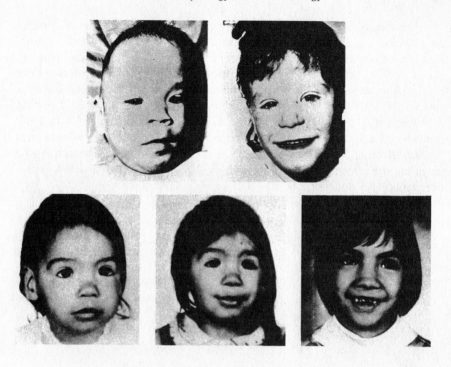

mothers who do not smoke. The cause is not heredity but intrauterine environment. The tiny liver of the fetus cannot process alcohol as rapidly as the mother's can, so alcohol levels may be higher in the infant. It seems most likely to occur in the first trimester of gestation, especially if binge drinking produces high levels of blood alcohol at a crucial point in the development of the infant's central nervous system. But since the nervous system is by no means fully developed by the end of three months, and since there is some evidence that even moderate blood levels can produce defects, mothers are well advised not to drink at all during pregnancy. The catch is that most women learn they are pregnant only after missing a menstrual period, by which time they may be six weeks along. It is wise to avoid alcohol if they are planning to have a baby, or at least limit themselves to one drink maximum (not average) a day so that blood alcohol never rises notably. The June 13–17, 1982, AMA House of Delegates meeting adopted the stance of "NO drinking if pregnant" (*Alcoholism Report,* June 30, 1982, X [17]: 7).

Other psychoactive drugs should also be avoided, since the synergistic effect of alcohol with nicotine or marijuana can be fivefold. Cocaine is known to pass through the placental membrane into the fetus and not return, so it may build up to a higher level than in the mother. It may also show up in breast milk. There is good research evidence that cocaine causes birth defects.

The tragedy is that this is the most preventable of birth defects. It ranks as the third leading cause of birth defects and causes more defective babies each year than thalidomide did in its entire history. The odd facial features are as nothing compared to the permanent mental retardation. Perhaps we can learn a prevention lesson from the hippie era, when they were not worried about what LSD was doing to their own brains but stopped dropping acid when they learned it could harm their unborn babies. NIAAA in 1987 published *Program Strategies for Preventing Fetal Alcohol Syndrome and Alcohol-Related Birth Defects*, DHHS no. (ADM) 87–1482. Research is now revealing the effects on the sperm of high BAL in the father just before impregnation (Robe, 1982, pp. 80–81).

Sources

The literature on the effects of alcohol on the body is prodigious. The best sources are the works listed as "Series" at the beginning of the General Bibliography, which deal in great detail with specific aspects of the physiological effects of alcohol on the body and with the methodology of investigating them, the Journals listed there, and the special reports to the United States Congress by NIAAA entitled *Alcohol and Health*—all of which provide extensive bibliographies. The 16-mm. half-hour film *Medical Aspects of Alcohol: I,* by Max A. Schneider, M.D., is both informative and graphic, almost indispensable in the classroom.

ALCOHOL AND THE BRAIN

For good summaries see Blum and Payne (1991), Blum and Topel (1986), Parsons et al. (1987), Porjesz and Begleiter (1983), Topel (1985), West (1986), and the works of Henri Begleiter, Floyd Bloom, John Ewing, Mark Gold, Yedy Israel, Robert Myers, Boris Tabakoff, and Ralph Tarter, to name but a few.

A FEW OTHER USEFUL SOURCES

"Alcohol and Cancer," special issue of *Alcohol Health and Research World,* Spring 1986, 10(3):3–75.
Alcohol and Nutrition, NIAAA Research Monograph no. 2, 1979.
Andreasen, Nancy, *The Broken Brain* [excellent overview of recent developments in brain biochemistry as related to psychiatry, including addiction].
Edwards, G. et al. (eds.), *Alcohol-Related Disabilities,* World Health Organization, Geneva, 1984 [especially the article by M. M. Gross].
Geokas, M. C., et al., "Symposium on Ethyl Alcohol and Disease," *Medical Clinics of North America,* January 1984.
Israel, Y. and J. Mardones (eds.), *Biological Basis of Alcoholism.*
Rubin, E. (ed.), *Alcohol and the Cell.*
Smith, James W., and Ruth E. Little, "Alcohol Abuse in Medical Practice," in Carr and Dengerink (eds.), *Behavioral Science in the Practice of Medicine.*
Sudduth, William, "The Role of Bacteria and Enterotoxemia in Physical Addiction to Alcohol," *Journal of the International Academy of Preventive Medicine,* 1977, 4 (2):23–46; or in *Microecology and Therapy,* 1989, 18:77–81.
Tygstrup, N., and R. Olsson, *Alcohol and Disease.*
Wallgren, H. and H. Barry, *Actions of Alcohol,* 2 vols.

ALCOHOL AND BEHAVIOR

Bennett, A. E., *Alcoholism and the Brain.*
Birnbaum, I. M., and E. S. Parker (eds.), *Alcohol and Human Memory.* Lawrence Erlbaum Associates, Hillsdale, NJ, 1977.
Eidelberg, Eduardo, "Acute Effects of Ethanol and Opiates on the Nervous System," in R. J. Gibbins et al. (eds.), *Research Advances in Alcohol and Drug Problems,* vol. 2, pp. 147–76.
Finch, J. R., *Psychiatric and Legal Aspects of Automobile Fatalities.*
Highway Safety Research Institute, HIT LAB Reports, University of Michigan, Ann Arbor, 1970 and following years.
Linnoila, M., et al., "Effect of Alcohol on Accident Risk," *Pathologist,* 1986, 40(8):38–41.

Milner, G., *Drugs and Driving: A Survey of the Relationship of Adverse Drug Reactions, and Drug-Alcohol Interaction to Driving Safety*. Swetz & Zeitlinger, Basel and Sydney, 1972.

O'Farrell, T. J., and C. A. Weyand, *Alcohol and Sexuality: An Annotated Bibliography on Alcohol Use, Alcoholism, and Human Sexual Behavior.*

FETAL ALCOHOL SYNDROME

Jones and his colleagues published their observations on the fetal alcohol syndrome in *Lancet* in 1973 and so piqued the interest of clinicians and researches that publications on the subject have been proliferating since then. Ample references are in "Alcohol-Related Birth Defects," *Alcohol Health and Research World*, 1994, 18(1), entire issue, including an overall view by Ann P. Streissguth, pp. 74–81, and evidence on fetal damage from other drugs and polydrug use during pregnancy by Nancy Day and Gale Richardson, pp. 42–48. A good popular and scientific presentation with bibliography is *Just So It's Healthy* (rev. ed. 1982) by Lucy Barry Robe, who also points out the mixed messages that the alcohol beverage industry sends expectant mothers. See also Abel (1984), Stimmel (1982), West (1986).

On fetal alcohol effects (FAE), see *Alcohol and Birth Defects: The Fetal Alcohol Syndrome and Related Disorders*, NCADI, 1987; *Alcohol and Research World*, entire issues 1985, 10(1) and 1994, 18(1); and Hammer et al. (1987).

Larger bibliographies are those by Abel, *Fetal Alcohol Syndrome: An Annotated Bibliography* (1986); Gantner (1984); Russell and Blume (1985); NIAAA in Blane and Hewitt (1977), Appendix I; S. Landesman-Dwyer, L. S. Keller, and A. P. Streissguth, "Naturalistic Observations of Newborns: Effects of Maternal Alcohol Intake," *Alcoholism: Clinical and Experimental Research* (1978), 2:171–77; Claren and Smith (1978); and R. H. Warner and H. L Rosett, "The Effect of Drinking on Offspring: An Historical Survey of the American and British Literature," *JSA* (1975), 36: 1395–1420.

CHAPTER 5

Other Drugs: Physiology and Pharmacology

THE PRECEDING OVERVIEW of the physiology of alcohol is an excellent starting point for the study of the impact other drugs have on the body, as the health consequences resulting from excessive alcohol consumption provide a dramatic example of the physiological damage resulting from drug addiction. However, of the wide variety of drugs in addition to alcohol, each drug has its own impact on the physiology of the body. A complete overview of drug abuse and addiction requires an examination of the psychoactive effects, physiological impact, and abuse potential associated with the principal classes of addictive and abused drugs. Note that "psychoactive" means mind-altering, not just mood-altering.

Before discussing the physical effects of drug abuse in greater detail, it is important to note that guidelines for the use of psychoactive and dependency-producing drugs in medical practice have been established. The Comprehensive Drug Abuse Prevention Act of 1970 placed a number of drugs of abuse under federal regulation. That Act, which remains in force today, provided a comprehensive framework to control substances named in the act. Substances named by the act were placed under direct regulation of an agency created by the act, the Drug Enforcement Administration (DEA). Five schedules were established for categorizing drugs. Table 3 describes the schedules.

Opiates

Opiate drugs can be of synthetic or natural origin. The widespread use of opiates in medicine for the control of pain (and diarrhea) has led to the development of a variety of synthetic opiates in addition to those—codeine and morphine—that are derived directly from the opium. Synthetic opiates vary in strength, duration of action, and potential for abuse.

Opiates may be taken via a number of routes, including orally, injection, smoking, and sniffing. The route of administration used depends on the drug being taken. Even after an opiate is in circulation in the blood, it may take a considerable amount of time before it gains access to the brain. The delay in reaching the brain is due to the fact that many opiates are slow to pass a protective lining of the brain's blood vessels called the *blood brain barrier.*

The blood brain barrier presents an internal obstacle to reaching the brain,

Table 3 Schedules of Controlled Substances as Defined by the Comprehensive Drug Abuse Prevention and Control Act of 1970

Schedule	Criteria	Example
Schedule I	Drugs with high abuse potential lacking therapeutic utility or adequate safety for use under medical supervision	Heroin, marijuana, LSD, peyote, PCP, THC, mescaline, Psilocybin
Schedule II	Drugs with high abuse potential that are currently accepted in medical practice despite high physical and psychological dependence potential	Cocaine, morphine, opium, Benzedrine, methadone, codeine, methamphetamine
Schedule III	Drugs with moderate abuse potential that are currently utilized in medical practice, despite dependence potential	Some Barbiturates, amphetamine, glutethimide
Schedule IV	Drugs with low abuse potential that are currently accepted in medical practice despite limited dependence potential	Phenobarbital, Miltown, Darvon, diazepam (Valium)
Schedule V	Drugs with minimal abuse potential that are currently used in medical practice despite limited dependence potential	Cough medicine with small amounts of narcotic

which acts to protect the brain from the toxic action of substances circulating in the blood. The blood brain barrier also effectively excludes many drugs. As a result, the desirability of many psychoactive drugs, in terms of both therapeutic uses and illicit uses, may hinge on the drug's ability to travel rapidly to specific locations in the brain. Morphine, for example, can take up to an hour to reach the brain. Heroin, in contrast, reaches the brain many times faster. Given the fact that the abuse potential of a psychoactive drug is related to the speed of action of the drug, it is no surprise that heroin is considered a drug of choice by addicts when compared with morphine (the same relationship can be seen with stimulant drugs when comparing amphetamine to methamphetamine).

Opiate agonists (drugs like morphine, heroin, and codeine), whether synthetic or natural in origin, act by binding to opiate receptors found on the surface of brain cells (neurons). Opiate anatagonists, like *naloxone (Narcan)* and *naltrexone (Revía),* bind to opiate receptors and are capable of blocking the physical effects of opiate agonists like morphine and heroin. Several subtypes of opiate receptors have been identified, including a mu receptor (involved in physical dependence, analgesia, and respiratory depression) and a kappa receptor (involved in producing spinal analgesia and pupillary constriction).

The discovery of drugs with the ability to bind selectively to these receptors has allowed for the development of drugs with mixed opiate agonist and opiate antagonist qualities like *nalbuphine (Nubain)*. The drugs are especially intriguing in that they offer the ability to block pain impulses (analgesia) while not producing many of the psychoactive qualities that opiate addicts identify as desirable.

Opiate agonists produce a broad physical action, including euphoria, analgesia, sedation, respiratory depression, constriction of the pupils, vomiting, slowing of the heart, and constipation (Katzung, 1992). It should be noted that death by respiratory depression presents one of the greatest overdose risks associated with the use of opiate agonists.

Tolerance develops with frequently repeated administration of opiate agonists. As tolerance develops, the addict becomes physically dependent. Once physical dependence has developed, opiate agonists must be used on a regular basis to prevent the onset of withdrawal (physical abstinence syndrome), and a higher dose is needed if the original response is to be replicated. The interval between the use of opiates in a dependent individual depends on the length of action of the drug they are dependent on. Heroin addicts, for example, experience craving for heroin in as short a time as six hours after last using it. Addicts using the synthetic opiate agonist methadone (a long-acting drug used in treating heroin addicts) can go up to twenty-four hours before they experience a craving for methadone (Ray and Ksir, 1993). The use of an opiate antagonist in a physically dependent individual will induce withdrawal.

Stimulants

Cocaine and *amphetamine* act both in the central nervous system (the brain and spinal cord) and in the peripheral nervous system (the series of fibers coursing to muscles, glands, and organs as well as fibers carrying information from sensory structures back to the brain). Cocaine's peripheral actions, which include acting as a local anesthetic to block nerve impulses, make it useful in eye and oral surgery. Amphetamine's therapeutic actions include its role in the treatment of attention deficit disorder and narcolepsy (a condition in which an individual involuntarily falls asleep during the day). The central nervous system actions of cocaine and amphetamine, including their ability to induce positive mood states, euphoria, and behavioral activation, make them sought after by illicit drug users. Cocaine and amphetamine can be taken by several routes, including snorting, injection, and smoking.

Cocaine acts in the brain and in sites in the peripheral nervous system to modify the functioning of neurons releasing the neurotransmitters dopamine, norepinephrine, and serotonin (more specifically, one of cocaine's known actions is its ability to block the reuptake of dopamine, norepinephrine, and serotonin from synaptic clefts). These neurotransmitters are involved in a number of important actions in the brain, including their roles in the control of mood states and motor (muscle) functioning. Toxic reactions to cocaine are not uncommon and are compounded by highly variable absorption, distribution, and elimination of the drug. Amphetamine, like cocaine, acts to disrupt the normal functioning of the neurotransmitters norepinephrine and dopamine (its effect on serotonin systems remains unclear). Amphetamine acts to potentiate the natural actions of dopamine and norepinephrine.

Physically, acute cocaine or amphetamine use results in widespread activation of the central nervous system and of the sympathetic division of the autonomic nervous system (that branch known to control "fight or flight" responses in humans). Toxic levels of cocaine or amphetamine may produce anxiety, trembling, dilated pupils, muscular hyperreactivity, and psychosis. Additionally, high doses of cocaine or amphetamine may cause hyperthermia (high body temperature), seizures, and high blood pressure. Untreated, abnormally high blood pressure may lead to life-threatening ruptures of major arteries including the aorta (the major artery leaving the heart) and the brain. Some "designer drugs" with chemical structures similar to amphetamine may cause a similar pattern of symptoms when taken in toxic doses. Additionally, *Khat,* a plant used in East Africa and the Middle East for its amphetamine-like qualities, also has been found to produce amphetamine-like side effects if taken at high doses (Widler et al., 1994).

Consumption of alcohol in conjunction with cocaine increases the risk of heart failure (cardiac arrhythmia), which is often fatal. Combining alcohol and cocaine produces an especially lethal by-product—cocacetylene (Rose, 1994). Cocacetylene has been found to have a toxic action on the muscle of the heart. Other stimulants, like amphetamine, do result in the buildup of cocacetylene when combined with alcohol.

Behavioral and psychological correlates of high-dose cocaine or amphetamine use may range from anxiety and mood swings to delirium, hypervigilance, paranoia, repetitive behavioral mannerisms (stereotypy), and psychosis. Aggressive responses may accompany the psychotic state. Many of those behaviors become more pronounced as tolerance develops and the drug dose increases. Abrupt withdrawal from cocaine or amphetamine is not, in most cases, life-threatening. However, sleep disturbances, changes in appetite, and depression may follow.

The lack of a distinct physical withdrawal syndrome has led some researchers to describe cocaine and amphetamine as not addicting. Even in the absence of a distinctive physical withdrawal syndrome, however, high-dose stimulant users—especially those smoking or injecting the drug—display an increasingly intense behavioral dependence on these drugs.

Nicotine and Smoking

Nicotine, a naturally occurring substance isolated from the tobacco plant in 1828, has attracted increasing attention because of its addictive role in smoking and in other forms of tobacco dependence. Nicotine, unlike other naturally occurring substances like cocaine from coca and morphine from the opium poppy, is virtually never administered in its pure form, and no specific therapeutic action has been determined for nicotine.

Nicotine can be taken several ways, including chewing, sniffing, and smoking tobacco. Chewed tobacco releases nicotine, which is then absorbed through the membranes of the mouth. Sniffing tobacco, in the form of snuff, results in absorption across the nasal membranes. The most common route of administration of nicotine, however, is through smoking tobacco which releases vaporized nicotine for inhalation. Once in the respiratory tract, vaporized nicotine dissolves into the lining of the mouth and lungs. Cigarette smoke differs from pipe and cigar smoke in that it is acidic. The acid nature of cigarette smoke causes it to be better absorbed in the lungs. Pipe and cigar smoke, on the other hand, are more easily absorbed from the mouth. That is why cigar and pipe smokers don't inhale.

Nicotine initially concentrates in the brain following smoking, and nicotine can cross most membranes, including passage into the breast milk of nursing mothers. Nicotine is eliminated from the body through excretion in the urine and by metabolism. Smokers metabolize nicotine faster than nonsmokers. Nicotine increases heart rate and blood pressure, and constricts blood vessels in the skin. The constriction of blood vessels in the skin results in a drop in skin temperature.

Nicotine has been identified as the addictive agent in tobacco dependence and has also been found to be an effective reinforcer of behavior in laboratory animals—just like cocaine and heroin. Many of nicotine's psychoactive effects, including a sustained attention span and behavioral arousal, occur within seconds of inhaling nicotine (Henningfield et al., 1985).

In addition to nicotine's effects on the body, other ingredients inhaled when smoking tobacco can cause a whole host of other health problems. Smoking has been implicated in chronic bronchitis and emphysema; lung, bladder, and oral cancers; acute hypertension; and the development of cardiovascular disease. The carbon monoxide inhaled during smoking reduces the amount of oxygen reaching the tissues of the body. Smoking increases the risk of blood clots and strokes. No wonder smokers have been found to die five to eight years, on average, younger than nonsmokers (Parakrama and Taylor, 1991). Smoking presents a health risk to nonsmokers too. Secondhand smoke has been found to cause cancer in those who breathe it on a regular basis, and babies born to smokers, on average, are smaller in birth weight and size than those born to nonsmokers.

Surprisingly, even after all the research conducted on tobacco use, only recently has nicotine been publicly acknowledged as addicting (Surgeon General Report, 1988). Although the focus of most research on tobacco involves the use of cigarettes, the risk of addiction is not limited only to those who smoke cigarettes. The use of any form of tobacco—whether by chewing or by smoking pipes or cigars—can result in an addiction to nicotine. When addicted tobacco users stop, some of the symptoms of withdrawal include agitation, weight gain, difficulty concentrating, and insomnia.

Marijuana

The means by which marijuana's active ingredient, Delta-9-Tetrahydro-cannabinol (Delta-9-THC or THC), produces the psychoactive characteristics associated with the use of marijuana are not well understood. What is known is that the highly fat soluble Delta-9-THC is rapidly absorbed from the surface of the lungs when marijuana or hashish is smoked, and physical effects rapidly follow. An experienced user will notice the effects of the drug almost immediately. When taken orally (for example when marijuana is cooked into foods), the onset of action is significantly slower, often taking more than an hour after eating before psychoactive effects are noticed.

Delta-9-THC easily enters the brain and is then redistributed to fatty tissues throughout the body. Elimination of THC is slow, with metabolites of THC taking many days, even months, to leave the body. Chronic use is associated with cardiovascular changes, including increased pulse rate (Katzung, 1992) and an increase in blood pressure in high-dose users. Reddening of the conjunctiva of the eye (red eye) is characteristic of THC intoxication. There is growing concern over the potential risk for lung cancer in chronic marijuana smokers, although evidence supporting such a claim is unclear. It should be noted, however, that the chronic smoking of marijuana, like tobacco smoking, exposes the user to tars and other toxic ingredients that have been found to pose significant health risks in tobacco smokers.

Marijuana's psychoactive effects are difficult to categorize. Marijuana is mildly sedating, analgesic, and hallucinatory. In some individuals, marijuana will induce tension and anxiety. Panic reactions are not uncommon. A typical "high" may involve euphoria and a "mellow" feeling of satisfaction. As the drug experience progresses, the user may drift into a "relaxed, dreamlike state of introspection" (Katzung, 1992). The peak drug effect occurs about twenty minutes after smoking marijuana and lasts about three hours.

Chronic marijuana users, who have used the drug for decades, are not uncommon in the United States. Some still question whether or not marijuana is "addicting." Physical dependence on marijuana seems likely, as a mild withdrawal syndrome has been noted in high-dose users. Physical tolerance to the effects of marijuana has been substantiated (Ray and Ksir, 1993). One of the most alarming conditions associated with chronic marijuana use is an *amotivational syndrome*. A loss of motivation and interest in outside activities has been noted in regular users of marijuana. The cause of this behavioral change has not been identified, although, given the slow rate of elimination of THC, chronic intoxication by Delta-9-THC or a related metabolite may be likely.

Hallucinogens

The drug LSD is related to mescaline (from the peyote cactus) and Psilocybin (from Psilocybin mushrooms or "magic mushrooms") in its psychoactive effects and pharmacological actions (Katzung, 1992). The exact mechanism of action by which LSD and LSD-like compounds produce hallucinations is unknown, but it appears to involve a decrease in the activity of serotonergic neurons, possibly inhibiting the release of serotonin from neurons.

Taken orally, often by licking a sugar cube or in Jell-O, only very small amounts of LSD are needed to induce a hallucinatory state (less than two thousandths of a gram per kilogram of body weight). LSD-like drugs create a broad range of perceptual disturbances, which can include visual and auditory hallucinations and a shift in time perception.

Hallucinogenic drugs also produce a number of physical effects, including weakness, tremor, and nausea. Because LSD and related compounds stimulate the autonomic nervous system, users commonly display dilated pupils, slightly increased blood pressure, increased heart rate, and behavioral arousal. No known fatalities have occurred as a result of the physical effects of using LSD. The psychoactive effects of LSD and LSD-like drugs may last for several hours. The intensity of the hallucinogenic experience depends greatly on the setting and expectations of the user.

The use of LSD-like hallucinogens may have lingering behavioral effects. Some reports have linked the long-term use of LSD to a state of chronic psychosis (Glass and Bowers, 1970). It is important to note that, although cases of psychosis have been reported in individuals using hallucinogens like LSD, it is impossible to determine whether the individuals involved would have become psychotic with time even in the absence of the drug.

Another event often linked with the use of hallucinogens, especially LSD, is the occurrence of flashbacks. A flashback occurs when elements of the drug experience intrude into the consciousness of the user sometime following the drug experience. Why flashbacks occur is the subject of debate. Theories abound about the release of residual amounts of LSD stored in fat cells as being responsible. Some evidence suggests that flashbacks are more common in people who have had an intense negative experience with the drug or who have used LSD on a number of occasions. Although frequent users appear to become tolerant to the hallucinatory characteristics of these drugs, little evidence exists to suggest that the use of LSD results in physical dependence on hallucinogens.

Another frequently mentioned hallucinogenic drug is *PCP (Phencyclidine)*. Introduced in 1957, the drug was originally described as inducing a state of "dissociated anesthesia." PCP and a related drug, ketamine, were advertised as producing anesthesia without loss of consciousness. Early on it was noted that some patients receiving the drugs described a hallucinatory state on waking, especially with PCP. As a result, PCP was withdrawn from the market for use in humans, but it is still used in veterinary medicine. By the mid-1960s, PCP was being sold illicitly, often as LSD or pure THC. PCP can be taken orally, injected, snorted, or mixed with tobacco or marijuana and smoked (sherms).

The use of PCP can result in psychosis, and overdoses on PCP can be life-threatening. PCP has been rumored to produce violent behavior in its users.

No doubt, a person on PCP may be difficult to subdue or arrest, if for no other reason than the fact that techniques of physical restraint depend on pain stimuli, while PCP acts as a pain blocker or anesthetic (Ray and Ksir, 1993). Whether or not PCP induces violent behavior remains unclear. PCP does appear to be dependency-producing, despite the fact that many users report negative experiences.

Sedatives and Hypnotics

Sedative drugs have in common an ability to depress the functioning of neurons, thereby reducing anxiety or inducing sleep. Many sedatives, including alcohol, barbiturates, and benzodiazepines, accomplish this by potentiating the actions of the inhibitory neurotransmitter GABA (Gamma-amino-butyric acid), a neurotransmitter found to be involved in anxiety and sleep functions. Ideally, sedatives should potentiate the inhibitory actions of GABA enough to decrease anxiety without inducing unwanted drowsiness. Hypnotic compounds act to inhibit activity enough to induce sleep, which is often accomplished by increasing the dose of a sedative.

A number of compounds that can induce sedation and hypnosis have been isolated. However, those compounds also frequently cloud the consciousness of the user long after the therapeutic utility of the sedative has ended or when the hypnotic user wakes up. Even more serious is the fact that many drugs used for sedation and hypnosis present a serious overdose risk, and their sedative action can be synergistically increased by consuming them with alcohol. As a result, most of the sedative compounds used earlier in this century for sedation and hypnosis (for example, many barbiturates, methaqualone, and glutethimide) have fallen out of use. Taking their place are drugs of the benzodiazepine class—now the drugs of choice for both sedation and hypnosis.

Most modern sedative-hypnotic drugs are given orally. The rate of absorption of these drugs from the stomach and small intestine varies depending on the type of drug, as does the duration of action of specific drugs. Many hypnotic drugs, for example the sleep-inducing benzodiazepine Flurazepam, break down into psychoactive metabolites. Breakdown metabolites may take hundreds of hours to be completely eliminated from the body. The extended length of action can result in daytime sedation. Sedative drugs, for the most part, are dependency-producing, and addiction to them is not uncommon. In general, drugs with short durations of action tend to produce fast-moving, severe withdrawal syndromes, while those with longer durations of action produce a gradual withdrawal of long duration (Katzung, 1992).

Physical dependence is rare with benzodiazepine drugs and much more common with the older sedatives, like the barbiturates. Many people use sedative-hypnotic drugs in a manner similar to another sedative, alcohol. As with alcohol, low doses of these drugs produce a period of initial disinhibition, which, at higher doses, is superseded by drowsiness. As a person becomes intoxicated on a sedative, other signs similar to being drunk appear. At higher doses, the person may slur speech or stumble and fall. Over time, tolerance develops to the behavioral effects of these drugs, but not to the physical effects, like respiratory depression. As a person increases the dose of a sedative to overcome behavioral tolerance, he moves closer and closer to the dose needed for physical overdose. The situation becomes especially dangerous if alcohol is used in conjunction. The combined effects of the sedative and alcohol on respiration can be fatal (see Figure 3 in the previous chapter).

When a physically dependent sedative user stops using the drugs, a withdrawal syndrome similar to that seen in alcoholics can occur. Symptoms of sedative-hypnotic withdrawal include anxiety, tremors, twitches, nausea, and vomiting. Convulsions may occur; in severe cases, delirium and psychosis may also develop. For short-acting sedatives, withdrawal may be short in duration but intense. For individuals addicted to longer-acting sedatives, a lessened symptom profile is to be expected. An intense withdrawal state may last for more than a week (Katzung, 1992). Untreated, the withdrawal from sedative-hypnotics can be fatal because of convulsions. Medical treatment is advised to stabilize the individual.

Sources

Agurell, S., et al. (eds.), *The Cannabinoids: Chemical, Pharmacologic and Therapeutic Aspects.* Academic Press, Orlando, FL, 1984.

Glass, G. S., and M. B. Bowers, "Chronic Psychosis Associated with Long-term Psychotomimetic Drug Abuse," *Archives of General Psychiatry,* 1970, 23:97–103.

Goulart, F. S. *The Caffeine Book: A User's and Abuser's Guide.* Dodd, Mead, New York, 1984.

Henningfield, J. E.; K. Miyasato; and D. R. Jasinki, "Abuse Liability and Pharmacodynamic Characteristics of Intravenous and Inhaled Nicotine," *Journal of Pharmacology and Experimental Therapeutics,* 1985, 234:1–12.

Julien, Robert M., *A Primer of Drug Action.* 5th ed. W. H. Freeman, San Francisco, 1988.

Katzung, B. G., *Basic and Clinical Pharmacology.* 5th ed. Appleton & Lange, Norwalk, CT, 1992.

Kreek, M. J., and B. Stimmel (eds.), *Dual Addiction: Pharmacological Issues in the Treatment of Concomitant Alcoholism and Drug Abuse.* Haworth, New York, 1984. [*Advances in Alcohol and Substance Abuse,* vol. 3, no. 4]

Lakoski, Joan M., et al., *Cocaine: Pharmacology, Physiology and Clinical Strategies.* Telford Press, 1990.

Parakrama, C., and R. Taylor, *Concise Pathology.* Appleton & Lange, Norwalk, CT, 1991.

Ray, Oakley, and C. Ksir, *Drugs, Society, and Human Behavior,* 6th ed. Mosby, St. Louis, 1993.

Rose, John D., "Cocaethylene: A Current Understanding of the Active Metabolite of Cocaine and Ethanol," *American Journal of Emergency Medicine,* 1994, 12:489–90.

Surgeon General's Report, *The Health Consequences of Smoking: Nicotine Addiction.* DHHS Pub. No. (CDC) 88-8406, U.S. Government Printing Office, Washington, DC, 1988.

Widler, P.; K. Mathys; R. Brenneisen; P. Kalix; and H. U. Fisch, "Pharmacodynamics and Pharmacokinetics of Khat: A Controlled Study," *Clinical Pharmacology and Therapeutics,* 1994, 55(5):556–62.

PART TWO

ADDICTION

CHAPTER 6

Patterns and Symptoms

A NY OF US could suffer the effects depicted so far of alcohol and other drug misuse on our health, driving, social relations, and pocketbook, whether addicted or not. This chapter will address the development of addiction, using alcoholism as a model. The approach will be descriptive rather than explanatory, leaving to Chapter 7 any considerations of causality. The focus here is on *what* addiction is, not *why*. The distinction is important, for much needless quibbling about types is really mistaking description for explanation.

Types of Alcoholics

Alcoholics differ over the whole range of human variation in physiological and psychological characteristics. No two people are exactly alike. Each alcoholic is a unique individual, so that there is a temptation to resign ourselves to the existence of 10 million alcoholisms in a population of 10 million alcoholics. Alcoholism itself is not a single disease entity any more than cancer is, but a multiple illness, which amply justifies a growing trend toward use of the term *alcoholisms*.

With those facts in mind, it is clearly a serious mistake to assume that a "true" or "typical" alcoholic must be much like the one you know—or the one you are. The result, of course, is that the patient may not be able to identify with the accepted archetype, so will feel either left out or confirmed in his or her denial of being an alcoholic at all. The mere fact that the counselor or older AA member can't imagine an alcoholism different from the one with which he or she is familiar does not disprove its existence.

The best-known classification is that presented by the late E. M. Jellinek in *The Disease Concept of Alcoholism* (1960, pp. 36–41). Jellinek deliberately identifies his various types of alcoholics by letters of the Greek alphabet, to avoid names that might imply theories as to cause or nature. Whether or not one accepts his scheme, it is so much a part of the literature that one must be familiar with it in order to read or converse intelligently in the field. Note that these are not stages of progression, that is, from Alpha to Beta and so on.

The Jellinek Types of Alcoholisms

Alpha. This is purely psychological dependence on alcohol. These people have poor frustration tolerance or inability to cope with tensions. They use alcohol to boost morale, block out reality, bolster self-confidence, or relieve emotional or bodily pains. They drink too much and at the wrong times, which may result in offense to others, family squabbles, absenteeism from work, and a drain on the family budget. They can be called problem drinkers, but Jellinek rejects the term here because it can include the physically dependent. There is little or no progression and no physical addiction or withdrawal symptoms (although there can be some of the nutritional deficiencies of alcoholism). Hence Jellinek was reluctant to call it an illness per se (p. 37), although he definitely says it is alcoholism (p. 41). Some call it a symptom of mental conflict, but it is a symptom that has become the disease in its own right. At least 10 to 15 percent of AA membership is of this type (p. 38). Psychotherapy can help with the conflict, but medication would only lead to dependence on more alcohol or other drugs. Alpha alcoholism may develop into Gamma alcoholism, Jellinek says, but it can also continue for thirty or forty years with no progression (p. 37). Addictions to compulsive gambling and marijuana seem to involve this psychological vulnerability.

Beta. This is characterized by *social* dependence on alcohol, without either psychological or physical dependence. The usual problems from excessive drinking arise, including nutritional deficiencies and organic damage such as cirrhosis and gastritis. These alcoholics are often seen in general hospitals, where their physical ailments are all too often treated without remedying the drinking habits that caused them. They seldom join AA. The cause of their drinking is largely sociocultural or situational and is common in occupations where "everybody" gets drunk every weekend. This "everybody does it" feeds denial. In any case, heavy social dependence should not be dismissed lightly; it is one of the main obstacles to long-term rehabilitation of chronic alcoholics. Jellinek says this Beta type is alcoholism (p. 41), and it meets the third element of our working definition, because there is interference with important life functions. Both Alpha and Beta may involve some loss of control, but this is not paramount in either type.

Gamma. This is the chronic, *progressive* type of alcoholism most commonly seen in American males. It usually begins with psychological dependence and progresses to physical dependence. There is progressive loss of control over *how much* one drinks; except in the later stages, one can usually still choose *when* to drink or not, but once started there is little or no control over when to stop: "One drink is too many and a thousand are not enough." There is usually an increase in tolerance, and in the middle stage it may reach a remarkable level. There may be shakes or tremors for days after withdrawal. In the late stages withdrawal symptoms are severe, and tolerance drops irreversibly to below one's initial level so that a single drink is quite toxic. This is the classic instance in which the habitual addiction *is* the disorder. Searching for reasons why these people drink is superfluous; they drink because they are addicted to alcohol. This type is most responsive to the AA approach, but anything that will break the habit pattern can be useful: Antabuse (disulfiram), aversion conditioning, a religious conversion, or intensive treatment with a strong emphasis on understanding the nature of the illness and good physical rebuilding—any approach that attacks the pathological drinking as the primary disorder, on which all of the foregoing approaches agree.

Because members of Alcoholics Anonymous were the most available and cooperative when Jellinek did his research, the majority of his two thousand subjects reported histories that conform to this type. He observed that Alcoholics Anonymous "naturally created the picture of alcoholism in their own image" (p. 38), and in spite of his great admiration for AA he warns sternly that we must not let this selective sampling deceive us into imagining that the Gamma is the only typical or true alcoholic.

Delta. This is often called the *maintenance* drinker: the alcoholic who has lost control over *when* he or she drinks rather than *how much*. Inability to abstain, rather then inability to stop once they start, is the characteristic. Unlike the Gamma type, Deltas cannot "go on the water wagon" for even a day or two; yet they seldom appear to be drunk. Are they alcoholics? Yes, they show increased tolerance and even go into severe withdrawal symptoms (DTs) if deprived by accident or other circumstances, though they may have never been drunk in their lives. Social attitudes that favor regular drinking seem to play a major role. This is the commonest type of alcoholism in France and such other wine-drinking countries as Chile and Peru, and perhaps among American women. Or one can be a member of the three-martini-lunch bunch, the executive who must have alcohol to get through the day. One patient, told to cut out salt and alcohol as a routine treatment for high blood pressure, promptly went into DTs, although alcoholism was not suspected. Deterioration is so gradual that the Deltas do not realize that they don't feel very good most of the time; changes in family relationships are likewise so subtle that nobody recognizes the problems. Because their drinking rarely precipitates a crisis that would bring them to AA, they are not highly visible in the fellowship. Another reason is that they cannot identify with the distressing and sometimes amusing experiences other alcoholics recount from their drinking escapades.

Epsilon. This is the *periodic* or binge drinker, who abstains without difficulty for long periods but once started drinks heavily until passing out in a stupor. The period of abstinence may be a week, a month, or a year. It may be regular or varied in length. Epsilons differ from the Gamma type who is between drinking bouts in that they may experience no craving or struggle to maintain sobriety. They may serve liquor in their homes with no temptation to indulge.

No meetings or slogans are necessary. Often the spouse knows the telltale signs that signal the approach of a binge, but once the time comes there seems to be nothing anybody can do to avert it.

Called *dipsomania* in Europe, periodic alcoholism is a most puzzling type, about which little is known, as Jellinek, for one, noted. The dependence seems to be both psychological and physical. The loss of control is baffling. Research on this type is obviously difficult, and understanding may not be achieved for a long time to come.

Other Classifications

Zeta. Some have added a sixth type to Jellinek's five: Zeta alcoholics, in whom even small amounts of alcohol evoke violent, erratic behavior. This idiosyncratic response to alcohol is akin to the old psychiatric term *pathological intoxication* or "mad drunk" and may not be a true type of alcoholism.

Other classifications get into questions of causality and will not be pursued here. Partington and Johnson (1969), Pattison (1973), and many others have found different personality types among alcoholics, which may be useful in choice of treatment but add little to our understanding of alcoholism. Jellinek wrote that there are many other types of alcoholism, more than there are letters in the Greek alphabet. The point is not to put people into neat boxes, but to emphasize that alcoholics differ among themselves. Some may be a combination of two types or may shift from one type to another over time.

Common Characteristics

More useful to our understanding is an examination of some experiences that most alcoholics have in common, in ways and degrees that, of course, will vary. Wallace (1986) has given us an excellent explanation of those experiences, which we can do no better than to summarize. His approach is especially useful because it helps us understand many things often dismissed as mere denial when they are better called confusion, or perhaps ignorance or misinformation. No doubt the two are interwoven, but denial seems to imply some willful refusal or dishonesty. This implication mars the feeling of respect and trust between client and counselor. Wallace's approach may aid in avoiding this.

Confusion

Contrary to what he or she may have heard, the alcoholic did not get drunk each and every time or experience unpleasant effects on each drinking occasion. Many report periods of normal social drinking in between alcoholic binges. All have some happy memories of boisterous good times—due, in part, to retroactive falsification, whereby any human being tends to remember the pleasant and forget the unpleasant. Thirty years later they are still pursuing that pleasant "glow" they recall from early drinking experiences, and the incongruity between illusory images from the past and their present misery adds to the confusion. Cocaine and heroin addicts spend their lives trying vainly to recapture that first high.

Diagnosis is confusing enough to the objective professional, so it is no wonder that the alcoholic cannot apply to himself or herself the welter of diagnostic criteria with all the "ands" and "ors" that naturally leave open the possibility that they do not fit. Because of differences in drinking patterns and social customs, many a criterion would not be conclusive if taken by itself. Lastly, the alcoholic looks out at the world and sees a lot of drinking and even drunkenness, and a lot of people in far worse shape; surely those others are the alcoholics. "If they don't admit it or go to treatment, why should I?"

Search for Magic. Another significant part of the alcoholic's thinking is the vague, unfounded hope that if one searches hard enough and long enough, one can find a way to control and enjoy drinking. Even acceptance of the label "alcoholic" does not mean acceptance of the true nature of alcoholism in all its implications. Full participation in a good recovery program like Alcoholics Anonymous quells this subtle hope and keeps one conscious that the only sensible answer is not to drink. But the occasional resurgence of what AA calls "stinking thinking" shows that hopes for realization of this wild possibility are never quite dead.

Who Am I? Again, the alcoholic leads a sort of dual life. When sober, he is a fine, upstanding citizen whose life and values are quite different from what comes out during the drinking and its aftermath. This is not just self-delusion; the alcoholic really is a different kind of person from what the alcoholic behavior attests to. What am I really like? What sort of person? The alcoholic does not know not only what is wrong with him, but even who he is.

Feelings

Despite great individual differences, practically all alcoholics experience remorse, guilt, shame, and self-hatred. Their self-esteem sinks very low and often is shattered entirely. Feelings of loneliness and alienation are common. Depression and feelings of hopelessness, futility, and a sense of meaninglessness in their lives are typical. The depression is, of course, only augmented by alcohol.

Coping Devices

It is not surprising that all this leads the alcoholic to develop some rather elaborate, if subconscious, escape and defense mechanisms or coping devices. Unlike neurotics, alcoholics do not profit from common psychotherapeutic practices of getting their feelings out in the open. But some insight may be helpful, provided the analysis is combined with a strong emphasis on the nature of compulsive addiction itself. Thus omnipotence and grandiosity can be seen as simply attempts to cope with their sense of helplessness. At the beginning of Chapter 5 of *Alcoholics Anonymous* (1976), alcohol is described as "cunning, baffling and powerful." Research is still trying to elucidate the precise biochemistry of addiction, but every alcoholic has experienced the truth of that description. Hutchison (1994) has given a delightful parody of C. S. Lewis in exposing many deceptions in his *Screwtape Letters on Alcohol.*

Rationalization. A broad term for much of the devious thinking the alcoholic employs, rationalization does not mean rational thinking, but very irrational or emotional thinking. Most common is the ability to find reasons why one should have a drink: to relax, to get some sleep, to celebrate, to avoid offending someone, or just to keep someone company. This is confirmed by the euphoric recall of only the good effects of drinking. It seems impervious to logic when an observer notes the contradictions involved: We have a drink to relax and one to pep us up; a tall cool one in the summer and one to warm us up in the winter. Which does alcohol do? We talk about being fogged up with alcohol, and taking a drink to clear our head. We have a drink because our team won or because it lost; at a wedding or at a funeral; because we are married, or divorced; happy or sad. The alcoholic can always come up with a thousand reasons to take a drink, when in reality there is not one valid reason to do so. The fact that you must use a drug because you feel hot or cold, high or low, means you need it to be "normal," and that is one definition of addiction.

Projection of Blame. This is another favorite defense mechanism. The spouse, the boss, the parents, the police, "the system"—anyone or anything except alcohol must be to blame for all their miseries. The addict/alcoholic is often skillful at drawing others into this delusional system, especially a spouse or lover who sympathizes and thus becomes an enabler, as described in Chapter 9. Or the alcoholic may subtly maneuver the other to provoke a fight, which then becomes an excuse for drinking. Other coping devices the alcoholic may indulge in include chronic failure, accident proneness, pleas for sympathy, and neurotic perfectionism.

Denial. Much of what a counselor is tempted to ascribe to denial is really honest confusion in the alcoholic's mind, as described previously. Nonetheless there is some truth in the statement that alcoholics suffer from a fatal disease whose primary symptom is denial that they are sick. Denial is rationalization, emotional blindness, kidding ourselves, "honest self-deception." Not the only ones capable of it, alcoholics seem to excel. Certainly a high IQ doesn't help. Our experience, confirmed by numerous recovered alcoholics now working professionally in the field, is that the more intelligent alcoholics are, the more adept and devious they are at denial.

None of us is an impartial judge in his or her own case. Father Ralph Pfau (Father John Doe) tells of nearly shaking to pieces waiting for the minute hand to hit twelve so he could drink, while assuring himself that he was not an alcoholic because he had heard that an alcoholic was one who drank before noon. One woman, drunk for four years and vomiting blood for the last three, said, "I had no idea I had a drinking problem." In a nation where 4 percent of the population are alcoholics, only 0.1 percent of those questioned characterized *themselves* as even heavy drinkers. More recently, self-reports of alcohol consumption totaled just half the actual amount sold in the United States. The first twenty minutes of an intake interview are often taken up with listening to how much the client does *not* drink. Alcoholics have developed such an elaborate alibi system that they are almost incapable of recognizing the role that alcohol plays in their problems. They tell us, "But I'm different" while they die of what Pursch has called terminal uniqueness. The list is endless: I can't be an alcoholic because I'm too young; because I only drink beer; because I don't drink before 5:00 P.M.; because I am Jewish; because I am a clergyman; and, of course, "because I can quit any time I want to" (see Anderson, 1981).

Denial by Others. It is not only the patient who plays these mental games. As Kellerman describes in the now classic booklet *Alcoholism: A Merry-Go-Round Named Denial* (1973), the family and others are drawn into this rationalization in an effort, often quite subconscious, to avoid facing the fact of alcoholism. The mother tells herself and her children that Daddy is not "one of those" and fools herself that the neighbors don't know. One mother found baking soda, glass tubing, metal mesh, and a small torch in her daughter's bedroom, yet refused to believe that her lovely fifteen-year-old girl was using crack. After a binge the alcoholic may give the spouse an extravagant present or otherwise try to make up; not only does this reinforce the denial by the spouse, but by accepting the favor the spouse reinforces the alcoholic's own denial. In industry the foreman covers up for the alcoholic employee, and many companies are still denying there is any problem in their ranks.

Professionals are involved in the denial system also. The physician, social worker, lawyer, and clergyman all assure the spouse that his or her partner is too nice a person to be an alcoholic. In one study 91 percent of the clergy saw a need for alcohol programs in the nation, but only 40 percent saw a need in their own congregation. The rabbi says, "You can't be one. Jews don't become alcoholics." Lisansky (1974), in the *Bulletin of the American College of Physicians,* called alcoholism "the avoided diagnosis" and points out how many physicians either miss the diagnosis or treat only the effects and not the alcoholism, even if recognized (on surgeons, see Zuska, 1981). Until recently the news media tended to skip any mention of the role alcohol played in various crashes and other tragedies. Even in the helping professions some pay lip service to the disease concept of alcoholism but persist in evasive approaches and uncomfortable feelings about alcoholics.

Symptoms

Because at least the Alpha and Delta types may show no progression, the word *progressive* does not appear in our working definition of alcoholism, as it does in some. The charts usually used to graph the development of the illness are based on the work of Jellinek, who admits that his sample was heavily biased toward a predominance of Gamma-type alcoholics and is therefore not typical of all. Even when progression occurs, it does not follow a uniform pattern. The steps may be reversed in order, or some steps may be omitted. Symptoms progress, too; something that was minor in an early stage may appear later in a different form or to a greater degree, just as Monday's cough may be Friday's pneumonia. The symptoms have widely different meanings for different individuals or in different social contexts: "hitting bottom" might mean to one alcoholic finding oneself in jail or suicidal, while for another it might be burning the toast once too often.

Rate of progression varies also. It tends to be more rapid for some individuals and among certain races, probably because of a physiological predisposition. Generally it is faster for women than for men and faster in very young alcoholics. Some alcoholics take thirty or forty years to reach the chronic stage. Others plateau at the middle stage indefinitely. Chronological age is less important than stage of development of the illness. Rate of progression with drugs other than alcohol varies: eight months for cocaine versus 15–20 years for alcohol, and still more for marijuana.

For all of those reasons, it is preferable to stop referring to early, middle, and late stages and simply talk of mild, moderate, or severe problems. *DSM-IV* reflects this shift in thinking.

Tests

A definition tells what alcoholism is; diagnostic symptoms are a description, how it is recognized. For practical use in identifying alcoholics and problem drinkers during an initial interview or after apprehension on a drunk-driving charge, many questionnaire-type tests have been developed. They are easily administered and scored.

W. R. Miller (1976) reviewed some two hundred attempts at such scales. The best known are the Michigan Alcoholism Screening Test or MAST (Favazza and Pires, 1974; Selzer, 1971) and the Mortimer–Filkins Test or HSRI test (Jacobson, 1976a, 1976b), which is the most thoroughly researched. After much experimentation, the Substance Abuse Subtle Screening Inventory (SASSI Institute, 1988) has been introduced; it is designed to resist efforts to fake or conceal (especially by those who are test-wise). It also measures denial, adolescent addiction, and codependency on separate scales. Computer use of special scales of the MMPI can yield useful information. A complex, computer-analyzed blood test that can identify alcoholism, and even hereditary disposition to the illness before onset or long after cessation of drinking, is scientifically feasible based on the information in Chapters 4 and 7; it needs only to be made technologically and economically practical. Urine analysis reveals only drug use, not abuse or addiction; hair analysis gives a history.

The older definition and criteria developed by NCA and AMSA (NCA Criteria Committee, 1972, 1976) combined medical and behavioral symptoms. Their emphasis on late-stage, organic symptoms can unfortunately feed denial in the early or early-middle stage alcoholic. Later modification by NCADD and ASAM remedies this (NIAAA, 1991). Many are alcoholic when they take their first drink. Moreover, a majority of alcoholics never progress to the end stage, but remain miserably stuck on a "plateau" or middle phase, neither progressing to obvious deterioration nor able to get out of their pathological pattern of drinking (Jacobson, 1976a; Pattison, 1967, p. 130).

Signs of High Risk

It is easy to diagnose alcoholism as a severe problem. The challenge is to recognize the early signs, so important in secondary prevention (early intervention). That is not always easy, since the symptoms vary widely and are often subtle.

Persons at High Risk of Alcoholism. The fact that the statistical probability for certain groups to develop alcoholism is quite high should alert us. Epidemiological and sociological studies show that the following factors indicate high risk for the development of alcoholism. There is not complete agreement on the extent of risk for each factor.

A family history of alcoholism, including parents, siblings, grandparents, uncles, and aunts

A history of total abstinence in the family, particularly where strong moral overtones were present and, most particularly, where the social environment of the patient has changed to associations in which drinking is encouraged or required

A history of alcoholism or teetotalism in the spouse or family of the spouse

Coming from a broken home or a home with much parental discord, particularly where the father was absent or rejecting but not punitive

A lack of leisure activities that do not involve drinking

Origin from cultural groups (for example, the Irish, Native Americans, and Scandinavians) having a high incidence of alcoholism

Having female relatives of more than one generation who have had a high incidence of recurrent depressions

Heavy smoking (Heavy drinking is often associated with heavy smoking, but the reverse need not be true.)

A tendency to use other psychoactive drugs

Confused and inconsistent attitudes about one's own drinking, even with no conflict about drinking by others

Problem Drinking, or Mild Alcoholism

Some alcoholism is characterized by the following symptoms:

Increased tolerance. One feels proud of being able to hold one's liquor. Hangovers may be minimal or absent. The trouble at this point is that you can't tell which of the one in twelve drinkers will turn out to be alcoholic, so the high tolerance is reassuring rather than alarming, which only starts the process of denial.

Using alcohol for its effect rather than merely enjoying it. One learns early the pampering effects of alcohol and uses it for relief of tension, fatigue, disappointment, or self-consciousness. Some alcoholics get this on the first drink, and never have to make a transition from social lubricant to psychological dependence. Others undergo an unconscious learning process as reinforcement enhances the discovery.

Thus almost from the start, alcohol means a little more to the alcoholic than to others. This is so true that research indicates it can be a useful, though not infallible, diagnostic tool: Most of us can't remember our first drink, but many alcoholics can.

Preoccupation with drinking. Thinking about the next drink, planning the next drink, worrying about whether there will be drinks at the party or whether there will be enough.

Having a few before leaving home. One begins to select companions, restaurants, and recreational activities largely according to whether alcohol will be available: "Do you go bowling where beer is not served?"

Gulping and sneaking drinks. Always ready for the second round before everybody else, the alcoholic is looking for an effect when others are still just getting acquainted. This is gulping in a social way, but if things are slow one can volunteer to help the hostess and thus gain access to the kitchen or bar where one can sneak an extra drink. At a restaurant, the alcoholic orders a double.

Excuses for drinking, as detailed earlier in this chapter under "Rationalization."

Personality change, both cognitive and emotional, after a few drinks: pleasant to mean, imprudent, irrational, and so on.

Moderate Alcoholism

At some time, many alcoholics stop boasting about how much they drink and begin to lie about both amount and frequency. Actually, some of this is not a lie but simple confusion or forgetting; the alcoholic cannot recall how much he or she had. Some forgetfulness may be due to repression. Some of it may be due to blackouts as described in Chapter 4, Section C. Vagueness when asked about how much one drinks can be a telltale sign: "Not very much" and "a couple now and then" are not typical of the truly moderate drinker, who is more able to say specifically "one glass of wine at dinner."

Blackouts, in our opinion, have been exaggerated as a diagnostic sign. Other research does not confirm the importance suggested by Jellinek's chart. Blackouts rarely give a false positive (having them means one is an alcoholic) but often a false negative (one can be an alcoholic without them). More important, the very nature of a blackout precludes one's being aware of having it: One does not remember that one does not remember. Unless someone else explicitly refers to an incident that happened at eleven o'clock the evening before, one may not advert to the fact that she or he can remember nothing of the period from ten until midnight. Also, blackouts are often listed as an early sign of alcoholism, but for the above reasons they may not enter the picture until a canceled check or auto accident reveals an embarrassing hiatus in the memory. Such a blackout can be a rather disturbing or terrifying experience, although by then the illness may be so entrenched that the only reaction is to sedate the anxiety with more alcohol.

Drinking more than one intends may be a sign of loss of control, but it does not mean that one gets drunk every time one drinks. One may rarely get drunk, thus avoiding the stereotype of alcoholism. This symptom is very often misunderstood, causing much confusion. The genteel housewife who pours her wine from a carafe so she can drink like a lady doesn't intend to empty it and would be totally baffled at the suggestion that she was "one of those" (skid-road) alcoholics. The husband who starts out for the party telling his wife, "I'm only going to have two tonight, honey," really means it; they are both confused when this powerful man ends up having twelve.

Drinking alone is a misleading term. One may be quite alone in the hubbub of a crowded tavern but deny that this is drinking alone. It is not so much that the alcoholic's friends have left him or her, although the alcoholic may think so. Rather, the alcoholic has left them. Later, they will leave in fact.

Other symptoms are notable personality change upon drinking—the person who gets violent or vicious after a few drinks is probably headed for serious trouble over a lifetime—and "telephonitis" (lengthy conversations on the telephone).

There may be little visible interference with job performance, but some marital discord is likely. Unreasonable resentments, irritability, suspicions, and self-pity are common. Physical signs can include acid stomach with use of lots of antacids, insomnia, morning cough, sweating, elevated blood pressure, and high pulse rate. But the physical signs of addiction are not usually apparent.

Moderate alcoholism shows signs of increasing psychological dependence, and signs of physical dependence now begin to be observable. Hiding bottles or protecting the supply is a sure sign; one cannot bear the thought of not being able to have a drink if needed. The need will occur after a period of deprivation, usually in the morning but not necessarily. A fine hand tremor appears, developing later into "the shakes" of real withdrawal.

The excuses for drinking grow into an elaborate alibi system, often centered on blaming the spouse. A "geographical cure" means changing jobs or cities, blaming the boss as the focus of the alibi system. A job below one's training and education is a clue. Going on the water wagon periodically and even going to a dry-out spa or AA briefly in an attempt to prove "I can quit any time I want to" are symptomatic of the problem, but there is no real surrender at this point. Changes in drinking pattern are equally futile: switching brands, drinking only beer, only with friends, or whatever. Resolutions and broken promises only increase the family frustration and produce feelings of guilt and desperation in the alcoholic. Pomposity, bringing extravagant presents home, or the grandiose gesture of buying drinks for everybody in the bar betrays the guilt and inner loss of self-respect. The alcoholic may not be eating properly, but signs of severe malnutrition have not yet become grossly apparent.

Severe Alcoholism

Description here will be brief, both because the signs are all too obvious and because detailing them seems melodramatic. They include loss of family and job, trouble with bill collectors and the law, and some of the myriad physical illnesses listed in the final section of Chapter 4. Need or dependence now is palpably physical; one is caught in the vicious circle of not being able to start the day without a drink. Ethical deterioration sets in, with moral behavior at a level unthinkable a few years earlier; for example, sexual promiscuity, or the professional who neglects clients or patients. Irrational thinking, wide swings of emotion, persistent remorse, and vague, nameless fears and anxieties all occur. Tolerance may drop irreversibly below the initial level, so that a small drink inebriates even after years of sobriety. Prolonged benders or constant inebriation are typical.

One way for those of us who are not alcoholics to attain some grasp of the power of this obsessive-compulsive addiction is to look at what an alcoholic will consume when desperately needing a drink. Bay Rum shaving lotion, Listerine, vanilla or lemon extract, various cough syrups, and other patent medicines are all known to contain large amounts of ethyl alcohol.

More toxic, with methanol or worse, are canned heat (Sterno), paint remover, liquid shoe polish, and the like. One desperate hobo drank a mixture of white (unleaded) gasoline and milk.

Not That Bad. We conclude this section with the warning that emphasis on these severe problems can feed the alcoholic's denial and postpone acceptance of treatment. "Not that bad yet" is a phrase too often on the lips of alcoholic and spouse or employer. Alcoholics should not be encouraged by the fact that they still have a job or their health (really?) and have never been arrested or drunk paint thinner. The reason for our high success rates in treatment and rehabilitation is that we are getting them into treatment before brain deterioration sets in and while job, family, and self-respect—all of which have no motivating force once lost—are still there.

Progression

At the beginning of this section on symptoms we noted many reasons for avoiding overemphasis on progression. Is there any justification for including a progression chart?

The daily experience of many counselors indicates that, with all the pitfalls, it is still useful to chart alcoholic progression as it occurs in those many Americans who fall into the Gamma-type category, provided the foregoing variables and cautions are kept in mind. It can be a forceful tool in working with both the alcoholic and the family. The Glatt chart (Figure 4) helps to penetrate denial and provides a means for the alcoholic to understand what is happening and where it will probably end. It gives the counselor a basis for assessment of the case and gives the client something to identify with. Familiarity with the common symptoms is a necessary tool in the kit of any professional and an important part of public education about the illness. Granted that some blindness to alcoholism symptoms is due to denial, the extent of ignorance still rampant about the signs of developing alcoholism is incredible. Attending open AA meetings, one hears constantly, "I was hooked on alcohol and didn't know it," and this has been estimated to be true of 80 percent of alcoholics. The spouse shows equal ignorance; one wife claims she didn't even know her husband drank until he came home sober one night.

The old Jellinek (1952) progression chart (on which Figure 5 is based) shows innate tolerance increasing during the early or mild stage, remaining relatively high during the middle (moderate) stages, and dropping sharply at the late (severe) stage. We give just a schematic diagram in Figure 5 without listing the symptoms, because they vary in position. The most common chart, often called a dip chart, is based on the work of the British physician M. M. Glatt (1974b, pp. 334–35). While it does not show tolerance changes, it has the advantage of showing the signs of recovery. In Figure 4 we give our modification with more detail (see pp. 104–5). The same cautions apply, namely that one may skip or reverse some steps.

Figure 4 Alcohol Addiction

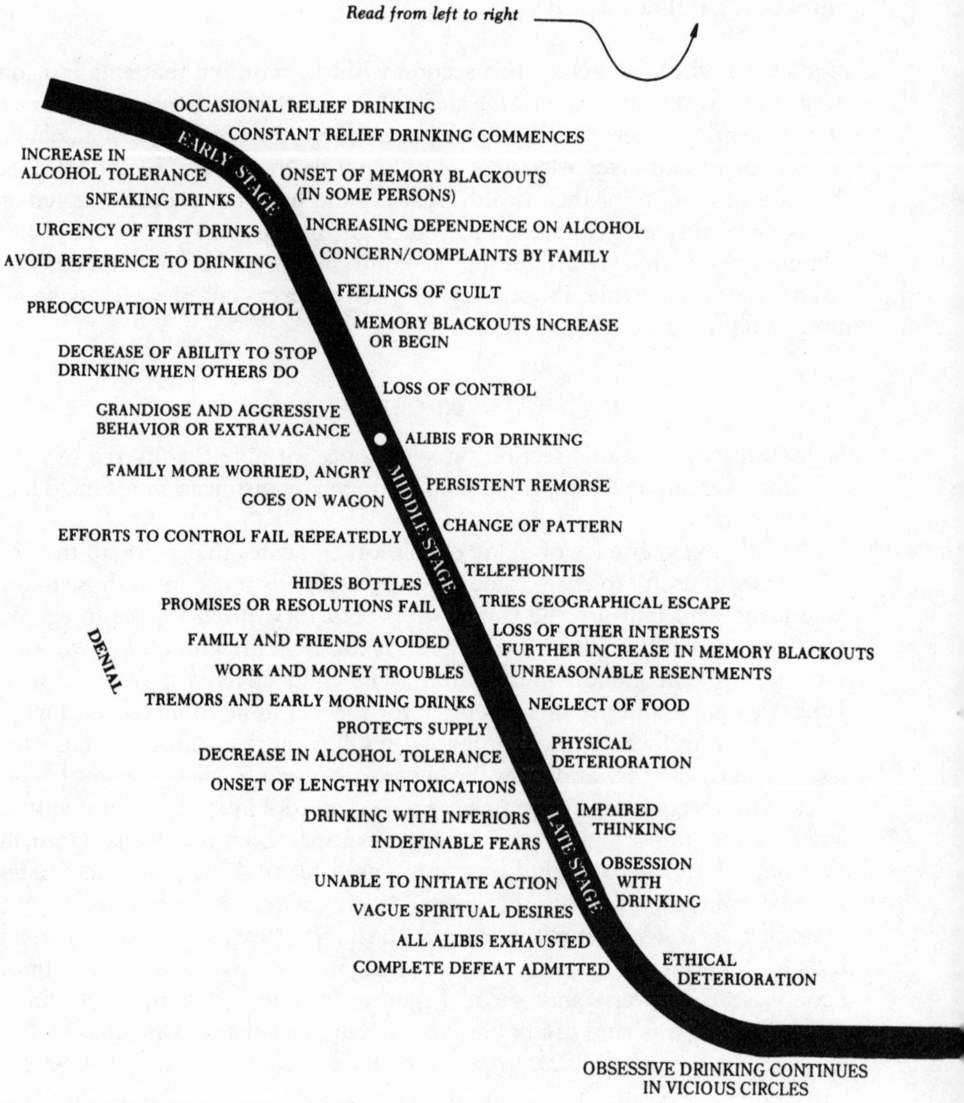

Read from left to right

OCCASIONAL RELIEF DRINKING

CONSTANT RELIEF DRINKING COMMENCES

EARLY STAGE

INCREASE IN ALCOHOL TOLERANCE

ONSET OF MEMORY BLACKOUTS (IN SOME PERSONS)

SNEAKING DRINKS

URGENCY OF FIRST DRINKS

INCREASING DEPENDENCE ON ALCOHOL

AVOID REFERENCE TO DRINKING

CONCERN/COMPLAINTS BY FAMILY

FEELINGS OF GUILT

PREOCCUPATION WITH ALCOHOL

MEMORY BLACKOUTS INCREASE OR BEGIN

DECREASE OF ABILITY TO STOP DRINKING WHEN OTHERS DO

LOSS OF CONTROL

GRANDIOSE AND AGGRESSIVE BEHAVIOR OR EXTRAVAGANCE

ALIBIS FOR DRINKING

MIDDLE STAGE

FAMILY MORE WORRIED, ANGRY

PERSISTENT REMORSE

GOES ON WAGON

EFFORTS TO CONTROL FAIL REPEATEDLY

CHANGE OF PATTERN

TELEPHONITIS

HIDES BOTTLES

PROMISES OR RESOLUTIONS FAIL

TRIES GEOGRAPHICAL ESCAPE

LOSS OF OTHER INTERESTS

FAMILY AND FRIENDS AVOIDED

FURTHER INCREASE IN MEMORY BLACKOUTS

WORK AND MONEY TROUBLES

UNREASONABLE RESENTMENTS

DENIAL

TREMORS AND EARLY MORNING DRINKS

NEGLECT OF FOOD

PROTECTS SUPPLY

DECREASE IN ALCOHOL TOLERANCE

PHYSICAL DETERIORATION

ONSET OF LENGTHY INTOXICATIONS

DRINKING WITH INFERIORS

IMPAIRED THINKING

INDEFINABLE FEARS

OBSESSION WITH DRINKING

LATE STAGE

UNABLE TO INITIATE ACTION

VAGUE SPIRITUAL DESIRES

ALL ALIBIS EXHAUSTED

COMPLETE DEFEAT ADMITTED

ETHICAL DETERIORATION

OBSESSIVE DRINKING CONTINUES IN VICIOUS CIRCLES

THE ROAD TO RECOVERY

ENLIGHTENED AND INTERESTING WAY
OF LIFE OPENS UP WITH ROAD
AHEAD TO HIGHER LEVELS THAN
EVER BEFORE

FULL APPRECIATION OF
SPIRITUAL VALUES

GROUP THERAPY AND MUTUAL HELP CONTINUE

CONTENTMENT IN SOBRIETY

FIRST STEPS TOWARDS
ECONOMIC STABILITY

CONFIDENCE OF EMPLOYERS

INCREASE OF EMOTIONAL CONTROL

APPRECIATION OF REAL VALUES

FACTS FACED WITH COURAGE

REBIRTH OF IDEALS

NEW CIRCLE OF STABLE FRIENDS

NEW INTERESTS DEVELOP

REHABILITATION

ADJUSTMENTS TO FAMILY NEEDS

FAMILY AND FRIENDS
APPRECIATE EFFORTS

DESIRE TO ESCAPE GOES

REALISTIC THINKING

RETURN OF SELF-ESTEEM

REGULAR NOURISHMENT TAKEN

DIMINISHING FEARS OF THE
UNKNOWN FUTURE

APPRECIATION OF POSSIBILITIES
OF NEW WAY OF LIFE

CARE OF PERSONAL APPEARANCE

ONSET OF NEW HOPE

START OF GROUP THERAPY

PHYSICAL OVERHAUL BY DOCTOR

GUILT REDUCTION

RIGHT THINKING BEGINS

SPIRITUAL NEEDS
EXAMINED

MEETS HAPPY SOBER ALCOHOLICS

STOPS TAKING
ALCOHOL

TOLD ADDICTION CAN BE ARRESTED

LEARNS ALCOHOLISM IS AN ILLNESS

HONEST DESIRE FOR HELP

—Modified from M.M. Glatt

Figure 5 Basic Scheme of Jellinek Progression Chart

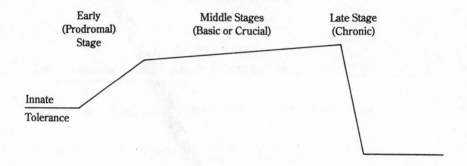

Sources

In spite of a proliferation of charts and lists of symptoms, the literature on progression is sparse; this may be due to great variability (from none to highly predictable) that makes generalization impossible. See Fillmore (1988), *Alcohol Use Across the Life Course: A Critical Review of 70 Years of International Longitudinal Research*. The works of M. M. Glatt and E. M. Jellinek have been noted.

The question of types seems equally elusive. Pages 35–41 of Jellinek's *The Disease Concept* (1960) are brief. Two articles in the *Quarterly Journal of Studies on Alcohol* are Joan K. Jackson, "Types of Drinking Patterns of Male Alcoholics" (1958), and J. Rimmer et al., "Alcoholism vs. Diagnosis and Clinical Variation Among Alcoholics," *QJSA*, 1972, 33:658–66. See also Jacobson (1976a), Morey and Blashfield (1981), and Schuckit (1995b).

Regarding denial, useful items are Anderson, *The Psychopathology of Denial* (1981); Hutchison, *Screwtape Letters on Alcohol* (1994); Kellerman, *Alcoholism: A Merry-Go-Round Named Denial* (1973); and Wallace's chapter 1 in Estes and Heinemann (1986). Hazelden pamphlets include *Dealing With Denial*, Heilman's *Dynamics of Drug Dependency*, and Weinberg's *Why Do Alcoholics Deny Their Problem?*

CHAPTER 7

Causality of Addiction

S O FAR THIS BOOK has been descriptive rather than explanatory. Now we must face the hard question of etiology, or what *causes* addiction. Only thus can we dispel some of the myths and folklore that persist even among degreed professionals. Attacks on our calling alcoholism a disease usually stem from a misunderstanding of *what kind of disease* alcoholism is. A simplistic medical model of disease only provokes useless quibbling; a total-person or biopsychosocial model can clear the air. A fresh appreciation of this model in terms of its complex causality will dictate our treatment rationale, our prevention strategies, and our legal handling of the problems.

The current fashion of asserting with a kind of scientific hauteur that the cause of alcoholism is unknown misses the fact that although we do not fully understand it and more research is needed, we do know a great deal about the etiology of alcoholism. Along with the work on brain biochemistry mentioned in Chapter 4, Vaillant's *The Natural History of Alcoholism* (1983) and Madsen's *The American Alcoholic* (1973) are mostly about causality, and they may be among the best books written so far on alcoholism.

Again we distinguish: We are not asking why people drink, or even why they get drunk. Some people deliberately get drunk for a variety of reasons, but they are not alcoholics. Alcoholics can always give a reason why they drink: Our team won, or our team lost; it's too hot, it's too cold; women alcoholics drink because they have nothing to do at home, or because they have too much to do in a career. Analyzing the reasons why alcoholics drink is really a waste of the therapist's time. The alcoholic will play along with this for a year, drinking meanwhile or ready to start again. Craving? Many an alcoholic will admit they never crave alcohol. Taste? I like the taste of T-bone steaks, but I don't eat them to the point of ruining health, job, and family. One could go on forever, or stop short with a simple answer, euphoria—you drink to feel good. (In late-stage alcoholism it would be better expressed "to feel less bad.") The fact is that most alcoholics began to drink for the same reasons as everyone else: custom, to relax, to be sociable, whatever. The real question is not why they drink, but why do they *continue* to drink when by all reason and common sense they should not; that is, why do they drink alcoholically?

Complex Causality

To ask *the* cause of someone's being an alcoholic implies that there is just one cause. This explains why some assert that the cause is unknown. Simplistic thinking can be a trap. For example, if there were no alcohol, there would be no alcoholism. True, and if there were no money there would be no bank robberies. The fact that only one in a dozen drinkers becomes alcoholic poses the real question: Why are some drinkers alcoholic? The very fact that there are different types of alcoholics and different kinds of alcoholisms would rule out a simple answer. The question is complex, and the burden of this chapter is that alcoholism is the result of many different causes, so generalizations are impossible. Shakespeare says, "Some are born great, some achieve greatness, and some have greatness thrust upon them." The same could be said of alcoholism. In one case it might be an inborn predisposition; in another case alcoholism might be achieved by excessive drinking for psychological reasons; and a third case might exemplify situations whereby some have alcoholism thrust upon them by a sociocultural situation.

Nearly all discussions of causality of addiction pit one theory against another, as if the reader must choose one to the exclusion of others. Why not combine them? There is probably a grain of truth in each, or intelligent persons would not propose them. It is relatively easy to go through each theory and point to evidence that shows it cannot explain all alcoholism. It is also fruitless.

Let us, then, not only try to accept the evidence for a variety of theories, but assume that two or more causes can work together in the same individual, and in different proportions in different individuals. It may be that no one cause is sufficient to trigger alcoholism. Jack London's autobiographical *John Barleycorn* details thirty-five years of alcoholic drinking in which he never liked the taste; he began drinking in his teens to prove he was a tough he-man and ended up addicted to the drug. Addiction involves the whole person's behavior, not just physical dependency. There is always the problem of what differences are the result of alcoholic drinking rather than the cause of alcoholism. Feedback loops may result in mutual reinforcement between physical and psychological causes, making it impossible to disentangle where the circle began. It may be that certain physiological factors, either hereditary or acquired, are combined with some psychological or sociocultural factors to produce alcoholism. And however all this comes about, the alcoholic ends up *habituated* to using alcohol in harmful ways, which result in a psychophysiological state that is unconscious, involuntary, and a self-reinforcing vicious circle.

We shall group the areas of causality under five headings. Note that these five etiological or explanatory factors do not parallel Jellinek's five descriptive types. At least for the purposes of this chapter, any type of alcoholism could be caused by any combination of causal factors, and in any proportion (see Chaudron and Wilkinson, 1988).

Sociocultural Factors

Three can be no alcoholism (active, not potential) if there is no drinking. We have seen that different societies have different cultural attitudes toward drinking and drunkenness, which greatly affect their drinking patterns. To ignore the importance of social pressures toward drinking in the etiology of alcoholism is to ignore facts. Craig MacAndrew and Robert Edgerton, in *Drunken Comportment,* and studies of various American Indian tribes show that to be true not only of drinking but also of intoxicated behavior. All this surely contributes to the development of alcoholism and at least partially accounts for different rates of alcoholism.

Most Vietnam soldiers who took heroin in concentrations far above street level doses were able to kick the habit easily when they returned to close contact with friends and family and productive jobs. (The fact that only a small minority of those exposed to heroin became addicts may also point to differences in physiological vulnerability, which is also suggested by one report that 70 percent of cocaine addicts had alcoholic parents.) Some theories try to explain the low rate of alcoholism among Orthodox Jews as entirely due to ethnic pride and strong attitudes against drunkenness. If there is marriage with a gentile, the next generation will differ biologically, but when an Orthodox Jew leaves that culture and subsequently becomes alcoholic, the change is sociocultural and not hereditary for that individual. If 57 percent of all Scotch in the United States is sold to blacks (who are about 14 percent of the population), this argues for social prestige as a strong factor. The Italians and the French, both Mediterranean and wine-drinking peoples but with different rates of alcoholism, differ notably in their attitudes toward drinking outside mealtimes and especially toward drunkenness. Women seem more influenced by social factors. Joel Fort (1973, p. 100) says that "sociological causes are preeminent"; although we might not agree entirely, we cannot rule them out.

Psychological Factors

When alcoholism first began to be seriously studied in modern times, the most common explanation was that the alcoholic drank to sedate some deep inner psychological conflict or to avoid some psychic stress, or that it was simply a behavior disorder symptomatic of the sociopathic personality. That has been proved false for 70 to 80 percent of alcoholics, as we shall see in the next chapter. But we must recognize that even in the research of Milam and others reported there, some alcoholism is the symptom of an underlying psychopathology. Too ardent a devotion to the concept of physiological addiction can cause grave errors in diagnosis.

Next, psychological factors can notably alter the effects of alcohol. The research on marijuana shows that subjective factors such as expectancy and social setting largely determine the effects. Double-blind studies by Marlatt

(1987), Nathan (1983, 1988), and others show that reactions may depend on whether people *think* there is vodka in the orange juice or not. *The New Yorker* once carried a story of a New Mexico tribe in which a group mistook root beer for real beer and proceeded to get quite inebriated. Some iatrogenic disorders are due to the power of suggestion. We know that the amount of alcohol consumed is not nearly as important as one's reaction to the drug, and this may vary for both psychological and physiological reasons.

Partial Cause

No research has found an "alcoholic personality" that is *the* cause of alcoholism. Nevertheless, psychological factors certainly play a part in all alcoholism and may be the main cause in some (Gottheil, 1987; Orford, 1985; "Vietnam," 1988). We noted in Chapter 1 that psychological dependence may be more devastating than physiological addiction. Compulsive gambling illustrates all too well the relevant psychology. The higher rates of alcoholism among drinkers from traditionally "dry" peoples, religious or ethnic, may well be due in great part to excessive guilt when they do drink. Parental models are a powerful influence on behavior, as evidenced by the number of mothers who treat their children exactly as their mothers treated them, in spite of loud resolves that they would never do so. An old adage in Alcoholics Anonymous says, "It's not your drinking that makes you stinking, it's your thinking." Sobriety is recognized as being much more than mere abstinence from alcohol. Chapter 5 of the book *Alcoholics Anonymous* (1976) is a marvel of psychology, and we have used it quite successfully for problems other than alcohol.

Most personality traits usually found in alcoholics are more the effects of prolonged drinking and reaction to drinking problems than they are the cause of alcoholism. They include immaturity, selfishness, dependence, frigidity or impotence, hypersensitivity, paranoid thinking, low self-esteem, and many others. Since we do not identify alcoholics before they develop the illness, research on personality characteristics prior to onset is difficult (Blane and Leonard, 1987; Rivers, 1994). Obsessive-compulsive traits, rigidity of thinking, low frustration tolerance, perfectionism and impulsiveness, and short-term goal orientation are often listed and may be either cause or effect. Ambivalent attitudes and confused thinking about the use and abuse of alcohol may be causal.

Some Theories. Research by Donovan and Marlatt (1988) and others shows a "learned helplessness" in alcoholics with little internal locus of control— they develop the conviction that external forces run their lives. David Mc-Clelland proposed a theory that explains alcoholism in terms of drive for power, frustration, and feelings of inferiority, using the psychology of Alfred Adler. Others propose an inner conflict between dependency and aggressive drives. Andrew Weil, in *The Natural Mind* (1972), theorized that man has an innate need to get high, which he will satisfy chemically if he cannot achieve it in more natural ways. All these are more accepted today than Freud's theories of slow suicide from a death instinct, fixation at the oral stage, or latent homosexuality. Of those three Freudian theories, the first may have some slight foundation, the second does not explain why the oral gratification must be from alcohol and not any nipple, and the homosexual theory was pretty well refuted when some state laws were changed to allow women to drink in bars—and the alcoholics went right on drinking without paying any attention to the sex of whoever was on the next barstool.

Physiological Factors
Addiction to a Drug

Dr. Stanley Schacter of Columbia University, a respected clinical and experimental psychologist, reported four years of research on heavy smoking (1977) with the conclusion that we can forget all the nice psychological theories about "something to do with my hands" or Freudian oral gratification: "We smoke because we are physically addicted to the drug nicotine, period." Addiction to the drug alcohol as an explanation of why alcoholics drink alcoholically is not a new idea, having been stated in ancient times, and then through the nineteenth century by doctors Rush, Trott, and others. The psychiatrist Harry Tiebout, who is said to have known more about alcoholism than any other psychiatrist of his time, was writing this in 1944 and 1945. Frederick Lemere, a longtime staff psychiatrist at Shadel Hospital, published an article to the same effect in a 1956 psychiatric journal. Jellinek's *Disease Concept* in 1960 and his writings as early as 1945 contained much of the same idea, but the alcohol world was not ready to listen for several reasons. Behaviorism, with its stress on conditioning, had dominated American social science for decades. The old psychiatric and psychological theories were there first, so were hard to dislodge. Alcohol was a controversial enough beverage without the added stigma of being an addictive drug. The notion of selective addiction had not been developed, and there was no biological evidence such as we have today that differentiates alcoholics from other drinkers.

Most previous theories, such as that of Tintera on hormones or Roger Williams on nutrition, were unable to account for all alcoholism and thus were summarily dismissed instead of being integrated into the total picture. Jellinek had postulated an unknown X factor, which sent researchers scurrying off to discover a single defect when there are actually many factors. Differences in metabolism did not show up in sufficient degree to explain all alcoholism. Low tolerance also proved unsatisfactory, partly because *good* tolerance is a sign of alcoholism (Goodwin, 1978a, pp. 127–29; 1978b, p. 10). The person who is allergic to alcohol, gets the Chinese flush, or otherwise feels uncomfortable or even sick after one drink, is not likely to drink enough to develop alcoholism. The supposed X factor is turning out to be not a simple defect but a combination of differences in liver and brain, which are often excess (for example, high tolerance and a thickening of the bowel) rather than defect, followed by eventual decompensation as nature can no longer adapt.

Vulnerability to Addiction

The notion of immunity versus susceptibility is familiar in biology. We are all exposed to the tubercular bacillus daily but have built up sufficient immunity to be relatively safe. Diabetes runs in families, and although the parallel is not perfect, the similarity to alcoholism is striking in many ways. Roger Williams, in his book *Biochemical Individuality* (1969) and its more popular version, *You Are Extraordinary,* shows that humans differ markedly from each other in both anatomy and physiology, contrary to what the textbooks might lead us to suspect: Organs are not located according to the anatomy diagrams; some people are color-blind or left-handed. We know that some people get stimulated by sedatives, and a few get depressed by speed. Why should we assume that all react in the same way to alcohol?

Experiments show that even within the same species, some animals adapt to alcohol at once, some slowly, and some never do. Some mice get high on alcohol, some do not. Roger Williams bred strains of rats that resembled Jellinek's Gamma, Delta, and Epsilon types. Research with humans is much more difficult, because we cannot control all factors and "make" alcoholics, or measure every bit of food and drink since birth. Why do some teens get cirrhosis in eighteen months, and Churchill not in ninety years? Vulnerability and immunity are not black and white boxes, but a continuum with all shades of gray in between. The research team may require years to identify and isolate just one enzyme out of the fifty or sixty involved, then even longer to understand its biochemistry and transfer this knowledge from the laboratory to the living person (see Popham, 1968).

Many Factors Involved. But progress is being made. We now have massive evidence that alcoholics differ physiologically from nonalcoholics, especially in both brain and liver. Many of the differences seem to be present at birth or to continue even after two years of sobriety. Contrary to the notion of a single X factor, we saw in Chapter 4 that every organ of the body can be affected by alcohol and can also enter into the body's handling of alcohol. The body begins almost at once to adapt, so that a slight withdrawal takes place every time blood alcohol subsides. Since the obvious severe signs of withdrawal do not appear until late stages, we forget that it occurs throughout the drinking history and that much of the bodily distress is due to the adapted cell's need for alcohol to function normally.

Hormonal secretion from the adrenal glands is different in the alcoholic. The liver is less able to store sugar and use it gradually, resulting in extreme swings of blood sugar level. The enzyme action in the liver differs, for example, by using catalase rather than alcohol dehydrogenase, or an abnormal form of ADH, or by developing the MEOS. The work of Lieber and others on amino acid and liver enzyme differences may yet distinguish alcoholics from heavy drinkers, when the cause-effect time relations are fully worked out. This is congruent with the adoption studies to be mentioned under "Heredity" which apply to alcoholics but not heavy drinkers. Following the discovery by Heath that alcohol alters the pleasure center in the limbic system of the brain, Myers and Melchior (1977) put tetrahydropapaveroline (THP) into the brains of rats, with the result that they no longer would switch back but permanently preferred alcohol. Strains of mice that do not prefer alcohol can be converted into alcohol-craving mice by damaging their livers with carbon tetrachloride. We cannot assume perfect similarity of mice and humans, but these facts suggest that the alcoholic liver burns alcohol in place of sugar. The hereditary aspect is reinforced by evidence that the cousins of alcohol-preferring rats develop changes in the brain rapidly upon exposure to alcohol, so that they take in twenty times their prior amounts of alcohol.

The work of Hans Selye described in *Stress* (1956) highlights innate differences in tolerance and adaptability, and is complemented by Sudduth's (1977) enterotoxemia hypothesis, wherein neurotoxins from bacteria in the gastrointestinal system are both increased by alcohol and sedated by more of the same, in a vicious circle. This conforms to the discovery of Bruel and LeCoq long ago (1939, 1947) that alcohol given intravenously does not produce the same effect as when orally ingested. Both lines of thought are congruent with the important role the liver plays in our immune system.

Most important may be the interaction of alcohol in the brain with innate psychoactive substances such as dopamine and serotonin (see Andreasen, 1985). We may have either too little or too much of these natural drugs. This seems related to the fact that alcohol seems to be more a stimulant for alcoholics than for others, and with the fact that drinking often produces anxiety rather than sedating it. Davis and others (1970) had reported on the relation of alcohol and dopamine, Ewing in 1976 compared levels of the relevant enzyme dopamine betahydroxylase (DBH) with response to alcohol. Nonalcoholics with low DBH levels tend to feel bad when they drink, a difference also found to vary with race. Lundquist (1975) stated that Yedy Israel's work on the permeability of nerve-cell membranes in the lower midbrain may be crucial, as the alcoholic differs *initially* from the nonalcoholic because the alcoholic's nerve tissue prefers the alcohol molecule to the sugar molecule, much as a key fits a lock. These receptor sites may be hypersensitive or may have either excess or lack of natural blockers. Changes here may account for the gross drop in tolerance seen in very late-stage alcoholism. We cannot recount all the details here, and much is still unknown. But the exciting fact is that a cohesive picture of addiction is emerging, as parts of the puzzle fall into place. In the next chapter we shall see how even the psychological research confirms the notion that alcoholism is due in large part to physiological factors, and in relatively few cases is it merely symptomatic of personality disorder.

Hereditary or Acquired?

The physiological factors mentioned above, which are at least a part of the cause of alcoholism, may be either acquired or innate. The difficulties in trying to get hard data on alcoholics before they are identified as patients leave us with the old chicken-or-egg problem. Heredity and environment are inseparable in real life, and practically impossible to disentangle in research.

Some Acquired. Even when the biological characteristics of alcoholics are the result of drinking, this still leaves the notion of physical addiction as a cause of alcoholism. Whether or not there is hereditary predisposition, there will be tissue adaptation with subsequent decompensation, the interaction between the chemical and the organism. Psychological and sociocultural forces are causal factors to the extent that they induced the prolonged drinking, which in turn caused the biological changes. The oxygen deprivation, magnesium loss, and general electrolyte imbalance in the brain plus the enzyme and structural changes in the liver, along with poor diet, are bound to cause deterioration in time, and nature can compensate only so much. Psychological dependence would then be more obvious in the earlier stages of the progression, and physical addiction would become apparent only later in the disease, although the physical vulnerability may have been developing very early.

Theoretically, any person who drinks hard and long enough could produce these changes and "achieve" alcoholism, even though originally not so disposed. Actually, some people seem to have such high immunity that they die of other things first, so we never know. Again, drinking is not the only way these differences can be acquired. Gastric resection, brain injury, cross-addiction to other drugs, damage to the liver by carbon tetrachloride or the like, and other traumata all have been cited as increasing vulnerability to alcoholism. But is it always acquired?

Some Hereditary. Heredity was long a taboo subject in the alcohol field, because it smacked of the old idea that "this child is doomed to be a hopeless drunkard like his father." Behaviorism, in its stress on environmental conditioning, had scoffed at the exaggerated hereditarianism of earlier evolutionary theory. Not until the invention of the electron microscope and discovery of the DNA molecule, along with other advances in the science of genetics, was there a renaissance of emphasis on heredity. As this has moved into the alcoholism field, the attitude is not hopelessness but rather, "Forewarned is forearmed." Today there is a strong prevention emphasis on children of alcoholic ancestry as high-risk candidates for addiction. One authority reported that 70 percent of his cocaine addicts had alcoholic parents.

That alcoholism runs in families is well known. The old explanations were the alcoholic environment, imitation of a parental role model, or reaction to the stressful situation. But research has controlled for these in a variety of ways, and many lines of evidence point toward biological predisposition to alcoholism as being inherited regardless of parental environment. Notice we say predisposition, for alcoholism is not inherited as a unit Mendelian trait. At no time do we imply heredity is the sole cause of alcoholism, as some incautious authors seem to do (e.g., Fitzgerald, 1988). Overemphasis on heredity can be dangerous, as people can drink themselves to death while believing they are immune because they see no alcoholism in their ancestry. Hereditary vulnerability and alcohol ingestion may combine as part causes. Drinking depends on many psychosocial factors, as we have seen. But the reason only some drinkers become alcoholics, and many of those early on or from the very start of their drinking, is closely tied to biological lineage. A child with an alcoholic father or brother has a 25 percent chance of being an alcoholic, which is five to eight times the incidence in the general population (Goodwin, 1978a). The probability goes much higher if there is alcoholism in both lines of ancestry. Grandparents as well as parents must be considered, since many hereditary diseases can skip a generation.

How do we know it is hereditary and not parental environment? After all, the child speaks the same language as the parents, but nobody would argue that this is biological. In a special focus issue of *Alcohol Health and Research World,* Winter 1987–88, 12 (2), Petrakis (1985) and Schuckit (1987) summarize the evidence from many studies using several different approaches (see Vaillant and Milofsky, 1982, and "Sources" at the end of this chapter). Adoption at birth or within six weeks into a different home removes the child from the alcoholic parent and that environment. Such children develop alcoholism at three to five times the rate of the adopting parents or of adopted children from nonalcoholic parentage. Some of the best studies here are from Scandinavia, because records of adopted children are more readily researched in those countries. Familial predisposition is specific for alcoholism and not on a continuum with heavy drinking (Goodwin, 1978b, p. 4, whose findings are important because he began his research with an open bias against heredity). Ironically, one study (Schuckit, 1976b) showed a higher rate of alcoholism when the children of alcoholic parents were adopted into nonalcoholic homes than when raised by the alcoholic parent. The environmental argument that alcoholics come from broken homes is refuted by the fact that the rate of alcoholism in this case is not above that shown by the genetic findings. Yet siblings or half-siblings raised by the alcoholic parents were twice as likely to have broken homes as those adopted out, and to be in poorer socioeconomic conditions. A social worker never deliberately places a child into an alcoholic adoptive home and is duly horrified at the error, but researchers following up on such cases found that the rate of alcoholism in the adopted child echoed the alcoholism in his biological ancestry, not the adopting home. Research on adoption and on twins does not imply any greater frequency of alcoholism when either of those factors occurs; researchers merely take advantage of these "natural experiments" when they can find them.

Studies of *identical twins* show more than twice the likelihood of alcoholism in the other twin when one is alcoholic than in *fraternal twins,* showing the influence of the identical genes. *Half-sibling* studies, where the children have one parent the same and one parent different, show a higher incidence of alcoholism when the common biological parent is alcoholic than when the other is. *Genetic marker* studies show that alcoholism follows hereditary lines as indicated by the other characteristics known to be gene-linked, for example, blood type (Hill et al., 1975), salivary secretions, PTC taste response, color blindness, and so on. Schuckit (1979, 1987) found that offspring of alcoholic ancestry get higher acetaldehyde levels when they first drink than do controls. The work of Begleiter and colleagues (1984) and other researchers on evoked brain potentials shows similar EEG patterns even in long-abstinent alcoholics, and in alcoholics' children seven, eight and nine years old, before they ever take a drink. Interesting is the observation that when two people meet in AA and marry after years of sobriety, their children are biologically vulnerable even though the parental environment has been healthy.

Most of the earlier research was done on males, but new evidence is being found in girls as well as boys. Social factors may play a larger role in females, and the lower likelihood for women of being diagnosed as alcoholic may skew the statistics. Both male and female children of alcoholic ancestry show distinctive brain wave patterns. Parsons and others (1987) have other evidence that females can inherit a predisposition to alcoholism also. Propping and colleagues (1982) even report more hereditary findings in women than in men.

Roe (1944), for years the only research purporting evidence against the heredity hypothesis, has been criticized on many scores: It was based on a very small number; there was no objective definition of alcoholism; the children were adopted late rather than shortly after birth; the parents were not comparable; and it was done while the adoptees were young adults so that three of the twenty were later discovered to have developed alcoholism after the study was published, and we don't know how many more could have in their lifetime. One can only say that if this was the best the antihereditarians could bring forth, they did not have much of a case. More recent opposition to heredity is from those who seem to think that heredity must be the sole cause of all alcoholism if it is to be considered at all, instead of recognizing that it is a part cause in perhaps half the cases, as Jellinek once postulated.

What is inherited? Most of the items mentioned above under the subhead "Many Factors Involved" seem to be inheritable. Sudduth stresses that bacterial endotoxins vary greatly with inherited immune systems. This may be cardinal, along with DBH, differences in the membranes of brain cells, neurotransmitters, and blockers. Differences in glucose metabolism and liability to hypoglycemia (hepatic or alcoholic, not true type) are tied to the fact that some twenty isoenzymes or variants of ADH have been discovered by Li (1984) and his associates, among others. Cloniger (1983) has identified two types of alcoholism with reference to heredity. Tarter and his associates (e.g., 1984) report several lines of research. Ongoing work will no doubt throw more light in time.

Race. The question of racial vulnerability is a thorny one. We acknowledge the importance of cultural attitudes and drinking customs, but we cannot avoid the mounting evidence that biological factors play a part. We saw that it is simplistic to look merely at metabolism rate and fallacious to seek low tolerance as a danger signal when just the opposite is true. One study on rate of metabolism among Native Americans involved waiting ninety minutes after ingestion, thereby missing the most critical time for important behavioral reactions to alcohol (Bennion and Li, 1976). There is always the question of cause versus effect. But studying racial differences is not racism, just biology. As with sickle-cell anemia among blacks, knowledge about alcoholism differences among various races can be used in preventive efforts if objectively presented.

The research is difficult, and much more needs to be learned. There is always the scarcity of good criteria for racial identity, more so as intermarriage and migration obscure racial lines. We said earlier that one cannot lump all members of one racial designation into a single group of Chinese, Italians, blacks, or Irish. A further complication is that hereditary diseases, including alcoholism, often skip a generation. The "Chinese flush," an innate reaction much like that to Antabuse, has been reported in 60 to 83 percent of Orientals (even babies) and about 5 percent of Europeans; it may account for some of the differences. An atypical form of ADH was found in 90 percent of one sample of Japanese livers. This, combined with a defect in their ALDH, causes faster production and slower metabolism of acetaldehyde, which means higher residual levels. We know that rates of alcoholism are very high among Eskimos and Native Americans, especially of northwestern North America, and higher among peoples of northern European stock than those of Mediterranean extraction. Alcohol-related deaths make the Native American mortality rate in the state of Washington the highest in the nation. The rate of alcohol-related deaths among the native populations of Alaska is about twice that of nonnative (Kelso, 1977, vol. 4, pp. 135–43). High rate of alcoholism correlates with early onset in many peoples, in contrast to low rate and late-life incidence among others. Schaefer, Ewing, Paredes, Hanna, and many others are pursuing the problem from various angles.

Rather than attempt further details, let us outline briefly one hypothesis (Milam, 1974; Milam and Ketcham, 1981) that might explain why racial differences could be in great part biological rather than purely sociocultural. We see a definite correlation between low rates of alcoholism and length of time in which a given people have been exposed to alcohol. Some groups have had alcohol since before recorded history, perhaps 60,000 years or 2,400 generations according to one archeologist. Northern Europeans have probably had alcohol in any quantity for only about 2,000 years, and North Americans less than 400 years and even as little as 150. This is tied to agriculture, since nomadic tribes can hardly get enough wild berries or honey to make a difference. Since alcohol affects both fertility and longevity, including infant mortality, the natural selection process over thousands of years could have allowed elimination of the alcoholics and the survival of the fittest, yielding low vulnerability to alcoholism among the Mediterranean peoples: Jews, Greeks, and southern Italians. Since alcoholic Eskimos average fewer children than nonalcoholic Eskimos, this same kind of selective breeding could occur eventually, but it is not biologically possible in the short time that they have been exposed to alcohol. (Those American tribes who had alcohol but used it only in controlled ritual or even ceremonial drunkenness did not have free access to enough alcohol in a way that could affect the gene pool or alter susceptibility to alcoholism, regardless of how many centuries it continued.)

One could attribute these differences to the amount of time different groups have had to develop social controls and drinking customs, but this theory does not square with what we know about heredity or with what we know about social factors and the psychological strengths and weaknesses of these races. Communist China has little alcoholism, whereas Russia has a high rate. Sweden has a high rate of alcoholism in spite of cradle-to-grave care, whereas the very word "ghetto" tells of two thousand years of stress and persecution that should have given the Jews a high rate of alcoholism, if that is the cause. The Native Americans prior to their use of alcohol were a strong people, as were the Eskimos, who survived in a hostile climate. On the other hand, Jews have the highest rate of schizophrenia and a high rate of anxiety neurosis, and Italians have the highest rate of manic-depressive psychosis, so the low rate of alcoholism in these latter peoples can hardly be credited to low psychiatric vulnerability. Lastly, the higher rate of alcoholism among the American Catholic clergy than among the Mafia is more easily explained by their respective proportions of Irish and Italian lineage than by cultural principles.

Moral and Spiritual Factors

If only for the sake of completeness, we must at least raise the question as to whether the moral and spiritual changes observed in some alcoholics may be part cause and not merely the effect of the alcoholic drinking. This is a delicate subject, to which we shall return in Chapter 19, and certainly there is no need for a lot of false guilt to arise here, because most alcoholics had no idea they were heading for alcoholism during most of their drinking. We would not have dared to ask the question in the early post-Prohibition days. But the field may be mature enough now to look at the issue dispassionately.

The shift in moral and spiritual values that alcoholics experience in their drinking days is a psychological fact, regardless of whether there is moral responsibility for it. Most of the deterioration to which we refer here is no doubt effect rather than cause. But alcoholism is an illness of the whole person. We shall see in Chapter 19 that alcoholics may be unconsciously seeking to fulfill their spiritual needs with alcohol. Today there is a new emphasis on moral values in psychotherapy (Andrews, 1987). The most widely successful approach to recovery, Alcoholics Anonymous, is an intensely spiritual program, and its Twelve Steps are a very practical means of refurbishing one's moral life. Religion may be one factor in the relatively low rate of alcoholism among Jews.

Learning and Habit

Behavioral learning theorists have thrown much light on the development of alcoholism. Keller uses the phrase "disorder of behavior" in his definition of alcoholism. Pathological drinking behavior is certainly at the heart of alcoholism. Is it redundant to say that alcoholics drink that way because they are alcoholic? It is not nonsense if we examine the precise nature of habit.

Habit is a key concept in personality (Royce, 1964, Chapter 3). What kind of person we are is well summed up by Aristotle and William James as a "bundle of habits," but only if one understands the term in its full richness as a psychophysiological disposition: persistent, dynamic, unconscious, and often irrational. Habits can be cognitive, volitional, emotional, perceptual. Habits are largely learned or acquired, but some run so deep that if we understand their nature we will not lightly suggest that they can be easily unlearned, if at all. Deeply rooted in the nervous and endocrine systems, human habits involve physiological changes as well as learning.

Learning

Most people do not find the taste of alcohol initially pleasant, and nobody knows ahead of time what that first drink will do for him or her. One *learns* to drink alcohol and is reinforced by its immediate effects. To say that this or that life trauma caused Mary's alcoholism is true only if we recognize that Mary learned that alcohol soothed life's hurts.

Lester (1966) said that animal experiments had not provided us with a good model. Mice rarely get drunk, and even dogs that do so don't become alcoholics. One could argue that Masserman's (1950) cats did not develop true neurosis and the rats who learned to drink when they went to college in the experiments of Roger Williams didn't really prefer alcohol if they could get sugar water. Some suggest that pigs may become alcoholics, which at least has symbolic value. But serious researchers like Ting-Kai Li now maintain that animals can be good research models for at least some aspects of the problem (see McLearn et al., 1981; Mello, 1973).

Nevertheless, what we know about animal and human learning, with alcohol and in other ways, tells us much about the nature of alcoholism. Even when not primary, learning by reinforcement of the escape value of alcohol may be a part factor. Anxiety, tension, and guilt melt away with a few drinks, at least temporarily. Some alcoholics learn only this, and not that the troubles always come back worse.

Timing is important in learning, as any student of behavior modification knows. Drinking is reinforced quickly by a lift or glow or euphoria or tran-

quility or whatever. It need not always work, as the facts of intermittent reinforcement show. One does not hit the jackpot every time, but an occasional
win keeps the compulsive gambler coming back. Alcoholics have selective
amnesia: They remember the good times and forget the misery, looking for
that illusory euphoria—when all that alcohol brings is trouble. Research by
Smart (1968) shows alcoholics have a different sense of time from others: "A
long time" is quite relative.

Timing is why a hangover does not cure alcoholism. The reason hangovers do not deter the alcoholic is the same reason you don't spank a child on
Friday for eating cookies on Tuesday: If the reinforcement is to be effective it
must be closely associated with the behavior. For the alcoholic, drinking feels
good; next morning's hangover feels bad and is associated with not drinking;
a drink makes one feel good again. The associative learning is clear. What we
would need is an alcohol that made one feel bad immediately upon drinking,
then good upon withdrawal. Alcoholics seem to get a quicker lift or euphoria, but it wears off sooner, leaving an incentive to keep drinking. One recovered alcoholic says:

> Why doesn't the hangover act as an aversion? A hangover acts as a
> powerful negative reinforcing stimulus or punishment for the act of
> not drinking. He associates the way he feels with the fact that he is
> not drinking. This punishing reinforcement is not absent entirely
> when the hangover subsides. If he is not drinking, he is uncomfort-
> able a great deal of the time, and for many weeks, sometimes
> months. Many alcoholics drink to maintain a normal comfort level.
> Not all are seeking the euphoric level; they merely need a relief from
> the discomfort the absence of alcohol brings on.

Characteristics of Habit

Habit is *powerful*. One can resolve, pray, promise, but habit will triumph
over all these unless outside leverage is brought to bear. It can lie dormant for
years. One who has not ridden a bicycle since childhood rides off at once
without having to relearn. Compulsive gambling and heroin addiction afford
comparable examples. One cigarette can rekindle a habit that the smoker
paid a heavy price to extinguish. Associative learning is powerful here, as
there is nothing physically necessary about the morning paper and a second
cup of coffee that demands a cigarette. Heavy smokers have more knowledge
and negative attitudes about smoking than nonsmokers; 90 percent want to
quit. Yet the habit persists. I am reminded of my grandfather's story of meeting an old Irishman on the road on a Saturday evening; "Pat, where are you
going?" "Sure and I'm going down to the village to get drunk, and Lord, how
I *hate* it." But he went, and he got drunk.

We concluded Chapter 6 by citing examples of how the compulsion can
drive one to drink everything from canned heat to antifreeze in rusty water.

Denatured alcohol used in nonbeverage products contains exceedingly bitter compounds to make them undrinkable. Despite this, some people continue to drink those products. Such is the power of habit.

Unconscious. One feature of habit is that it diminishes freedom of choice and, in the extreme case, can eliminate it. Loss or diminution of control is a sign of alcoholism; the alcoholic is not as free in the choice to avoid drink as one without the habit. Being unconscious, the habit is part of us awake or asleep, adverting to it or not. Being conscious of the alternatives is essential to choice. The effectiveness of AA is partly due to keeping one conscious of the fact that one is an alcoholic. Drinking for an alcoholic is irrational, but the unconscious nature of habit means this need not be brought before the bar of reason.

One reason for the irrationality of habit is that it develops unconsciously over a period of time. Nobody deliberately and consciously chooses to become an alcoholic. The AA *Grapevine* for January 1978 tells of a psychological experiment that, apocryphal or not, illustrates the point. In the experiment, a healthy frog is placed in a pan filled with water whose temperature is raised so gradually that the rate never goes above the threshold or JND (just noticeable difference) below which an organism cannot make discriminations. The frog can never sense the increase, so although free to jump out at any time he stays until he is boiled to death. No wonder Step 2 of AA speaks of a need to be restored to sanity by some power greater than ourselves. Another example of animal behavior, closer to the self-reinforcing mechanism of the alcohol habit, is the actual work of Olds (1960), who connected the bar in a rat's Skinner box usually producing a food pellet to an electrode implanted at the brain center for sexual orgasm. Yes, the rat continued to press the bar until successive orgasms caused him to die of exhaustion (some student always says, "What a way to go!"). (Interestingly enough, dopamine or L-dopa will prevent this.) The continued drinking of the alcoholic is not less irrational, and certainly does not involve a high level of conscious choice.

Functional Autonomy. Habit implies a learned need; we become dependent on alcohol. Why we do becomes irrelevant after a while. And this fact points to the main characteristic of habit pertinent to our understanding of alcoholism. The Harvard psychologist Gordon Allport says that a habit develops functional autonomy, which is just a fancy way of saying that habit becomes its own dynamism, a law unto itself regardless of origin. Note that it is the alcoholism that becomes autonomous, not the alcoholic. Vaillant (1983, p. 177) says it goes on "automatic pilot." Drinking itself now leads to more drinking. Hence the self-perpetuating habit itself, and not the original motive, becomes the main target of change. What we need is not analysis of why one drinks but treatment that breaks the habit of alcoholic drinking. An example is the sailor who, at age sixty-five, comes for help on a decision whether to continue sailing. He originally went to sea at fifteen because he hated his father. Meanwhile he has sailed for fifty years, so that sailing has become his very life. His entire set of habits centers upon the open sea and the adventure of far places. We say he has salt water in his veins. All his thoughts, feelings, and memories concern sailing. Is there any point in asking him whether he still hates his father? The parallel with alcoholism therapy is obvious.

It is the self-dynamism or functional autonomy of habit that explains, in great part, the answer to the question with which we began this chapter. Why does an alcoholic drink alcoholically? Gone are the reasons that our team won or our team lost; they didn't even play. An alcoholic drinks because he is an alcoholic. A combination of causes culminates in this vicious circle of wanting more of the very substance that creates the problem. Even in those cases that began as symptomatic of some psychological conflict, it is "a symptom that has become a disease," in the words of Tiebout long ago. Our next chapter examines the propriety of this designation.

Sources

Not only is the literature here prodigious, but any attempt at selection means omissions that are bound to offend some. In addition to references to the General Bibliography cited through the chapter, we list a few useful items.

Galizio, Mark, and S. Maisto (eds.), *Determinants of Substance Abuse: Biological, Psychological, and Environmental Factors.*

Goodwin, D. W. et al. (eds.), *Longitudinal Research in Alcoholism.*

Gottheil, Edward, et al. (eds.), *Etiologic Aspects of Alcohol and Drug Abuse.* Contains ample references, e.g., in Dwight B. Heath's chapter "Sociocultural Perspectives on Addiction."

Jellinek, E. M., *The Disease Concept of Alcoholism.*

Keller, Mark, *Some Views on the Nature of Addiction.*

Kissin, B. and H. Begleiter (eds.), *The Pathogenesis of Alcoholism: Psychosocial Factors.* Vol. 6 of *The Biology of Alcoholism.*

Lemere, Frederick, "What Causes Alcoholism?" *Journal of Clinical and Experimental Psychopathology,* 1956, 17:202–6.

Madsen, William, *The American Alcoholic: The Nature-Nurture Controversy in Alcoholic Research.*

Mello, N. K., "Some Issues in Research on the Biology of Alcoholism," in William Filstead, J. Rossi, and Mark Keller (eds.), *Alcohol and Alcohol Problems: New Thinking and New Directions,* pp. 167–91.

Milam, James R., *The Emergent Comprehensive Concept of Alcoholism,* and Milam and K. Ketcham, *Under the Influence.*

Vaillant, George, *The Natural History of Alcoholism.*

Vaillant, George, and E. S. Milofsky, "The Etiology of Alcoholism: A Prospective Viewpoint," *American Psychologist,* 1982, 37:494–503.

Wallace, John, *Alcoholism: New Light on the Disease.*

HEREDITY

The special focus issue of *Alcohol Health and Research World,* Winter 1987–88 (vol. 12, no. 2), Rose and Barret (1988), and the items in our General Bibliography under Goodwin, Petrakis, Marcia Russell, Schuckit (1987), and Vaillant and Milofsky (1982) all contain extensive references, as do most of the other authors cited in that section of the chapter. See also items listed by Begleiter, Bohman, Cruz-Coke, Eriksson, Hasselbrock, Kaij, Lemere and Voegtlin, Mardones, Partanen, and Reed.

CHAPTER 8

Addiction as a Disease

THIS MAY WELL BE the most important chapter in this book. A great engineer once said, "There is nothing so practical as a good theory." Understanding what kind of illness addiction is has very important practical applications. Philosophy of treatment, goals of prevention, length of recovery period, and attitudes regarding return to life in a drinking society all depend on one's conception of the nature of alcoholism. Actually, the foundation for this concept was laid in Chapter 7, which must be read in conjunction. Addiction was portrayed there as a complex psychophysiological dependence upon alcohol that ends up being its own obsessive-compulsive dynamism. Should this be called a disease? If so, what kind of a disease is it?

Recent quarrels about calling addiction a disease pit the physiology of addiction against the psychology of habit. We combine them into a whole-person unity instead of opposing them in an outmoded dualism of mind and body.

History

Seneca in ancient Rome observed a difference between being drunk by choice and inability to choose, which Chaucer quoted in the fourteenth century. In 1849 the Swedish physician Magnus Huss introduced the term "alcoholism." Rush and Trotter had hinted at it earlier, and the concept of alcoholism as an illness began to be discussed in the late nineteenth century in both Europe and America.

In 1933 the words "alcohol addiction" and "alcoholism" were included in standard American disease nomenclature (Keller, 1976b, p. 1697). The World Health Organization acknowledged alcoholism as a medical problem in 1951. In November 1956, the House of Delegates of the American Medical Association declared alcoholism an *illness* treatable in general hospitals, and in 1957 the American Hospital Association concurred. In its Clinical Sessions of 1966 the AMA used the term *disease,* which is also in a 1965 statement by the American Psychiatric Association and in a joint statement of September 16, 1969, from the American Bar Association and the AMA. The question of calling addiction a disease was pretty well settled within the addiction profession. The field had been echoing the title of Jellinek's 1960 book but NCA's Board of Directors on April 16, 1983, passed a resolution dropping the term "disease concept," which implied that it was just somebody's idea or theory.

Apparent exceptions to this consensus were really outside the field (e.g., Fingarette, 1988, who admits that he never treated a single alcoholic patient). But misrepresentation in the media of an April 20, 1988, U.S. Supreme Court decision in the *Traynor/McKelvey* case stirred up the controversy again for a while. Actually, the Court explicitly said that it had no intention of ruling on whether alcoholism is a disease, but only to resolve a conflict of laws within a very narrow construction regarding the time limit of veterans' benefits. Meanwhile the Veterans Administration was spending more than a billion dollars a year to treat alcoholics in its hospitals, which presumably treat diseases. On October 20, 1988, Congress cleared up the confusion by ruling out the term "willful misconduct."

Two 1966 U.S. district courts of appeal had raised the hopes of most workers in the field that the U.S. Supreme Court would soon declare it unconstitutional to jail an alcoholic for drunkeness, on the grounds that it is cruel and unusual punishment to jail one for exhibitng the symptoms of a disease. But in the 1968 case of *Powell* v. *Texas* our highest court ruled otherwise in a close five-to-four decision. (One reason the Court gave was that facilities for treating impoverished alcoholics are woefully lacking throughout the country. Instead of using the lack of existing treatment facilities as a reason for putting alcoholics in jail, the Court might have put the burden on the public for developing adequate facilities, much as the great civil rights decisions forced the issue of racial justice. Eventually this began to happen because of the passage of the Uniform Act, to be discussed in Chapter 20.) *Powell* v. *Texas* suggested that the 1968 disease concept was too narrow and stimulated rethinking of the whole problem. Rethinking, however, does not imply rejection of the term. But let us review the pros and cons of calling addiction a disease and see where that leads us.

Pros and Cons of Calling Addiction a Disease
Pro

It was a great step forward to replace the view of alcoholism as a crime, a species of moral depravity or weak will, with the view that it is an illness to be understood and treated rather than punished. Calling alcoholism a disease encouraged a professional attitude among doctors, nurses, social workers, the police and courts, and hospitals. We don't punish a disease. Marvin Block, M.D., headed an AMA team to educate physicians and hospital administrators, and addiction is now included in their national examination. The term has been important in getting medical insurance coverage for alcoholism treatment and acceptance of occupational alcoholism programs for employees.

Stigma. Calling addiction a disease has great psychological advantages for the victim who is sincere about helping himself. It disarms denial, enabling one to

admit needing help; nobody takes out his own appendix. It facilitates the realization that one is different, that one cannot drink like others. It removes
the sting of the moral degeneracy or weak will theories; it replaces guilt with
the self-respect that is so essential for coming back. It reassures alcoholics
that they are not crazy. It makes alcoholism seem less ghostly and mysterious;
it makes it something we can fight. It is face-saving for the family, too. "Mom
is sick" sounds acceptable. Lastly, in the area of prevention and public education it reduces the social prestige of the early symptoms and dispels a lot of
folklore about drinking and the macho image.

Alcoholism has been compared to diabetes. Like all comparisons, this
one limps, but there are similarities. Neither alcoholism nor diabetes is cured,
but both can be controlled. Both have aspects of compulsion, and both involve behavior that is socially acceptable for others but harmful to the victims. Both have evidence for inherited physiological predisposition.

These are *sick* people, regardless of whether this is cause or effect. Some
argue that a disease ought to be more identifiable, but they focus too much on
the early stages, where other diseases also escape detection. What the doctor
said was a cold on Monday and the flu on Tuesday is finally seen as pneumonia on Friday. Some alcoholism does follow a somewhat identifiable course of
progression, at least within a variety of types, which makes it a syndrome
with fair predictability if untreated. There are many varieties of cancer, many
of them undetected in early stages.

Con

It is necessary to examine the arguments contrary to the term "disease," even
if one favors it, for several reasons. We must be able to answer the objections
of insurance companies, which do not want to include medical benefits and
industrial interests, which do not want to pay premiums for such coverage.
We have to be able to defend in court that fact that our client is sick, not a
criminal. We have to answer the fallacious arguments against the term disease
as well as recognize its true weaknesses.

Invalid Arguments. We have already noted that some of the arguments are
fallacious—for example, that alcoholism must be a single disease entity like
smallpox rather than a multiple illness like cancer. Madsen points out that no
two snowflakes are alike, but that does not prove there is no such thing as
snow. The same holds for the argument that it does not have a single cause;
many diseases have multiple causality. Some argue it is not a disease because
it is not 100 percent hereditary. But many diseases have heredity as only part
of their total etiology, and some may not be hereditary at all. Fingarette argued that the term disease was used by treatment people to exploit the profit
motive, yet numerically the largest group favoring it are in AA, which is free.

Calling it a disease does *not* absolve one from all responsibility, and we
shall see in Chapter 19 just how and where moral principles apply. The rela-

tion between habit and free choice is very complex and subtle, and we need a balance between powerlessness over being alcoholic and responsibility for what we do about it. People differ: Some can quit on their own, others cannot. Resisting temptation may require great skill in mobilizing motivation and outside assistance. AA supplies both, but it is not a simple matter of will power.

You don't buy disease in a bottle; you buy a drink. Similarly, you can't give up a disease but you can give up drinking. Both arguments confuse alcoholism with drinking, as warned against early in our first chapter. Drinking is not alcoholism any more than going to church is fanaticism or bigotry. One does not choose whether or not to be an alcoholic. Would you tell a hay fever victim just to use will power and not sneeze?

Some argue that to call addiction a disease implies that it is hopeless; but many diseases are eminently treatable, including addiction. Alcoholism is not an allergy, in the technical sense of antigen-antibody response, but many diseases are not allergies. (To say alcoholism is "like" an allergy may be a useful analogy, which helps some people and harms no one.) It is sometimes said that the disease concept is incompatible with certain treatment approaches, from aversion conditioning to the spiritual program of AA. That is not true. AA tradition prohibits espousing any causes, but members usually accept the term disease and even insist on it. The same is true of those who prescribe Antabuse or aversion techniques, which can quite logically be used to fight a disease. It is naïve to argue that alcoholism cannot be a disease because it is self-inflicted; any experienced physician has seen many self-inflicted illnesses. Lastly, Fingarette argued that it is not a disease because it is hard to draw a line between heavy drinking and alcoholism. Madsen (1988) answered that one cannot draw a line on the continuum between constipation and diarrhea, but that does not prove that dysentery is not a (fatal) disease.

Like Diabetes. The comparison with diabetes does limp, as all analogies do. There is no insulin and no natural need for alcohol as there is for carbohydrates. More important are the psychological differences: The diabetic does not get the same degree or lift or sedation from sweets that the alcoholic gets from alcohol, nor does he experience the same compulsion, go to the same extremes, bring the same tragic harm to his family, or undergo the drastic personality changes we see in alcoholics. One bite of a rich dessert may make it psychologically harder for the diabetic to refuse a second bite, but there is not the quick effect on the brain that makes the alcoholic unable to refuse a second drink. Nonetheless, the analogy does have some value.

Reasons Contra. Some agruments against calling addiction a disease cannot be dismissed as fallacious. One still caught up in the web of denial and rationalization can use it as an excuse—"I'm sick, feel sorry for me, I can't do anything about it"—and to avoid all responsibility for recovery": "I'm sick; you cure me." (Those phrases do not usually come from the alcoholics we see in treatment. Like the diabetic, they know they must cooperate in the recovery process.) The alcoholic might excuse himself from all responsibility for debts incurred and injuries inflicted, on the grounds that he was sick. Prevention efforts can be harmed because people use the term "disease" to excuse heavy drinking instead of exerting social pressures against it—again a confusion of drunkenness with alcoholism.

The disease label can feed the denial of early-stage or upper-class Gamma-type alcoholics who identify the disease with the skid roader, since they see no serious physical symptoms in themselves (yet). As a self-fulfilling prophecy, it can generate a fatalistic hopelessness in those who do not understand it is a treatable illness. Yet AA is largely a story of hope, not negativism.

Even if applicable to primary alcoholics, it may be that *secondary* alcoholics fare worse under a disease model, which may cause one to misdiagnose when mental illness is the primary disorder. In family therapy it creates a false dichotomy of "You're sick, I'm well" thinking. It creates guilt feelings in the spouse who divorces the one he or she vowed to keep "in sickness and in health." It can slight the importance of sociocultural factors, miss the psychology of addiction, and omit the whole spiritual dimension. It can lead some to think that once drinking stops, all problems are solved—which we shall see in Chapter 16 to be false.

Lastly, the word *disease* suggests full acceptance of a purely medical model. While this may have the advantage of motivating physicians to treat the alcoholic in a nonjudgmental way, cognizant that relapse is common in any chronic disease, it has some distinct disadvantages. In spite of the recent rapid growth of ASAM and a general awakening of interest among the medical profession, several surveys have revealed that the average American physician is still both reluctant to treat alcoholics and often ignorant about addiction. This is not said in disrespect; it is based on reports from the medical profession itself. As one medical school dean put it, his students, until recently, had fewer clock hours of instruction on alcoholism than on some obscure tropical diseases they will never see. Medical models tend to put the physician in full charge, focus almost exclusively on physical damage, and perpetuate a medical "revolving door," which is more humane than the drunk tank but equally ineffective for long-range treatment. It implies that nonmedical persons are "amateurs" unable to treat the illness; yet AA, with more than 2 million members, has been probably the single most successful approach, and other group therapies, recovery houses, and outpatient centers staffed by trained but nondegreed professionals are achieving recovery rates far better than the old medical methods. Worst of all, "medical" suggests "medication"—substituting another addictive drug like Valium or Xanax for alcohol. The result, as a member of ASAM told his medical colleagues, is that "your patients don't get better, they just *smell* better." Pursch (1985) writes that treating alcoholism with Valium is like treating lung cancer with cigarettes.

Biopsychosocial Disease

Rather than a naïve acceptance because "everybody says" it is a disease, addiction must be understood in the full light of its many-faceted nature and complex etiology. We need not choose between heredity and environment or between medical model and psychological approach. A holistic view takes into account all aspects. We need a nice balance between biochemistry and psychology, between addiction and habituation. Addiction is more than physical, and learned habit goes deeper than psychology. Most human behavior is a complex result of physical, psychological, social, and learning factors. Alcoholic drinking is no exception.

Some seem to feel that as high as 90 percent of true alcoholics are not physically addicted, at least in the mild or moderate states. Those theorists are using manifest criteria such as withdrawal symptoms, but we have seen that from the onset of drinking there may be subtle adaptive changes occurring in both liver and brain. Older people who develop alcoholism as a reaction to crises of retirement may have been physiologically vulnerable all along, but their bodies had never been exposed to heavy doses of alcohol. The youth who smoked to prove he or she is mature ends up thirty years later addicted to the drug nicotine, though the original motive has long since gone. Nobody can say when psychology ended and physiology took over. It makes no difference whether the alcoholic hides bottles because the dependence on alcohol is psychological or because it is physical. If one needs alcohol to feel "normal," that *is* addiction.

It would be simplistic to say that 70 to 80 percent of all alcoholism is physical or that 20 percent of alcoholics are psychiatric cases. In the former group physiological addiction may be primary, but psychological and sociocultural factors are also at work. In the latter group stress or conflict may be the main cause, but inherited vulnerability and the dynamism of acquired habit also contribute. Granted multiple causality in each case, with the various factors contributing in different proportions for individuals even within the same category, present evidence seems to favor roughly the above proportions.

Dis-ease

The question is the appropriateness of calling this complex phenomenon a disease. Note that health is not a mere absence of disease, but vice versa. Health is functioning according to the design of nature. Disease, illness, sickness, malady, ailment, and disorder are really synonyms; all mean a lack of this integral and purposive functioning. Dis-ease is lack-of-ease in functioning. Alcoholism is a state of not being able to function "with ease" in regard to alcohol. The decision not to drink does not eliminate the disease, any more than the decision not to eat strawberries eliminates the allergy; the inability to handle alcohol endures.

What's In a Name? Troublesome connotations make any word a poor choice. Thus "disease" connotes bacteria, and hence is inappropriate for alcoholism. We might wish that Jellinek had chosen one of the other synonyms, but none is quite satisfactory. "Illness" again connotes only the physical to some people, missing the psychological and spiritual dimensions of alcoholism. A holistic view of human nature avoids mind-body dualism and puts the disorder in the whole person. "Sick" for many connotes mental illness, and for this reason would be misleading because alcoholism is usually the primary pathology rather than symptomatic of mental disorder. "Behavior disorder" connotes a purely learned reaction, which can be unlearned, missing the peculiar psychology and physiology of addiction, which is an apparently irreversible habit state even when the act or behavior is controlled as in abstinence. There seems to be no *word* that will please everyone, but this does not invalidate the *fact*.

Is Drug Addiction a Disease? The terms disease and addiction have been overworked, ignoring important differences in both substances and people. But one can rightly object to the inconsistency of calling heroin misusers addicts and not calling alcoholics addicts. Addiction is addiction, even though those addicted to the other drugs may differ notably from alcoholics in life-styles, average age, ethnic background, and medical problems. In June 1987, the AMA declared all chemical dependencies to be disease. Addiction is a state of the total person, a way of living. Compulsivity or dependence, not physical adaptation, is cardinal. If you take twenty drinks and quit, you may suffer withdrawal, but you are not alcoholic unless you go back and do it again. Cocaine addicts do not experience withdrawal. One could ask, Is compulsive gambling a disease? It is certainly sick behavior. Whether you call the addiction a disease or not, you can substitute gambling for alcohol or heroin and get exactly the same tale of repeated promises, threats of divorce, relapses, remorse, resolutions, renewed efforts, wrecked lives and families. Pathological gambling even shows patterns of brain activity similar to that found in those addicted to alcohol and other drugs (*Psychology Today,* April 1986, 20, 4:9), and other parallels among all addictive behaviors are being noted as research reveals a common pleasure center in the brain. It may seem to be stretching the word a bit to call this disease, but the concept seems clear enough. Addiction is a physical, psychosocial, and, as we shall see, spiritual disease.

Emerging Consensus

The alcohol field is seen by some as divided. At the risk of sounding arrogant, it might be more accurate to say that the split is not within the ranks of alcohol specialists so much as between those who understand alcoholism and those who don't. There is a real consensus among those working in the field. Theoreticians have showed a renewed interest in the work of Tiebout, rereading Jellinek, capitalizing on the broad perspective of social scientists like

Madsen, who put a balanced but strong emphasis on physiology and heredity, and accepting the views of psychiatrists and psychologists like Vaillant and Wallace, who have rejected the older psychiatric theories in the light of both psychological and biological research. Top officials of the American Psychological Association have joined NIDA in this position (*APA Monitor,* July 1994, pp. 24, 29). The evidence in the previous chapter on liver and brain differences in alcoholics seems a confirmation of this view. The evidence for a hereditary factor reinforces it from another angle. The convergence is partly because degreed people are coming out of their traditional clinics and working in recovery programs that use newer and more successful approaches based on the experience of recovered alcoholics. Only social scientists who have never actually worked with a suffering alcoholic or a desperate spouse seem to cling to the deviant opinion.

Pathological Drinking Is Primary

The consensus is holistic, psychobiological, and biopsychosocial—with variations, of course. There is substantial agreement that alcohol is an addictive drug, so that the concepts of tissue tolerance, cellular adaptation, withdrawal, and the rest all apply. Moreover, the whole psychology of addiction also applies: the notions of compulsion, augmentation, habituation, denial, learning, and sociocultural pressures.

But chiefly it considers alcoholism as a pathology in its own right, not merely a symptom of something else. The American Medical Association's interpretation of alcoholism as a disease says that "the treatment primarily involves merely not taking a drink," and we must presume that physicians are treating illness and not just symptoms. But they add that "most alcoholics cannot break the cycle alone." Treatment facilities and AA report high rates of success, whereas, according to Tiebout, psychiatry had helped only 3 percent of alcoholics, and Chambers said 2 percent. The reason is that the mechanics of psychotherapy may be inherently self-defeating. If the anxiety and tension are the result of drinking and are what ultimately bring alcoholics to treatment, then reduction of these may function more to sustain drinking than to promote recovery. Worse, a probing psychotherapy can be very threatening and can literally drive one to drink. The patient often continues to drink while the psychotherapist is trying to uproot the causes. "Meanwhile the patient gets sicker and sicker," said Dr. Luther Cloud, then president of NCA, with agreement from Dr. Marvin Block, chairman of the AMA Committee on Alcoholism.

This concept is not new. The psychiatrist Tiebout was writing about alcoholism as a primary disease as early as 1944 (see Sources). Jellinek (1952) said:

> The aggressions, feeling of guilt, remorse, resentments, withdrawal, etc., which develop in the phases of alcohol addiction are largely consequences of the excessive drinking. . . . By and large, these reactions

to excessive drinking—which have quite a neurotic appearance— give the impression of an "alcoholic personality," although they are secondary behaviors superimposed over a large variety of personality types which have few traits in common [p. 683].

More recently, the *Harvard Medical School Mental Health Letter* (July 1987, p. 2) said, "It is usually useless to solve other psychological or social problems first and hope that drinking will then stop . . . they are more likely to be effects than causes of drinking."

Toxicity, Not Personality. The literature is full of reports on psychological tests of alcoholics that exhibit a formidable array of psychopathology. We would indeed be inclined to infer from this that one is an alcoholic because of personality problems, especially because alcohol is a tranquilizer. Unfortunately, most of those tests were administered during the first ten days of sobriety. Milam (1974) and Farmer (1973) were among the first to challenge the apparently obvious inference by repeating the tests after three months of sobriety. Milam used standard personality tests like the Minnesota Multiphasic Personality Inventory (MMPI) on three different populations, from skid-roaders to upper class; Farmer replicated his study using the Bender-Gestalt, a test sensitive to brain damage. The results were consistent: Between 70 and 80 percent of the "alcoholic personalities" in all these studies turned out to be quite normal when residual toxicity had been given a chance to subside. Only about 20 percent were personalities that may have caused the alcoholism.

Bean-Bayog (1988), Ludwig (1987a, 1987b), and Nathan (1988) have confirmed this stand, which is consistent with the reports of EEG brain wave changes and brain CAT scan tests that require up to six months or even two years to return to normal after drinking ceased, and with the psychometric research of Mellor and associates (1986). It also coincides with the fact that 90 percent of alcoholics can be color blind ten days after drinking, but most will recover normal vision in time (Smith and Brinton, 1971). In 1983 Dr. Douglas Talbott at Ridgeview Institute for alcoholic physicians in Georgia reported 87 percent returned to normal personality profiles. His may be a select patient population, but in any case the fallacy of testing toxic brains is clear.

Marty Mann, commenting favorably on the research of Milam, related how for five years she thought she was crazy, and when psychiatrists did not confirm this she decided that "my insanity is of such a severe nature they don't dare tell me"—only to discover that she was perfectly normal after getting sober. Unfortunately, the psychiatric label often clings to the patient even after a return to normalcy. Many an alcoholic has spent a fortune on psychiatric analysis, only to discover that his or her symptoms disppeared with direct treatment for alcoholism.

Westmeyer (1976, p. 27) and Mello (1972) subscribe to the common opinion that there is no such thing as the alcoholic personality. There is no research evidence that proves that the psychopathology observed in alcoholics precedes and causes alcoholism. Contrariwise, psychometric research (Milam, Farmer, Mellor et al.; Rohan, White, White and Porter), as well as the experience of psychiatrists working with alcoholics (Tiebout, Fleming, Lemere, Heilman), shows that recovery from alcoholism results in disappearance or marked diminution of those symptoms, which are therefore logically effect and not cause. Even the minority who will need psychotherapy can be neither identified nor treated until the residual toxic effects have disappeared. Success is highest in therapies that attack the drinking-habit pattern itself, whether by Antabuse, aversion conditioning, AA, or whatever. The analysis of personality defects in Chapter 5 of *Alcoholics Anonymous* is aimed at prevention of relapse and handling guilt problems, not at the original causality. The focus is on helping the alcoholic to avoid drinking, which is seen as the basic problem. (Always fascinated by psychiatry, it took Bill W. until 1968 to admit that Dr. Silkworth was right on this point, according to histories of AA.)

Needless Psychologizing. Paresis or syphilis of the brain was called "the great simulator," because it can imitate the symptoms of any psychosis. Brain tumors can do the same, and so can alcohol. Hence the need for retesting three months after sobriety. We don't treat paresis by inquiring why one went to a brothel where the syphilis was contracted. Epilepsy, diabetes, leprosy, and tuberculosis are all diseases that were attributed to low morals or personality traits until the medical truth was discovered—which took still longer to be commonly accepted even by medics. Very few personality traits have been identified as existing prior to alcoholism rather than subsequent to it. One of them is a slightly higher average IQ, which would only confirm the idea that alcoholism is not caused by inferior personality. Some cognitive and learning deficits prior to onset seem to be related to paternal alcoholism and hence not truly psychological causes. The reseach of Mueller and Klajner (1984) shows that alcohol does not really help drinkers to escape unpleasant memories. If we blame shyness and being left out for causing alcoholism, what about the individual who develops alcoholism because of being very popular and always invited to parties? Adolescent alcoholics are immature and confused; but so are most adolescents. The reason why only some become alcoholic would seem to lie elsewhere, since nearly all adolescents drink.

Analyzing causes can be a game both psychotherapists and alcoholics love to play, with little profit. Various motives can be augmented or facilitated by the alcoholic state, just as a minor remark gets blown up into a horrendous attack when one is sick or tired. The psychological causality is in no proportion to the effect, which must be attributed in great part to the physical condition. Here again the question is not Why does one drink?—for which the incident could be reason enough—but Why get drunk? The reason for that is not in the incident but in the augmentation that facilitates the basic disposition to drink alcoholically, much as you get a bigger knee jerk if you tense your arms.

The adage *in vino veritas*—when one is in his wine cups the truth comes out—is sometimes taken as evidence that alcoholism is the result of inner repressed urges or conflicts. To begin with, there seems to be a contradiction here. Does alcohol sedate the repressed material, or the inhibitions that prevented it from coming out? Actually, both may be true. Alcohol is a tranquilizer, and it can also act as a "truth serum" by sedating inhibitions so that defenses are down. But what comes out is not necessarily the "true" personality but a toxic version: drug-affected emotions and irrational thinking or behavior. The result can be most unrepresentative of the person's true inner feelings. In any case, there is no proof that what comes out is somehow the cause of alcoholism rather than the effects of alcohol. Moreover, if alcohol is a stimulant initially, especially for alcoholics, they would therefore seem less likely to use it to sedate inner conflict. MacAndrew and Edgerton (1969) showed that in many cultures alcohol does not sedate inhibitions.

Alcoholism Is Cause, Not Symptom. All this parallels what we saw in Chapter 4, C: that the alcoholic does not drink because he is impotent, but is impotent because he drinks. "Stinking thinking" can lead to a relapse, but it is no more the cause of alcoholism than "diabetic thinking" is the cause of diabetes. One of the few longitudinal studies is by the Harvard psychiatrist George Vaillant (1977, 1983), who studied more than six hundred men for forty years, starting as college sophomores in 1940. He came to a similar conclusion, that "alcohol is the antithesis of a tranquilizer and the average alcoholic does not drink because his childhood was unhappy; he is unhappy because he drinks." To put it another way, alcoholism is indeed usually a symptom—of a deep, underlying *drinking* problem!

Practical Applications
Implications for Therapy

You don't *counsel* a caterpillar on how to fly; you wait for physiology to change it to a butterfly. By the same token it is ridiculous to attempt depth psychotherapy before a toxic brain clears, nor are addicts ready for "hot seat" encounters or insight therapy. They need to learn that they are sick, not weak or crazy or morally bad people. Dredging up the past may only produce guilt and remorse, which can do more to occasion a relapse than to promote sobriety. Addicts need to learn that their irrational behavior is the result of the illness. Drinking out of remorse for drinking too much is not very sane.

But it is equally irrational to attack the behavior instead of the alcoholism (see Beasley, 1987; Vaillant, 1981). We know cases where patients, in danger of death from alcoholic seizures upon admission, were referred to the psychiatric ward because of their alcoholic hallucinations. In other cases four or five major complications of alcoholism were treated, such as liver disease and bleeding ulcers, without any attempt to treat the alcoholism that caused them all. In still others social workers attributed to "bad luck" a string of accidents, lost jobs, bad marriages, and the like without once seeing whether they might be the result of alcoholism rather than the cause of the drinking. Zuska (1981) berates his fellow surgeons for misdiagnosing fractures and other traumata as primary instead of as mere symptoms of alcoholism, which is the underlying pathology. A woman who wanted and obviously needed hospitalization for her alcoholism was refused by one psychologist who said, "She just wants mothering." Pursch (1985) loves to twit his fellow medics about missing the primary diagnosis with the quip that one alcoholic suffering from alcohol-induced gastritis had so many stomach X-rays that he got addicted to barium!

Prevention

The understanding of addiction as a disease is seen by some as inimical to prevention efforts. On the contrary, since it points to physiological differences as a reason why only one in twelve drinkers becomes alcoholic, it should answer the frequent question. "Why don't you drink like others do?" It is not that alcoholics don't want to, but that they can't. They may have the same reasons for drinking as everybody else, but their reactions to alcohol are not the same. Urging them to drink responsibly is futile. Many responsible drinkers develop alcoholism, and many irresponsible drinkers do not, even though drinking heavily all their lives.

Research on the many physiological factors mentioned in the previous chapter could give the examining physician palpable objective evidence of early alcoholism whereby he could penetrate the alcoholic's denial, without haggling over subjective factors or a rationalized drinking history. The differences are often imperceptible except in retrospect, and much of the early adaptation is nonpathological; tolerance is not a defect but a plus. Thus it is important for people at the onset of drinking to be aware that they may be more vulnerable than others if their ancestry suggests this.

Heredity is now being studied as a causal factor in schizophrenia and manic-depressive (affective) psychosis, but in these the precipitating environmental causes are nebulous and diffuse. In alcoholism we know exactly what the agent is: alcohol. Prevention can thus be much more specific. What is inherited is not a compulsion to drink, so learning and sociocultural factors still play a part. An orthodox Jew who leaves his orthodoxy does not change biologically but may develop alcoholism, whereas a Native American is not necessarily an alcoholic in spite of his biological heritage. But just as a disposition to diabetes or an allergy to strawberries can run in a family, so those of alcoholic ancestry should be told that statistically the chances are much higher that alcohol is dangerous for them. This avoids both moralistic and racist overtones. If my body breaks out in ugly red hives every time I eat strawberries, the safest answer is not to eat strawberries. This does not make me bad or weak, just physiologically different. And if my compulsion for strawberries is so strong that I cannot avoid them without help, then I should take Anti-strawberry-abuse and join Strawberries Anonymous.

Rehabilitation

Focus on addiction as not only a primary but a *chronic* disease has important implications for long-term recovery. Where before they drank because of alcoholism, alcoholics must now stay sober in spite of alcoholism (Madsen). It may take years for the body to return to normal, if ever. Adaptation can be so profound that even after two years of sobriety alcoholics may need a little alcohol to approach normal on some functions. The drop in tolerance common in late stage alcoholics seems to be irreversible. And even after years of sobriety, a relapse does not put them at the start of social drinking, but at the stage where they were when they quit.

Other drugs will likewise act on this chronic condition. We mentioned the recovered alcoholics who relapse when given a painkiller by the dentist and have seen long-recovered alcoholics whose doctor prescribed tranquilizers after a mild heart attack relapse into alcoholic drinking within three weeks and death in six months. It is not true that one drink will always trigger a relapse, but sooner or later, if continued, the drinking gets out of control. Hence the only realistic goal in therapy is to avoid the first drink. (It is often asked how the recovered alcoholic priest can drink wine at Mass without relapse. McSherry [1986] showed that individual priests differ. But many recovered priests agree that a thimbleful of dry wine at Mass is neither physiologically nor psychologically an adequate stimulus for a binge: The few molecules of ethanol when diluted in many pints of blood are unable to make any impact on the brain, and for a priest who believes that the wine is the blood of Christ it is simply *not* "a drink." The problem is the bottle of wine in the sacristy, but that is the same problem every recovered alcoholic has of living in a society where alcohol is always available. Lay people can pass if it bothers them.)

Enduring Disposition. Habit is a state of disposition, a quality of the person, semipermanent in nature. Actions come and go, but the habit is disposing us to a certain way of acting at all times. Thus a man is good or wise even though sound asleep and performing no acts of goodness or wisdom, because when he awakes he does not start from zero to acquire these dispositions but has had them all along. Hence a person says, "I *am* an alcoholic" rather than "I was" even though sober for twenty years. They know they are the kind of person who will not drink in moderation over the long haul but are disposed to drink alcoholically. After twenty years of no hives, I still say, "No thanks, I am [not was] allergic to strawberries."

Recovering? For the above reasons, members of AA often prefer to call themselves "recovering" rather than "recovered," lest the latter term cause them to let down their guard as if the process were over and the disposition were no longer there. (Forty years ago "cured" was forbidden and "recovered" was insisted upon, for exactly the same reason!) This is perfectly intelligible within the fellowhsip. However, the *AA Guidelines* (Alcoholics Anonymous, 1994, p. 5n.) warn that others may interpret "recovering" to mean that one is still drinking and recommend "recovered" as more intelligible to outsiders. The title page of their "big book" and the usage throughout confirms this. Marty Mann strongly concurred, saying that "not recovered" after thirty-seven years means that AA doesn't work. The public is happy to fly with a recovered pilot but not with a recovering one. The word *recovering* could cost one a job if the person hiring did not understand this language, antidiscrimination laws notwithstanding.

Can Recovered Alcoholics Be Conditioned to Drink Socially?

Under such titles as Harm Reduction or Moderation Management, this old question has been resurrected. We psychologists know that conditioning is limited in its ability to produce behavioral changes. To attempt to condition alcoholics to drink socially may be asking of behavior modification more than it can do. Actually, most uses of conditioning in this field have been to create an aversion *against* drinking, to condition alcoholics to live comfortably in a drinking society, and to learn how to resist pressure to drink. Steps 4 through 10 of AA use what psychologists would describe as reinforcement, operant conditioning, modeling, and incompatible response method. In this we have been reasonably successful, since this is in accord with the physiology and psychology of addiction. But can we turn recovered alcoholics into social drinkers?

Davies (1962) and Cain (1964) started the discussion, but except for some work by Mendelson and Mello no scientific research had been attempted until 1969, when Mark and Linda Sobell, two psychologists at Patton State Hospital in California with no clinical experience in treating alcoholics, attempted to modify the drinking of chronic alcoholics, not as a treatment goal but just to see whether it could be done at all. Some others thought one value of controlled drinking experiments could be that the patient learns for himself what he has not been able to accept from others, namely that he cannot drink in moderation—giving all this extra scientific help might destroy the rationalizations of the alcoholic who still thinks he can drink socially "if I *really* tried." Lastly, some have tried to avoid polarization by suggesting a compromise whereby total abstinence is the agreed goal for treating alcoholics, but experiments on Moderation Management or Harm Reduction continue for *non*-alcoholic problem drinkers and drunk drivers.

Failure. With the exceptions noted, the literature is a record of failure (Maltzman, 1994; Wallace, 1990b). Although never quoted by advocates of controlled drinking, Cain (1962), Davies (1963), and Selzer (1963), whose research Cain had cited, all repudiated it except as a speculative concept and stated that the only realistic goal in treatment is total abstinence. The prestigious British alcoholism authority Griffith Edwards (1985, 1994) reviewed the work of Davies and concluded that it disproved rather than confirmed the Sobell position. Drs. Ruth Fox, Harry Tiebout, Marvin Block, and M. M. Glatt were among the thirteen authorities who responded to the Davies article in a special reprint from the 1963 *Quarterly Journal of Studies on Alcohol* to the effect that never in the thousands of cases they had treated was there ever a clear instance of a true alcoholic who returned to drinking in moderation. Maltzman (1987a, 1987b, and references in each) pointed out various errors and fallacies in such attempts. Ewing (1975; Ewing and Rouse, 1976) was determined to prove it could be done by using every technique known to behavior modification, but also did careful and lengthy followup. Where others had reported success after periods as short as three months and several after a year or so, at the end of nearly four years every one of Ewing's subjects had gotten drunk, and he called off the experiment with the declaration that it would be unethical to attempt any more. The most thorough research (Helzer et al., 1985) studied five- and seven-year outcomes on 1,289 diagnosed and treated alcoholics, and found only 1.6 percent were successful moderate drinkers. Of this tiny fraction, most were female and all showed few clear symptoms of true alcoholism. In any case, it would be unethical to suggest to any patient a goal with a failure rate of 98.4 percent.

The furor aroused by the Rand report (Armor, 1976) was modified by a second report (Polich et al., 1980), which largely eroded the original findings. The Rand report and other studies have been criticized (*Alcoholism Report*, July 9, 1976; Emrick, 1977; Orford, 1978) for covering too short a time period, for using inadequate care in followup, for subjective reporting, small number, sampling fallacies, lack of control group, and employing absurdly artificial settings. The Sobells (1987) tried to defend their work, but questions remained about selective sampling and adequate criteria, as well as the validity of their followup. Madsen concluded one of the better reviews of the Sobell experiments by saying, "In no place does the experiment domonstrate that a single alcoholic has learned to control his drinking totally" (1988). Finally, Pendery and Maltzman (1982) exposed the failure of the Sobell work in *Science*, using hospital and police records and direct contact to show that nineteen of their twenty subjects did not maintain sobriety in social drinking, and the other was probably not a true alcoholic to begin with.

Most attempts in this matter fail to separate adequately true alcoholics from alcohol abusers or problem drinkers, which makes reports of success misleading. Nor can we know how many of the latter may progress into true alcoholism. Again, many researchers lumped all alcoholics together, ignoring the fact that they are of many different types. Thus craving is entirely different in a progressive Gamma, a maintenance Delta, and a periodic Epsilon. Craving also varies with the individual; it may not automatically be set off with one drink, but can build up. Pattison and the Sobells (1977) seem to make a "straw man" of the disease concept by incorrectly assuming that alcoholism is always progressive, that alcoholics are all of one type, and that craving, compulsion, and loss of control are uniform all-or-none phenomena (Maisto, 1977). There is a vast difference between a nonalcoholic getting drunk and an alcoholic doing so; for the former it may be a minor incident, but for the latter it is pathological behavior. The research of Peter Nathan indicates that whereas others may be able to use internal cues (subjective feelings of intoxication) to estimate BAC while drinking, alcoholics cannot; so this method of control is not available to them.

Loss of Control. A major fallacy concerns loss of control (Keller, 1972). In fact, *all* alcoholic drinking is "controlled" drinking, until the last deteriorative stage. There is some partial control at various stages and at some periods, so experimenters took too literally the idea that one drink always means getting drunk. Madsen suggests (1973, pp. 68–69), and quotes Marty Mann to corroborate, that this misinterpretation resulted from listening to the preventive philosophy of Alcoholics Anonymous rather than to the actual experiences of members. His own research shows 97 percent of AAs reported ability to quit drinking after one drink at some stage and under sufficient motivation, yet every one of them knew that if they continued they would eventually lose control. Many research projects set out to disprove the "one drink" hypothesis in laboratory or hospital settings so artificial and with criteria so wooden that nobody with real experience in alcoholism could take the results seriously. As Madsen says, any heavy smoker can avoid smoking during High Mass.

Conclusion. It is unfair to imply that all researchers advocate social drinking for alcoholics. One need not question the sincerity of the experimenters, but one can question their good judgment and their unconscious motives. Nobody with lengthy experience in treating alcoholics would find it hard to agree with Dr. Ernest Noble, former director of the National Institute on Alcohol Abuse and Alcoholism (NIAAA), that "it would be extremely unwise for a recovered alcoholic to even try to experiment with controlled drinking." To ask a recovered addict to engage in "responsible heroin shooting" or a compulsive gambler to just play for small amounts is to ignore the whole psychology and physiology of addiction. Even if a tiny fraction of alcoholics could in fact return to normal drinking, most alcoholics, through denial and rationalization, would immediately place themselves in that fraction and fail. Physiology aside, the compulsive gambler had better be motivated to accept the idea that he should avoid gambling entirely.

Add to this the statement of Dr. Nicholas Pace, former president of NCA, that "you can't teach a sick liver to drink again," and recall what happened when Myers put THP into rats' brains and they changed from alcohol-avoiders to alcohol-seekers. Alcoholism is not a simple learned behavior that can be unlearned, but a habitual disposition that has profoundly modified the whole person, mind and body. This explains the admitted failure of psycho-analysis to achieve any notable success in treating alcoholics, and renders vapid the notion of Claude Steiner in *Games Alcoholics Play* (1972) that the alcoholic is a naughty child rather than a sick adult. Even the Sobells' claimed successful cases are now reported to have given up controlled drinking. For them abstinence is easier (Caddy, 1979)—trying to take one drink and stop is sheer misery. The reason is that one cannot "unlearn" the instant euphoric reinforcement that alcohol gives. Once you have turned a cucumber into a pickle, you cannot change it back.

Sources

Vaillant (1983) reviews the pros and cons of calling alcoholism a disease, as did Selden Bacon in his chapter "Concepts" in Filstead et al. (1976, pp. 88–96, 112–16). Beasley (1987), Bean and Zinberg (1981), Keller (1976b), Jolyon West (1984), and Wallace (1990a) are enlightening. A good overall comment is the article by M. M. Glatt, "Alcoholism Disease Concept and Loss of Control Revisited," *British Journal of Addiction*, 1976, 71:135–44. Shaffer (1984) and Shaffer and Burgess (1981) cover many addictions. One can purchase from NCADD a package of nine important contributions by H. M. Tiebout as "The Tiebout Papers" (for titles see General Bibliography). Jellinek's classic *Disease Concept* (1960), Madsen's *The American Alcoholic* (1973), Milan (1974), and Milam and Ketcham (1981), have been referred to. A broadening perspective is given in F. P. Seeburger, *Addiction and Responsibility: An Inquiry into the Addictive Mind* (1993).

On the question of conditioning alcoholics to drink socially, among the many sources cited in the text the following are probably the most incisive:

Madsen, William, *Defending the Disease of Alcoholism: From Facts to Fingarette* (1988).

Maltzman, Irving, "Controlled Drinking and the Treatment of Alcoholism," *JAMA*, 1987a, 257(7):927.

———, "In Reply," *JAMA*, 1987b, 257(23):3229.

———, "Why Alcoholism Is a Disease," *Journal of Psychoactive Drugs*, 1994, 26:13–31.

Pendery, M. L., and I. Maltzman, "Controlled Drinking by Alcoholics? New Findings and a Reevaluation of a Major Affirmative Study," *Science*, July 9, 1982, 217:169–75.

Wallace, John, "Controlled Drinking, Treatment Effectiveness, and the Disease Model of Addiction: A Commentary on the Ideological Wishes of Stanton Peele," *Journal of Psychoactive Drugs*, 1990, 22:261–84.

CHAPTER 9

The Spouse and Family
of the Addict

PROBABLY THE GREATEST ADVANCE in the treatment of alcoholism and other drugs in the past few decades has been the application of family systems theory such as that of Murray Bowen, Salvador Minuchin, Gregory Bateson, Virginia Satir, and Peter Steinglass. As a result, treatment centers are reporting a 40 to 60 percent increase in success rates. The family is compared to a mobile, of which each hanging piece is affected in a delicate balance by the movement of each other piece. Some treatment centers have a special wing or building exclusively for the spouses of addicts to live in during part of the patient's treatment period, and some *require* the spouse to be in treatment for part of that time. If that is not possible, at least participation in a family group therapy session is made a condition for visitation rights. Often the year of weekly family groups afterward is more effective than the intensive inpatient therapy (see Friedman and Granick, 1990). If the addiction is to illegal drugs, the family psychodynamics are the same, but the impact on the family is often worse because of the associated crime and violence.

"The family of the alcoholic *needs help as much as or more than* the alcoholic" seems better than the older saying "as sick as or sicker than the alcoholic." The spouse and family became involved in a mighty tug-of-war wherein the alcoholic desperately clung to the drinking while the spouse and family tried to diminish or stop it. The alcoholic as patient was the center of attention, while the spouse was viewed as Enabler or Provoker, and the children were neglected. We now recognize that it is futile to rehabilitate an alcoholic who returns to a family environment that is still sick. Treatment can even separate them, since an alcoholic growing psychologically and spiritually through AA actually grows away from a spouse who is not growing in pace through Al-Anon.

Regardless of the impact on the recovery of the alcoholic/addict, treatment of the family is important in its own right. Actually, they can often profit from treatment first. The sequence is: (1) drinking, (2) spouse reacts, (3) more drinking, (4) spouse overreacts. When we eliminate 2 and 4, through counseling or Al-Anon or both, the drinker cannot blame the spouse and has to face 1 and 3 as the problem. The recovery of the alcoholic then sometimes occurs as a welcome by-product, even though not the primary or direct objective. All this, of course, applies to the families of those addicted to drugs other than alcohol, contrary to the older opinion that family treatment for other addictions was irrelevant.

Research and Theories

During the past few centuries when the alcoholic was the focus of attention, the spouse was almost totally neglected or merely pitied. The spouse was always presumed to be the wife; the husband of the alcoholic woman was ignored entirely. When studies began to be published, they assumed that the wife was a neurotic person who married an alcoholic husband to satisfy some unconscious need to be needed, a mothering or protective impulse which could be gratified by taking care of a suffering alcoholic.

Dr. Joan Jackson challenged this concept in her now classic paper, "The Adjustment of the Family to the Crisis of Alcoholism" (1954), reprinted in this chapter. Although our comments are updated to account for current research, we decided to leave the original paper intact—you don't revise Hamlet. It has been confirmed by the research of others. We retain Jackson's wording, since her research was on the wives of alcoholics. The principal thrust of her research was to show that although a few wives of alcoholics may indeed marry because of unconscious neurotic needs, the majority were normal personalities at marriage, and the neurotic behavior they exhibit is the result of living with alcoholism, rather than its cause. This parallels a similar shift in alcoholism theory that we saw in chapters 7 and 8, away from psychopathology as cause of addiction and toward a recognition that usually the psychopathology is the result. A similar consensus now reigns, and recent developments have focused on the children of these dysfunctional families, seen in Chapter 10.

Patricia Edwards and associates (1973), Orford (1975), and Paolino and McCrady (1977) have systematically reviewed the controversies in the research on wives of alcoholics and have rightly insisted that the matter needs to be put in the broader perspective of psychosocial research, which includes other types of marital problems as well as alcoholism. However, it is not necessary to make a dichotomous choice between the old *predisposing personality* theory and Jackson's *reaction to stress* theory. The wife of an alcoholic is an individual, and we must avoid stereotypes. Moreover, we recognize that with the decline of the traditional nuclear family, the typical roles do not always apply.

Predisposing Personality

Older theories contended that certain types of women marry alcoholics in order to satisfy deep unconscious needs. The wife, at the time of her marriage, was depicted as an insecure person who expected her husband to be strong and dependable, or as a domineering person looking for someone to mother. And so we had the stereotypes of Controlling Catherine, Wavering Winnie,

Suffering Susan, and Punitive Polly. These symbolized psychological explanations of why the wife either married an alcoholic husband in the first place or continued to live with him in spite of the misery of an alcoholic marriage, and would even include decompensation whereby she could not stand his sobriety upon recovery and would subconsciously seek to have him drink again. (A parallel can be made for husbands of alcoholic wives: the long-suffering martyr who mothers and spoils his child-wife; the husband who leaves furious, but comes running back; the unforgiving and self-righteous husband; and the punishing, sadistic variety. So we have Coddling Charlie, Bewildered Bennie, Unforgiving Freddie, and Sadistic Sam.)

No psychologist can deny the "need to be needed" or that it is a factor in some alcoholic marriages. Long before Robin Norwood's *Women Who Love Too Much* (1985), psychologists knew that the wife may have a reaction formation to her own emotional deprivation in childhood and be determined to shield others from it. The teenage daughter of an alcoholic father may receive the attention he no longer gives his wife. As a result she may grow up thinking that she can manage an alcoholic through love, and so ends up marrying one. When we asked one daughter of an alcoholic why she married one, she replied, "I knew what buttons to push."

Reaction to Stress

The theory of a predisposing personality has largely given way to another view, one that recognizes that living with an addict generates instability, indecisiveness, guilt feelings, hopelessness, and a host of other reactions in an otherwise normal personality (Asher, 1992; Bepko and Krestan, 1985; Paolino and McCrady, 1977; Reddy, 1978, p. 28). Certainly these qualities in a spouse should not be presumed at the outset to be the cause of the drinking problems.

Because spouses usually come to the initial interview feeling that the alcoholic drinking is their fault, it is best not to start with a history that is only depressing and would reinforce those guilt feelings. Even when the wife's behavior is inappropriate and bizarre, we cannot assume that she is driven to act in this manner by an unconscious need to have her husband drink. It may be that the wife's behavior is motivated by more immediate concerns: to release situationally induced tension and to stabilize the family. If it precipitates further drinking by the husband, that is not necessarily the unconscious intent of the spouse.

Before Marriage

During courtship, the suitor tends to be on his best behavior. Problem drinking is hidden, or simply is not seen because love is blind. In talking with wives of alcoholics one is astounded to hear that they suspected nothing, although any novice familiar with the early stages could have seen many warning signs of alcoholism. In other cases the alcoholism began only after marriage. These facts seem to have been overlooked in the older theories about marrying to fulfill neurotic needs, since these women did not marry known alcoholics. In cases where some awareness is reported, both wife and relatives indulge in a "love conquers all" brand of thinking, believing that "marriage would straighten him out," whereas things only get worse once the honeymoon is over.

Stages in Family Adjustment to Alcoholism

For simplicity of language, and because most of the research has been done on the wife of the alcoholic, we shall refer to her as the spouse. It is clear that the chances might be equal that the alcoholic is a woman and the spouse her husband. Similarly, our emphasis on variety of patterns and individuals should preclude any wooden interpretation of the following seven stages. They are presented as examples of how the family reacts, not as a rigid sequence of events. As such, they support Jackson's adjustment hypothesis even if the patterns vary. It is true that much of this is based on the perceptions of the wives; but these subjective phenomena are in themselves data, psychological facts that must be looked at. Most of what follows is in Jackson's own words; the authors take credit for only the shortcomings.*

1. Denial and Minimizing

Usually the first experience with drinking as a problem arises in a social situation. The husband drinks in a manner which is inappropriate to the social setting and the expectations of others present. The wife feels embarrassed on the first occasion and humiliated as it occurs more frequently. After several such incidents she and her husband talk over his behavior. The husband either formulates an explanation for the episode and assures her that such behavior will not occur again, or he refuses to discuss it at all. For a time afterward he drinks appropriately and drinking seems to be a problem no longer. The wife looks back on the incidents and feels that she has exaggerated them, feels ashamed of herself for her disloyalty and for her behavior. . . .

Eventually another inappropriate drinking episode occurs and the pattern is repeated. The wife worries but . . . in attempting to cope with individual episodes, she runs the gamut of possible trial and error behaviors, learning that none is permanently effective. If she speaks to other people about her husband's drinking, she is usu-

---

* Joan K. Jackson, "The Adjustment of the Family to the Crisis of Alcoholism," reprinted by permission from *Quarterly Journal of Studies on Alcohol,* 1954, vol. 15, pp. 562–86. Copyright © by Journal of Studies on Alcohol, Inc., New Brunswick, NJ 08903.

ally assured that there is no need for concern. . . . Some friends convince her that her problem will be solved as soon as she hits upon the right formula for dealing with her husband's drinking.

During this stage the husband–wife interaction is in no way "abnormal." In a society in which a large proportion of the men drink, most wives have at some time had occasion to be concerned, even though only briefly, with an episode of drinking which they considered inappropriate. . . . On the whole, a man reacts to his wife's suggestion that he has not adequately controlled his drinking with resentment, rebelliousness and a display of emotion which makes rational discussion difficult. The type of husband–wife interaction outlined in this stage has occurred in many American families in which the husband never became an excessive drinker.

Jackson here anticipates Orford (1975) by two decades.

The romantic illusions of courtship days dominate the wife's thinking in this first stage. She tells herself that he is too intelligent to be an alcoholic, forgets what he was like before problem drinking began, clings to false hopes that things will change or that it's really not that bad. She believes his excuses and accepts his promises. Reproof is met with resentment, which usually puts her on the defensive instead of him.

2. Tension and Isolation

Stage 2 begins when the family experiences social isolation because of the husband's drinking. Invitations to the homes of friends become less frequent. When the couple does visit friends, drinks are not served or are limited, thus emphasizing the reason for exclusion from other social activities of the friendship group. Discussions of drinking begin to be sidestepped awkwardly by friends, the wife and the husband. . . .

Isolation is further intensified because the family usually acts in accordance with the cultural dictate that it should be self-sufficient and manage to resolve its own problems without recourse to outside aid. Any experiences which they have had with well-meaning outsiders, usually relatives, have tended to strengthen this conviction. The husband has defined such relatives as interfering and the situation has deteriorated rather than improved.

With increasing isolation, the family members begin to lose perspective on their interaction and on their problems. Thrown into closer contact with one another as outside contacts diminish, the behavior of each member assumes exaggerated importance. The drinking behavior becomes the focus of anxiety. Gradually all family difficulties become attributed to it. (For example, the mother who is cross with her children will feel that, if her husband had not been drinking, she would not have been so tense and would not have been angry.) . . . The family feels different from others and alone with its shameful secret.

Attempts to cover up increase. The employer who calls to inquire about the husband's absence from work is given excuses. The wife is afraid to face the consequences of loss of the husband's pay check in addition to her other concerns. Questions from the children are evaded or they are told that their father is ill. The wife lives in terror of the day when the children will be told by others of the nature of the "illness." She is also afraid that the children may describe their father's symptoms to teachers or neighbors. Still feeling that the family must solve its own problems, she keeps her troubles to herself and hesitates to seek outside help. If her husband beats her, she will bear it rather than call in the police. (Indeed, often she has no idea that this is even a possibility.) Her increased isolation has left her without the advice of others as to sources of help in the community. If she knows of them, an agency contact means to her an admission of the complete failure of her family as an independent unit. . . .

During this stage, husband and wife are drawing further apart. Each feels resentful of the behavior of the other. When this resentment is expressed, further drinking occurs. When it is not, tension mounts and the next drinking episode is that much more destructive of family relationships. The reasons for drinking are explored frantically. Both husband and wife feel that if only they could discover the reason, all members of the family could gear their behavior to making drinking unnecessary. . . . On her part, the wife begins to feel that she is a failure, that she has been unable to fulfill the major cultural obligations of a wife to meet her husband's needs. With her increasing isolation, . . . each failure to help her husband gnaws away at her sense of adequacy as a person.

Periods of sobriety or socially acceptable drinking still occur. These periods keep the wife from making a permanent or stable adjustment. During them her husband, in his guilt, treats her like a queen. His behavior renews her hope and rekindles positive feelings toward him. Her sense of worth is bolstered temporarily and she grasps desperately at her husband's reassurance that she is really a fine person and not a failure and an unlovable shrew. The periods of sobriety also keep her family from facing the inability of the husband to control his drinking. . . .

Family efforts to control the husband become desperate. . . . Many different types of behavior are tried but none brings consistent results. . . . Threats of leaving, hiding his liquor away, emptying the bottles down the drain, curtailing his money, are tried in rapid succession, but none is effective. Less punitive methods, as discussing the situation when he is sober, babying him during hangovers, and trying to drink with him to keep him in the home, are attempted and fail. All behavior becomes oriented around the drinking, and the thought of family members becomes obsessive on this subject. . . . Long-term goals recede into the background and become secondary to just keeping the husband from drinking today.

There is still an attempt to maintain the illusion of husband-wife-children roles. When father is sober, the children are expected to give him respect and obedience. The wife also defers to him in his role as head of the household. Each drinking event thus disrupts family functioning anew. The children begin to show emotional disturbances as a result of the inconsistencies of parental behavior. During periods when the husband is drinking the wife tries to shield them from the knowledge and effects of his behavior, at the same time drawing them closer to herself and deriving emotional support from them. In sober periods, the father tries to regain their favor. Due to experiencing directly only pleasant interactions with their father, considerable affection is often felt for him by the children. This affection becomes increasingly difficult for the isolated wife to tolerate, and an additional source of conflict. She feels that she needs and deserves the love and support of her children and, at the same time, she feels it important to maintain the children's picture of their father. . . .

In this stage, self-pity begins to be felt by the wife, if it has not entered previously. It continues in various degrees throughout the succeeding stages. In an attempt to handle her deepening sense of inadequacy, the wife often tries to convince herself that she is right and her husband wrong, and this also continues through the following stages.

The family has now become obsessed with the drinking problem. The question "Why does he drink?" is not only pointless but implies guilt on the part of some or all in the family. Augmentation takes place as tension mounts, so less is required to set off an emotional explosion.

3.   Frustration and Disorganization

The wife begins to adopt a "What's the use?" attitude and to accept her husband's drinking as a problem likely to be permanent. Attempts to understand one another become less frequent. Sober periods still engender hope, but hope qualified by skepticism; they bring about a lessening of anxiety and this is defined as happiness.

By this time some customary patterns of husband-wife-children interaction have evolved. Techniques which have had some effectiveness in controlling the husband in the past or in relieving pent-up frustration are used by the wife. She nags, berates or retreats into silence. Husband and wife are both on the alert, the wife watching for increasing irritability and restlessness which mean a recurrence of drinking, and the husband for veiled aspersions on his behavior or character.

The children are increasingly torn in their loyalties as they become tools in the struggle between mother and father. If the children are at an age of comprehension, they have usually learned the true nature of their family situation, either from outsiders or from their mother, who has given up attempts to bolster her husband's position as father. The children are often bewildered but questioning their parents brings no satisfactory answers as the parents themselves do not understand what is happening. Some children become terrified; some have increasing behavior problems within and outside the home; others seem on the surface to accept the situation calmly. . . .

When the wife looks at her present behavior, she worries about her "normality." In comparing the person she was in the early years of her marriage with the person she has become, she is frightened. She finds herself nagging and unable to control herself. She resolves to stand up to her husband when he is belligerent but instead finds herself cringing in terror and then despises herself for her lack of courage. If she retaliates with violence, she is filled with self-loathing at behaving in an "unwomanly" manner. She finds herself compulsively searching for bottles, knowing full well that finding them will change nothing, and is worried because she engages in such senseless behavior. She worries about her inability to take constructive action of any kind. She is confused about where her loyalty lies, whether with her husband or her children. She feels she is a failure as a wife, mother and person. . . .

The wife begins to find herself avoiding sexual contact with her husband when he has been drinking. . . . Her husband, on his part, feels frustrated and rejected; he accuses her of frigidity and this adds to her concern about her adequacy as a woman.

It is of interest here that marriage counselors and students of marital adjustment are of the opinion that unhappy marriage results in poor sexual adjustment more often than poor sexual adjustment leads to unhappy marriage. . . . The wives of the inactive alcoholics report that their sexual adjustments with their husbands are currently satisfactory; many of those whose husbands are still drinking state that they enjoyed sexual relationships before the alcoholism was established.

By this time the opening wedge has been inserted into the self-sufficiency of the family. The husband has often been in difficulty with the police and the wife has learned that police protection is available. . . . However, guilt and a lessening of self-respect and self-confidence accompany this method of resolving emergencies. . . .

In Stage 3 all is chaos. Few problems are met constructively. The husband and wife both feel trapped in an intolerable, unstructured situation which offers no way out. The wife's self-assurance is almost completely gone. She is afraid to take action and afraid to let things remain as they are. Fear is one of the major characteristics of this stage: fear of violence, fear of personality damage to the children, fear for her own sanity, fear that relatives will interfere, and fear that they will not help in an emergency. Added to this, the family feels alone in the world and helpless. The problems, and the behavior of family members in attempting to cope with them, seem so shameful that help from others is unthinkable.

The wife has lost her self-confidence and is unable to do any long-range planning. Her indecisiveness allows her to call the police when he beats her up, then refuse to press charges when they arrive. She may even begin to drink herself now for relief. The children feel guilty, since they have been shushed so often that they think it is their noise that causes Daddy to drink.

4. Attempts to Reorganize; Shifts in Roles

Stage 4 begins when a crisis occurs which necessitates that action be taken. There may be no money or food in the house; the husband may have been violent to the children; or life on the level of Stage 3 may have become intolerable. At this point some wives leave, thus entering directly into Stage 5.

The wife who passes through Stage 4 usually begins to ease her husband out of his family roles. She assumes husband and father roles. This involves strengthening her role as mother and putting aside her role as wife. She becomes the manager of the home, the discipliner of the children, the decision-maker. . . . She either ignores her husband as much as possible or treats him as her most recalcitrant child. Techniques are worked out for getting control of his paycheck, if there still is one, and money is doled out to her husband on the condition of his good behavior. When he drinks, she threatens to leave him, locks him out of the house, refuses to pay his taxi bills, leaves him in jail overnight rather than pay his bail. Where her obligations to her husband conflict with those to her children, she decides in favor of the latter. As she views her husband increasingly as a child, pity and a sense of being desperately needed by him enter. Her inconsistent behavior toward him, deriving from the lack of predictability inherent in the situation up to now, becomes reinforced by her mixed feelings toward him.

In this stage the husband often tries to set his will against hers in decisions about the children. If the children have been permitted to stay with a friend overnight, he may threaten to create a scene unless they return immediately. He may make almost desperate efforts to gain their affection and respect, his behavior ranging from getting them up in the middle of the night to fondle them, to giving them stiff lectures on children's obligations to fathers. . . . It seems to be a desperate effort to regain what he has lost, but without any clear idea of how this can be accomplished—an effort to change a situation in which everyone is seen as against him; and, in reality, this is becoming more and more true. . . .

The children, on the whole, become more settled in their behavior as the wife takes over the family responsibilities. Decisions are made by her and upheld in the face of their father's attempts to interfere. Participation in activities outside the home is encouraged. Their patterns of interaction with their father are supported by the mother. Whereas in earlier stages the children often felt that there were causal connections between their actions and their father's drinking, they now accept his unpredictability. "Well," says a six-year-old, "I'll just have to get used to it. I have a drunken father."

The family is more stabilized in one way but in other ways insecurities are multiplied. Paychecks are received less and less regularly. The violence or withdrawal of the father increases. When he is away the wife worries about automobile accidents or injury in fights, which become more and more probable as time passes. . . .

During this stage hopes may rise high for father's "reform" when he begins to verbalize wishes to stop drinking, admits off and on his inability to stop, and sounds desperate for doing something about his drinking. Now may begin the trek to sanitariums for the middle-class alcoholic, to doctors, or to Alcoholics Anonymous. Where just the promise to stop drinking has failed to revive hope, sobriety through outside agencies has the ability to rekindle it brightly. There is the feeling that at last he is "taking really constructive action." In failure the discouragement is deeper. . . .

The wife, finding she has managed to bring some semblance of order and stability to her family, while not exactly becoming a self-assured person, has regained some sense of worth which grows a little with each crisis she meets successfully. . . . On some occasion she may be able to approach social agencies for financial help, often during a period when the husband has temporarily deserted or is incarcerated. She may have gone to the family court; she may have consulted a lawyer about getting a restraining order when the husband was in a particularly belligerent state. . . .

Often she has had a talk with an Al-Anon member and has begun to look into what is known about alcoholism. If she has attended a few Al-Anon meetings, her sense of shame has been greatly alleviated as she finds so many others in the same boat. Her hopes rise as she meets alcoholics who have stopped drinking, and she feels relieved at being able to discuss her problems openly for the first time with an audience which understands fully. . . . She exchanges techniques of management with other wives and receives their support in her decisions.

She learns that her husband is ill rather than merely "ornery," and this often serves to quell for the time being thoughts about leaving him which have begun to germinate as she has gained more self-confidence. She learns that help is available but also that her efforts to push him into help are unavailing. . . . Blaming and self-pity are actively discouraged. In group discussions she still admits to such feelings but learns to recognize them as they arise and to go beyond them to more productive thinking. . . . With new friends whom she can use as a sounding board for plans, and with her growing acquaintance with the alternatives and possible patterns of behavior, her thinking ceases to be circular and unproductive. Her anxiety about her own sanity is alleviated as she is reassured by others that they have experienced the same concern and that the remedy is to get her own life and her family under better control. . . .

The drinking behavior is no longer hidden. Others obviously know about it, and this becomes accepted by the wife and children. Already isolated and insulated against possible rejection, the wife is often surprised to find that she has exaggerated her fears of what would happen were the situation known.

5. Separation, Escape

Stage 5 may be the terminal one for the marriage. In this stage the wife separates from her husband. Sometimes the marriage is reestablished after a period of sobriety, when it appears certain that the husband will not drink again. If he does revert to drinking, the marriage is sometimes finally terminated but with less emotional stress than the first time. If the husband deserts, being no longer able to tolerate his lack of status in his family, Stage 6 may be entered abruptly.

The events precipitating the decision to terminate the marriage may be near-catastrophic, as when there is an attempt by the husband to kill the wife or children, or they may appear trivial to outsiders, being only the last straw to an accumulation of years.

The problems in coming to the decision to terminate the marriage cannot be underestimated. Some of these problems derive from emotional conflicts; some are related to very practical circumstances in the situation; some are precipitated by the conflicting advice of outsiders. With several children dependent on her, the wife must decide whether the present situation is more detrimental to them than future situations she can see arising if she should leave her husband. The question of where the money to live on will come from must be thought out. If she can get a job, will there be enough to provide for child care also while she is away from home? Should the children, who have already experienced such an unsettled life, be separated from her to be cared for by others? If the family still owns its own home, how can she retain control of it? If she leaves, where can she go? What can be done to tide the family over until her first earnings come in? How can she ensure her husband's continued absence from the home and thus be certain of the safety of individuals and property in her absence? These are only a small sample of the practical issues that must be dealt with in trying to think her way through to a decision to terminate the marriage.

Other pressures act on her to impede the decision-making process. "If he would only stay drunk till I carry out what I intend to do," is a frequent statement. When the husband realizes that his wife really means to leave, he frequently sobers up, watches his behavior in the home, plays on her latent and sometimes conscious feelings of her responsibility for the situation, stresses his need for her and that without her he is lost, tears away at any confidence she has that she will be able to manage by herself, and threatens her and the children with injury or with his own suicide if she carries out her intention.

The children, in the meantime, are pulling and pushing on her emotions. They think she is "spineless" to stay but unfair to father's chances for ultimate recovery if she leaves. Relatives, who were earlier alienated in her attempts to shield her family but now know of the situation, do not believe in its full ramifications. They often feel she is exaggerating and persuade her to stay with him. Especially is this true in the case of a "solitary drinker." His drinking has been so well concealed that the relatives have no way of knowing the true nature of the situation. Other relatives, afraid that they will be called on for support, exert pressure to keep the marriage intact and the husband thereby responsible for debts. Relatives who feel she should leave him overplay their hands by berating the husband in such a manner as to evoke her defense of him. This makes conscious the positive aspects of her relationship with him, causing her to waver in her decision. If she consults organized agencies, she often gets conflicting advice. The agencies concerned with the well-being of the family may counsel leaving; those concerned with rehabilitating the husband may press her to stay. In addition, help from public organizations almost always involves delay and is frequently not forthcoming at the point where she needs it most.

The wife must come to terms with her own mixed feeling about her husband, her marriage and herself before she can decide on such a step as breaking up the marriage. She must give up hope that she can be of any help to her husband. She must command enough self-confidence, after years of having it eroded, to be able to face an unknown future and leave the security of an unpalatable but familiar past and present. She must accept that she has failed in her marriage, not an easy thing to do after having devoted years to stopping up the cracks in the family structure as they appeared. Breaking up the marriage involves a complete alteration of the life goals toward which all her behavior has been oriented. It is hard for her to rid herself of the feeling that she married him and he is her responsibility. Having thought and planned for so long on a day-to-day basis, it is difficult to plan for a long-term future.

Her taking over of the family raises her self-confidence but failure to carry through on decisions undermines the new gains that she has made. Vacillation in her decisions tends to exasperate the agencies trying to help her, and she begins to feel that help from them may not be forthcoming if she finally decides to leave.

Some events, however, help her to arrive at a decision. During the absences of her husband she has seen how manageable life can be and how smoothly her family can run. She finds that life goes on without him. The wife who is working comes to feel that "my husband is a luxury I can no longer afford." After a few short-term separations in which she tries out her wings successfully, leaving comes to look more possible. Another step on the path to leaving is the acceptance of the idea that, although she cannot help her husband, she can help her family.

When staying is intolerable and leaving seems impossible, the wife may try to get the counselor to make the decision for her. The answer, of course, is that she must make it herself. The counselor can assist her to work through the problem by facing squarely the consequences of separation, not to dissuade her but to help her look at them realistically. Only when she has consulted a lawyer, made decisions about the house, worked out a budget based on feasible income, and has projected schooling for the children should the decision be finalized. The counselor can then support her in her decision. Once proposed, she must be fully prepared to go through with it. The word *divorce* should never be mentioned before this point, lest it be written off as a mere idle threat. Unfulfilled threats amount to just nagging.

6. Reorganization Without the Alcoholic

The wife is without her husband and must reorganize her family on this basis. Substantially the process is similar to that in other divorced families, but with some additions. The divorce rarely cuts her relationships to her husband. Unless she and her family disappear, her husband may make attempts to come back. When drunk, he may endanger her job by calls at her place of work. He may attempt violence against members of the family, or he may contact the children and work to gain their loyalty so that pressure is put on the mother to accept him again. Looking back on her marriage, she forgets the full impact of the problem situation on her and on the children and feels more warmly toward her husband, and these feelings can still be manipulated by him. The wide circulation of information on alcoholism as an illness engenders guilt about having deserted a sick man. Gradually, however, the family becomes reorganized.

Most important is that the shift in roles described in Stage 4 now becomes complete. The wife is father and mother. She is disciplinarian, budget manager, and often the sole wage earner. The children have learned to obey only her, and ignore the father. They may be bitter against him, unless they have joined a group like Alateen and learned emotional detachment. The wife still needs her Al-Anon meetings, for not all problems are solved by separation.

7. Recovery and Reorganization with the Alcoholic

For years the spouse has prayed, begged, and hoped—always with the expectation that if the drinking would only stop, everything would be all right. Now the alcoholic has gone to treatment, joined AA, and things seem worse! There are many reasons for this paradox. Alcohol loses the role of scapegoat. The couple must face problems they haven't faced in years, discovering that not all their problems were caused by drinking. They have not really communicated for a long time, and have to learn how to talk with each other. (Hint: Don't say, "Now we are going to discuss . . ." as that will almost certainly evoke a negative response. Just start talking, preferably at a well-chosen time and place.) The mistrust that has built up for years does not dissipate overnight. He knows he is going to make it this time, but she has been burned too many times to feel his inner confidence. When he demands love from his wife, her frigidity stems not from bad will but from spontaneous feelings.

> [It] was pointed out that in earlier stages most of the problems in the marriage were attributed to the alcoholism of the husband, and thus problems in adjustment not related directly to the drinking were unrecognized and unmet. . . . Irritation or other signs of growing tension were viewed as indicators of further drinking, and hence the problems giving rise to them were walked around gingerly rather than faced and resolved. Lack of conflict and lack of drinking were defined as indicating a perfect adjustment. For the wife and husband facing a sober marriage after many years of an alcoholic marriage, the expectations of what marriage without alcoholism will be are unrealistically idealistic, and the reality of marriage almost inevitably brings disillusionments. . . .
>
> The beginning of sobriety for the husband does not bring too great hope to the family at first. They have been through this before but are willing to help him along and stand by him in the new at-

tempt. As the length of sobriety increases, so do the hopes for its permanence and efforts to be of help. The wife at first finds it difficult to think more than in terms of today, waking each morning with fear of what the day will bring and sighing with relief at the end of each sober day.

With the continuation of sobriety, many problems begin to crop up. Mother has for years managed the family, and now father again wishes to be reinstated in his former roles. Usually the first role reestablished is that of breadwinner, and the economic problems of the family begin to be alleviated as debts are gradually paid and there is enough left over for current needs. With the resumption of this role, the husband feels that the family should also accept him at least as a partner in the management of the family. Even if the wife is willing to hand over some of the control of the children, for example, the children often are not able to accept this change easily. Their mother has been both parents for so long that it takes time to get used to the idea of consulting their father on problems and asking for his decisions. Often the father tries too hard to manage this change overnight, and the very pressure put on the children toward this end defeats him. In addition, he is unable to meet many of the demands the children make on him because he has never really become acquainted with them or learned to understand them and is lacking in much necessary background knowledge of their lives.

The wife, who finds it difficult to conceive of her husband as permanently sober, feels an unwillingness to let control slip from her hands. At the same time she realizes that reinstatement of her husband in his family roles is necessary to his sobriety. She also realizes that the closer his involvement in the family the greater the probability of his remaining sober. Yet she remembers events in the past in which his failure to handle his responsibilities was catastrophic to the family. Used to avoiding anything which might upset him, the wife often hesitates to discuss problems openly. At times, if she is successful in helping him to regain his role as father, she feels resentful of his intrusion into territory she has come to regard as hers. If he makes errors in judgment which affect the family adversely, her former feelings of being his superior may come to the fore and affect her interaction with him. If the children begin to turn to him, she may feel a resurgence of self-pity at being left out and find herself attempting to swing the children back toward herself. Above all, however, she finds herself feeling resentful that some other agency achieved what she and the children could not.

Often the husband makes demands for obedience, for consideration and for pampering which members of the family feel unable to meet. He may become rather euphoric as his sobriety continues and feel superior for a time.

Gradually, however, the drinking problem sinks into the past and marital adjustment at some level is achieved. Even when this has occurred, the drinking problem crops up occasionally, as when the time comes for a decision about whether the children should be permitted to drink. The mother at such times becomes anxious, sees in the child traits which remind her of her husband, worries whether these are the traits which mean future alcoholism. At parties, at first, she is watchful and concerned about whether her husband will take a drink or not. Relatives and friends may, in a party mood, make the husband the center of attention by emphasizing his nondrinking. They may unwittingly cast aspersions on his character by trying to convince him that he can now "drink like a man." Some relatives and friends have gone so far as secretly to "spike" a nonalcoholic drink and then cry "bottoms up!" without realizing the risk of reactivating patterns from the past.

If sobriety has come through Alcoholics Anonymous, the husband frequently throws himself so wholeheartedly into AA activities that his wife sees little of him and feels neglected. As she worries less about his drinking, she may press him to cut down on these activities. This is dangerous, since AA activity is correlated with success in Alcoholics Anonymous. Also, the wife discovers that, though she has a sober husband, she is by no means free of alcoholics. In his Twelfth Step work, he may keep the house filled with men he is helping. In the past her husband has avoided self-searching; and now he may become excessively introspective, and it may be difficult for her to deal with this.

If the husband becomes sober through Alcoholics Anonymous and the wife participates actively in Al-Anon, the thoughts of what is happening to her, to her husband and to her family will be verbalized and interpreted within the framework of the Al-Anon philosophy and the situation will probably be more tolerable and more easily worked out.

The illusions the spouse has had about the alcoholic, the marriage, and herself continue to create serious difficulties during the readjustment process. The more idealized these were in her romantic illusions, the greater the disillusionment. For this reason the family defenses cannot be dispensed with at once, for they cannot tolerate the hurt when unmasked until time has softened it and new strengths have developed. The family is rarely at the same stage of illness as the alcoholic, who in turn may get well faster than the family.

The families of the *steady* drinker or *regular* periodic drinker usually readjust faster than the family of the irregular periodic. The families of the former learn what to expect, develop patterns of reaction, have less guilt, and are less easily manipulated by the alcoholic. The irregular periodic drinker has them in a constant turmoil, feeling very helpless and confused, and more easily manipulated because the alcoholic can somehow make them feel they must be responsible for his periodic binges. The resulting mistrust and confusion make the process of readjustment very difficult. Since he was an irregular periodic, it takes longer to be convinced that drinking will not start again.

Unwitting Sabotage. The reversal of roles that took place during the drinking was natural and necessary. The spouse had to take charge; the children had to obey her and ignore the alcoholic. But resistance to a change back to original roles after recovery would seem illogical. Isn't this return what the spouse has been waiting for? Consciously, yes. However, there are many advantages to the spouse from the reversed roles. To revert back means to lose control of the money, to lose authority and power, to no longer be the martyr with good grounds for self-pity. She resents the fact that others have succeeded after she had tried harder than anyone else—"Why did he do it for them when I am the one who loves him?" He gets praised for his successful sobriety, while nobody praises her for her heroic management during the difficult years. After sobriety the children can no longer play one parent off against the other and "work" the alcoholic for compensatory presents. All this adds up to powerful, if unrecognized, resentment at his sobriety and even a secret wish he would start drinking again.

The husband of the recovered alcoholic wife seems to be even more prone to this kind of subconscious illogic. With no controlled research, but with considerable confirmation from many recovered alcoholics and professionals in the field, our experience is that the role of husband as spouse is more reluctantly given up than when the wife is the spouse. He is the protector, the strong one, the martyr. All of his troubles and shortcomings can be blamed on having an alcoholic wife. In the beginning he may have found that she was most responsive sexually after a few drinks, and may fondly remember that rather than her later poor performance. Even cleaning up her vomit gives him a sense of superiority congenial to the male ego. When she recovers he can no longer baby her. In fact, when she ceases being dependent and asserts her true personality as a very capable woman, he may be totally inadequate to accepting this. For whatever reason, we have seen case after case where the husband blocks her attendance at AA meetings and subconsciously contrives a situation whereby she starts drinking again. Of course, he would deny this and protest loudly that he wants nothing more than to see her happily sober.

The psychodynamics here are very complex and subtle, which means that the counselor is wise not to attempt any conscious analysis with the spouse, be it husband or wife. Indirect means of support and constructive direction are more likely to be helpful. The spouse should be encouraged to attend Al-Anon when the alcoholic is at AA meetings and to get involved in the outpatient aftercare or group sessions that are a vital part of the followup treatment in any good facility now.

Decompensation or Readjustment? If compensation for unfulfilled needs is the underlying motive for marrying or staying married to an alcoholic, then attempts to undermine the recovery could be decompensation. This is plausible in those cases where the theory applies. However, the evidence suggests that most of the time these subconscious efforts are simply maladjustive reactions when a learned behavior pattern is threatened. Habit is resistant to change, and learned values can be powerful motivation. So the spouse who once poured bottles down the sink and did all the other wrong things may end up regretting the loss of power or self-pity which the drinking provided. Thus Jackson's Stage 7 is not necessarily support for the unconscious need theory.

Mutual Interaction

Although it is possible to become an alcoholic through solitary drinking and no interaction with other human beings, this is rarely the case. Almost always there are people around who are used by the alcoholic in manipulative ways to justify the drinking or delay any surrender to treatment. Besides the alcoholic, the spouse is the principal actor in this life drama but there are others. We prefer the term *drama* to *games*, for this is no fun, and nobody wins. All the world's a stage, and there is a great deal of role-playing here which must be unmasked if genuine relationships are to be restored. Otherwise the drama is always a tragedy.

J. Kellerman, in *Alcoholism: A Merry-Go-Round Named Denial* (1973), calls the players the Alcoholic, the Enabler, the Victim, and the Provocatrice. Others refer to a Patsy, a Rescuer, a Persecutor, a Connection, and an Agitator, which is the language of Eric Berne's Transactional Analysis as described in Chapter 6 of his *Games People Play* (1967). Alcoholic and spouse may reverse roles, for example each takes a turn at being the Victim or Patsy or at being the Persecutor. Any third person will usually make a triangle out of the relationship: A child can come between the spouses, or one spouse can set up rivalry between a child and the other spouse. The Agitator is adept at starting fights but avoids engaging in them. The Connection might be the friendly bartender willing to extend credit. The Patsy or Victim may be the spouse, foreman, business partner, or whoever ends up doing the alcoholic's work when he or she is absent or hung over. The Provocatrice or Persecutor is the spouse who ends up being blamed for all that is wrong in the marriage, in spite of heroic efforts to make the marriage work, which only provoke resentment in the alcoholic. Nagging, hiding bottles, withholding sex, bargaining, threatening, haggling over money, and moralizing are examples of these efforts. Alcohol through augmentation or facilitation causes a hypersensitivity and low frustration tolerance, which in turn is displaced or projected, as when the alcoholic kicks the cat or takes it out on the spouse, leading to a *folie à deux,* which makes their lives truly unmanageable.

The Enabler

By far the most damaging role is that of the Rescuer, or Enabler. The spouse is the chief agent here, but other rescuers may be the clergyman, physician, social worker, lover, or parent who always comes to the rescue and never lets the alcoholic feel the full consequences of the drinking. Lying to the boss, bailing out of jail, covering up before the children and neighbors, paying debts, and reassuring the alcoholic that he or she is "not that bad" are some of the things that enable the alcoholic to continue drinking and delay the moment of truth that leads to treatment. It is not a question of causing the continued drinking, but rather of being used by the alcoholic. In the case of the secondary rescuers, that is, the professionals, it may stem from a need to play God, or a sublimation of the rescuer's own anxiety and guilt. Regardless of motivation, the Enabler never allows the alcoholic to learn from his or her mistakes.

To learn from our mistakes is the hard way, but probably the only way most of us reach maturity is by shouldering responsibility. Hence it is cruel to act as Rescuer, and really kind to exert the "tough love" that forces the alcoholic to accept responsibility and do something about the drinking. This is never easy, and always somewhat risky. Alcoholics are sick people, and the illness sometimes involves a fair degree of paranoia. The sick mind twists everything to avoid facing reality and becomes ingenious in ways of shifting the blame. Two favorites are to accuse the spouse of infidelity and to alienate the children. Recently we had a case where the alcoholic accused his wife not only of infidelity, but of plotting his death so that she could get his money; the means of killing him she supposedly used was to provoke fights so he would drink himself to death!

Psychotherapy for any of this is impossible while the brain is still affected by alcohol, which means not only while the alcoholic is still drinking but also in the early days of sobriety. Depth analysis is totally inappropriate during the first phase of treatment. But the counselor should be able to recognize what is happening and to help the spouse handle some of the projected guilt and self-blame. Most important is to help the spouse abandon the role of Rescuer or Enabler and to confront the alcoholic squarely with the realities. More of this in Chapter 14.

Sources

Literature on families of alcoholics, including children of alcoholic parents, has proliferated so rapidly in the past few years that any attempt to list it all would be absurd. Literature on the children of alcoholic parents, including ACoA, is listed in the Sources for Chapter 10, that on Al-Anon and Alateen after Chapter 18.

The writings of Claudia Black, Murray Bowen, Edward and Pauline Kaufman, Joseph Kellerman, Peter Steinglass, Sharon Wegscheider-Cruse, and Janet Woititz are all recommended. An important source is *The Alcoholic Marriage: Alternative Perspectives,* by Thomas J. Paolino and Barbara S. McCrady, which reviewed all the major literature in the field and analyzed both theoretical approaches and research findings. Joan Ablon reviewed the literature in her chapter in B. Kissin and H. Begleiter (eds.), *The Biology of Alcoholism,* vol. 4, pp. 205–42. NCADI has a "Bibliography on Spouses of Alcoholic Persons." The *Family Dynamics of Addiction Quarterly,* edited by Gary and Ann Lawson, Aspen Publishers, began in 1991. Some other useful items are listed below.

Asher, Ramona M., *Women with Alcoholic Husbands: Ambivalence and the Trap of Codependency.*

Barnard, Charles P., *Families, Alcoholism and Therapy.*

Bepko, Claudia, and Jo Ann Krestan, *The Responsibility Trap.*

Curlee-Salisbury, Joan, *When the Woman You Love Is an Alcoholic.*

Drews, Toby Rice, *Getting Them Sober.* 3 vols. (The content is much more in line with Al-Anon than the title suggests.)

Elkins, M., *Families Under the Influence.*

Friedman, Alfred S., and S. Granick, *Family Therapy for Adolescent Drug Abuse.*

Lawson, G. W.; J. S. Peterson; and A. W. Lawson, *Alcoholism and the Family: A Guide to Treatment and Prevention.*

Maxwell, Ruth, *The Booze Battle,* and *Breakthrough.*

Middleton-Moz, Jane, and Lorie Dwinell, *After the Tears: Multigenerational Grief in Alcoholic Families.*

Orford, Jim, and J. Harwin (eds.), *Alcohol and the Family.*

Stanton, M. Duncan, and T. C. Todd, *The Family Therapy of Drug Abuse and Addiction.*

Worden, Mark, "Happily Ever After," *Focus on Family,* July/August 1985, 8(4):6–7, 38–39.

Zink, Muriel (pamphlets), *So Your Alcoholic Is Sober: Ways to Live More Comfortably with Your Alcoholic; Family's Guide for the 4th Step; Blueprint for the 4th Step Inventory; Silent Slippers: A Way out of Hiding; and Recovery: Turning Negatives into Positives.*

CHAPTER 10

Children of Dysfunctional Families

A MAJOR OFFSHOOT of the emphasis on family therapy has been the wildfire growth of the Children of Alcoholics (CoA) and Adult Children of Alcoholics (ACoA) movements—on which most of the research has been done—and more recently Adult Children Anonymous (ACA), which includes all addictions. Having an addict/alcoholic parent can have devastating effects on a child (Besharov, 1994). Some experts equate it to the post-traumatic stress disorder syndrome of Vietnam War veterans (PTSD). The symptoms may appear psychotic but are usually just situational, and caution in diagnosis is advised. With admitted variations, similar characteristics are observed in children from other types of dysfunctional families.

Co-dependency is a vague concept that has been overused by some treatment centers (M. M. Moore, 1995; Windle and Searles, 1991). In the pathological sense it means a dysfunctional and progressive life pattern focused on the addictive behavior of another person, characterized by denial, obsessive-compulsive behavior, and emotional repression (see Cermak, 1986). The term applies to both spouse and children and can include a boss or even a counselor. *Co-alcoholic* was the original term used to describe the effects on the family, becoming *co-dependent* when extended to families of other addicts. It was further extended in some contexts to *dysfunctional families* when similarities began to be observed among members of families in which there were other disorders, such as gambling, eating problems, domestic violence, and sexual abuse. Little of this was scientific research, most of it being merely anecdotal from participants in meetings of those from dysfunctional backgrounds. Mannion (1991) and Schuckit (1995c) point out that the concept has been inflated in a way that devalues its empirical and clinical usefulness, so some cautions are in order.

Co-dependence is not the same as alcoholism, in spite of similarities. Not all co-dependents are sick, nor are all children of these families disordered. A personality trait is not necessarily a personality disorder. A couple happily married for fifty years while retaining their individual identities may indeed grow mutually dependent, but that may be healthy and even beautiful. Or co-dependency can be a normal response to an abnormal situation. In dysfunctional families there is a lot of unhealthy behavior, and one study found that the whole family may suffer from psychosomatic and other illnesses that multiply their health costs by ten times that of matched controls. In a real sense the spouse and offspring may be addicted to the alcoholic, obsessed with the problem, yet psychologically unable to get out of it. But only the alcoholic suffers from alcoholism. Although needed treatment should not be denied a child with a serious disorder, when families are treated under certain medical insurance plans a child who is not mentally ill may acquire a psychiatric diagnosis that may haunt him in later life during a job screening or security check (Bissell and Royce, 1994, p. 54). Anne Wilson Schaef even published a book that makes all society out to be the victim of addiction—well-intentioned, but badly marred by unscientific generalizations.

On the other hand, some object to the term *co-alcoholic,* asking "Would you label someone a co-diabetic?" Our answer is that if the wife is always serving her diabetic husband's favorite rich desserts and saying "The doctor is too strict, you can have just a little" she is an Enabler and a Provoker and the term co-diabetic is quite justified. The fact that there are varied patterns does not mean they are healthy, any more than does the fact that not all cancers are the same. Jael Greenleaf correctly points out that the co-dependency of a child is not the same as that of the spouse, if for no other reason than that the child has no choice about the situation. The spouse may *feel* trapped, but the child *is* trapped.

Again, it is important to remember that the characteristics we shall describe are developed unconsciously, subtly, and over a long time—not deliberately. So there is no reason for blame or guilt (Dwinell, 1993). Nobody in the family quite realizes what is going on. Family members cling to earlier illusions of an ideal Daddy or "He's the best husband in the world when he isn't drinking." Denial, as discussed in Chapter 6, is insidious. One patient, after telling her story of both parents being alcoholics, was given the diagnosis of an Adult Child of an Alcoholic; she reacted angrily "I am NOT a child!" Many a daughter whose mother very kindly shielded her from the fact that her Daddy was a drunk ends up hating her mother for not telling her. Some children are loyal to the alcoholic (or sexually molesting) parent and hate the spouse. But they suffer terribly. While the alcoholic is often anesthetized by alcohol, the family bears the full brunt of its effects, which may include, besides guilt and confusion, battering, incest, and often verbal abuse more painful than a beating.

Since much of all this is unconscious, recovery takes time. The alcoholic may recover in one or two years, whereas the family may take two to five years (e.g., Middleton-Moz and Dwinell, 1986). The alcoholic until recently got more help than the family, found it easier to let down defenses than the spouse, and was praised for recovery, while the spouse tended to get blamed or at least felt guilty. Spouses can't understand why they don't feel good about their alcoholic's recovery, being unaware of the dynamics described under "Unwitting Sabotage" toward the end of Chapter 9. Homeostasis is a law of nature, even if it means clinging to an unhealthy situation. There is no quick fix for a family system that is dysfunctional in varied and complex ways, delusional, with no good role models, and in a self-perpetuating unconscious denial. The children have learned all too well the three rules described by Claudia Black: *Don't Tell, Don't Trust, Don't Feel.*

Children Coping

Children in dysfunctional families, alcoholic or otherwise, may become confused, withdrawn from other children, and afraid to bring companions home. They may be divided in their loyalty between their two parents and mistrusting of all adults. They are often inattentive in school, hostile and rebellious, lonely, insecure, defensive. They may feel neurotic guilt about their parent's drinking and develop a wide spectrum of psychosomatic disorders, such as skin rashes and stomach upsets.

They can be physically or sexually abused by the alcoholic/addict parent, but incest can also occur with the other parent. Neglect is a severe form of abuse; even battering or seduction is a form of attention. Incest victims feel dirty and find intimacy difficult or impossible. If they enjoyed the abuse, they feel guilty about that. They seem to get involved with other abusers, because they don't know any other way to relate. They find it hard to talk about and need to be gently led by such questions as "Tell me what it was like growing up in your house. Who disciplined you? How? What was your first sexual experience?" The counselor should not be overprotective or overly sympathetic.

These children may be happy at school early in the week and grow more tense as the weekend approaches. They may constantly fear being abandoned and may try to compensate with bizarre attempts to win or buy acceptance from the other children. They deny and conceal their parent's addiction, with boys more likely to be chivalrous about their mothers. They may act out their resentment and frustration with vandalism, truancy, shoplifting, early marriage, illegitimate pregnancy, eating disorders, or drinking or other drug abuse. In any case, diagnosis of any family problems should not be made without careful investigation of the role that alcohol and other drugs might play. And the worker should remember that giving alcohol or other drugs to a child is child abuse.

They may avoid alcohol entirely until their thirties or start drinking very early, but in either case they tend to become alcoholics at four times the general population rate and to marry alcoholics or those who become alcoholics at five times the rate of other children (Cermak, 1986, 1988). If the same sex as the alcoholic, they tend to become one; if the opposite sex, they tend to marry one. These facts, and unconscious denial, provide the irony for the poignant title of Claudia Black's classic book about the children of alcoholics: *It Will Never Happen to Me!* (1982).

Too often the serious symptoms just enumerated signal the first time anyone realizes that the children need help. The alcoholic/addict mother may have compensated by sending her children off to school well dressed and scrubbed, so that signs of neglect do not appear until problems are well advanced. Their experiences as children of such parents result in earlier maturity, so that detection is often delayed until symptoms become severe. Having to take responsibility as substitute parent, adjusting to frequent moves, learning to subsist in spite of poverty or desertion, and trying to prevent their parents' fights all may force them to learn how to cope with the world very early. They may be more aware of the cold facts of real life than their counselors.

It is generally agreed that when the mother has the problem the effects on the children are worse, since she is usually more often with them and more directly involved in their care. She may alternate between being cross and overloving; she may be belligerent while drinking and irritable during the hangover, with periods of loving overcompensation in between. She may fail to hear an infant cry or leave it wet and hungry, drop lighted cigarettes, hurt herself in falls, and otherwise keep the children in a constant state of anxiety, confusion, repressed rage, and rejection. She creates unreasonable and lasting guilt feelings in the children by seeming to blame them for everything. She often throws a burden on the oldest girl as a substitute mother, who shoulders it well at the time but later resents it bitterly.

Roles Children Adopt

Let us describe some typical roles taken on by children in dysfunctional families. These roles need to be understood as varying with individuals and families. Too-quick diagnoses without regard to individual and cultural differences are dangerous and unprofessional. Children may combine roles or switch from one to another. Though typically dependent on birth order, this too may vary; we recently had a family in which the second child was the Hero and the oldest the Scapegoat. Claudia Black first described these characteristics, and Sharon Wegscheider-Cruse developed a set of roles that are essentially parallel but with minor differences.

Responsible One (*Black*) or Hero (*Wegscheider*). Often called superkid or manager, this is usually the oldest child, especially if a girl. This child takes on a parental role, coming straight home from school to fix dinner, care for the younger children, and clean the house, and tries to stop parental fights. Contrary to the stereotype of the child of an alcoholic, the Hero usually does well in school and brings pride to the family in all areas. She or he seems well adjusted, may be a good athlete, and may become the confidante of the nonalcoholic parent. Only later in life does the sometimes overwhelming sense of responsibility and need to "fix" everything and everybody become manifest.

Scapegoat (*Wegscheider*) or Acting Out Child (*Black*). This is the stereotype of the identified "child of an alcoholic" juvenile delinquent and is usually the second oldest, especially if a boy. The family almost welcomes these behavioral problems, because blaming them takes the focus off the real problem, which is the alcoholism. This child gets in trouble at school, with alcohol or other drugs, with the law, and with the other children in the family. He or she may run away from home or be placed in foster or juvenile homes. If a girl, she may be sexually promiscuous and get pregnant early or may get married as a teen. If a boy, he may be placed in a military school. Either may project the image of the "born loser" and antisocial. Because they want attention, they often respond well to treatment.

Adjuster *(Black)* **or Lost Child** *(Wegscheider)*. This is often the middle or only child, who is usually quiet and spends a lot of time alone. It may be more often a girl. Lonely, helpless, and afraid, this child is unable to express desires, opinions, and fears; any form of participation is a losing proposition. Lost children often have a vivid fantasy life and are very shy. In a group they tend to take both sides if they speak up at all. They pretend not to understand what is expected of them and may have somatic symptoms or develop hearing difficulties, stuttering, or asthma. They usually either avoid intimacy or become victimized in relationships. Because they are quiet and not troublemakers, they often go unnoticed. They are usually the hardest to reach and work with. Once reached, they will need time to build trust; too aggressive an approach will scare them off.

Mascot *(Wegscheider)* **or Placater** *(Black)*. Almost always the youngest child, often "cute" and spoiled by parents and siblings, this child provides the comic relief in a tense family system by playing the clown. She or he is the safety valve and becomes an expert at it. Such children are afraid to be taken seriously, are very insecure, and will always look for a protector. The Mascot tends to be high-strung and hyperactive, nervous when there is silence, and often compulsively busy but unable to concentrate for long on any one project. He or she is highly prone to addiction, especially to minor tranquilizers.

Children often identify with the various role designations quite readily: "I'm a Hero" or "I'm a Scapegoat" can come rather easily. But even the most skilled counselor may find it nearly impossible to get the child to recognize and accept the inner feelings that accompany those roles. It may take at least two years to do so. They must be approached carefully, focusing on the child's reaction to the drinking and drugging and without negative implications about the parent. Drawing pictures, or coloring books like those developed by Claudia Black, may make it possible for younger children to express what they cannot verbalize. Sharing in Alateen groups (see Chapter 18) can help older children.

Use of the Roles

Many of the skills children develop in these roles are very functional, if not downright necessary for survival in a confusing, unstable family system. Their behavior is their only defense against feelings of rejection, fear, anger, hurt, and guilt. But they pay a high price for that security. Always ready for the next crisis, they lose the spontaneity and freedom from care which children need. They have no time or life-space for play or creativity. Most important, the atmosphere of family denial creates a mistrust of their own experience, to the point where they may think they are crazy. They tend to confuse reality and fantasy. Inconsistency and unpredictability in the family system breed serious insecurity in children. They learn not to trust anyone, not to share, not to allow feelings to be felt. Repressed emotions and poor communication skills make interpersonal relationships later in life difficult or impossible.

Many lists of characteristics of these children have been compiled, based on the research and clinical experience of the above-mentioned authors. They generally include the following:

1. We have an overdeveloped sense of responsibility and want to "fix" everything and everybody, confusing love with caretaking. Or we may become very irresponsible, caring for nobody.
2. We have a low sense of self-esteem, becoming "people pleasers" who lose our own identity in the process and feel guilty when we stand up for ourselves. We thus become victims ourselves and are easily manipulated.
3. We develop alcoholism or some other compulsive disorder and/or marry someone who has the same, being extremely loyal even in the face of evidence that the loyalty is undeserved.
4. We have difficulty having fun or enjoying intimate relationships, unable to feel or express normal feelings.
5. We may lie when it would be just as easy to tell the truth and have difficulty following projects through to completion.
6. We feel isolated, uneasy with authority figures or criticism, and afraid of angry people.
7. We may become addicted to excitement and frenetic activity, or stoical and apathetic.
8. We are dependent personalities who are terrified of abandonment or loss, and whose feelings largely reflect those of the other person—I look to you to see how I am feeling.

Adult Children (ACoA or ACA)

Most significant is the rapid growth of the Adult Children movement, based on the fact that seemingly mature adults at thirty, forty, or fifty have never faced and resolved the emotional problems and habits they developed as children growing up in a dysfunctional family. Often they discover this only during treatment for addiction or co-dependence, or in training to be addictions counselors. (A high percentage of workers in the helping professions seem to be unconsciously acting out their childhood caretaker roles, as in one claim that 83 percent of nurses are children of dysfunctional families.) In such cases they are well advised to settle their present addiction or co-dependency issues first, before they tackle the problems that arise out of their childhood; thus some good ACoA groups and Dr. Janet Woititz recommend that they not join ACoA or ACA until they have been in a regular AA or Al-Anon group for at least one year.

Started in 1977 by some ex-Alateens, the ACoA movement has gone through two developmental stages. When the research on children of alcoholics first became widely known, there was a tendency to focus on identifying roles and their characteristics as described above, with the result that meetings were sometimes little more than "ain't it awful" sessions in which the members bemoaned the fact that they were victims of unfortunate childhood experiences. This is not said in criticism, but simply noting what were probably the growing pains of a necessary early phase.

Happily, the ACoA movement has progressed to a second, more constructive stage. As we noted above, their coping skills served them well as children struggling to survive the family turmoil. For instance, they handle crises well. Being a Hero or a Scapegoat does have advantages, and the task at hand is how to utilize the skills and insights acquired from those experiences. ACoA meetings now accept and focus on how these CoA characteristics can be used positively to get on with their lives. Thus therapy becomes learning new skills and practicing them, or applying old survival skills to present life situations.

ACoA groups, especially those that base their program on the 12 Steps of AA, have demonstrated remarkable psychological and spiritual growth in their members. Al-Anon meets those needs for many, while others find that ACoA has additional aspects that are helpful. But there need be no incompatibility between them, and the old AA slogan "cooperation but not affiliation" applies. In general, those ACoA groups who use the AA 12 Steps or the Al-Anon format seem to function more effectively than those who do not.

Otherwise there can be amateurish psychologizing instead of solid spirituality and a tendency to blame ACoA status for what could be the members' own responsibility. The word "disease" can too easily become an excuse for being victims instead of responsible adults, leading one cynic to coin the term "Whiners Anonymous." At least two national authorities maintain that ACoA groups should always have a professional present.

In any case, the 12-Step program as a way of life seems necessary because of the persistent, habitual nature of the characteristics taken on in the different roles. As one ACoA put it, "It's not so much the terrible things that happen to us in childhood that hurt us; it's the things we continue to do to keep them from happening again." It takes time and persevering effort to change those habits. Often the parent's drinking itself was less serious a problem for the child than the yelling, conditional and inconsistent love, sheer neglect, and parental addictions to work, food, and television, which seem to be more common among alcoholics. Those things damage emotional health in a child, though they may not surface until an adult relationship such as marriage is attempted decades later. Although the title probably should have been "Women who don't know how to love, i.e., how to receive," many CoA women married to alcoholics react to Robin Norwood's book *Women Who Love Too Much* with "That's the story of my life."

Sources

Literature on this topic is proliferating at a rate that defies keeping current. The best bibliographical source is *Children of Alcoholics: A Review of the Literature,* edited by Marcia Russell and Sheila Blume and published by the Children of Alcoholics Foundation, PO Box 4185, Grand Central Sta., New York 10163, which also publishes a *National Directory of Resources for Children of Alcoholics.* Grace M. Barnes (1982) and NCADI have also published bibliographies. Thomas W. Perrin of Perrin & Treggett edits the *CoA Review* and has a large list of publications, as do Health Communications (which edits *Changes,* an ACoA journal), Hazelden, CompCare, Johnson Institute, and others listed in the Appendix.

Dr. Ruth Fox (1962, 1968, 1972) and Margaret Cork's *The Forgotten Children* (1969) pioneered the research. Later came Claudia Black (herself the child of alcoholic parentage, as are most of these leaders), Sharon Wegscheider-Cruse, Robert Ackerman, Janet Woititz, H. Gravitz and J. Bowden, and Timmen Cermak. Cathleen Brooks described the situation graphically in her paperback *The Secret Everyone Knows.* Judith Seixas and Geraldine Youcha, *Children of Alcoholism,* is based on research. Jane Middleton-Moz and Lorie Dwinell's work reflects deep clinical experience.

The new positive thrust of ACoA described in this chapter is exemplified in the more recent writings of Sharon Wegscheider-Cruse, Claudia Black, Janet Woititz, Timmen Cermak, Rokelle Lerner, Wayne Kritsberg, and Robert Subby; the many publications emanating from Thomas W. Perrin; and perhaps most importantly Robert Ackerman's *Growing in the Shadow* (1986), Timmen Cermak's *A Time to Heal: The Road to Recovery for Adult Children of Alcoholics* (1988), and the work of Herbert Gravitz and Julie Bowden: *Guide to Recovery,* revised as *Recovery: A Guide for Adult Children of Alcoholics* (1987).

We list a few items in addition to those mentioned in the chapter and those listed under the above authors' names in the General Bibliography.

Al-Anon Is for Adult Children of Alcoholics, The Al-Anon Focus, and *Al-Anon Sharings from Adult Children*—Al-Anon pamphlets.

Bean-Bayog, M., and B. Stimmel (eds.), *Children of Alcoholics.* Vol. 6, no. 4, of *Advances in Substance Abuse,* 1988.

Beattie, Melody, *Codependent No More.* Harper & Row, New York, 1987.

Besharov, Douglas J., *When Drug Addicts Have Children: Reorienting Child Welfare's Response.*

Black, Claudia, *Double Duty: Dual Dynamics Within the Chemically Dependent Home.*

Brown, Stephanie, *Treating Adult Children of Alcoholics.* John Wiley, New York, 1988.

Deutsch, Charles, *Broken Bottles, Broken Dreams: Understanding and Helping Children of Alcoholics.* Teacher's College Press, Totowa, NJ, 1982.

Dwinell, Lorie, *We Did the Best We Could: Help for Parents of Adult Children.*

Friedman, Alfred S. and S. Granick, *Family Therapy for Adolescent Drug Abuse.*

Hindman, Margaret, "Child Abuse and Neglect: The Alcohol Connection," *Alcohol Health and Research World,* Spring 1977, pp. 2–7, and other articles in same journal.

Lewis, David C., and C. Williams (eds.), *Providing Care for Children of Alcoholics: Clinical and Research Perspectives.* Health Communications, Deerfield Beach, FL, 1986.

Mannion, Lawrence, "Co-Dependency: A Case of Inflation," *Employee Assistance Quarterly,* 1991, 7(2):67–81.

Marlin, Emily, *Hope: New Choices and Recovery Strategies for Adult Children of Alcoholics.* Harper & Row, New York, 1987.

McConnell, P., *Adult Children of Alcoholics: A Workbook for Healing*. Harper & Row, San Francisco, 1986.

Metzger, L., *From Denial to Recovery: Counseling Problem Drinkers, Alcoholics, and Their Families,* Chapter V, on developmental issues in children of dysfunctional families.

NIAAA, *A Growing Concern: How to Provide Services to Children from Alcoholic Families*. PH 196, NCADI, 1983. Good on ethnic and cultural aspects.

Orme, Terry C., and J. Rimmer, "Alcohol Abuse and Violence Against Children or Women," *JSA,* 1981, 42(3):273–87.

Perrin, Thomas W., *I Am an Adult Who Grew up in an Alcoholic Family*.

Russell, Laura, *Alcoholism and Child Abuse Insights*. Thomas W. Perrin, East Rutherford, NJ, 1984. A remarkably shrewd study.

Vannicelli, Marsha, *Group Psychotherapy with Adult Children of Alcoholics*.

Windle, Michael and John S. Searles, *Children of Alcoholics: Critical Perspectives*.

CHAPTER 11

Special Groups

I N THIS CHAPTER we survey briefly the addiction problems of a few groups of people who, among others, have been neglected in the research until recently or who merit special attention.

Women

Long neglected and underestimated, addiction problems among women are finally receiving the attention they deserve. Roth's two volumes (1991), Perez (1994), and Wilsnack and Wilsnack (1994) show how far we have progressed. Of course much more needs to be done, and the picture is changing rapidly. Any definitive treatise on the subject should probably be written by a woman, although some research indicates that the gender of a therapist is less important than sensitivity to women's issues.

Early in Chapter 1 we listed many names in support of our belief that if fully reported the number of women alcoholics would really equal that of men, an impression confirmed by 40 percent of private physicians in one survey (Jones and Helrich, 1972). Male patterns, cirrhosis of the liver, and quantity-frequency of alcoholic beverage consumption are all misleading as indicators of female alcoholism. Women drink less beer than men, and more wine and hard liquor. Although gin drinking and sherry sipping are an old story among women, there is definite evidence that the rate and amount of drinking by women has increased considerably (Fuchs and Stampfer, 1995). Alcoholic beverage advertising is aimed more at women than formerly. Greater freedom for women has included greater freedom to drink. Patricia McGuire (1977) depicts graphically the double pressure women are under to maintain a wife-mother role while competing in the business world. However, to blame either the women's rights movement or the ills it opposes as the sole cause of female alcoholism is simplistic; if some statements made by *either* side were true, all women would be alcoholic!

Myths and stereotypes about alcoholic women die slowly (Roth, 1991). The fact that their needs and problems are different from male alcoholics does not necessarily make them sicker. Schuckit (1995a) argues that differences are due to societal roles and biology, not that alcoholism is a unique disorder in women. Here we see the old double standard still operating: A man engages in "frequent extramarital relations," but a woman is "promiscuous." Another fallacy is to lump all women alcoholics into one category, when actually they vary in type and pattern as much as men. Media stereotypes that portray women alcoholics as weak, inferior, sexually loose, or drinking because they don't feel feminine only deter a woman from going into treatment, because that would imply admission that some or all of this was true of her.

A false sense of chivalry and the harsh stigma attached to a woman with an addiction problem tend to perpetuate her problems by weaving a protective circle of silence around her rather than urging her to seek treatment. Instead of diagnosing her alcoholism problem, the physician will all too often prescribe tranquilizers, with the result that up to 87 percent of women alcoholics are cross-addicted. Because the pills potentiate with alcohol, they need to drink less, and this feeds their denial. In addition to prescription drugs, cross-addiction to illegal drugs was reported in 51 percent of women patients in one study. Men are reluctant to recognize alcoholism as a primary illness in women; rather, they tend to see it as a symptom of something else, and male professionals seem more easily caught up in the web of the woman's denial (Kimball, 1978, pp. 37–42). For these and other sociocultural reasons, their denial may be more complex and subtle, and their shame and suffering worse. But prognosis is as good as that for men, or better.

Hypotheses that women drink because of feelings of dependency, to increase feelings of power, and to increase a sense of femininity, among others, are contradictory and lack experimental verification (Wilsnack and Beckman, 1986; Wilsnack, 1974). There are many unnecessary psychiatric referrals of alcoholic women patients. Some investigators assert that women, more frequently than men, start drinking heavily to cope with a specific life crisis, but that may be because the question is asked in a manner that elicits the expected response in women who are naturally looking for an excuse. Such psychologizing usually suffers from the problem of confusing cause with effect; in any case, it is not too helpful, because alcoholics are always happy if the researcher furnishes them with a reason to drink. What of the women who lost a baby and did not become alcoholic?

Physical differences between male and female drinkers cannot be ignored. When women try to keep up drink for drink with men, their smaller size and higher proportion of body fat causes a higher BAC. Whereas men are more inclined to munch and snack while drinking, women are often dieting to stay thin, so they drink on an empty stomach. This results in both malnutrition and quicker absorption of alcohol into the bloodstream. Menstruation can cause a higher blood alcohol level from the same amount ingested. Since estrogen and progesterone levels drop during the premenstrual period, tolerance is lessened while tension and depression increase. Women tend to progress more rapidly into middle- and late-stage alcoholism than men do, as the physiological changes seem to occur in a shorter time span. They seem more prone to high blood pressure and faster liver damage. Hormonal changes and vitamin or mineral deficiencies connected with menopause seem to cause special problems. The fetal alcohol syndrome (FAS), a source of birth defects in the children of drinking mothers, was described in Chapter 4.

Divorce rates for alcoholic women are much higher than for alcoholic men. Nonalcoholic wives are more likely to remain with their alcoholic husbands than the nonalcoholic husbands with their alcoholic wives, although the oft-quoted ratio of ten to one is questionable. Men seem unable to perceive the economic problems of the recovering woman. Far more than men, women alcoholics report a history of depression associated with their alcoholism, and this in turn leads to a greater use of psychoactive drugs, including more alcohol, with a greater suicide rate. A fairly typical survey says 98 percent of women in treatment described themselves as sexually dysfunctional, 63 percent had been victims of rape or incest before age fourteen, and 91 percent claimed they had strong spiritual needs not addressed in treatment.

For treatment, too few programs have aimed specifically at the needs of women, Most women alcoholics still find themselves in treatment programs primarily designed for and run by men, where their feelings may run from fear of rape to embarrassment at walking down the corridor in a bathrobe. The treatment center is often located in a part of the city where women do not feel safe. Two surveys of women working in alcoholism rehabilitation in two states evoked a unanimous response that women do better in all-women facilities. Women need to feel comfortable with themselves and are reluctant to discuss their problems in mixed company. Hence all-women groups are important, especially in early recovery. Later, coed groups may be helpful in integrating them back into mixed society. The coed centers that report good success rates are those where the proportions of men and women among both patients and staff are approximately equal. Women need good role models at all levels to motivate recovery. Dr. Margaret Mantell (1995) has developed a series of workbooks specifically for women, useful for long-term and spiritual recovery.

Lastly, child care seems to be a principal need in the treatment of women. Because the mother is with the children more hours of the day and the father is less able to shield them, it is generally conceded that children of alcoholic mothers suffer worse effects than children of alcoholic fathers. In any case, mothers cannot profit fully from treatment if they are worrying about their children's being with someone else. Family live-in arrangements are expensive, but this is a growing trend and is worth the expense.

Youth

During the drug scare of the late 1960s, parents who learned that their child was involved in a drinking problem were inclined to reply. "Thank God, it's not drugs." Now journalistic sensationalism has portrayed alcohol as the new teenage drug menace. Adolescents have always drunk too much, so this is not new. For most adolescents, drinking is an important part of growing up in our culture. Alcohol has always been the main drug of abuse among teenagers. One 1952 study showed 17 percent of high schoolers drank to forget their troubles. During the 1960s, one-third were drinking at least once a week and 5 percent daily. Soon 93 percent of high school senior boys and 87 percent of the girls reported having been intoxicated at least once, and 60 percent of them reported having used marijuana.

Most important is the polydrug complication. Some adolescent alcoholics use only alcohol, but combination with one or more other drugs is more common. High prevalence of poly-addiction has lowered the age at which many individuals so afflicted must get help if they are to recover. Criminal and gang activities are usually connected with traffic in illegal drugs. Reportedly, a million youths each year run away from home. Most return in a few days when they find that street life is lonely and brutal, but many wil die of alcohol and other drugs.

Drinking Versus Alcoholism

A 1988 NCA report found that 11 percent of high school seniors are alcoholic, 30 percent say that most or all of their friends get drunk at least once a week, and 37.5 percent admit to heavy drinking within the previous two weeks; 100,000 fifth- and sixth-graders (ten and eleven years old) get drunk at least once a week, and 4.6 million youngsters eighteen and under are in trouble with alcohol and other drugs. True alcoholism is relatively rare in preadolescents, but it does occur as young as age seven. Cases of DTs have been reported at age nine, and at least one death from cirrhosis.

Whereas some decades ago only about one-half to two-thirds as many girls drank as boys, that gap has practically disappeared. Accurate figures are hard to obtain, and researchers differ in their definitions of drinking, heavy drinking, and problem drinking. Some of the increase may reflect merely the fact that drinking is more out in the open now. Most surveys are done in schools, and it is known that the rates are even higher among school dropouts. On the other hand, data gathered on juvenile delinquents must not be generalized to all adolescents. There is some evidence that alcohol use has leveled off, but there is little change in the use of LSD, heroin, and other opiates, and an increase in the use of inhalants. Alcohol use has not declined and remains by far the principal drug of abuse among youth.

If the rate of use is leveling off now, it may be because it has reached the maximum. If 93 percent of all high school seniors drink, there are not many left, and most of the small remainder probably will never drink. The median age to start drinking in America is now under thirteen years, which means that more than half our young people have been initiated into this rite of passage before they enter high school. We are not talking about a sip from the parent's glass. Fifth- and sixth-grade teachers report that pupils in those grades, that is, as much as half the youngsters nine, ten, and eleven years old, bring bottles to school, drink during noon hour or recess, and show obvious signs of intoxication in the classroom. One-fifth of high school students get drunk at least once a month. Depending on definition, some 10 to 20 percent of adolescents report alcohol problems, including 8 percent with blackouts.

Is this alcoholism? No, the majority of kids at the Friday night kegger will never become alcoholics. Some will wreck cars and will maim others. Some will suffer other adverse effects in schooling or jobs. One study showed that upon entry into college one-third reported some impairment due to alcohol abuse. Among adolescents, more than anywhere else, the distinction between alcoholic and problem drinker is useful. Using adult criteria to diagnose alcoholism in adolescents is misleading. Most adolescents get into a little trouble. Being stopped by the police is not the same as being arrested, and even an arrest for being a minor in possession of alcoholic beverages is not alcoholism or even problem drinking. Most important, labeling a young peson as an alcoholic may be a self-fulfilling prophecy. Forcing them into treatment may only induce them to conform to adult expectations. Among juvenile delinquents alcoholism may be symptomatic of schizophrenia, of a depressive disorder, and especially of antisocial personality. Differential diagnosis is often difficult.

It is often asked, where do they get it? Youthful ingenuity finds many sources, including shoplifting or having an older person buy it for them. But very often it is the parental liquor cabinet. Each parent thinks the other parent drank it, without suspecting the children.

Adolescent Alcoholism Differs from Adult

Differences between alcoholism among adolescents and among adults involve most of the usual features of adolescence: rebellion against parents, poor coping skills, fewer responsibilities, hormonal changes of puberty, adolescent confusion. Adolescent alcoholism seems to be more closely tied to heredity. As with others, asking adolescent alcoholics why they drink is a waste of time. Adolescents say that adults drink to reduce anxiety or relieve personal problems, but rarely give this as a reason for their own drinking. A 1986 NCA report said 30 percent of fourth-graders (nine-year-olds) and 60 percent of seventh-graders (twelve-year-olds) feel pressured to drink. Peer pressure and seeking adult status are no doubt very important in nonalcoholic adolescent drinking, but the adolescent alcoholic seems to drink for the effect. There seems to be less of the controlled drinking of adult alcoholics; most say they drink to get high, and 52 percent of adolescent problem drinkers drink simply to get drunk. Progression seems more rapid, and organic damage, especially to the central nervous system, seems to be greater because the brain is still in formation. There is a lot of denial on the part of both the individual and society: "It can't happen that young" or "They'll grow out of it." They are worse as drinking drivers because they are inexperienced both as drivers and as drinkers. Because of smaller body size and lower tolerance, it usually takes less alcohol to inebriate them.

Treatment

Although many facilities now accept adolescents, there are relatively few exclusively devoted to treating adolescent addiction. Merely applying an adult program to adolescents is ineffective, and unethical because special knowledge and competence regarding adolescents is lacking (Bissell and Royce, 1994, p. 20). If the treatment setting is perceived as simply imposed on them by adults, it is resented. AA lacks appeal because adolescents see it as simply another authority put-down by their elders. Younger AA groups are still mostly young adults in their twenties and not for teenagers, so there is a real need here. Adolescent alcoholics are often harder to motivate because they have not faced serious crises, saying, "I'll do something about it when it gets that bad" when they hear the stories of older AA members. They seem to need longer treatment and have a higher relapse rate, because immaturity makes successful rehabilitation difficult; most seem to have to learn the hard way. Lastly, it is harder for them to reenter their society after treatment without receiving scorn from their peers who drink. (See G. Ross, 1994.)

Parents of adolescents in trouble with alcohol and other drugs are often not much help, as in their frustration they often take an either-or position and cannot recognize that there is a middle road between coerciveness and condoning (Ables, 1977; Meyer, 1984). The parents are advised to seek help for themselves and only secondarily for the user (Huberty and Huberty, 1976).

The Elderly

Even as late as 1974 the NIAAA Second Special Report *Alcohol and Health* conveyed the impression that alcohol might be good for old people, as many physicians used to feel. Alcoholism among the aging has been underestimated partly because the picture is complicated and partly because of a reluctance to show "disrespect" by suggesting that a number of senior citizens are alcoholics. And whereas men tend to get into troubles that expose their alcoholism, the alcoholic woman may remain hidden for years. You won't find alcoholism if you don't look for it, and current thinking now recognizes that alcohol and polydrug problems can be a serious danger in old age. One experimental "happy hour" in a nursing home was abandoned when it was found that a few beers did not alleviate the pain and loneliness but rather awakened addiction, increased incontinence, and produced many other problems. Important complications in research include the following: Alcohol damage is easily confused with the usual physical deterioration of aging; lower tolerance in old age means less observable quantity consumed; and there is great potential for poly-addiction among older people.

Since "old" is a relative term, we shall arbitrarily speak of alcohol problems among those sixty-five and older. The older alcoholic is generally someone without evidence of severe antisocial or psychiatric problems. But there seem to be two distinct subpopulations here. One group comprises those who began drinking as a reaction to the loneliness, depression, and lowered ego connected with retirement, widowhood, and general diminishing functions of aging. The alcohol problems began in midlife or late life and were not just a progression of early alcoholics living into old age. (One reason for this, of course, is that many alcoholics do not reach old age.) Progression in this group may be fairly rapid, although it may be that the early- and middle-stage symptoms were dismissed as "just old age" and the alcoholism was not diagnosed until the person went into withdrawal. The other group are those who have been drinking for a long time, with alcohol problems progressing over the usual span. These latter usually exhibit greater organic damage. In either case, today's greater longevity means a larger population of elderly alcoholic/addicts (Graham et al., 1995).

Polydrug

Cross-addiction or polydrug abuse among older people should always be suspected (see Moore and Teal, 1985; Simonson, 1984). Overmedication is common, since this 10 percent of the population uses 20 percent of the prescription drugs sold in this country, most of which potentiate with alcohol. Old people tend to hoard and swap drugs, and otherwise use them in nonprescribed ways. If they can use the sanction of "doctor's orders" for either alcohol or other drugs, it is easy to rationalize overuse. They refuse to believe that sleeping pills, diet pills, and many psychoactive drugs lose their effectiveness after five days or, at most, two weeks. They may become quite crafty at obtaining prescriptions from different doctors or having them filled at different pharmacies. Many nonprescription drugs contain large amounts of alcohol, and the combination of Nyquil or Geritol with Scope (mouthwash) can yield a 60-proof intoxicating beverage that leaves a clean breath! One alcoholism treatment center reported 85 percent of their older female patients were polydrug abusers. And a significant factor remains "iatrogenic alcoholism," which Blume (1973) describes as being initiated by the physician who recommends alcohol as a tranquilizer.

Elderly people respond well to treatment, perhaps because they appreciate the added attention. But they seem to be more difficult to identify and get into treatment, requiring special outreach efforts. They may have pre-Prohibition attitudes. Besides, society still tends to take the attitude that they should still be allowed to drink up their last days in peace and die. When younger people drink, they affect more people. When the elderly drink, they just become more isolated. Alcoholism accentuates the loneliness and suspiciousness of old age. A further tragic complication arises in a social welfare system that all too often excludes the elderly alcoholic from some old-age services because of the alcoholism, and from some alcoholism services because of the old age.

Racial Minorities

The most controversial and emotion-laden area of addiction problems is that of racial minorities (Trimble et al., 1992; Watts, 1989; Watts and Wright, 1983). This brief overview is drawn largely from minority sources or from personal experiences of the senior author, who more than once found himself the only white person in a group discussing these problems. Even so, he is aware that one cannot encompass, much less please, all the subgroups that fall under this heading. The chief racial minority groups in this country are the native American Indians, the blacks, the Hispanics, and the Asian Americans. Each of these general headings includes numerous subgroups so diverse that one blushes to lump them together. Again, growing up knowing three black families well rooted in the West made us aware that there can be greater differences between Far West and Deep South in both races than between black and white.

Native Americans

By far the most literature and research concerns the aborigines of our land (see "Sources"). Here again diversity precludes any easy generalizations. Even the term *native American* is insisted upon by many groups in the Southwest, while in the Pacific Northwest *Indian* is their own choice. This diversity only accentuates the basic theme of these pages: Any attempt to deal with problems in people of a particular culture must exhibit genuine sensitivity to the language, the customs, and the thinking of that culture. This does not mean that only a member of that subgroup can work efficiently with them, but it does mean that success is contingent upon being recognized as one who understands and accepts them as they are. This involves study, compassion without condescension, and, above all, the ability to listen.

American Indian leaders have long recognized that "alcohol is killing our people," and they lead the other minorities in their efforts to acquire training and develop programs. The "drunken Indian" stereotype is both unfair and self-defeating, but the severity of the problem is undeniable. Figures vary with the tribe and with one's definition of alcoholism, but it is common to see reports of male alcoholism as high as 80 or 85 percent, and rates of 35 to 55 percent among females. Some Alaskan villages report that up to 95 percent of all adults, male and female, are full-blown alcoholics. The suicide rate among young Eskimo males is twenty-five times the national average. Urban, village, and reservation natives are affected, but life-styles are so different that again the approaches must be specific, and generalizations are unwarranted. Again, illegal drugs are becoming more used among many native tribes, while peyote has always been used in the Southwest.

Alcohol is a factor in 75 percent of Indian deaths, 80 percent of their suicides, almost the only remaining prevalence of tuberculosis, and a homicide rate three times the national average (Baker, 1986; *Alcohol Health and Re-*

search World, Summer 1985, 9[4]:66–67). Half of their high school students drop out because of alcoholism. Indian reservation women have thirty-six times more cirrhosis than white women (Wilsnack and Beckman, 1986, p. 126) and have FAS babies at seven times the rate of white women (*Alcoholism Report,* March 18, 1985, p. 4). Prohibition of Indian drinking was the law from 1832 to 1953, and its only effect besides high profits for the bootleggers was to force secret and fast drinking. Customs vary and generalizations cannot be made, but some Indian languages have no separate verb for distinguishing "to drink" from "to get drunk." This reflects an uncritical acceptance of drunken behavior as well as widespread group pressure. Refusal to drink is a rejection of one's brother Indians or a denial of Indian identity.

Etiology. There is no one reason for the prevalence of alcoholism among these people. Forty-two theories have been listed under the headings of cultural, social, economic, biological, psychological, and combination. They include defiance of prohibition, lack of drinking norms, cultural disruption, governmental paternalism, poverty, poor self-image, exploitation by the white man, and biological vulnerability. The learned helplessness mentioned under psychological factors in Chapter 7 is for Indians an internalized oppression. Combination theories center on the concepts of either a vulnerable person or a conducive environment. Certainly all these factors are important as partial causes, and we need not choose one to the exclusion of the others. Purely psychological explanations seem to ignore the fact that before the white man brought his whiskey, the native American Indian was a proud, brave person who had developed high competence in coping with a difficult environment. Their current high rates of cirrhosis and other ills are clearly the result of drinking, and although there is no doubt a vicious circle at work, one must look hard at the evidence that for many of their problems alcoholism is the cause rather than the effect. It is not simply a matter of tolerance or different rates of metabolism, as there is no one "X factor" that explains alcoholism. Research on this point has tended to use simplistic logic, apparently because of reluctance to abandon behavioristic prejudice against heredity. On the other hand, it may be that some of the evidence for rapid intoxication by Indians was a simulated drunkenness, which the Indians put on for the benefit of the white observer (Lurie, 1971; see also Leland, 1976, and Westermeyer, 1974).

Treatment. Failure of earlier treatment programs should be interpreted less as a sign that the clients were hopeless or uncooperative than as a sign of our failure to involve the Indians themselves in the development of programs within their own specific cultures. A totally different concept of time and an attitude that the white man's helping efforts were mere interference are two characteristics of Indian thinking that were ignored. The success of the Alkali Lake Village people in north central British Columbia shows that the natives can do it themselves, as shown in their film *The Honour of All,* in which a nearly-all-alcoholic village became 95 percent nonalcoholic through a strictly grassroots effort with no help from authorities.

Because of a natural reluctance to go to the white man's agencies, special outreach efforts must be made to contact native Americans, preferably through their own people. Understandably reticent about exposing either their inner feelings or their problems before a Caucasian group, they must be treated in centers where they can help each other within the traditions of their own culture. Use of the sweat lodge and native medicine men can be effective (Jilek, 1982). Every meeting on Indian alcoholism I have attended began with an invocation of the Great Spirit, and we must be careful to preserve the tradition of Alcoholics Anonymous, which gives them full freedom to speak "as they understand Him." *Help for Ourselves,* an adaptation of the 12 Steps of AA to Indian thought, with beautiful Indian colored artwork, was developed by the Umatilla tribe and republished by CompCare. AA World Services in New York has AA materials in simple English, suitable for work with semi-literate peoples (and signing for the deaf).

African Americans

Although Watts (1986) has compiled a fine bibliography, the research literature of alcohol problems among blacks is less extensive than for native Americans, with the first book, by J. K. Larkins, appearing in 1965, followed by that of Frederick D. Harper (1976), whose important findings include the following:

Problem drinking is most common among young urban black males. Cirrhosis of the liver is twice as prevalent in blacks as in whites. A much higher percentage of black women are total abstainers as compared with white women, and blacks generally tend to drink either heavily or not at all. Drinking among blacks is more social than solitary and is more status-conscious, as evidenced by the high proportion of Scotch consumed. Black alcoholics admitted to hospitals and clinics show a stronger motivation for treatment, fewer complaints, and greater cooperation during the treatment process than do white alcoholics. They express less need for separate treatment than for special outreach programs, since they are less likely to seek out treatment. They also need better long-term care, including family treatment. Black alcoholics often feel uncomfortable at meetings of Alcoholics Anonymous dominated by whites, and the AA program is most successful for them when developed within black communities.

Writings by such black authors as Harper, Fred T. Davis, Jr., and Donald Phelps concur in linking alcoholism among blacks to problems of poverty, and there is some evidence that upper-middle-class blacks have better attitudes and behaviors regarding alcohol than their white counterparts. But all stress that there is no simple solution, and rather than just separate addiction programs for blacks, they say, it is important that the entire health delivery system recognize their special needs and problems and be more sensitive to cultural differences. As Watts (1985) points out, most important is the development of *prevention* programs aimed specifically at these and other minority races. (One prominent black authority says that black radio stations have three hundred times the liquor ads that white stations carry.) June J. Christmas, M.D., a black female psychiatrist who led the mental health services for New York City, warned (1978) that members of any race must not be lumped together to the neglect of important differences within the subgroups, and that not merely minority but all personnel at all levels must make a real effort to understand the values, modes of communication, standards of behavior, and peculiar conditions of minority clients.

Hispanics and Asian Americans

Still less research or pertinent literature has been developed regarding Hispanics and those whose ancestry is Chinese, Japanese, Filipino, and of other Pacific peoples. The language problems alone are formidable, and we can only emphasize that more consideration must be given to both treatment and prevention. As with the blacks and Indians, excessive drinking and drugging among youth is a large and growing problem. Cultural differences and fear of discrimination make them particularly inaccessible to prevention and outreach programs, and special efforts must be made. For example, a Hispanic man might not let a worker even talk to his wife, much less let the family get into treatment. Rates of alcoholism and alcohol problems among Latinos are reported to be about twice those of the rest of the U.S. population. As noted earlier, there is enormous variation within each of these racial categories.

The Military

The military services have long condoned, and at times encouraged, the use of alcoholic beverages. Customs and traditions peculiar to the soldier's environment almost dictated alcohol abuse in the past. With a "machismo" image, the hard-fighting soldier was stereotyped as a hard-drinking soldier. Even in more modern times, the military services had made regular liquor rations available to soldiers, sailors, and especially airmen. Social life in the military was frequently centered on drinking activities, from the low-priced "happy hour" to more elegant parties where both officers and their wives were under heavy social pressure to drink. Either from ignorance or from pride in the corps, alcoholism in the armed forces was somewhat of a military secret. The alcoholic serviceman had been generally stereotyped as the combat-hardened veteran with many years of service, the career man who had held responsible positions until he began to drink excessively. Frequently he was protected and retained without treatment until retirement.

This picture began to change in December 1972, when investigations of alcoholism in all branches of the military accelerated, culminating in the April 8, 1976, report to Congress by the comptroller general of the United States entitled: "Alcohol Abuse Is More Prevalent in the Military Than Drug Abuse" (MWD 76-99). Some of the findings showed that alcoholism and alcohol problems among officers and enlisted personnel, both male and female, were far higher than previously reported, and much above comparable civilian populations. Earlier impressions that drinking was a problem among enlisted men far more than among commissioned officers were corrected by evidence that the officers are just more protected and less liable to disciplinary action. Overseas duty, boredom, and loneliness seem to create greater drinking problems for both service personnel and their spouses.

All this is now undergoing drastic change. Programs of education, prevention, intervention, and treatment were initiated for the armed forces, starting with the Navy. Most important for long-range prevention have been attempts to counteract the image of the hard-drinking fighter and to reduce the easy availability of cheap alcoholic beverages (see Sources). Rates of consumption have notably decreased.

Veterans, especially those from the Vietnam War, cannot be treated for their addiction problems apart from the post-traumatic stress syndrome they may also suffer. This complicates both diagnosis and treatment in various and subtle ways, requiring a long time to discover and deal with ("Vietnam," 1988).

Skid-Road Alcoholics

The stereotype of the alcoholic as a skid-road bum has so dominated American thinking and legislation that one is inclined to focus on its negative effects: fostering denial in other alcoholics as well as among professionals and obscuring the fact that 97 percent of alcoholics are "respectable." But these roughly 300,000 indigents are human beings and deserve our consideration. Although for the many who have suffered permanent, irreversible brain damage, the most we can do is humane treatment and custodial care, a fair proportion are not "hopeless" and can respond to enlightened treatment methods (Fagan and Mauss, 1986). This means longer recovery time and more adequate followup rehabilitation.

Since the implementation of the Uniform Alcoholism Intoxication and Treatment Act, the problems faced by the homeless alcoholic and by the society that wants him or her off the streets have been somewhat changed but not eliminated. In more than half the states, being drunk in public is no longer a crime, so arrests have become less frequent. However, alcoholics in this category are different from other alcoholics in some important ways, have significantly different kinds of problems in treatment, and pose continuing difficulties for all those who exercise social control.

Here again we must avoid generalizations. Only about 30 percent of skid-road residents are alcoholic, the remainder living there either by choice or out of financial necessity. They include many older permanent residents and some nonalcoholic transients. Among the alcoholics there are many distinct subgroups with different characteristics, designated by such names as bum, character, wino, rubby-dub (those who habitually drink nonbeverage alcohol), and lush. The lush tends to belong to a bottle gang, which has a very definite unwritten protocol and rules of conduct.

Skid-road alcoholics comprise a wide range of intelligence and mental status, from former bank presidents and professional men to mentally retarded or of borderline intelligence, and including some with simple schizophrenia or sociopathic personality. They have their own language with subtle shades of meaning. For example, Spradley (1988) found them distinguishing fifteen kinds of tramp. Contrary to some romantic myths, most are not pleasantly drinking their lives away but are engaged in a grim struggle for survival. Physically they are very sick men as a group. Thorough physical examinations of one hundred successive cases yielded a report that sounded like an encyclopedia of medical pathology: every organ, every known disease, many undiagnosed fractures and badly healed wounds (Ashley et al., 1976).

Although nobody chooses to be an alcoholic, some skid-roaders apparently choose that way of life. But most are there as a result of circumstances, low intelligence, personality disorder, or alcoholism. It may be a combination of any or all of these, with alcoholism a principal factor. Jackson and Connor (1953a) found that some want to break out of the pattern, but they have little in the way of alternatives available. The skid-road alcoholic is not necessarily an irretrievable derelict or at the final stages of a drinking career. They need hope, patience, understanding, a longer than usual treatment program, retraining to become employable, and a great deal of help in finding a place to live and a job and a new way of life. What they do not need is a social system that perpetuates and implicitly encourages their dependence, while continuing to provide them with money to drink.

Other Groups

Until recently, physicians, nurses, and members of the clergy who suffered from alcoholism or other drug addiction were perhaps the subject of local gossip, but they were not formally recognized as alcoholics by their professions, nor were formal attempts made to understand them and to help them. As the stigma has lifted, more and more of these professionals have come out of the closet. Increasingly, professional concern is expressed and appropriate actions are considered (Bissell and Haberman, 1984). In addition to a Physician Assistance Program at AMA and an Impaired Physician Committee in most state medical associations, there is a group called International Doctors in AA (IDAA) for physicians and dentists, a treatment facility just for physicians (Caduceus Hall at Ridgeview Institute in Smyrna, Georgia), and information available through ASAM. Bissell and Skorina (1987) researched women physicians who were addicted.

Impaired nurses now have their own state and national committees (Sullivan, Bissell, and Williams, 1988). Pharmacists, psychologists, attorneys, and judges have been slower to organize help for their impaired fellow-professionals, but the scene is changing and peer help is becoming available. Teachers seem to be one of the hardest professions to help.

There are at least two groups for recovered clergy: Recovered Alcoholic Clergy Association (RACA), and the National Catholic Council on Alcoholism and Related Drug Problems (NCCA). Both are quite ecumenical, but the former is predominantly Episcopal and the latter largely Roman Catholic, including religious sisters and brothers. Considerably less has been written about them than about physicians, yet clergy who attend 12-Step groups and have been open about their occupation are warmly welcomed by fellow members (Fichter, 1981; King and Castelli, 1995; NCCA, 1960; Sorensen, 1976).

Both medical professionals and clergy share with other alcoholics, apparently to an even greater degree, their tendency to poly-addiction. They seem especially vulnerable to the combination of alcohol with such prescription drugs as tranquilizers, sleeping pills, and reducing pills.

Dual Diagnosis. Patients with both addiction and mental disorder are getting more attention, whereas formerly these patients were shunted back and forth fruitlessly between the mental health and addiction workers. Diagnosis here is difficult, since alcohol causes symptoms that look like mental disorder, especially affective disorder or manic-depressive psychosis. On the other hand, addiction workers must realize that some anxiety and phobic states, for instance, can be discrete disorders and not drug-related (see Alterman, 1985; Daley et al., 1994; Freed, 1982; Levy and Cohen, 1992; Meyer, 1986; N. S. Miller, 1994; D. F. O'Connell, 1990).

Disabled. In 1988, NCADI published a list of programs and organizations that offer assistance to physically and mentally disabled persons who also have addiction problems. *Alcohol Health and Research World* devoted its entire Winter 1980–81 issue to the subject. The deaf and hearing-impaired have special needs, since so much of addiction treatment is in groups, including the 12-Step programs. Even those who read lips well miss a great deal, since by the time they focus in on the speaker someone else is talking. Unlike the blind person who may feel very much a part of a group, the deaf often feel isolated and perhaps a bit paranoid. The rapidly growing literature on the relation of alcoholism and other drug addictions to *eating disorders* (bulimia, anorexia) and *sexual disorders* (compulsive child abuse, incest, and so on) is beyond the scope of this book, as is the counseling of addicted homosexuals (Finnegan and McNally, 1987).

Sources

Gary W. Lawson and Ann Lawson, *Alcoholism and Substance Abuse in Special Populations* (1988) covers fifteen major high-risk groups and is the first such book to deal with all the topics in this chapter. NIAAA Alcohol and Health Monograph No. 4, *Special Population Issues,* 1981, DHHS Pub. No. (ADM) 82-1193, has good documentation but is out of print.

WOMEN

Paula Roth, *Alcohol and Drugs Are Women's Issues* (1991); R. Wilsnack and S. Wilsnack (eds.), *Gender and Alcohol* (1994); Sharon Wilsnack and Linda Beckman (eds.), *Alcohol Problems in Women* (1986); and Stimmel (1986) all have bibliographies; Chalfant (1980) is an annotated bibliography. *Alcohol Health and Research World* has special focus issues: "Drinking and Drinking Problems among Women" and "Patterns of Women's Use of Alcohol Treatment Agencies," Winter 1984–85, 9(2):3–25; "Women and Alcohol," Fall 1978, 3(1); "Women in the Workplace," Spring 1983, 7(3); "Women and Alcohol," 1994, 18(3). The growing literature on this topic was reviewed and evaluated by Beckman (1975), Gomberg (1977), and Lindbeck (1972).

Fascinating are Robe, *Co-Starring: Famous Women and Alcohol* (1986), and the history by Marian Sandmaier (1992). A well-written and sympathetic journalistic work is Hornik's *The Drinking Woman;* see also the writings of Sheila Blume, Jonica Homiller, Bonnie-Jean Kimball, Jean Kirkpatrick, Muriel Nellis, Muriel Zink, and Geraldine Youcha. Many women have found the Hazelden book *Each Day a New Beginning* helpful daily reading. More technical books dealing with women addicted to alcohol and other drugs are by Eileen Corrigan, *Alcoholic Women in Treatment* (1980); Dowsling and MacLennan (eds.), *The Chemically Dependent Woman* (1978); M. Greenblatt and M. A. Schuckit (eds.), *Alcoholism Problems in Women and Children* (1976); Oriana Kalant (ed.), *Alcohol and Drug Problems in Women* (1978); Mondanaro, *Treating Chemically Dependent Women* (1989); Perez, *Counseling the Alcoholic Woman* (1994); and United States Department of Health and Human Services. *Advances in Alcoholism Treatment Services for Women.* Government Printing Office, Washington, DC, 1983.

YOUTH

There is a vast literature on youth and alcohol abuse. Grace Barnes (1982) cites nearly 5,000 publications. The United States Department of Justice (1985) has a topical bibliography. An excellent review, which is both comprehensive and evaluative, is provided by Blane and Hewitt, *Alcohol and Youth: An Analysis of the Literature, 1960–1975.* Hyde (1988) and Heuer (1985) appeal to youth. DuPont (1984) helps parents face the connection between alcohol and other drugs. Useful are Beschner and Friedman (1986), Brook et al. (1985), Glassner and Loughlin (1986), Gordon and McAlister (1982), Isralowitz and Singer (1983), Jaynes and Rugg (1988), Johnston (1986), MacDonald (1984), and G. Ross (1994). A special focus issue of *Alcohol Health and Research World,* Summer 1983, 7(4) is on "Treatment Services for Youth," and the Summer 1975 issue had an overview on "Young People and Alcohol," pp. 2–10. Globetti's "Teenage Drinking" (1977) provides a brief perspective. Jessor and Jessor (1975, 1977) have done important longitudinal research. Barnes in "The Development of Adolescent Drinking Behavior" (1977) evaluates the data on family influences on what the young person does about drinking.

THE ELDERLY

There is a substantial and growing body of publications drawing attention to the problems of substance abuse among the elderly. Grace Barnes and colleagues (1980) compiled an extensive bibliography. We list Abrams and Alexopoulos (1987); Atkinson (1984); Freund and Butler (1982); Funkhauser (1977–78); Gottheil (1985); Graham et al. (1995); Mishara and Kastenbaum (1980); Moore and Teal (1985); Marc Schuckit's "Geriatric Alcoholism and Drug Abuse" (1977); Sherouse (1983); Simonson (1984); and *Alcohol Health and Research World*, Spring 1984, Summer 1979, and Spring 1975 issues.

MINORITY GROUPS

Joseph E. Trimble et al. (eds.), *Ethnic and Multicultural Drug Abuse* (1993); Thomas Watts, *Alcoholism in Minority Populations* (1989); and a special issue of *Alcohol Health and Research World*, Winter 1986–87, 11(2) are on minorities. The NCADI staff compiled "Ethnicity and Alcohol: Resource Listing" in *Alcohol Health and Research World*, Summer 1980, 4(4):31–33.

For one reason or another, Americans have been concerned for well over a century with the drinking of American Indians. As a result there is voluminous literature on that subject, much of it interdisciplinary in nature, dealing with such diverse areas as the role of drinking in Indian culture, its effects on Indian health, economics, and psychology, and in their relationships with the majority. Patricia D. Mail and her colleagues gathered all this material into a comprehensive bibliography (Mail and McDonald, 1981). There is also *Alcohol Problems Among American Indians and Eskimos: Bibliography*, from the National Clearinghouse for Alcohol Information (NCALI, SAB 1-C-2). For critical evaluation of the literature, see the many writings of Dwight B. Heath, which have ample bibliographies. For an overview of the extent of the problem and the kinds of actions taken to solve them, see Hamer and Steinbring, *Alcohol and Native Peoples of the North* (1980); Kelso's volumes (1977); Manson, *New Directions in Prevention among American Indian and Alaska Native Communities* (1982); and the reports of three task forces to the Indian Health Service, which were published in 1972 under the title, *Alcoholism: A High Priority Health Problem*.

African American alcoholism sources are listed in the annotated bibliography by Watts (1986). Peter Bell and J. Evans, *Counseling the Black Client: Alcohol Use and Abuse in Black America* (1984) is authoritative. The writings of Frederick D. Harper deal with what research has been done and suggest where future research efforts could be directed most effectively. See also Bourne (1973), Brisbane and Womble (1985), Brunswick and Tarica (1974), Christmas (1978), Dawkins (1980), Maddox and Williams (1968), and Watts (1983, 1985). There are studies dealing with drinking patterns of black youth listed in Blane and Hewitt's *Alcohol and Youth: An Analysis of the Literature, 1960–1975*.

Writings with respect to other minorities are less plentiful. Although occasional references occur in papers about alcoholism among Americans of Asian or Spanish-speaking origins, there has been little systematic study of alcoholism, although it is known to occur; little written about the use of treatment facilities, though they are thought to be underutilized by these groups; and some literature on general drinking practices. The literature on Hispanic Americans is listed by Gilbert et al. (1993) and in Paine's excellent study, "Attitudes and Patterns of Alcohol Use Among Mexican Americans: Implications for Service Delivery" (1977), and M. Jean Gilbert and Richard Cervantes, *Mexican Americans and Alcohol* (Spanish Speaking Mental Health Research Center, UCLA, 1987). Of interest might be Richard Stivers, *A Hair of the Dog: Irish Drinking and American Stereotype*, and Bickerton and Sanders (1976) on Hawaii.

THE MILITARY

Alcohol Health and Research World, Winter 1981–82, 5(2):2–17 has references. *Alcoholism: The National Magazine,* March–April 1985, 5(4):15–23 is on the Navy program. A comprehensive analysis is by J. R. Long, I. E. Hewitt, and H. T. Blane, "Alcohol Abuse in the Armed Services: A Review. I. Policies and Programs," *Military Medicine,* 1976, 141:844–50, and "II. Problem Areas and Recommendations," *Military Medicine,* 1977, 142:116–28. See also the entire Winter 1977 issue of *Military Chaplain's Review.*

SKID-ROAD ALCOHOLICS

The entire Spring 1987 issue of *Alcohol Health and Research World* is devoted to the homeless. Fagan and Mauss (1986) is encouraging. Ashley et al. (1976) presents the medical picture. The following throw very important light on the characteristics and special problems of the skid-road alcoholic, despite the fact that some are out of date with respect to the relationships between this kind of alcoholic and the police because of the Uniform Act (Chapter 20): Bahr, *Skid Row* (1973); Blumberg et al., *Liquor and Poverty: Skid Row as a Human Condition* (1978); Pittman and Gordon, *The Revolving Door: A Study of the Chronic Police Case Inebriate* (1968); Rubington, *Alcohol Problems and Social Control* (1973); Spradley, *You Owe Yourself a Drink* (1988); and Wiseman, *Stations of the Lost: Treatment of Skid-Road Alcoholics* (1980).

OTHER GROUPS

The best research on alcoholic *physicians* is by Bissell and Haberman (1984). *The Care and Management of the Sick and Incompetent Physician,* by Green et al. (1978), also throws light on the problems of alcoholic physicians, as do Glatt (1977), John (1978), Steindler (1977), and Twerski (1986). Useful is *Intervention with Colleagues in Health Care and Other Professions: How to Help Those in Trouble with Alcohol/Drugs,* by Linda R. Crosby and LeClair Bissell (1989).

For the most part alcoholic *clergy* are not discussed in print. Recent exceptions are King and Castelli (1995), the writings of Fichter, and Sorensen's *Alcoholic Priests: A Sociological Study* (1976). Although not for general circulation, the NCCA has published *The Blue Book* annually since 1949 and has collected some of its best articles in *Alcoholism: A Source Book for the Priest.*

PART THREE

PREVENTION
and
INTERVENTION

CHAPTER 12

Prevention

WE HAVE COMPLETED our survey of the problems arising from excessive use of alcohol and other drugs. As it was only a survey, it left many questions unanswered. But the big question remains, What are we to do? This second half of the book is a brief look at some solutions.

Quite understandably, the humane thing to do seems to be to help the sick person. This is important, and a large portion of the remaining chapters will be devoted to treatment and rehabilitation. But at the risk of being accused of insensitivity to the suffering addict and family, we put an even higher value on prevention (Cahalan, 1991; Donohew et al., 1991; DuPont, 1984, 1989).

You do not win a war by treating its victims. No significant public health problem was ever solved by treatment. If Jonas Salk had not developed his vaccine, today we would be treating polio with computerized iron lungs. Smallpox has been practically wiped off the globe, not by daubing the pockmarks with medicine but because Jenner discovered vaccination. Would physicians who say, "I don't believe in preventive medicine. I leave that to the Disease Control Centers in Atlanta" be practicing good medicine? Prevention is the responsibility of all professionals. The analogy is trite but still appropriate: Putting the bulk of our addiction funds into treatment rather than into prevention is like stationing an ambulance at the bottom of the cliff instead of erecting a barricade at the top.

Although law enforcement is a necessary part, and legalization would only send youth a message that drugs are okay and make drugs more available to children, effective prevention must focus largely on demand rather than supply. As we saw in the history of Prohibition worldwide, and as the failed "war on drugs" attests, the profit motive will guarantee a supply as long as there is a demand. But what if the pushers threw a party and nobody came? It is possible. Already there has been a shift in the national mentality regarding drinking and driving, and drunkenness at parties. The fear of AIDS is changing the habits of intravenous drug users. We are offered a choice of nonsmoking sections in restaurants, so why not a nondrinking section for those offended by alcohol's sight, smell, and effects on behavior?

"Just say NO" is simplistic, and scare tactics alone will not do the job. Alcoholics must be taught that they cannot drink moderately, and others who cannot follow the USDA guidelines of two drinks per day for men and one drink per day for women should abstain just for health reasons. Women who drink two or more drinks a day have a much higher mortality rate than do women who abstain (Fuchs and Stampfer, 1995). Most "controlled drinking" programs recommend drinking levels that actually have serious health consequences, besides the danger of becoming addicted.

In our present polydrug culture, moreover, we need to enlarge our target to include the misuse of other drugs. This is reflected in the NCADD Prevention Policy statements and in combining the prevention activities of NIAAA and NIDA into the Center for Substance Abuse Prevention (CSAP, formerly OSAP) with its newsletter *Prevention Pipeline,* begun in 1988.

Mention of funds usually raises the question of what it all will cost. But the real question is how much it will save. In 1993 alcoholism cost this country more than $148 billion. Preventing even a small part of that loss would save far more than the total we have spent so far on prevention. Regardless of cost, heroic efforts and huge expenditures on treatment are like bailing a damaged ocean liner with a teacup if society continues to turn out alcoholics/addicts faster than we can rehabilitate them. The answer seems to lie in the community rather than in institutions, in long-range prevention rather than in stopgap measures.

But is prevention possible? Certainly not with 100 percent success. But that is no reason not to try; it says only that we need to learn from the failures (Cahalan, 1987; Nathan, 1983) and to be realistic in setting goals. One problem is that this is measuring a nonevent, something we keep from happening and hence hard to observe. Another problem is that it takes time, and the gap between effort and results makes it hard to see the relation. Critics who expect instant results should recall that it took more than two hundred years for Jenner's vaccination to wipe out smallpox. Some point to one means that was not the answer instead of recognizing that prevention requires a massive effort at all levels and by all segments of society. One drop of water won't make a hole in a stone, but enough drops can. Thus, warning labels alone might not deter, but they can contribute to a shift in public attitude as part of the big picture. Today we have more than 40 million ex-smokers in the United States; 66 percent fewer high school seniors in one study used multiple drugs; and 90 percent of Americans are drinking less than formerly, so prevention is more possible than the pessimists think (see Botkin, 1995; Falco, 1992; Wechsler et al., 1994).

Prevention does not mean a return of Prohibition. It must be made clear that what is to be prevented is alcoholism and alcohol problems, not drinking. Warning labels do not infringe on freedom, but rather enhance it by making possible an informed choice based on facts the public has a right to know.

Current terminology distinguishes primary, secondary, and tertiary prevention:

Primary prevention means to forestall or reduce the incidence of new cases in a population at risk before the development of the disease. In other words, stopping it before it gets started.

Secondary prevention, or early intervention, refers to measures taken to arrest or interrupt the progression of symptoms before they reach the moderate or severe states.

Tertiary prevention is actually treatment and rehabilitation, which prevents further progression of the illness and the spread of its effects to others.

Primary Prevention
Direct Prevention

Specific, or *direct,* primary prevention aims at removing or blocking the causes of addiction. It is much more than just education or information. Toward this goal the NCADD Prevention-Education Committee lists strategies that attempt to:

1. Alter public attitudes, sociocultural factors, and environmental conditions conducive to alcohol and other drug misuse
2. Educate the community, especially high-risk populations, concerning the addictive properties of the drug alcohol and the varying susceptibilities of individuals to its use
3. Influence positively the individual's decision-making skills regarding use, misuse, or nonuse
4. Provide adequate role models and other means of developing social skills and ways of coping with stress so as to include alternatives

This is obviously a big order. But Muslims, Jews, Buddhists, the Pioneer Society in Ireland, and Maoist China all exemplify the fact that patterns of excessive use can be changed (Keller, 1976a, p. 14). There have been massive changes in our own country in the last three centuries regarding patterns of use, preferred beverage, place and amount of consumption, age and sex of consumer, tolerance of drunkenness, and many other aspects of drinking. For the most part those changes have come about not through legislation but through social groups and personal motives, including religion. Government *control* has been largely a failure, but much might be accomplished if we could agree on methods and objectives and then use government *help.*

Indirect Prevention

Nonspecific, or *indirect,* primary prevention refers to means that are not aimed directly at addiction but have its prevention as a desired by-product. For example, improving the quality of life and developing adequate social skills and better ways of coping with stress are legitimate goals in themselves, but they may also be cultivated in the hope that thereby some problems may be prevented instead of just picking up the pieces afterward.

If stress were the only cause of alcoholism, freeing people of any need to anesthetize themselves against stress would be a full solution. But the fact is that life does bring stress—"ecstasy without agony is baloney." What we really need is to help young people develop better ways of coping with stress so they will not turn to alcohol and other drugs.

Adolescence is an awkward age, and adolescents are socially clumsy. It is easier to dull one's sensitivity than to develop social graces. Drinking in the formative years atrophies the development of coping mechanisms and social skills. Psychologists know from imprinting experiments that some needs must be met at a certain developmental stage or it is too late. That may hold as well for social skills, if not developed during adolescence because of reliance upon drugs as a substitute or escape. Add the evidence that the nervous system is still in its formative stages during the teen years, and the importance of delaying the use of alcohol until maturity becomes even clearer. The big problem is to convey this to young people without putting a premium on drinking by making it adult behavior, a sign of maturity, which they will immediately try to prove by drinking.

Public Health Model

Since there is no one cause of addiction, there will be no one way of prevention. Complex etiology demands multiple preventive approaches. Using a public health model, we can list strategies according to their relation to the *agent* (alcohol, other drugs), the *host* (that one in ten or twelve users who seems most susceptible), and the *environment* (conditions conducive to interaction of the host with the agent). To the question of which is most important, we answer "Which is the most important leg of a three-legged stool?"

The Agent: Alcohol, Other Drugs

Decriminalization of now-illegal drugs has appeal because of the crime and violence they bring. But those who look at the big picture see it as simplistic. What would be saved in prison and law enforcement costs would be multiplied in health costs. NCADD says that repeal would send a wrong message to youth and would increase the number of addicts. The Harrison Act did actually decrease drug addiction in this country.

Alcohol, like tobacco, is a different problem, partly because its use is so deeply embedded in our culture, as we saw in Chapter 3. Prohibition was an infringement on personal freedom in a part of normal life, a status other drugs do not share. Even if in theory nobody is absolutely immune, in practice we know that many people drink all their lives without developing alcoholism. That makes it difficult, if not impossible, to eliminate alcohol entirely. Yet it is still true that there would be no alcoholism without alcohol, and many are taking a second look at the relation between per capita consumption of alcohol and rates of alcoholism, on which research was begun by

S. Ledermann (1956). It is true that the alcoholic will always get liquor, regardless of cost or availability, but we are talking here about primary prevention, before one becomes alcoholic.

To some this smacks of prohibitionism, but instead of a curt dismissal it deserves careful research to assess the effect of limiting times and place of purchase, legal age of purchaser, and price in relation to available income. Although per capita consumption is not always in direct proportion to alcoholism rates, much evidence indicates that the relation is hardly zero. In fact, some claim there is more evidence in favor of restricting access to alcohol as a basis for prevention than for any other preventive measure. Formerly dismissed as an approach the public would not stand for, the feasibility of setting restrictions appears to be enhanced by an increase in the number of those who favor them. The very mention of such an approach naturally sparks powerful lobbying from the alcoholic beverage industry. In any case, it must be accomplished largely through public acceptance rather than simply by law. No aspect of prevention can be effective in isolation from the total picture.

The Ledermann hypothesis favors moderate legal restraint on availability (Beauchamp, 1980; Olson and Gerstein, 1986). Some argue for legal restraints keyed to a uniform distribution model, in opposition to a bimodal model targeting a high-risk population (e.g., Single and Storm, 1985). Perhaps the two theories are not that irreconcilable in practice. Decrease in overall availability could reduce consumption among the high-risk group before they develop alcoholism, especially if combined with a "forewarned is forearmed" approach that the bimodal model favors. We need to try combining efforts instead of putting them in opposition. Attitudes and life-styles are changing so rapidly, especially among young drinkers, that prevention efforts cannot be focused exclusively on the host without regard to the environment and to availability of the agent (see "Regulation of Sale" in Chapter 20).

The Host

Even though we do not understand fully the biochemical mechanisms of immunity and susceptibility, we have a fair amount of data that identify certain populations as at high risk of alcoholism if they drink. We said in Chapter 7 that no child is doomed by heredity to be an alcoholic. Individuals differ, but we know that statistically the children of alcoholic ancestry are much more vulnerable. We must also mention truants and school dropouts, and native American youth, among others. Liver enzyme tests or EEG may eventually enable us to identify those more likely to develop alcoholism, who would then be educated as to the nature of the illness without using scare tactics. We should capitalize on the current interest in nutrition, physical fitness, and good health habits. An obstacle here is the almost invincible optimism of youth; young people tend to think they are invulnerable, even when confronted with examples from their own age group.

Another approach is law. The legal drinking age was lowered in many states as part of a move to accord adult status to young men involved in the unpopular Vietnam War. It now seems that several assumptions were false: (1) that most teenagers were already drinking, so changing the law would not alter their drinking patterns; (2) that removing the motive of rebellion might actually reduce their alcohol consumption; (3) that alcohol-related auto crashes by teenagers would not increase; and (4) that lowering the legal age to eighteen would not affect the high school population, because those over eighteen would have left school. Various researchers have shown all four assumptions to have been wrong. The trend toward a lower legal age was reversed in many states with positive results (Valle, 1986; Wagenaar, 1983, 1993), and a uniform minimum drinking age of twenty-one is saving many lives (see "Sources" for Chapter 20).

The Environment

Social pressures to drink, and sometimes to drink heavily, converge on us from all sides. When the Bud Light advertising budget is twenty-five times that of the NIAAA prevention and education budget, and the alcoholic beverage industry in the United States spends about $2 billion a year, or $5.48 million a day, on advertising, those businessmen presumably get what they pay for: $2 billion worth of pressure on us to drink. They claim it is not aimed at consumption but only at choice of brands, yet the net effect cannot help but promote drinking rather than abstinence. (Actually, the ads are aimed at adding new drinkers and at heavy drinkers; if everybody practiced moderation as the ads pretend to advocate, the alcoholic beverage industry would lose nearly half its business.) One issue of *Ms.* magazine contained twice as many ads for liquor as for cosmetics. College newspapers in 1988 had thirty-four times as much space in ads for beer as for books. The atmosphere this creates is bolstered by the attractive cocktail waitress who appeals to your machismo with the subtle implication that you are not much of a man if you don't order up; by the modeling of parents who make hospitality synonymous with offering a drink; by the portrayal of alcohol drinking on television shows out of all proportion to the actual rate as compared with nonalcoholic beverage use; by our tolerance and even admiration of excessive drinking; and by slogans and customs that make the nondrinker feel unsophisticated and antisocial.

Customs. Given that alcohol is a drug, we are a nation of pushers. Suppose you invite me to dinner and serve carrots as a vegetable, which I politely refuse. You do not spend the rest of the evening telling me that I *must* have a carrot, that I can't fly on just one carrot, to have one for the road, be a man and have a carrot, and on and on. Ridiculous, of course. Yet that is exactly the way we all too often treat a guest who wishes to drink moderately or not at all. It is as if we are afraid of being thought stingy or inhospitable or morally overrighteous, of looking as though we favor prohibition or are against fun. The host urges "one more won't hurt you," when he has no idea whether or not his guest is developing a problem, or he cries "bottoms up" without ever considering whether some in the group should not continue drinking. Rarely does "a drink" mean anything except alcohol. There seems to be something contradictory about giving bottles of liquor as Christmas gifts (a custom that the NCADD discourages) or a beer mug inscribed "Drink Healthy."

A salient feature of this environment is its inconsistency. Instead of saying generic or analog drugs, we say "designer drugs," which conjures up an image of fashionable good taste when we should be portraying them as dangerous and depressing, not glamorous. We require the listing of ingredients on food and drugs but not on alcoholic beverages. We even put on cocktail parties to raise money to fight alcoholism! We still have a double standard regarding women and alcohol misuse. Even our jokes reveal a certain uneasiness and mixed attitudes about drink and drunkenness. Drinking straight gin is considered vulgar, but the very, very dry martini is sophisticated—and practically straight gin. Adult luncheon groups that welcome a speaker who expatiates on "youth and drugs" will reject the suggestion of a speaker to talk about "middle age and martinis." We are not sure whether Joe is the life of the party or an embarrassment. We deplore the problems that alcohol causes, yet fear to lose the revenue that alcohol taxes bring in. And those who work in the alcoholism field know that heavy drinkers are not the jolly people we hear described in the popular drinking songs; we see much more of loneliness, tension, fear, anxiety, frustration, and resentment. Most alcoholics and other addicts tell of chasing a myth, vainly trying to recapture that first "high."

Such inconsistency, combined with divergence in use patterns, makes impractical the suggestion of those who feel that alcoholism can be prevented by simply letting children grow up learning how to drink moderately. That might make sense in a population that has consistent attitudes, does not condone excess, and attaches no great social significance to drinking. Even there it does not seem to work too well for the one group with whom we are concerned, the alcoholics. Social and recreational use may be the reason why others drink, but even in adolescence those who are headed for trouble with alcohol seem to be those who drink for the effect. Apparent contradictions in the research regarding parental models might be explained in this way: Research that describes youthful drinking as an imitation of adult drinking has often been done where adult social drinking is the norm, whereas studies that ascribe youthful drinking to rebellion have usually been conducted where adult abstinence is the norm. Moreover, adults have been more permissive about adolescent drinking because of their concern over adolescent misuse of other drugs.

The Media. Full pages of color in the slick magazines advertise hard liquor as linked to adventure, sexual attractiveness, or sophisticated entertainment (Jacobson et al., 1983; Kilbourne, 1985). Television ads associate drinking beer

with masculinity and with driving (Postman et al., 1988; Lieberman and Orlandi, 1987). Athletes often serve as models for youth, and for years American youth has been exposed, often during broadcasts of athletic events, to
famous athletes advertising a favorite beer. Beer has always been popular
with young people. Wine coolers appeal largely to the youth market, and
many do not realize they often contain more alcohol than beer. Chocolate
liquor bottles containing a syrup that can be as high as 13.6 percent alcohol
are sold as candy to children, with no sales restriction or warning. A few
years ago the industry introduced drinks of 30 proof, almost four times the
alcoholic content of beer, with flavors for adolescent tastes: chocolate,
mocha, strawberry, banana. So in spite of disclaimers by the alcoholic beverage industry, there seems to be little doubt that this barrage of advertising is,
in great part, aimed at young people, regardless of the legal age for drinking.
Significant is one research which reports that small children showed a higher
recognition rate for Joe Camel than for Mickey Mouse. A 1995 survey revealed a 33 percent increase in smoking among eighth- to twelfth-graders, attributed to the $6 billion advertising budget of tobacco companies.

Quite apart from advertising, several studies of prime-time television
shows (e.g., DeFoe and Breed, 1983) reveal that the drinking of alcoholic beverages has been portrayed on the screen with a frequency that is totally unrepresentative of American drinking practices. Coffee and soft drinks are
both consumed far more frequently than alcohol in real life, yet the impression conveyed by television has been that the exact reverse is true. Moreover,
drinking alcohol was found to be pictured as not only a constant feature of
American life but refined, manly, or useful in relief of stress, with no suggestion that for some it could be highly addictive and for all potentially dangerous. That is changing, thanks to the Caucus for Producers, Writers, and
Directors, which started a reversal of the trend in 1983 with a white paper for
the Entertainment Industries Council entitled "We've Done Some Thinking."
Dorn and South (1983) contains an annotated bibliography on this topic.

Another encouraging note is the revised Code of Advertising Standards
adopted by the Wine Institute (1988), which could well serve as a model of
responsible advertising for the entire alcoholic beverage industry. Subscribers
to the code agree not to use athletes or other youth heroes to advertise their
products, not to imply health or problem-solving benefits, not to exploit sex,
and not to appeal especially to youth, among other laudable undertakings.
Yet beer ads continue to feature ex-athletes, which they have claimed are not
athletes because retired, although the reason for their appeal is precisely that
they are athletes!

Secondary Prevention

Addiction can be prevented from developing into serious problems through
intervention, whereby it is interrupted in its problem or moderate state. Although not as ideal as primary prevention, it may be more realistic in our

present state of knowledge. The American Cancer Society has not conquered cancer yet, but it has saved a lot of lives by early detection and treatment. The elements in successful secondary prevention include public education, which will both alert to the dangers and make treatment more acceptable; the education of key persons such as physicians, nurses, clergy, social workers and others as to the early signs of alcoholism; and development of skills in intervention or confrontation.

Public Education

The communications media can do more than the classroom to educate the public, but all avenues must be used. The distinguished citizens who have publicly identified themselves as recovered alcoholics have done much to break down the stigma and make treatment for alcoholism no more a disgrace than treatment for appendicitis. Alcoholism and smoking are now being recognized as our nation's biggest public health problems, and myths that clouded the early signs are being dispelled. Smoking is no longer a mark of sophistication but leads to social ostracism. But much more needs to be done. An objective, scientific approach, rather than scare tactics in the classroom or a preachy, moralizing tone in the pulpit, must be combined with a nationwide effort to change the image of drinking in both entertainment and advertising. Ignorance is still widespread. We hear too often, "I was married to an alcoholic for twenty-five years and never knew it." One patient was drinking a fifth of vodka a day for more than a year before her husband had any idea she had a drinking problem.

Early Detection

Industry and business (Chapter 13) can provide a key source of secondary prevention. People who are on the job are still motivated; the addiction can be caught before there is deterioration of the brain or other organs, and a good policy can set up strategies for getting them into treatment.

Courts, especially *family* and *traffic* courts, are good places for early detection and intervention if judges, attorneys, and court workers are skilled in detection and alert enough not to be fooled into thinking that other problems are the cause of the drinking instead of its result. We cannot assume that all persons arrested for drunk driving or sued for divorce are alcoholics, but the question of drinking or other drug problems should be explored. Deferred prosecution or diversion plans may put the suspect into an Alcohol Information Program (AIS) or treatment clinic instead of jail, which solves nothing and may only perpetuate the problems. One judge has the DUI offender write out a detailed essay on the twelve hours preceding his arrest, indicating not only the amount of alcohol consumed but all the circumstances that may have contributed to the consumption.

Physicians and *nurses,* especially public health nurses and other outreach workers, can uncover many cases of hidden addiction and get the patient into treatment before it becomes a serious problem. Now that some knowledge of alcoholism is required in the licensing examination for physicians, we have to look at making it a requirement for psychologists, lawyers, social workers, and other professions.

Teachers and *counselors* in schools must become aware of early signs. Gulping and sneaking drinks are typical symptoms of early alcoholism, and for youngsters they have a thousand special meanings. A drop in school grades, sleepiness in the classroom, irritability, and many other signs may tip off an alert teacher or counselor to look for incipient drug problems.

Driver education classes are a prime opportunity for alcohol education. Teenagers are highly motivated at the time of obtaining their first driver's license, and much more likely to be impressed by scientific facts about the effects of alcohol on behavior than by scare lectures on how their liver will look forty years from now. The factual approach can show that alcohol causes more problems than alcoholism and that addiction is not confined to the late organic stages but includes psychological or social dependence and other aspects of interest to the adolescent.

Bartenders can be a great source of referrals. They should be trained to spot potential alcoholism and should be considered allies rather than opponents of the alcoholism field.

Tertiary Prevention

Since tertiary prevention is actually treatment and rehabilitation, one might ask how it can be considered prevention if the addiction has already occurred. First, it prevents further damage to the addict and those affected, and prevents relapses. Next, it prevents further ill effects on the children and the spread of harm to others not yet affected. Third, it gives a model of addiction as a treatable illness, thus motivating others to seek help. Last, it prevents the addict from recruiting others to his rationalizations and instead adds weight to the trend toward abstinence or nonabuse.

All of the above aspects of prevention need to be considered as applying not merely to the addict, but also to the family and the community. Prevention includes, for example, educating a personnel manager to the idea that a recovered alcoholic is a far better employment risk than a hidden drinker.

Means of Prevention

No one means will be effective. Authoritarian answers imposed by experts have little hope of success. What is needed is a well-orchestrated cooperation of both public and private agencies, schools, churches, police, the media, the professions, business, the whole community (see Alexander, 1990).

Information

Factual information is basic to all prevention efforts. Myths must be dispelled, and there are probably more myths and false folklore about alcohol than about any other drug. The information must be correct, current, and objective; otherwise credibility is lost. We must remove the mystery about why people drink and stress that the principal reason most people (including alcoholics) drink is for euphoria, which makes alcohol a psychoactive drug.

But mere facts can be quite ineffective. We learned this in the big drug scare of the late 1960s, when schools rushed into a program of factual information that not only failed to prevent but often added fuel to the flames. Some youngsters learned how to shoot heroin into the vein, and others learned about glue sniffing or other things they would never have dreamed of without this "drug education" (Bard, 1974; Brecher, 1972). We have abandoned a stress on mere facts, showing students the different colored pills and the like. After all, most heavy smokers know more about smoking than the nonsmoker, and most have tried to quit: 90 percent in one survey had tried more than once. Doctors and nurses know more about drugs than most other people, yet their rate of addiction problems are worse than for others. The horrors of delirium tremens in the vague distant future make no impact on the optimism of youth. Important as facts are, mere knowledge has never guaranteed behavior, any more than knowing how to do it makes one shoot par golf.

Early. Since alcoholic beverages are readily available and known to the smallest child, there is not the same danger in giving information about alcohol as there is about other drugs. Hence the information can be given very early (Lecca and Watts, 1991). The preschooler can recite or sing all the beer ads from TV and tell you what brand of whiskey his daddy drinks. The five-year-old knows that what her mommy is drinking while she irons is not Seven-Up but gin. High school is too late to start, as most have their attitudes formed by age nine (fourth grade), and half our youngsters are drinking by age thirteen. The average age when cocaine use begins is fourteen, so education should begin by age twelve or earlier. But it must be field-tested: "Alcohol free" meant "free alcohol" to some eight-year-olds.

Education

Imparting facts is only a small part of the educational process. Drug education is the development of appropriate habitual knowledge, principles, attitudes, and motivated *behavior.* It may be formal or informal, in the classroom, through mass communication media, or in homes. One study showed 50 percent of the children already had attitudes formed at home, and 30 percent more from religion. The question is whether drug education is using the best that we know about the education process. It is certainly more than having a speaker come in once a year, or writing one more curriculum guide nobody uses.

Unenforceable laws against underage drinking are not the answer, but neither are scare tactics, biased opinions, or what students perceive as just one more authoritarian figure telling them what to do. Studies showing that many adolescents lower their rate of drinking after reaching legal age suggest that at least some adolescent drinking is just rebellion. Some advocate low-risk drinking, but kids *like* to take risks. *Self-activity* of the learner is an established principle of educational psychology. Instead of telling them, let them find out and tell us. There is plenty of factual material available today. Talking *with* students is much more effective than talking *at* them. Another neglected principle is *individual differences:* Adolescents are not all the same, and adolescent alcoholism is not the same as adult alcoholism.

That is one reason why Alcoholics Anonymous warns its members that if they are invited to a school they should not give the same type of talk they might give in meetings. The students cannot identify with the recital of either drunken escapades or misery. Sometimes their reaction is, "I'm going to drink and have all those adventures, and if I get into trouble I'll join AA and then everybody will admire me."

Three possible approaches can be rejected:

1. Total abstinence. This is unrealistic in a drinking society, and denies personal freedom.
2. Avoid the question, because it is controversial. This would force the schools to abandon nearly all teaching, since most subjects arouse some difference of opinion. What is conveyed is not the personal value judgment of the teacher but a basis for choice. To exemplify how divergent and controversial views can be, note that while white parents are being permissive about alcohol and very concerned about abuse of other drugs, some Indians are telling their children to use peyote and avoid alcohol.
3. "Responsible drinking." The slogan sounds good, and this approach certainly would make a lot of fifth-graders happy. But there are many reasons for rejecting it. It puts a premium on drinking as proof of responsibility and subtly implies that nondrinking is a mark of irresponsible people. It assumes that everybody drinks, which is not true, because a sizable minority of Americans do not drink at all, and over 70 percent do not drink more than once or twice a month. It assumes that everybody *should* drink, confusing average with normal and giving no freedom to minorities. Worse, it assumes that everybody *can* drink, ignoring the one in ten or twelve who cannot drink without problems. It ignores the role of drinking in the etiology of alcoholism. Every alcoholic does a lot of "controlled" drinking before reaching a severe state, and none would admit to being an irresponsible drinker. Even if "responsible drinking" were not a possible trap for the rest of us, it is totally inappropriate for the group we are most concerned about: the potential alcoholics.

Instead, what is needed is drug education integrated into all subjects in a factual way that leaves pupils free but gives the basis for an informed choice. That is the ideal, but in reality it requires that teachers all be not only well informed but have their own attitudes well in hand. They must be able to admit the diverse opinions of a pluralistic society, with no emotionalism and with no pretense that differences do not exist. Education can be done not only in health education classes but in literature, history, chemistry, biology, sociology, economics, psychology, or anywhere from kindergarten through senior high school. It should not be just about addiction, but about drugs and alcoholic beverages and the problems caused. Misuse exposes people to injuries, fights, arrests, pregnancy, venereal disease, and AIDS. Alcohol harms athletics, driving, study, friendships, dating, and sex—one survey reported 77 percent of college students found alcohol use offensive in the opposite sex.

Alcohol-specific education is needed, not mixed in with education about other drugs. Otherwise we foster the erroneous assumption that alcohol is used in the same context as other drugs, instead of being socially acceptable. We lose sight of the fact that the kinds of decisions made about drinking are often quite different from decisions about other drugs. When lumped with other drugs, alcohol tends to be minimized and taken for granted instead of being seen as our main drug problem, and focus on populations at high risk for alcohol problems is lost.

Rather than how to drink, what is needed is to teach how to live in a drinking society, how to make responsible decisions or personal choices about use and nonuse of alcohol. Young people need to develop refusal skills. Instead of just saying NO, which seems like a lifetime or moralistic stance, they can say, "Not now" or "Not tonight" or "I'll have a Coke, please." They need to learn how to have fun without drinking and still keep their friends. They need to see that they are being cheated if they pay the beer company to advertise its product on their T-shirt, instead of having the beer company pay them. In other words, independent decision-making means more than being swept into the assumption behind the liquor industry's slogans such as "Know your limits"—that everybody should drink to their limit. It means being your own person, not needing a chemical to feel normal. The aim is not to make people feel guilty if they drink but to help them not feel guilty if they don't drink. Rather than, "It's not OK to drink," which would be prohibition, we need "It's OK not to drink," which gives them choice. School-based programs that focus on social influences, such as peer-resistance training or changing social norms, show the most promise.

Decision-making Skills, Values Clarification

Popularized in the writings of Louis E. Raths and Sidney B. Simon in the 1960s, values clarification enjoyed a vogue in which it was mistakenly touted as some kind of magic, then debunked as a passing fad. Both reactions are mistaken. It is not moral relativism, teaching that any behavior is permissible as long as you clarify your values to justify it. Rather, it can be used to promote objective values, not just mere feelings, as the basis for choice. We need to learn to decide what is more important than what. Starting with "how alcohol touches your life," one can go on to learn how to ask, "Is it worth it?" The danger of alcoholism forty years from now is small motivation; we need to assess our values and motives for our actions right now.

Peer counselors can play a role in this as in other approaches. Young people will often be more effective with those their own age than older people are, because they are more trusted and because they know the age level. Note that a "peer" is not necessarily the same age: twelve-year-olds will take it better from a sixteen-year-old than from someone who is thirty.

Alternatives

A most valuable part of prevention is helping people to realize that there are alternatives to drugs, that you don't have to drink to have fun. A natural high can be a bigger thrill and can leave you with happy memories instead of a hangover. As one learns interpersonal skills, there is less need for alcohol as a social lubricant. One cynic has suggested that we anesthetize ourselves with martinis at social gatherings because we can't stand each other. Certainly we don't need alcohol if we truly enjoy someone's companionship and are doing something that we and our companions find pleasurable in itself.

Enjoyable activities need not be expensive. Dancing, sports, camping and hiking, hobbies, volunteer work in institutions, and a thousand other things can be enjoyed for their own sake and actually go better without alcohol. Drinking should never be the sole or even the primary function of a social activity, but at most an incidental accompaniment, which is optional and could be dispensed with if need be. There are many recipes for attractive nonalcoholic drinks to enhance a party. Beer consumption at the Friday night keggers on one college campus was cut 37 percent just by having the favorite soft drinks very visible and ice-cold. There is a new interest in spiritual growth, which should be exploited. Young people especially need to learn how to turn on to life, to cope without a chemical crutch, to develop a zest for living.

Enhancing Self-esteem

One of the biggest reasons why young people find it hard to make their own choices about drinking instead of letting the crowd sway their behavior is that they lack a sense of self-worth. If they have confidence that they are somebody who deserves respect, who can live their own lives and not worry about what others think, they can say, "No, thank you" with poise and self-assurance. Avoiding what is too much for you becomes the norm, regardless of others.

Role Models

The learning that flows from unconscious imitation must not be ignored. "What you are shouts so loud I can't hear what you say" is still true. Attractive role models must be provided—for example, by bringing out that many top athletes and popular girls do not drink or take drugs at all. Youngsters take their idols from the sports and entertainment worlds, but more than we realize they model themselves on those around them, including both peers and parents.

Changing Public Attitudes

Lastly, a key factor in prevention is to reverse current public attitudes about drinking and drunkenness. Instead of looking upon drinking as a social necessity and a sign of sophistication or manliness, and pushing drinks as a sign of hospitality, we need to see those attitudes as both silly and dangerous. A school education program can scarcely be effective if the parents and the community at large are still set in the opposite opinion and customs. Parent-Teacher Associations have joined with the Jaycees in a national educational effort, and local cooperation can often be enlisted simply by inviting the parents to find out what their children are being taught about "the number-one drug among youth." Those parents who say they don't want their child talking about the drinking that goes on at home should be informed that children do talk regardless. Parents and business can cooperate in objecting to advertising and entertainment programs that push drinking or tolerate drunken behavior.

But is it possible to change public attitudes? It is not easy, and Prohibition made it a lot harder. But it can be done, and *has* been done with regard to other things. We take air travel for granted, for instance, and forget that not too many decades ago people were saying that human beings were not meant to fly. Today nonsmoking is becoming almost a prestige symbol instead of making one a social outcast. Whereas earlier research showed that on college campuses a minority of students who drank excessively set the norms for the whole campus, now sororities and fraternities are having alcohol-free rush week and have dropped drunken behavior as part of hazing. A clear campus policy is needed (Gehring and Geraci, 1989). The push for a drug-free workplace, warning labels, the banning of stadium sales and happy hours where two drinks are sold for the price of one, the serving of nonalcoholic wines and beers in bars and restaurants, and intolerance of driving after drinking are examples of how public attitudes have shifted in the past decade.

"You don't drink! Why not?" puts the nondrinker on the defensive. The burden should be reversed: "You drink, why? I don't need it." Business ought to show that alcohol is not necessary for success in certain jobs, such as selling. We need to point up the inconsistency of looking down on an Indian custom of drinking to get drunk while we condone the bachelor party, which often has exactly the same intent. Instead of too much emphasis on drunk driving and alcoholism, we have to stress positive things, such as alternative forms of entertainment, how to handle somebody who wants to drive while impaired, how to promote good family relations. To be a good host or hostess one must learn some basic rules: (1) Always offer soft drinks and/or coffee as choices; never force your guests to have to ask. (2) Serve some food so that one need not drink on an empty stomach. (3) Don't push drinks, or serve doubles, or rush refills. (4) Serve dinner on time; don't prolong the cocktail hour. (5) Don't allow an intoxicated guest to drive home; call a taxi, or take him or her home yourself. Ideally, we can look forward to the day when one can order a plain ginger ale without fear that some ignoramus will spike it with vodka and without having to pay an exorbitant price just because it is served in a bar.

Drug abuse prevention programs have proliferated at both national and local levels, faster than we can enumerate here. We mention the Partnership for a Drug-Free America, D.A.R.E. to Keep Kids off Drugs (Drug Abuse Resistance Education), and Community Anti-Drug Coalitions of America. NCADD gives an annual meritorious award to one of the many ingenious prevention-education programs developed by their local and state affiliate councils.

Primary prevention involving such massive changes in attitude will take a long time, so we must not expect instant results. We must keep the long-range goal in sight, which should not be hard if we recall Chapter 1 on the magnitude of the problem.

Sources

CSAP and SALIS and the Prevention/Education office of NCADD are prime bibliographical sources (see Appendix). *Alcohol Education Materials: An Annotated Bibliography,* by Gail Milgram (1981), is a series of bibliographies covering 1950 to 1981. A good review of prevention efforts with ample references is NIAAA, *Alcohol and Health: Sixth Special Report,* 1987, Chapter VI, with a well-documented review of advertising and other portrayals of alcohol use in the media. A broad view is in G. Armyr et al., *Alcohol in the World of the 80's: Habits, Attitudes, Preventive Policies and Voluntary Efforts* (Addiction Research Foundation, Toronto, 1982).

New prevention materials are coming out rapidly, some needing careful evaluation according to the concepts in this chapter and in such works as Cahalan (1973, 1987), Cox (1986), Grant and Ritson (1983), Nathan (1983), the chapter by Joseph R. Gusfield, "The Prevention of Drinking Problems," in Filstead et al. (1976), Bacon (1978), and that by Howard T. Blane, "Education and Prevention of Alcoholism," in Kissin and Begleiter, vol. IV (1975), pp. 510–78.

Alexander, Bruce K., *Peaceful Measures: Canada's Way Out of the "War on Drugs."*

Beauchamp, Dan E., *Beyond Alcoholism: Alcohol and Public Policy.*

Boswell, B., and S. Wright, *The Cottage Meeting Program.* Utah Alcoholism Foundation, Salt Lake City, 1976.

Donohew, Lewis, et al. *Persuasive Communication and Drug Abuse Prevention.*

Dorn, N., and N. South, *Message in a Bottle: Theoretical Overview and Annotated Bibliography on the Mass Media and Alcohol.*

DuPont, R. L., *Getting Tough on Gateway Drugs: A Guide for the Family.*

———— (ed.), *Stopping Alcohol and Other Drug Use Before It Starts.*

Eiseman, Seymour (ed.), *Focus on Alcohol.* Baywood Publishing, 1995. (Avoids traditional model.)

Falco, Mathea, *The Making of a Drug-free America: Programs that Work.*

Finn, Peter, *Alcohol: You Can Help Your Kids Cope—A Guide for the Elementary School Teacher* (NCA pamphlet.)

Globetti, Gerald, "An Appraisal of Drug Education Programs" in R. J. Gibbins (ed.), *Research Advances in Alcohol and Drug Problems,* vol. 2, pp. 93–122.

Lecca, Peter J., and Thomas D. Watts, *Substance Abuse Strategies and Preschool Children.*

Meyer, Roberta, *The Parent Connection: How to Communicate with Your Child about Alcohol and Other Drugs.*

Mills, K. C., et al., *Handbook for Alcohol Education: The Community Approach.* Ballinger, Cambridge, MA, 1983.

Nathan, Peter E., "Failures in Prevention," *American Psychologist,* 1983, 38:459–67.

National Council on Alcoholism, *Prevention Policy Handbook;* also *Curriculum Guides.*

O'Gorman, Patricia A., and Peter Finn, *Teaching About Alcohol.*

Rhodes, Jean E., and L. A. Jason, *Preventing Substance Abuse Among Children and Adolescents.* Pergamon, New York, 1988.

COLLEGE PROGRAMS

Anderson, D. S., and A. F. Gadaleto, *That Happy Feeling: An Innovative Model for Campus Alcohol Educational Programming.* Southern Area Alcohol Education and Training Program, Inc., 4875 Powers Ferry Rd., N.W., Atlanta, GA 30327.

Campuses Without Drugs (quarterly).

Dean, J. C., and W. A. Bryan (eds.), *Alcohol Programs for Higher Education.* American College Personnel Association Media, Southern Illinois University Press, Carbondale, II, 1983.

Engs, Ruth C., *Alcohol and Other Drugs: Self-responsibility.*

Gehring, D., and C. Geraci, *Alcohol on Campus.*

Gonzales, G. M. *BACCHUS (Boost Alcohol Consciousness Concerning the Health of University Students).* University of Florida, Gainesville, 1981.

Goodale, Tom (ed.), *Alcohol and the College Student.* Jossey-Bass, San Francisco, 1986.

Kraft, D. P. "College Students and Alcohol: The 50 Plus 12 Project," *Alcohol Health and Research World,* Summer 1976, pp. 10–14.

Maddox, G. L. (ed.), *The Domesticated Drug: Drinking Among Collegians.* College and University Press, New Haven, CT, 1970.

Mantell, Margaret M., "Student and Employee Assistance Programs: A Model for Secondary Prevention," *Labor–Management Alcoholism Journal,* 1983, 12(4):113, 124.

National Highway Traffic Safety Administration, *The Best Prevention: Model Alcohol and Drug Education Program.* NHTSA, Washington, DC, 1984.

North, G., *Alcohol Education for College Student Personnel.* 338 Student Services Bldg., Michigan State University, East Lansing, MI 48824.

Villanova University, *Alcohol and Drug Assistance for Students.* Villanova, PA.

Wanner, Craig, et al. (eds.), *Alcoholism on American Campuses.* Rutgers University, New Brunswick, NJ, 1983.

Wechsler, H. et al., "Health and Behavioral Consequences of Binge Drinking in College."

The Whole College Catalog About Drinking: A Guide to Alcohol Abuse Prevention. HEW Publ. No. ADM-76-361., U.S. Government Printing Office, 1976.

CHAPTER 13

EAP—Occupational Programs

S ECONDARY PREVENTION was defined in the previous chapter as early detection and intervention, preventing progression of the illness to middle or late stages. Perhaps the best opportunity for that is through occupational alcoholism programs. The current term is Employee Assistance Programs (EAP), for reasons that will become clear in the discussion of the broad brush approach at the end of this chapter. But it implies that employers cannot be alcoholics, too, yet NCA reports a 1983 study which showed that the rate of alcoholism is the same in the top third of earnings as in the bottom third. We include the armed services and government employees at all levels, from local to federal, as well as other occupations that are neither business nor industry, such as the professions.

The reason secondary prevention is so successful in occupational programs is twofold: The alcoholism is nipped in the bud before severe deterioration develops, and the person is highly motivated by the desire to keep a job. Hence there is much more to work with in the person than after brain damage or a loss of major incentives has occurred (Roman, 1990). Again, all that we say here also applies to drugs other than alcohol (Butler, 1993; Thompson, 1990).

"We don't have alcoholics in our company; we fire them" is a fairly typical response when the topic is first broached to corporate executives. There is a double fallacy here. First, any company of any size is almost certainly employing a number of alcoholics, whose presence is kept hidden through fear of the very policy just stated, which discourages them from seeking treatment. Second, the hidden drinkers, driven underground by the policy, continue as troublesome, half-efficient, accident-prone employees until they are terminated, often after some tragedy or expensive grievance procedures (Denenberg and Denenberg, 1991).

More enlightened employers recognize that in America 6 to 8 percent of the workforce at all levels is having problems with alcohol or other drugs; one study gave 5.7 percent as the most conservative estimate. It is statistically most improbable that any organization of sixteen persons will not have at least one alcoholic, or that a group of one hundred will not have about six alcoholics, or a company of one thousand about sixty alcoholics. They may range from bank presidents and chief surgeons to secretaries and maintenance personnel. Probably there are as many women as men, in proportion to numbers employed. The more denial there is from top-level management that a problem exists, the more likely it is that the problem is being kept hidden by both employee and immediate supervisor.

Costly Alternatives

Some executives see only three choices for themselves regarding an employee with a drinking problem: termination, early retirement, or continued employment of a half-person. All three are costly. (1) Termination is costly because valuable employees are lost by this policy. Their knowledge and experience are real assets to the company and represent a big investment in training. For example, the average client in the Great Northern Railroad's alcoholism program had been twenty-two years with that railroad. Workaholics are productive but vulnerable. (2) Early retirement is costly for the same reason, plus the fact that pension benefits must be begun earlier than budgeted. (3) But more costly than turnover is keeping the alcoholic on the job. Aside from humanitarian considerations for either the person or the family, let us examine the cost in hard dollars.

Economists talk about the cost of steel, but General Motors spends more in one year on health insurance than on steel to build cars. Excessive drinking was estimated in the 1950s to cost American business and industry annually some $7 billion. Those are not wild guesses. Two health economists at the University of California at Los Angeles, Luce and Schweitzer (1978), put the figure at $20.6 billion; NIAAA in 1986 said $44 billion. These figures are conservative. Many costs are not recorded, such as number of work errors. Some costs cannot be measured, such as employee morale or customer good will, and loss to the corporate image when a drunken executive lands on the front page of the local newspaper or makes unfulfilled promises during a blackout. But some we can count:

1. *Lost hours of work.* This can be through absenteeism, tardiness, or interruptions. Alcoholic employees average more than twice the sick leave of other employees. Time lost in arguments with fellows or supervisor is often not recorded, and the alcoholic in denial will say "I never missed a day of work."
2. *Half-work* on the job, through diminished efficiency or time-wasting habits. Closer supervision, correction of errors, and especially slowing down the whole production line are all costly.
3. *Wasted time* of supervisor and discipline board.
4. *Excessive sick benefits* and higher insurance premiums, usually paid by the employer. Recall from Chapter 4 the long list of ailments that can be due to alcohol.
5. *Costly errors* from either hangover or drinking on the job. Two actual examples will illustrate. A layout man ruined $30,000 worth of materials before a large press could be shut off. The vice president in charge of investments for a large insurance company returned from a three-martini

lunch and made a foggy-minded decision that cost the company $2 million.

6. *Theft.* Chemical dependence surely contributes to the $50 billion annual loss by employee theft.

7. *Accidents.* In addition to the worker who literally drops a wrench in the machinery, causing costly repairs and lost production time, there is a massive cost in personal injuries and damage suits. Allis Chalmers reports 56 percent of waste loss was eliminated after it put in a good company alcoholism program. The Oldsmobile plant of General Motors cut accidents by 82 percent. Most sensitive here is the transportation industry. The U.S. Department of Transportation estimated a loss of 34 lives and $28 million in 1983 by alcohol-related train accidents. Formerly there was reluctance to initiate a program for fear the public might take this as an admission there were alcoholics running the train or plane, with subsequent loss of patronage. Actually, just the opposite occurred. The president of the Great Northern Railroad five decades ago had the vision and courage to put in a program, with the result that his company had the best safety record in the country for five of the next six years. In contrast, another railroad, which did not put in a program, had two freight train wrecks within one year in which the engineers had been drinking. One shudders at the hundreds of lives lost if those had been passenger trains. The commercial airlines, the Air Line Pilots Association (ALPA), and the Federal Aviation Administration have all now recognized that a happily recovered alcoholic is a much safer pilot than a hidden alcoholic who is still drinking but afraid to ask for treatment for fear of reprisals. Some alcoholics have fewer accidents, but only because they are either absent or being so careful that they are less productive.

A simple yardstick to measure what all this probably costs an organization is to take 8 percent of all personnel and multiply that figure by 25 percent of the average annual salary. This gives $800,000 probable loss due to excessive drinking and other drug misuse in an organization of one thousand. In a small company of one hundred, the cost would be $80,000 per year. This formula applied to 94 million employed persons in the country yields just under $44 billion loss annually.

A Fourth Choice

From this it is clear that the question is not how much an occupational program would cost, but how much it would save (Scanlon, 1991). One company spent $65,000 on a program that saved them $750,000 in sick pay alone. ITT saved $30 million in ten years by putting in an EAP. Health costs for one employee dropped from $40,000 in one year to $450, after completion of treatment. It is expensive *not* to rehabilitate alcoholic/addict employees (Holder et al., 1992).

Because of early intervention, success rates in business and industry are usually higher than average. Recovery in 60 to 80 percent of cases is common, some companies reporting 85 to 90 percent, and the pioneer program in one of the companies listed below reports 93 percent success using stringent criteria. That this is good business policy is evidenced by naming some of the corporations that have adopted enlightened policies regarding alcoholic employees: DuPont Chemical seems to have been the first in 1942, Eastman Kodak in 1945, then Allis Chalmers, Burlington Northern R.R., McDonnell-Douglas, Standard Oil of California, Caterpillar Tractor, Kemper Insurance, Oldsmobile, American Airlines, Hughes Aircraft, Con Edison, and many members of the Bell Telephone system, starting with Illinois Bell.

Two elements are essential for success: a policy and a program. A policy without a program to implement it is just a sheet of paper. A program without a firm policy to back it up will never be effective, as the first-level supervisor cannot be sure of support from above.

Policy

A firm policy must be promulgated widely and clearly to educate the whole company: all members at all levels. A policy of "quit drinking or we fire you" implies that the employee *can* quit, missing the compulsive nature of the illness as well as the social respectability of alcohol. Instead of that negative approach, a positive policy states that addiction is a treatable illness entitling one to the same sick leave and benefits as any other illness, with no penalty or stigma attached to seeking treatment. Such a policy statement provides a basic frame of reference for the development of procedures and a guide for uniform administration by all concerned. It encourages the individual's voluntary use of the program and serves as a valuable training tool for all employees and managers.

The policy must state early that there is no intrusion on the private life or personal habits of the employee. The focus is on *job performance*, and relates to drinking or drugging on or off the job only to the extent that it affects job performance. It does not create a witch-hunt looking for drunks but offers assistance to those whose job is imperiled in whatever way. It must make clear that the fact of seeking help will not become a part of one's personnel record and will pose no threat to job security or promotion. In fact, the whole purpose is to save the job, and more importantly to save the person who, when sober, will be a far better candidate for promotion than when drinking. The U.S. Navy proved this by showing that 46 percent of those who accepted treatment were promoted, as against only 44 percent of the comparable Navy population.

Participation is voluntary, in the sense that the alcoholics make the choice. They fire themselves by refusing to take the necessary means to remedy deficient job performance. The policy must be clear that firm and consistent action will be taken on this basis. Saving the job and the person is always paramount, so the individual acts for his own good.

Cooperative Effort

Experience has shown it is important that the policy statement be drawn up by a joint effort of both labor and management. Otherwise the employee plays one off against the other like a child manipulating its parents. Even when at odds over the bargaining table on other isuses, labor and management can and do cooperate well here, because it is in the best interest of both parties. The union knows it is protecting the jobs and health of its members just as clearly as the organization knows it is protecting its image and fiscal viability. Although this is a matter of good management and not for negotiation at the bargaining table, it is important that labor be involved from the outset. Otherwise the policy could be misinterpreted as something imposed upon labor from above instead of a matter of mutual interest and concern.

A new joint committee in any company need not start from scratch in writing a policy. It can draw on the accumulated experience and readily available materials from many of the older firms named above and especially the Employee Assistance Professionals Association (EAPA, formerly ALMACA). Perhaps the most useful starting point can be a "Joint Union–Management Statement of Policy" in line with the policy positions already enunciated here, including the following among its principles:

> Addiction is defined as a disease in which a person's use definitely and repeatedly interferes with that individual's health and/or job performance.

> Persons who suspect that they may have a problem, even in its early stages, are encouraged to seek diagnosis and to follow through with the treatment that may be prescribed by qualified professionals, in order to arrest the disease as early as possible.

> Neither supervisors nor union representatives have the medical qualifications to diagnose a disease. Therefore, referral for diagnosis and treatment will be based on job performance, within the terms, conditions and application of this union–management agreement.

Top-level Endorsement. It is most important that the policy statement, although the work of a joint labor–management committee, be promulgated as having the endorsement of management at the highest level. Otherwise there will always be doubt about whether middle management will back up a supervisor who relies on it. It must apply to all levels, so that a president is faced with the same alternatives as anyone else.

Women. A proper policy does not single out women alcoholics, but neither does it make any special concessions to them. Both errors have been made in the past and constitute unjust discrimination. The old double standard is too often still operative even when the policy is clearly based on job performance. A woman may make a mistake on her job and is rated "not qualified," where a man making the same mistake simply "needs more training." Women may be more prone to polydrug misuse, but this in turn is usually the result of a patronizing attitude by a physician who looks on her complaints as psychosomatic, or by a psychologizing approach that more often analyzes "female" reasons for drinking instead of facing the nature of addiction in itself. Thus a forty-four-year-old office worker dressing for work one day realized she didn't remember where she worked; instead of recognizing blackout or alcoholic stupor, a therapist told her that she hated her job so much she had repressed it. Male protectiveness here can only harm the woman by avoiding the issue of alcoholism. On the other hand, sex discrimination has put added pressure on the woman who tries to climb the corporate ladder. She may compete at the bar as she has to elsewhere, drink for drink with the men, but her smaller size and hormonal differences put her at a distinct disadvantage in this dangerous competition.

Program

Even the best-written policy drafted by the best joint committee is fraught with difficulties. Developing a program takes time and expertise. After the policy is written and means of promulgation agreed upon, supervisors must be trained, treatment facilities selected, procedures arranged whereby the employee is referred to treatment through the medical department or personnel office, means of payment for treatment worked out, and record-keeping routines established as a basis for followup and evaluation. Many states now require that all group health insurance policies include coverage for alcoholism.

Job Performance Is the Criterion

As stated in the policy, decline in job performance is the basis for any action taken, and restoration of job performance to the proper level is the measure of success. That is crucial, because it takes supervisors out of the role of diagnosing or counseling and keeps them in their proper role. Besides expecting a function for which they are neither trained nor paid, any other approach invites untold problems. It can lead to arguments: "You were drunker at the staff party than I was." It introduces subjective and emotional factors into arbitration that do not fit with contractual agreements and union–management understandings. Unsatisfactory work performance is the concern of management; protection of the employee's job and health is the concern of labor. Both have the same result here: coercive action if alcohol or other drugs interfere with job performance of the employee or others (which is relevant because the alcoholic is more likely to get into fights or disturb others at their work). This criterion also applies to drinking behavior off the job that either cuts efficiency or reflects on the company. The alcoholic often carries his problem to the job in the form of hangovers, headaches, nervousness, money worries, and wage garnishments—all of which waste time and cut down productivity. Union's role and right is to be present during a supervisor–employee interview, to protect the employee from unjust action, and to assure that coercive action is clearly based on the work record of the employee.

Supervisors can thus be trained in a two-hour session to carry out the policy, since they do not need to be experts in addiction. Theirs is assessment of a problem, not the diagnosis of a disease. Their task has four functions: to observe, to record, to confront, and to refer. Their observations can be sharpened by alertness to on-the-job signs of alcoholism, especially early signs not usually recognized by those who think in terms of a falling-down drunk, or even bleary eyes and shaky hands. They must learn to document behavior precisely, so that confrontation is not a fiasco of assertions and denials. The exact dates of absences and tardiness, the excuses given for sick leave (fifty-three tooth extractions or three grandmothers' funerals are suspect), the exact time and place of fights and the name of the other party should all be recorded. Notes on the confronting interview should document the fact that the shop steward or other union representative was present.

The supervisor can look for and document many things not usually thought of as symptomatic of alcoholism. Absenteeism, especially on Monday mornings, is a late sign; the alcoholic knows enough to punch in bright and early so as to avoid having a record of Monday morning delinquency on file, at least until the illness has progressed to the point where this becomes very difficult. Personality change may be more important than physical signs at first: irritability, especially in one previously pleasant, moodiness, procrastination, sloppy dress, undependability, blaming others when things have been put off or done poorly, avoiding others. To be noted is improvement in personality after lunch or a break where one might sneak a drink from a thermos jug or in the washroom; this shows dependence on alcohol to function normally. There may be the usual signs of hangover: red or bleary eyes, hand tremors, flushed face, mistakes or errors in judgment, intolerance of fellow workers. Instead of a steady work pace, the alcoholic may work furiously for a while but spasmodically slów down in both quantity and quality of work. Excessive use of breath purifiers can be obvious, but so is always needing a loan until payday, and even having one's wages garnisheed. Being indignant at any mention of one's drinking is significant, as are drinking at lunch or arriving at work with liquor on the breath. Accident proneness can be due to either drinking or hangover. Drinking executives are harder to detect, since they are less supervised, enjoy the protection of their staffs, and can get away with doing less while continuing to do it well for a long time.

Confrontation is aimed at referral, not counseling or even diagnosis. After a warning session, likewise documented, the second interview puts it squarely to the employee: Either improve job performance or be terminated. It is strongly urged that the employee use the help provided by the company program, whether it be an employee assistance counselor, the medical department, or whatever. They are to do the diagnosis, not the supervisor, who without violating confidentiality can confer with the counselor and discuss the reasons for the referral. Since alcoholics are usually great con artists and the supervisor is naïve in this area, any other approach can eventuate in the alcoholic's convincing the supervisor that it is the supervisor who has the problem, or else the supervisor feels sorry for the employee and agrees to help out or cover up in ways that only prolong the alcoholism or defer real help. Promises, idle threats, resolutions, and bargaining are most ineffectual here. The supervisor should never ask why; stick to facts, not reasons. Moralizing and debating with the employee are to be avoided.

Forced Treatment Works. But doesn't the alcoholic have to hit bottom and want help before it is effective? That myth has been thoroughly exploded by occupational programs. Actually, it has long been known that most alcoholics come into treatment or AA under some duress: threat of job loss, divorce, ruined health, or the like. Nobody seeks help if there is no problem. A director of one large and successful treatment facility in the Midwest stated that every patient came in angry at being forced into treatment but left grateful that somebody cared enough to act for his or her own good. Research is not unanimous on the point, but most evidence suggests *higher* rates of recovery in forced treatment. That, of course, may be at least partially due to the earlier arrest of the illness. Pursch (1985) reports a 93 percent recovery rate among airline pilots, most of whom are coerced. The real danger is that not only the spouse but also fellow workers and the immediate supervisor will deny the problem or cover up for the alcoholic/addict, shielding him or her from higher management in a misguided form of help, which may actually be lethal. Thus the company may act as an Enabler. Whether it is called "tough love" or "constructive coercion," the experience of many programs confirms the fact that forcing an alcoholic into treatment as an alternative to job termination is saving jobs and lives as well as avoiding lawsuits.

Part of the policy, clearly promulgated and then rigidly adhered to, should be a statement on relapse. The Great Northern (now Burlington Northern) policy explicitly provides for rehiring once only, with no exceptions. With this policy, it reported 88 percent success in their original program after two thousand cases and 85 percent success in more than seven thousand cases since the merger. Experience has shown that deviations from such a policy backfire and create worse problems, as alcoholic/addicts are great at exploiting the system.

Confidentiality

A most important feature for the credibility of any program is that the employee must know that seeking help will not hurt a future career. In some programs the office and records are in the home of the addiction counselor, and in any case they should never be part of the personnel file. That is not the same as the anonymity tradition of AA, but there are some common features. The fact that the supervisor referred the employee to a counselor is a matter of company record, as is any subsequent job improvement or deterioration. But the diagnosis or nature of the treatment is strictly between the counselor and the employee, and even higher management has no right to that information. Exception could be made for proven imminent and serious danger to a third party, or to the employee himself or herself.

The above, of course, will vary with conditions and is sometimes governed by law. It is a particularly difficult problem in the armed services, but every effort should be made to protect the individual seeking treatment. The model Uniform Act provides for secrecy of records. Hotly disputed is the question of *mandatory testing;* see Chapter 20 under "Discrimination."

The Family

We have stressed that it is almost pointless to treat addiction and ignore the family environment in which the recovered person must live. Since the trend is toward family involvement in all treatment, occupational programs should be no exception. One company reported that its EAP saved 30 percent of health costs of the employees, but 40 percent of those for the family. The counselor, of course, must have the employee's permission to contact the spouse. It is usually granted once a good relationship has been established and the client is assured that cooperation is to his or her benefit. In some programs the alcoholism counselor and spouse form an AA and Al-Anon team, which has proved very effective. Family group sessions can add much to a program. Special provision for child care may be necessary.

Addicted Spouse. The program ideally should also provide for the alcoholic spouse of a nonalcoholic employee. This is job-related. If the spouse calls frequently during business hours or is just on the employee's mind as a source of worry, this cuts down performance. The employee is afraid or unable to take a trip for either vacation or company business, for fear the alcoholic spouse will burn down the house or have an accident. One is ashamed to bring the alcoholic spouse to the company picnic or office party. If there are children, the anxiety is increased. Al-Anon and Alateen (Chapter 18) can be a great asset to any rehabilitation program, without adding to the budget.

Followup

It is not sufficient to refer the employee to the proper source of help. The counselor must keep in contact for at least two years, being careful not to give the impression of spying or mistrusting. The contact should be friendly and encouraging, with the offer of help on any of the myriad problems that can linger after recovery. Legal, medical, family, and financial problems may plague the recovered person for some time. Loan sharks, child support or vis-

iting privilege wrangles, social pressures to drink, and the restoration of reversed marital roles described in the last section of Chapter 9 can all demand
continued support and counsel. Without being overprotective, the supervisor
must do everything to ensure that fellow employees welcome the recovered
employee back with warmth and encouragement, and to counteract any suggestion from the group that recovery means that the alcoholic can drink or
drug again.

Renewal. Education should always be a function of the program. An ongoing
training program is needed to bring new supervisors in line with the policy
and sharpen the referral skills of all. Promulgation to new employees, and an
occasional reminder for the entire organization, will keep both supervisors
and union representatives aware, so that the program does not die through
neglect. Promulgation of a policy means more than tacking up a copy once on
a company bulletin board. It should be mailed to the home (spouse?) of every
employee each year.

A much-neglected need is counseling for the supervisors themselves. They
may not want to refer to EAP: "This is just between us; we can work it out
together and nobody else need know." Like the spouse, the supervisor at any
level may become emotionally involved in the problem, get caught up in the
alcoholic's denial system, develop denial that the supervisor himself or herself
may indeed be part of the problem, experience guilt or anxiety, and be inept
at handling the situation when the alcoholic returns to work from treatment.
Even when well trained in confrontation and referral, the supervisor may
need individual counseling and help with these and other problems. Presumably the trained addiction counselor to whom the employee is referred can
also help the supervisor.

Evaluation. Although names are kept strictly confidential, records must be
kept so that number of cases and rates of success can be communicated to
higher management and indeed to the whole organization. That means establishing definitions and criteria in keeping with the policy statement, and avoiding bias in reporting results.

Referral Procedure

If, upon confrontation, employees agree to seek help, to whom does the supervisor refer them? It must not be assumed that the average physician, nurse,
psychologist, social worker, or counselor has specific knowledge and skills regarding alcohol and other drug addiction. It must be someone who knows
not only early signs and patterns of progression but also the tricks of denial
and manipulation by which an alcoholic can usually outmaneuver the un-
wary professional. Regardless of profession or title, the person must be prepared to recognize that perhaps 90 percent of the problems referred are
caused by alcohol or other drugs. And above all, one must not fall for the ra-

tionalization that the problems caused the drinking, when really the drinking caused the problems.

The location and title of this person will depend on the size of the organization and other circumstances. It would be impractical for a small company to establish its own program. A clear policy will provide a channel to resources available in the community, once the problem has been identified. A large organization could profitably have its own full program staffed by one or more addiction specialists, with AA and Al-Anon meetings on location. But even in this case, counselors must accept their limitations and possess a thorough knowledge of other treatment facilities for appropriate referral. In neither case does the supervisor refer to a person or office entitled with a diagnosis not yet made. Even those who reject a "broad-brush" approach agree on this.

Broad-brush is a term used to describe programs that do not carry the word alcoholism in their title but go by such names as employee assistance, occupational health services, or guidance and counseling. The opponents argued that the broad-brush approach only feeds denial, perpetuates the stigma, and weakens the whole prevention and educational effort (Roman, 1979). The proponents claimed that many people will accept the more neutral title who would refuse to walk through a door with "alcoholism" on it. They argued that as long as the counselor is skillful in diagnosing alcoholism once the client is inside, it will catch more alcoholics than a program whose title deters them. A strong consideration is polydrug abuse, since there are really very few "pure" alcoholics anyhow. As indicated previously, the two positions may not be as far apart as either side would make it appear, as a forthright policy on alcoholism—sometimes lacking in broad-brush programs—still calls for procedures that permit the supervisor to refer to a counselor without the supervisor's making the diagnosis.

Current EAP practice seems to indicate a preference for the broad-brush approach. This means that EAP counselors need greater expertise in polydrug, mental health, and other problems besides just alcoholism.

Sources

John J. Miletich (1988) has compiled an exhaustive bibliography on this topic. Much of the material quoted in this chapter is derived from long experience with private industry programs. Most of the companies mentioned in the text are willing to share with genuinely interested persons the excellent materials they have developed.

Useful material is often in pamphlet form, published by organizations such as NCADD, NIAAA/NCADI, the Christopher D. Smithers Foundation, EAPA, and insurance companies, such as Kemper and Metropolitan Life. In addition, EAPA publishes a journal. Information on certification of EAP professionals can be obtained from the Employee Assistance Certification Commission, 1800 N. Kent St. #907, Arlington, VA 22209.

This is an aspect of alcoholism on which there are also excellent 16 mm. films, including *Alcoholism; The Bottom Line; The Dryden File; Weber's Choice; One Company's Answer; We Don't Want to Lose You; Alcoholism: Industry's Costly Hangover; A Firm Hand; Business with a Twist;* and *Need for Decision.*

Alcohol Health and Research World, "Alcohol and the Workplace," 1992, 16(2):95–164, esp. W. J. Sonnenstuhl, 129–33.

Brisolara, Ashton, *The Alcoholic Employee.* Human Sciences Press, New York, 1979.

Butler, B., *Alcohol and Drugs in the Workplace.*

Christopher D. Smithers Foundation, three booklets: *The Key Role of Labor in Employee Alcoholism Programs; A Company Program on Alcoholism; Alcoholism in Industry.*

Denenberg, Tia S., and R. V. Denenberg, *Alcohol and Other Drugs.*

Mantell, Margaret M., "Student and Employee Assistance Programs: A Model for Secondary Prevention," *Labor–Management Alcoholism Journal* (NCA), 1983, 12(4):113, 124.

Masi, Dale A., *Designing Employee Assistance Programs.* American Management Association, New York, 1984.

Maxwell, Milton A., *The A.A. Experience: A Close-up View for Professionals* (largely for EAPs).

National Council on Alcoholism, *A Joint Labor–Management Approach to Alcoholism Recovery Programs* and *The EAP Manual.*

O'Donnell, M. P., and T. H. Ainsworth, *Health Problems in the Marketplace.* Wiley, New York, 1984.

Presnall, Lewis F., *Occupational-Counseling and Referral Systems.* Utah Alcoholism Foundation, Salt Lake City, 1981.

Roman, Paul (ed.), *Alcohol Problem Intervention in the Workplace.*

Scanlon, Walter F., *Alcoholism and Drug Abuse in the Workplace.*

Schramm, Carl J., *Alcoholism and Its Treatment in Industry.* Johns Hopkins University Press, Baltimore, 1978.

Sonnenstuhl, W. J. and H. M. Trice, *Strategies for Employee Assistance Programs: The Crucial Balance.* Cornell University, Ithaca, NY, 1986.

Standard Oil Company of California, *Special Health Services and Troubled Employee: A Supervisor's Guide* (booklet).

Thompson, Robert, Jr., *Substance Abuse and Employee Rehabilitation.*

Trice, Harrison, and Paul Roman, *Spirits and Demons at Work: Alcohol and Other Drugs on the Job.* 2d ed. New York State School of Industrial and Labor Relations, Ithaca, NY, 1979.

Wrich, Jim, *The Employee Assistance Program: Updated for the 1980's* (Hazelden booklet).

CHAPTER 14

Referral and Intervention

H OW DO WE GET PEOPLE into treatment? Perhaps the best answer is, "Any way we can." Individuals and situations differ. Referral is more than merely giving someone a name and phone number. All the skill and tact one can muster might be necessary to get the client to accept help, and a thorough knowledge of available facilities is essential to making an appropriate referral.

In social welfare agencies, alcoholics are said to be the most referred and the least helped of all clients. That is no surprise, if they are shunted from one agency to another instead of entering a system that tailors an integrated continuum of care for each individual. Too often they are lost in transition from one stage of treatment to the next. A good referral includes followup from detoxification through intensive treatment to rehabilitation and return to full life in the community. Continuum of care also means that it is rarely a matter of choosing one means to the exclusion of all others, but rather a sequence or combination of several.

Timing is vital in the referral process. Obviously, it is useless to discuss anything with a person who is intoxicated. But we must see them when they need help, not at our convenience. "Next Tuesday at two o'clock" often means "never" to a person in crisis.

Initial Assessment

A social worker with ten years' experience took our survey course in the fall quarter. The next spring term he stated, "I used to think about 5 percent of my caseload was alcohol-related problems; now I see it as 65 percent—and it's the same caseload!" On the other hand, the skilled alcoholism worker is alert not to presume that all clients are alcoholic. The spouse or clergyman may say so, but that does not make it true. Overenthusiasm may cause some to see every DUI offender or drunken adolescent as alcoholic; this only destroys the credibility of alcoholism workers in the eyes of judges and others. Snap diagnoses, sometimes over the telephone without having ever seen the client, often based on hearsay evidence or solely on amount of alcohol consumed, discredit the whole alcoholism profession. In spite of the stand we took on addiction as a primary illness, we must warn that it can cause the intake worker to miss a dual diagnosis, especially if one is not trained in mental disorders.

We have already pointed out that hanging the label *alcoholic* on a client may only get defenses up if he or she is in a denial phase. Rather, we just explore together whether excessive drinking is causing any problems in important life areas, or whether there is any basis to the complaints of spouse or employer. A good reason for avoiding the word *alcoholic* at this stage is the stereotype of the skid-road bum; we want to contact alcoholics while they are still "not that bad."

Sometimes inquirers will hide their own problem by beginning with "I have this friend . . ." while feeling out the counselor to test acceptance. Or she may say, "My husband says I drink too much," when actually it is she who is worried about her drinking. And to lie about one's drinking is a classic symptom of alcoholism; the counselor can usually double or quadruple the amount (a 1987 study said 81 percent don't tell their doctors they even drink). But it must not be assumed that the person is lying; one may be unaware of how much was consumed in a blackout, or may forget, or just be confused. He or she may sound very logical and convincing. The counselor who agrees that the client wouldn't drink excessively if only he or she could find the right job, or if only a spouse would be more responsive sexually, has been conned.

We must relate the drinking to the life history. For example, how likely is it that a string of bad marriages, lost jobs, accidents, and health problems is anything but the result of the addiction? Those who have never been fired because of drinking should be asked how often they quit first to prevent being fired. Alcoholics may be much more willing to talk about their sex life, and must be made to stick to the drinking history. Asked if they have ever quit drinking, they must be shown that this is a classic symptom, not proof of control. Why quit if no problem? The same must be said for good tolerance or ability to function better after a drink or two. Changing jobs, working below one's level of competence or education, loss of friends, and family disruption must all be related in the client's eyes to the drinking, contrary to the fine rationalizations the client may present.

Drinking problems in one's ancestry, heavy smoking and coffee consumption, breath purifiers, excessive makeup on the woman, bruises, puffiness, slight tremors or nervousness, and clamminess or perspiring are all telltale signs. Review the patterns in Chapter 6. Significant is the giving of reasons why one drinks, which the social drinker doesn't have to do. Relief from worry, depression, low self-esteem, tension, and any "use" of alcohol as opposed to merely enjoying it are symptomatic of alcoholism. Blaming the wife's nagging or the unreasonable boss usually betrays a drinking problem rather than explaining it away. Every clue must be brought to bear in order to unmask the denial and rationalization. Is it really true that the neighbors don't know? the children?

Selection of Treatment Approach

Once a diagnosis of alcoholism is made, a decision must be reached on where to go for help. A smorgasbord of choices only confuses the client; decide on the treatment modality and offer a choice of facilities within that category. A rule of thumb is: The sicker the client, the fewer the choices. If the exploratory evaluation has been well done, the authority of the counselor should emerge.

One must never accept the answer that treatment is too expensive. AA costs nothing and is available almost everywhere. Actually, treatment is the cheapest thing one can do about a drinking problem: A divorce, a lost job, a smashed car, a liability suit, or a big hospital bill for any of the medical complications discussed in Chapter 4, Section C, can all be more costly. A recent study shows that every dollar spent on treatment of addiction saves $11.54 in the long run. Most have no idea how much they spend on their addiction, often enough in one year to pay for treatment, which then gives them extra cash for the rest of their lives.

Knowledge of Facilities. Here specific and current information is essential, not guesswork. To keep a list up to date requires constant effort. One must know admitting procedures of hospitals, extent of group insurance coverage, policies of welfare agencies and major employers, and local meeting times and places of AA, NA, CA, and Al-Anon. One must know physicians and clergymen whose attitudes and knowledge about addiction can be relied upon, including psychiatrists and clinical psychologists who will help instead of complicating matters if called. Acceptability to the client may depend not only on cost but on tone or climate of a treatment center, or the personality of the therapist. Whether a bed is available must be checked, as well as the ability of the client to meet the financial arrangements at admission. Knowledge should include not only alcoholism facilities but other community resources: public assistance caseworkers, child care, food stamps, homemakers, medical coupons, social security benefits, skid-road centers, Medicaid and Medicare, senior citizens groups, and all kinds of helping agencies.

Skill in Selection. Equipped with this information, the counselor must still exercise judgement in picking a particular facility for this individual. Contrary to some mythology, a trip to the county detoxification ward will not scare the upper-class patient into doing something about his or her problem, but will probably scare him or her out of any other kind of treatment if he or she concludes that this is typical of all treatment facilities. Besides, it reinforces patients' rationalization that they are not "that bad" when they see the late-stage derelicts being treated. Conversely, hospitals may be threatening and "middle class" to some indigents. A coed facility may terrify a timid female patient. Some preparatory explanation, choosing the right group, and finding a suitable sponsor are paramount for a favorable introduction to AA. If there is a spouse or family, they should all be included and referred to Al-Anon and Alateen.

Severity of the addiction is a significant factor. Few alcoholics need medical detoxification, but a physical examination is always wise to rule out medical complications. A hospital may be the only choice if the patient is extremely ill. Those not quite so ill need a physical examination and structured residential treatment with good followup. Those with mild to moderate problems are often best treated in outpatient centers. Within those categories, the client may be offered a choice, but ordinarily should not be asked to choose between hospital and outpatient treatment, for instance. Psychotherapy is usually best postponed until there has been enough sobriety to see if it is necessary and to allow the brain to reach a point where the treatment can be effective.

Psychiatric assessment may be helpful in selection of treatment modality. The aggressive and stubborn patient usually has a good prognosis, as does the slightly neurotic. More severe mental disorder and sociopathy indicate a poorer prognosis. Adolescents are typically unstable, confused, and egocentric; of greater diagnostic importance is what they were like before the onset of drinking and drugging. But in any case we cannot assume all will respond equally well to the same approach. In addition to form of treatment and the psychological characteristics of the patient, the social components of the treatment setting may also be important. Extroverts do better in AA than introverts, while psychotics and borderline psychotics don't do well there. Other factors in suggesting a type of treatment are level of intelligence, family and job stability, active religious participation, and degree of emotional control.

It is a mistake for any one treatment center to attempt to handle all types of patients, either through a single approach or by trying to give a little of everything, for the simple reason that both client population and residential tone must be matched with the individual client. Good referral is better than bad treatment. Unfortunately we have not yet developed the matching process with scientific precision, but experience and good judgment along with a knowledge of the characteristics and client populations of each local facility can result in a fair degree of accurate matching.

A common mistake is to recommend outpatient treatment in a futile effort to save the client's job when intensive residential treatment is needed. This sets up the client for failure, and the job is lost anyhow. Since most alcoholics are short on self-confidence, they need maximum help and assurance of a successful outcome. If it comes to that, it is better to overtreat than to undertreat.

Objectivity. Membership in a particular profession may be a hindrance here, creating a tunnel vision unless specialized training in addiction has broadened one's horizons to the panoply of approaches other than one's own. Similarly, recovered alcoholics have a very understandable loyalty to the particular means that saved their lives, but this may blind them to the fact that what worked for them may be totally inappropriate for somebody else. This is true regardless of how they got sober; one hears equally enthusiastic loyalty to Antabuse, to AA, to aversion conditioning, or to any one of the many fine treatment centers throughout the country. It is the mark of the real professional to rise above personal bias and choose what is best for the client.

This is not only a matter of professional integrity; it may be crucial in saving a life. More than one alcoholic has turned suicidal after being told that AA, for instance, is the only way to sobriety; when AA fails to appeal, they decide they are hopeless and take their own lives. Some may need to buy time through Antabuse or aversion conditioning in order to achieve enough sobriety to profit from a program such as AA. Others may need to find out for themselves that they cannot do it alone and may need some physical leverage such as Antabuse, or some group support like AA.

Motivation for Treatment

It is now recognized that to say the client is not motivated is an escape on the part of the counselor. It is our job to motivate them (see Miller and Rollnick, 1992). There is much talk now of "early bottom" or "high bottom" or even "forced bottom." Since we know that forced treatment works, once we are sure of the diagnosis we do not passively sit by and let the patient hit bottom. Client-centered and nondirective approaches or timid, halfway measures are ineffective. A crisis can be forced. The effective motive will differ for each one: a divorce (not an idle threat), loss of job, finding oneself in jail. Loss of health may move one client, while another may say he wants to die anyway. But something can do it, if we can only find the key.

Some counselors are too quick to reassure, to relieve anxiety. At this point a little fear can be useful. To say "Don't worry" may feed denial and make the client feel good, but it doesn't save a person's life. Anxiety is not inappropriate when a life is threatened. Likewise, one must avoid being caught up in the client's web of excuses. And if it is the spouse who is the client, his or her anxiety and guilt should be utilized to get him or her some help whether the alcoholic/addict seeks help or not.

Someone else may have to make the decision. Many are far too sick to make a major decision regarding a terminal illness or to choose among a lot of alternatives. Of course, we have to motivate the person to cooperate, and eliminate the attitude of "What are *you* going to do about my drinking problem?" They must be motivated on the basis of their own welfare, not do it just for someone else's sake. This can backfire: "I'll get drunk and show you."

Intervention

Very often the most effective way to motivate a person to go into treatment is by a group intervention. The pendulum has swung from the opposite extreme of letting them hit bottom first, to a current fad of amateurs rushing in to do interventions. These must be carefully planned, under the guidance of one who is not only a trained addiction worker but one with special competence in intervention techniques. Of course, diagnosis must be certain, or tragic harm can be done to family relations. Timing is crucial: Just after a binge, when alcoholics are sick, sad, and sorry, is often the best time; don't wait until they are neither sad nor sorry, as they will feel little need for treatment. But many other factors may dictate a delay. Inappropriate persons must be screened out of the intervention team—those who might pounce on or browbeat the alcoholic. For those reasons the harsher term confrontation has been dropped. Most important, it must be done out of genuine *love*, not to satisfy one's own power needs (Ketcham and Gustafson, 1989).

Every member of the family over age five should come to the counselor's office for several sessions, where the process is explained and rehearsed for as long as four weeks. So that there are specific facts and not vague general allegations, it is useful to have each family member write out and read a list of times and events. Small children can play a part, since they know about it anyhow. It is powerful when Daddy's girl says, "Why do you drink that stuff when it makes you talk so funny or hurt mommy?" For whatever chivalrous reasons, a son may find it harder to face his alcoholic/addict mother, and husbands are usually more reluctant to confront their wives. Significant others besides family members may be able to make a useful contribution. The employer or a competent professional (physician, clergyman, friend) may add authority to the group. Experts disagree as to whether it should take place in the home or not, reporting high rates of success for each view.

The patient will try to play the interveners off against one another. Each must agree to maintain a united front; no party can feel sorry for the patient and spoil the unanimity. The counselor warns them what to expect: The subject will cry, accuse them of picking on him or her, of being unfair, of exaggerating. But they must promise not to settle for anything less than agreement to enter treatment. Sometimes there is refusal to enter treatment but a strong promise to join AA or NA. The team can agree only under a firm condition that if the alcoholic has a single drink he or she will enter treatment immediately. It must be explained that their fear of losing the person's love is unfounded; they will earn undying gratitude. There may be fear of failure, or that they will weaken and lose their nerve. Even if the person threatens to leave home, he should be told that it is better to do so sober and able to earn a living, so better to go to treatment first. The family must be warned not to be taken in by promises without agreement to a specific course of action, nor to allow the discussion to be diverted to other problems. They must not bluff, bargain, or debate. The tone must not be of anger or punishment, but of positive concern and hope.

In the planning session the group should face the fact that this will be an emotional drain; the counselor schedules a debriefing session for after the intervention. There they must agree to forget the past and hope for the future regardless of previous disappointments. The intervention team can become a support system when the person returns from treatment.

Although we have used this method successfully for decades (Lemere et al., 1958), it has been most usefully described in the writings and films of the Johnson Institute of Minneapolis. Its research and that of others shows that results with coerced patients can be superior to results with voluntary patients (Crosby and Bissell, 1989). Properly done, interventions succeed 97 percent of the time in getting the person into treatment, and the others plant a seed that may flower a year later. In a sense no intervention fails, because it educates the family and relieves them of the guilt of their codependency, regardless of whether the alcoholic gets help or not. The legal and ethical implications of intervention vis-à-vis informed consent are subtle, and lawsuits can occur.

Intervention can come from unexpected sources. We can train bartenders in the art of counseling alcoholic customers into treatment. A powerful ploy is to videotape alcoholics, with their permission, upon admission into the detoxification center or in arrests for drunk driving. Denial crumbles when they appear later with hair nicely done or clean-shaven and are confronted by the contrasting behavior and appearance on the tape.

The Drinking Test for Alcoholism

Most alcoholics can be reached through an explanation of the symptom progression charts, but a few whose denial prevents them from seeing that they have the symptoms of a disease can sometimes be reached by a test proposed by Marty Mann and others, whereby they find out for themselves. The test is only for alcoholics who are denying, and only after all other attempts have failed. After explaining that there is the same alcohol in a bottle of beer, a glass of wine, and an ounce of hard liquor (not a "drink" or cocktail containing more), give the client a strict quota of two of these drinks per day, every day, for six months.

If they can do this and never exceed two, they are probably not alcoholic. But they must be absolutely honest, making no exceptions and never transferring one day's ration over to the next day. It is not a valid test if someone else doles it out, or makes sure they stop or if they have to take such measures as leaving a party in order to keep within the quota. They must agree to come back if they exceed two even one time, for whatever reason or in whatever way. It may appear to be sending an alcoholic out to do more drinking, but for these cases it may be better than letting the client leave without any commitment, and it can convince them they are out of control.

Process of Referral

Instead of just giving a name and phone number, referral requires considerable attention to detail. Explicit instructions on how to get there may still not be enough, especially if shaky motivation fosters escape. In the light of good client–counselor rapport, actual transportation to the treatment facility can be considered an integral function of the counseling process rather than above and beyond one's duty. It is a more efficient use of the agency's time than losing the client after spending an hour or more motivating for treatment. At least the treatment center should be alerted to expect the client and agree to confirm arrival.

The client must be helped to know what to expect, as the fear of the unknown terrifies. Prior information on some detail about the personality or appearance of the therapist (for example, obesity or a beard) can engender a sense of confidence and prevent a negative impression. While generating a positive attitude, the counselor can warn that progress will not be instantaneous. Clients must be encouraged to realize that there is not so much a fear of facing reality without alcohol as inability to imagine reality without it, finding it hard to believe that they can function without a drink.

The counselor should avoid giving the impression that referral is a means of getting rid of the patient or a matter of last resort. Referral should be made while the relationship is good, not when it is going sour. The door should always be open for a return visit, and interest in the client's long-range recovery should be shown. If there is to be a next appointment, make the day, date, and time clear and explicit. In any case, a good rule is always to have the client walk out of the office with a card or pamphlet that has the counselor's name and phone number; it may be the bridge to sobriety when the client finds it in his pocket after a lost weekend, or at least some insurance against taking a drink when tempted. And to protect against violating confidentiality, the counselor must get a signed release if records are to be forwarded to the new facility.

Finally, referral is a two-way street. Too often alcoholism workers complain about lack of referral from other professionals but forget that they try to play God themselves and fail to refer clients to nonalcoholism agencies for problems that are beyond their scope.

Evaluation of Treatments

The referring counselor is not in a position to do evaluation research, but a few cautions may assist the counselor or inquirer in judging reports of claimed success.

There are four factors not quantifiable: First, each individual being unique, and alcoholism being so complex and variable with individuals, one can never be dogmatic about the effectiveness of any treatment for any individual. Second, a certain number of people are going to get well no matter what is done for them, just from the fact that somebody is at least paying attention to them. Third, spontaneous remission does occur in alcoholism, although rarely (Cary, 1989). Fourth, subjective bias and loyalty to one treatment modality may introduce subconscious distortions into one's perception of success rates.

When quantitative data are presented, a certain healthy scientific skepticism is justified in scrutinizing the claims that N number or percentage of cases have been successfully treated. Is N large enough to be valid? Is the sample a representative cross-section of the alcoholic population, or were selective factors at work? Does N include those who refused treatment or dropped out before completion? Comparable control groups are difficult to find, since we are reluctant to refuse treatment to some just for the sake of experimental design.

Most important is the time elapsed since completion of treatment. One year after discharge is the minimum time to have any significance. If a median time of sobriety is presented, one must look at how much the curve is skewed toward the short end of the sobriety period; that is, if a range of three months to one year of sobriety is given, a large number of cases may be bunched near three months and relatively few sober for nearly a year.

The criterion for success to be used is a matter of dispute. The final section of Chapter 8 made it clear that total abstinence is the only sensible goal to be proposed to patients, given the nature of the illness. Compared with total abstinence as a criterion, "improved" sounds too much like being just a little pregnant. A substitute addiction to tranquilizers would be a complicating factor.

The nature of the followup is crucial. Mail or secondhand reports that a subject is "doing all right" are too easily falsified by either the subject or the spouse who is ashamed to report failure. Purely negative criteria, such as not returning for treatment or not being arrested again, should not be taken as positive evidence of success: The subject may be in jail or in treatment somewhere else. Those who have died or are lost are sometimes allowed to appear as successes by the way the percentage of failures is reported.

Sources

The material in this chapter draws heavily on personal clinical experience. The items in the General Bibliography under "Intervention" (1988), Gallant (1987), Johnson Institute (1987), Johnson (1980, 1986), Ketcham and Gustafson (1989), Krupnick and Krupnick (1985), Marsh (1983), and M. Maxwell (1984) are useful and contain many references. One might also find it helpful to explore the social work journals. A Comp-Care pamphlet by Jon R. Weinberg, *Helping the Client with Alcohol-related Problems,* is an excellent guide for attorneys.

EVALUATION

Alcohol Health and Research World has a special focus issue, Winter 1988, 12(3):162–213 on treatment evaluation, with copious references for each article. Added evidence that treatment works is in D. C. Walsh et al., "A Randomized Trial of Treatment Options for Alcohol-abusing Workers" (1991). A very thoughtful essay about evaluation is "Methods for the Treatment of Chronic Alcoholism: A Critical Appraisal," by F. Baekeland, L. Lundwall, and B. Kissin, in volume 2 of R. J. Gibbins (ed.), *Research Advances in Alcohol and Drug Problems,* pp. 247–327. Throughout B. Kissin and N. H. Begleiter (eds.), *Treatment and Rehabilitation of the Chronic Alcoholic,* which is volume 5 of their *Biology of Alcoholism,* the methodological problems of evaluation are attended to.

PART FOUR

TREATMENT
and
REHABILITATION

CHAPTER 15

Overview of Treatments

T HE BRIGHT SIDE OF ADDICTION is recovery. Alcoholism is the most treatable of our major medical problems. We spend too much time saying "ain't it awful" and not enough on the joy of seeing people getting well, looking and feeling better, becoming taxpayers instead of tax liabilities, and on our high rates of recovery. After all, we never even ask, "What is your recovery rate?" in a cancer clinic! Studies from fifteen states indicate that money invested in treatment of addiction reduces future costs from medical complications, crime, accidents, and lost productivity.

Asking "Just what *do* you say to an alcoholic?" is like "Doctor, just how do you take out a gallbladder?" A cookbook approach is impossible. The "whole person" is a concept to which we often pay only lip service. Besides the addiction, each patient brings a unique set of other problems, which must be attended to if successful rehabilitation is to occur. We have already pointed out the need to assist the family with the problems they have developed as a result of living with an addict. Treatment thus becomes far more than the simple application of one approach to patient after patient.

Continuum of care means that for each patient an individualized treatment plan is formulated, providing for the gradual transition from detoxification through intensive treatment to long-range rehabilitation and restoration to normal living in the community. We can only list the stages briefly and make a few comments.

Detoxification

The percentage of alcoholics coming into treatment who need withdrawal from the drug alcohol in a hospital setting has been reported at 4 percent, 5 percent, or 7 percent—at most a small minority. But those few do need it very acutely, as it may be literally a matter of life and death. Getting blood alcohol level down to zero for other alcoholics is largely a matter of time and commonsense care. Much of this is being done now in subacute (not "nonmedical") dryout centers, which are not part of a hospital but have medical supervision and backup arrangements in case of need for quick transfer to a hospital. Withdrawal from tranquilizers and narcotics is practically never life-threatening, but all sedative/hypnotic withdrawal (such as from alcohol and sleeping pills) can be.

The decision whether to hospitalize depends on many factors. This *triage* decision is often made by an experienced nurse-practitioner or even by a police officer. Alcohol poisoning constitutes a medical emergency, especially since tolerance to a lethal dose does not increase proportionately to behavioral tolerance (Figure 3, in Chapter 4). Here a stomach pump, airway tube, life-support measures, and vigilance lest the patient choke on his or her own vomit are called for. Violent nausea may cause ruptured esophageal varices or Mallory-Weiss syndrome, and there is always danger of respiratory failure. Anyone drinking more than a fifth of liquor a day will certainly need medical supervision. Alcoholic seizures and DTs can be prevented by skilled medical management, which means specialized knowledge and experience the ordinary physician may not have. We noted in Chapter 4, Section B, that polydrug cases may exhibit a second withdrawal several days after the first is over, so other drug use must be routinely checked upon admission.

Numerous complications, including undiagnosed fractures and internal hemorrhage, may require hospital care but go unnoticed because the drug masks the pain. In addition, the smell of alcohol on the breath can cause a misdiagnosis of intoxication instead of diabetic coma, epilepsy, heart attack or stroke, brain injury or central nervous system disorder, uremic poisoning, or even acute psychosis.

Withdrawal by complete abstinence ("cold turkey") rather than by gradually tapering off is preferred if done at home, because neither the patient nor the family can control dosage well. But in either a hospital or a subacute detoxification center, the more addicted alcoholic is less liable to severe reactions if withdrawal is gradual. In these settings "tapering" may be appropriate. Many physicians borrow a principle from the established techniques of withdrawal from narcotics or barbiturates: the substitution of a calculated dose of a less addicting tranquilizer or sedative in controlled and decreasing doses to achieve withdrawal. Some experienced physicians even use decreasing doses of oral alcohol in a controlled environment to achieve DT-free withdrawal. Others prefer to give the ethanol intravenously, arguing that this route offers freedom from gastrointestinal irritation while giving less positive reinforcement for drinking. One very experienced physician tried four other drugs on one patient and finally gave ETOH to prevent fatal DTs, noting that the reason why alcoholics drink alcohol is because it works.

No matter which drug is chosen, it is mandatory that all staff personnel be aware of the dangers of substitute addiction, and protocol must include a finite date on which the patient is to be completely off such medication. Clearly a substitute addiction is neither helpful to the patient nor ethical for the physician. Hippocrates observed that "therapy" ought not make a patient worse.

Medical Management. In general, medical management of withdrawal is concerned with controlling or preventing (1) nausea and vomiting, (2) "shakes," (3) seizures of a *grand mal* type, (4) hallucinosis, and (5) sleeplessness. *Nau-*

sea and vomiting can be controlled with a nonsedative antinauseant such as Tigan. Some prefer frequent small doses of the phenothiazines (e.g., Thorazine) because of their sedation. *"Shakes"* and *seizures* can be managed with the benzodiazepine derivatives, such as Valium or Ativan, or with Xanax. Taractan, a phenothiazinelike drug, is also widely used because of its shorter half-life, but it does not have anticonvulsant effects and, in fact, may lower the convulsive threshold. Some have chosen to stay with the standard Dilantin for anticonvulsive management, using another rapidly absorbed, short-acting anticonvulsant in conjunction on the grounds that it requires three to five days of Dilantin to achieve therapeutic blood levels for seizure control. Others say this may be true in epilepsy but find that Dilantin itself controls alcoholic seizures from the start. The advantage of Dilantin is that it suppresses excitation without a rebound hyperexcitability. *Hallucinosis* is best controlled by vitamin B_1 (thiamine) and prevention or control of hypoxia to the brain. In practice this means management of pneumonias, obstructive lung diseases, anemias, and shock conditions concomitantly found with the condition of alcohol withdrawal. *Sedation* is perhaps most prudently managed by choosing a drug for control of either vomiting or seizures that has an adequate sleep side reaction. The $alpha_2$ agonist Clonidine is useful in detoxifying from opiates, followed by an opiate receptor antagonist like naltrexone (Revía) as a blocker.

Some general rules apply: If nausea and vomiting are present or if the level of consciousness is compromised, the intermuscular or intravenous route is preferable to anything given by mouth. Doses must be individualized and are known to vary with sex, age, smoking, body weight, and the health of the liver. Most drugs depend upon the liver for excretion, so duration of action of any such drug will be modified in the presence of reduced liver function. Whereas untreated DTs used to be more than 20 percent fatal, good nursing and adequate sedation have reduced this to zero in one hospital with more than fifty years' experience.

There is some evidence that addiction to alcohol and much organic damage are really due to the breakdown product of ethyl alcohol: acetaldehyde. For this reason those drugs that also break down to acetaldehyde, such as the barbiturates and paraldehyde, are suspect in managing withdrawal. Since paraldehyde is chemically almost identical with acetaldehyde, it should never be given to an alcoholic. Tranquilizers with no anticonvulsant capability and with high risk of addiction have little place in the management of alcoholism—for example, meprobamate (Miltown, Equanil). The patient needs to be educated to expect disturbance of sleep pattern for six months or more. Any sedative must be used sparingly, in a strictly controlled fashion, and must not lead to a new addiction.

Malnutrition and vitamin deficiency, especially of the vitamin B complex, have already been noted as common in alcoholics because of inadequate diet, excessive kidney excretion, and poor absorption from the gastrointestinal tract. For this last reason the needed vitamin supplement should be given either by injection or intravenously in the early phase of recovery. Later a good balanced diet with minimum added daily oral vitamins should suffice.

Decades ago Beard (Beard and Knott, 1969; Knott and Beard, 1967; Knott, 1986) exploded the myth that all alcoholics admitted to the hospital are dehydrated; the thirst may be from the drying effect of alcohol and from breathing through the mouth while unconscious, but mostly it is due to a shift of water from inside the body cells. The diuretic effect of rising BAC may be counteracted later by an antidiuretic hormone from the pituitary gland, which results in hyperfluidity (puffiness, edema) even if thirst is a complaint. Hence intravenous feeding of fluids is not indicated as a matter of routine, but only after true dehydration is diagnosed and overhydration is ruled out.

Excessive urination, perspiration, diarrhea, and vomiting all have contributed to loss of body salts. This will be aggravated by the presence of kidney dysfunction or diabetes mellitus. Screening should be done for abnormal sugar, potassium, or nitrogen in the blood. Although the literature speaks of magnesium deficiencies in alcoholism, it is prudent to avoid magnesium administration unless a deficit can be proved. Many American alcoholics self-medicate with magnesium-containing antacids, and deficiencies are rare; overdoses of magnesium can be lethal. Another caution is not to give iron unless iron deficiency is present. The alcoholic population has blood loss from the stomach or trauma plus folic acid deficiency as common causes of anemias. They also have a high incidence of liver damage. Inappropriate administration of iron can precipitate the irreversible condition of hemosiderosis.

Lastly, there is good evidence that plenty of TLC (tender loving care) can reduce the need for medical aids during withdrawal. Thus having a light in the room can prevent hallucinations, warm reassurance can reduce tremors, and understanding encouragement can dispel fear or despair, with resulting positive attitudes that speed up the body's recovery processes and can decrease the incidence of DTs. Another reason those features are helpful is that craving is largely psychological withdrawal. Good nursing, and the shared experience of recovered alcoholics with some training, can make a key contribution in this first phase of recovery (see O'Briant and Lennard, 1973). Note that "social (setting) detox" is not to be confused with "social model" treatment.

Treatment Methods

None of the above is really treatment for addiction, only for its immediate effects. The most important function of the detoxification center is not to bring the patient through one more crisis, but to serve as a bridge to definitive treatment, which should begin as soon as the patient's mental condition allows. A toxic brain can neither absorb nor remember the insights achieved in psychotherapy, nor can it project them for future behavior. There is ample research evidence (see Chapter 4, Section C, on the brain) to confirm the commonsense observation that this is true not only while the patient is still drinking but also for weeks after detoxification. Hence a short stay in a *recovery house* with light treatment and an introduction to AA has been found to be more practical than to rush severe-stage alcoholics directly into intensive treatment.

Treatment may involve several different modalities, and in any combination. Never should we think we are restricted to a choice of just one modality (Institute of Medicine, 1990a; Milkman et al., 1990; Moos et al., 1990). The individualized treatment plan should allow for flexibility if a change is required. It is clear from Chapter 8 that abstinence is the only realistic treatment goal for a true alcoholic.

Inpatient or residential settings have the advantages of better control over the patient and maximum opportunity to build up physical health, which are so important for the mental attitude of the patient (Walsh et al., 1991). Since the body of the alcoholic has adapted to the point of needing alcohol to function, the period just after withdrawal may require more difficult bodily adjustments than withdrawal itself and may thus need inpatient care even more from the third to the tenth day than during the first two or three days. A structured program puts order into the addict's life after perhaps years of irregular living habits. Diet, exercise, recreation, sleep, and medication can all be managed. An interdisciplinary team from the various professions should have a unified philosophy of treatment, which is important to avoid further confusing the patient, who is already confused enough. Length of stay should be dictated by the need of the patient, not by insurance coverage.

Outpatient treatment, however, even right from the start, has certain advantages (Crandell, 1988; V. Fox, 1974; Miller and Hester, 1986; Ruprecht, 1961). It is less expensive, does not create overdependency in patients but rather enlists their cooperation, may provide an occasion to involve the family earlier (for example, if they engage in transportation of the patient), does not give the impression that release from the hospital means the end of treatment, can be integrated with mission or shelter-type management (for example, the Salvation Army), is more acceptable to those who find a hospital threatening, and allows participation in a suitable local AA group, thus ensuring continuity.

Recent research has tended to pit outpatient against inpatient treatment, asking in effect the wrong question: "Which is better?" Well, which is better, a bandaid or major surgery? It obviously depends on whether you are treating a cut finger or acute appendicitis. The two might have equal effectiveness rates if appropriate placing always occurred. It may be that some reports of the superiority of outpatient treatment arise from the fact that the outpatient care is being done by certified counselors who know alcoholism and treat it as a primary illness, whereas the inpatient facility (even with JCAH approval) is staffed with psychotherapists clinging to an outmoded psychiatric approach. Certified counselors are not "amateurs"—see Chapter 21 on "The New Profession."

Alcoholics Anonymous

Twelve-Step programs such as AA, NA, and CA, to be dealt with in Chapter 17, are now recognized as being an important psychosocial treatment modality, not a religion. Numerically by far the most successful in dealing with alcoholics, AA does not always immediately appeal to every patient, and some preparation is often necessary for its attraction to work. If patients cannot stay sober for at least five days on their own, they will need some other help in breaking the habit-pattern so as to clear their heads enough to engage in the program. The 12 Steps can be an integral part of a treatment plan that includes prior or concomitant approaches (see Brown, 1985, by a recovered alcoholic who is also a Ph.D. psychologist).

Antabuse (Disulfiram)

In 1947 it was accidentally discovered that workers in the rubber industry had absorbed the sulfur compound disulfiram (tetraethylthiuram disulfide), which made them hypersensitive to alcohol, and by 1950 it was being marketed in America under the trade name Antabuse®. Temposil and Flagyl have been tried, but Antabuse remains the primary drug of this class and is now widely used with excellent results, in lower doses and with practically no side effects (R. Fox 1967a, 1973; Fuller et al., 1986; Martin H. Keller, 1976; McNichol and Logsdon, 1988).

Dr. Ruth Fox, certainly an ardent admirer of AA, made a strong case (1958) that far from any antagonism there is perfect compatibility between AA and Antabuse. It is simply a useful means of breaking the habit and buying sober time in order to participate in AA. One physician credits Antabuse with saving more than a quarter of a million lives, for which all alcoholics should be grateful. Purported dangers and side effects are largely related to its earliest use, when dosage was much higher than what is common now, and to the practice, now largely abandoned, of giving the patient a little experience of the Antabuse reaction as a deterrent. Label warnings are there largely to protect the maker in possible lawsuits. In short, one suspects that opposition to its use today could be symptomatic of denial or of resistance to the idea of sobriety. The fact that response to the suggestion of Antabuse serves as a good test of one's motivation for recovery lends credence to the suspicion.

Antabuse is not a psychoactive drug, so there is no danger of substitute addiction. It blocks the enzyme action necessary for the breakdown of acetaldehyde, a product of alcohol metabolism. Harmless as long as no alcohol is imbibed, it causes acetaldehyde to build up in the body if one drinks alcohol. The resulting reaction is characterized by flushed face, rapid pulse, pounding headache, difficult breathing, nausea and vomiting, sweating, blurred vision, etc. Since it takes at least five days for the Antabuse to be eliminated from the body, the alcoholic knows he will have this reaction if he drinks before that time. It thus acts as a guard against drinking, with the advantage that the decision is made only once a day, usually in the morning and away from the temptation to drink. That frees the mind of any consideration of drink for the next four or five days, or even up to two weeks.

Antabuse should never be taken without a doctor's prescription, based on a medical examination and the patient's consent after a clear explanation to the patient of how Antabuse works. The patient must be willing to use it as an aid toward desired sobriety. Otherwise he will resent it and soon find an excuse to stop. If given without his full knowledge, he might drink and precipitate a reaction. He must understand that he cannot take foods or medicines containing any alcohol (except foods cooked so that the alcohol has been evaporated out). Paraldehyde must be avoided. A few people do not absorb Antabuse into the bloodstream, which can be checked by a test of breath, urine, or blood.

Disulfiram is not a total therapy in itself but can be extremely useful in early stages of recovery. It cannot stop a person who wants to drink—all the patient has to do is stop taking the Antabuse for five days or longer—but it can help those who want to avoid alcohol and cannot do it alone. Some take it as insurance before holidays or stress times. The unwilling can pretend to swallow the pill and spit it out later, or even swallow it and vomit later. For this reason mandated Antabuse is crushed and given in orange juice. The impotence attributed to Antabuse is probably psychic, possibly also due in part to the sex partner's reaction to the bad breath it initially creates in some patients. There are very few, if any, for whom it is dangerous (McNichol and Logsdon, 1988), and in any case it is far less dangerous and damaging than alcohol, or even aspirin.

To those who call it a crutch, the obvious answer is that prescribing a crutch is good medicine while a broken leg heals, and alcoholism is a far more serious ailment than a fracture. Another answer is that some psychologists are horrified that AAs need the "crutch" of AA all their lives (not entirely fair, since AA is also a whole spiritual way of life). One ardent AA who got drunk every time he went off Antabuse decided that if epileptics take Dilantin all their lives, and heart patients take digitalis, it made sense for him to take Antabuse the rest of *his* life. Antabuse is particularly helpful for impulsive drinkers, whereas aversion conditioning may be preferable for those who experience craving.

Aversion Conditioning

In 1935 Charles Shadel, a recovered alcoholic, began treating alcoholics by establishing a conditioned response whereby the alcoholic experiences nausea at the sight, taste, or smell of alcoholic beverages. He compared it loosely to Pavlov's conditioning a dog to salivate at the sound of a bell. An injection of the drug emetine, which naturally produces nausea and vomiting, is used as the unconditioned stimulus. The conditioned stimulus is exposure to the whole range of alcoholic beverages, especially to one's favorite. That eventually produces a reaction of nausea even without the emetine, resulting in an aversion against drinking. It differs from Antabuse in being psychological instead of physiological, since it is the sight or smell of liquor that triggers the reaction and not the actual presence of alcohol in the body.

The idea goes back to ancient times, when the Romans tried to deter alcohol abuse by putting a tiny scorpion in the bottom of a wine glass. The reason that did not work is basic to understanding the Shadel process: Any amount of alcohol in the bloodstream would spoil the conditioning. Here any alcohol ingested is immediately vomited before absorption, and if some is accidentally absorbed the conditioning session is canceled. Timing is crucial here, as we saw when explaining why a hangover does not act as a deterrent. For the same reason, many attempts to use this approach in other treatment centers have shown poor results, since so much depends on precise technique.

Like disulfiram, aversion conditioning is not a total therapy. But, especially when coupled with other means such as AA and good followup, it has resulted in recovery rates as high as 78 percent for one year and 63 percent for four years using stringent criteria of total abstinence (Smith, 1979, 1982; Smith and Little, 1983, p. 436). It is not infallible, and patients are told that they can break down the conditioned response. It does not make it impossible for one to drink, but makes it possible for one not to drink. It is not a punishment but simply an associative learning process one freely chooses in order to counteract an undesirable habit. The aversion counteracts (1) the craving or appeal of alcoholic beverages and (2) the many stimuli that have conditioned the alcoholic to drink, for example at certain times or places. It serves to break the pattern and to provide a nondrinking life-style as a condition for pursuing permanent recovery. In common with Antabuse and 12-Step programs, it attacks alcoholism as the primary problem, assuming that even if it were originally due to some psychic trauma at age two, it is a little late to do anything about that, but something can be done about the pathological drinking. It must not be confused with attempts to condition alcoholics to drink socially.

A mild faradic sting (not convulsive electric shock) has been successfully substituted for emetine in the Shadel conditioning process when vomiting is contraindicated (Jackson and Smith, 1978). Covert sensitization, wherein the patient pairs a mental image of nausea and vomiting with an imagined drink, is reported to have some success but takes a great deal of time and is less effective unless the patient has a very vivid imagination.

Chemotherapy

The opiate receptor antagonist naltrexone (Revía, formerly Trexan), long used in treatment of opiate addicts, was approved by the FDA in 1995 as useful in the treatment of alcoholism. Neither a deterrent like Antabuse nor an aversion therapy, it acts as a blocker at receptor sites in the brain so that al-cohol does not produce its usual euphoric reward. Since it does not block other effects, it may harm the unmotivated patient who might try to override it in seeking for the euphoria. Preliminary tests show a 50 percent reduction in relapse, and reduced craving in some patients. It is nonaddictive, and NCADD and NIAAA have given it cautious approval, warning that it is not a full program of recovery. Patients need counseling as to its effects, side ef-fects, and noneffects. It must be prescribed by physicians with specialized training in addiction, and then only as an adjunct to psychosocial therapy such as AA. Selection criteria include a history of relapse, at least eight days of total abstinence before starting it, and freedom from active hepatitis or liver failure.

Antabuse, naltrexone, and aversion conditioning all differ in treatment role from the psychoactive (mind-altering) drugs sometimes vainly used in an attempt to treat alcoholism. We have stressed the danger of substitute addic-tion to sedatives and tranquilizers, while noting their legitimate use during withdrawal; they have no place in the long-term therapy of alcoholics. Even nonaddictive tranquilizers are more harm than help, since they can tranquil-ize to the point that the patient does not care very much about anything, in-cluding recovery. At one time LSD (lysergic acid) was used in the hope that the psychedelic experience would give a self-actualizing insight that would obviate any future need to drink. Several reviews (for example, Costello, 1969; Ditman, 1967; Smart et al., 1966, 1967) of the literature concur that the percentage of success is no better than without LSD; those few who get well are the stable personalities who recover from alcoholism regardless. The same is true of other hallucinogens; marijuana, if anything, seems to lead to relapse in recovered alcoholics. It seems better to let nature restore the bal-ance rather than tamper further with the complex brain biochemistry in ways that can backfire.

Methadone is a substitute for heroin and highly addictive; it has no coun-terpart in alcoholism treatment and is contrary to the usual philosophy of a drug-free goal. But police seem to be unanimous that it is the lesser of two evils, preventing an average of 147 crimes a year per addict.

Psychiatrists use a wide array of drugs for various neurotic and psychotic conditions: major and minor tranquilizers, antidepressants, stimulants, anti-psychotics, hypnotics, antianxiety drugs, and other drugs being developed continually. Many of them are addicting; a "nonaddicting" psychoactive pill is probably one that is too new for us to have found out the truth. Most po-tentiate with alcohol, and none are specific therapy for alcoholism. A few are used for treating conditions other than alcoholism; for example lithium or the tricyclic antidepressants (Aventyl, Elavil, Triavil, Tofranil, and others, but not the MAO inhibitors) may be legitimately prescribed for alcoholics who have affective (bipolar, manic-depressive) psychosis. The prescribing physician should be aware that the patient is a recovering alcoholic, and dosage must be carefully monitored. In general, patients need to be educated that amphetamines do not succeed in controlling weight and only make depression worse on the rebound; that sleeping pills and antianxiety pills only work for a short time; and that there is no magic pill for alcoholism.

Physical Rehabilitation

Psychosomatic medicine has taught us that feeling good physically can do wonders for mental attitudes. Recalling from Chapter 4 the damage that prolonged drinking can do to every organ of the body, it is clear that a large part of treatment is restoration to good physical health. Directors of treatment centers are often so occupied with specific therapies that they lose sight of the importance of the following.

Diet. Malnutrition and, especially, vitamin deficiency have been mentioned frequently. While avoiding fads, such as massive dosages of vitamins, a well-balanced diet is important. To avoid big fluctuations in blood sugar, avoid all refined sugar and carefully balance carbohydrates with proteins. (A badly damaged liver cannot handle the amino acids from too much protein.) Since meat, fish, eggs, and cheese are more expensive than macaroni and other staples of institutional food, this will increase treatment costs. The same is true of fresh fruits and vegetables. But the importance of eating well cannot be overemphasized. Food should also be attractively served, as the recovering alcoholic often lacks an appetite. Excessive coffee should be avoided.

Because the vitamin B complex is so important for neural functioning, its administration was observed to work dramatic improvement in routinely undernourished alcoholic patients. This led to the advocacy of massive doses of vitamins. Now a good vitamin supplement is certainly called for in these patients, but one cannot abuse nature with impunity. Megavitamin therapy using massive or gross doses became a fad, with predictable reactions. Except for people with inborn defects of vitamin metabolism, these massive doses have been shown to be not only unnecessary and useless, but also harmful and possibly fatal (for a good summary of the medical/scientific evidence, see "Nutrition as Therapy," Consumer Reports, January 1980, pp. 21–24). Thus large doses of vitamin B_1 may destroy vitamin B_{12}. Excessive vitamin C can destroy 50 percent or more of the vitamin B_{12} in a meal, cause kidney damage, and cause "rebound scurvy" in newborns of mothers taking massive doses, since nature apparently stops supplying it in the child. Vitamins A, B_3, B_6, C, D, and K can all harm the fetus (Robe, 1982, pp. 108–10). Several vitamins, including niacin, when taken in excess are known to cause liver and kidney damage, and vitamins A, D, and E in gross dosage have all been indicted. It is not true that only the fat-soluble vitamins are harmful, as if the water-soluble ones are just flushed out; the tubules of the kidney can be severely burned in the process. Careful reading of one popular book on megavitamins leaves the distinct impression that the "cures" are due not to megavitamins but to the well-balanced, low-carbohydrate, high-protein diet the book advocates.

Nevertheless, many nutritional diseases in alcoholics are treatable by vitamin therapy, when prescribed by a physician after a specific diagnosis. Thus pellagra, with its symptoms of diarrhea, gross skin disorders, and mental confusion often responds quickly to the vitamin B complex. The Wernicke-Korsakoff syndrome and beriberi are other examples. Polyneuropathy with impaired walking can be alleviated by vitamin B_1 treatment.

Recreation and Exercise. Alcoholics/addicts may have been getting little more exercise than sitting on a bar stool, and no other recreation than drinking. Along with good nutrition, they need help in developing ways to entertain themselves and opportunities for play (Myers, 1987). We can recommend outdoor exercise, a variety of sports, and an appreciation that walking is not only good physical exercise but also a way of getting back in contact with their world. Good conversation activates one's potential more than passively watching television. Hobbies, arts and crafts, music, and a library of books and magazines can all contribute to recovery. All this, along with a regimen of regular hours and good living habits, may have the added benefit of promoting a good night's sleep without any pills. Learning a trade or refurbishing old skills can serve the double purpose of occupying one's mind and preparing for future employment.

Education

One national study placed "learning about alcoholism" as the most important part of therapy. Mere passive attendance at dull lectures is not education, especially while the brain is still toxic. Nevertheless, it is of utmost importance that the patients be made to understand what alcoholism is, how their bodies react to alcohol, and the folly of trying to drink like other people. Much guilt and shame will be alleviated and a sense of self-esteem promoted through realization that "I'm neither weak-willed nor crazy, but just physiologically different from nonalcoholics."

Psychotherapy

Individual and group counseling have always been major components of alcoholism treatment. Each takes many forms. *Individual* counseling may range from the motivational counseling at referral or intake as described in the previous chapter, through intensive sessions with a trained addictions counselor during treatment proper, to depth psychotherapy for underlying problems later by a psychiatrist (M.D.), a clinical psychologist (Ph.D.), or a psychiatric social worker (M.S.W.). *Group* counseling most commonly occurs under a trained alcoholism worker in either inpatient or outpatient alcoholism treatment settings, but AA meetings may be considered a form of nonprofessional group therapy. Given that each human being is unique, there should always be individual contact with a counselor throughout treatment; lack of this is a severe deficiency in some treatment centers.

Individual Counseling. From its own literature, psychiatry, and especially psychoanalysis, admits a very poor rate of success as a therapy for alcoholism. That is so largely because of the old tendency to conceive of alcoholism as a symptom of inner conflict or escape from psychic stress, rather than as a primary pathology (see Chapters 7 and 8). Analysis of hidden motives or past causes is not only ineffective but can even worsen the drinking. At best, this approach only produces a better-adjusted alcoholic, not a recovered one.

However, at least 20 percent of alcoholism is secondary or reactive, and here the underlying psychopathology must be treated. "Just treat the addiction and everything else will clear up" is simplistic and dangerous. In addition, many recovered alcoholics will need psychotherapy for residual problems after sobriety has been achieved, and most will need some kind of counseling in vocational, marital, or other adjustments. Obviously this is best done by a therapist who understands the nature of addiction and the danger spots for a recovered alcoholic (see Lawson et al., 1984; J. A. Lewis et al., 1988; Metzger, 1987; and Royce, 1984, 1985a).

Group Counseling. There are some distinct advantages to therapy in small groups, whether AA or otherwise, which are largely composed of alcoholics who are either recovered or recovering (here the distinction is meaningful). There is a sense of belonging and acceptance that puts the newcomer at ease, a depth of understanding rarely achieved by one who has not experienced alcoholism personally, and a penetration of defensiveness and denial because an alcoholic is more likely to accept insights or criticism from a fellow alcoholic. (See Altman and Crocker, 1982; Corey and Corey, 1992; Edelwich and Brodsky, 1992; Flores, 1988; Perez, 1986.) Groups are often the best way to involve the family in treatment.

We must warn, however, that useful as a strong confrontation can be in getting a person into treatment, there is little place for it in recovery. The newly recovering person is too sick and lacking in self-esteem to be stripped of defenses when there is insufficient time to rebuild ego strength. Suicide can be the result. The Synanon "hot seat" approach may or may not be effective on hardened street-drug addicts, but it is inappropriate for most alcoholics.

Positive Therapy. Whether group or individual, it seems that the most appropriate psychotherapeutic modes are those that focus on the present and future rather than on the past. Examples are the reality therapy of William Glasser, the existential here-and-now logotherapy of Viktor Frankl, the rational-emotive therapy (RET) of Albert Ellis, and other such nonanalytic therapies. Self-management, positive motivation, and attitude change—especially in building up one's sense of self-esteem—are the cardinal features in most of those approaches, along with learning some good problem-solving techniques. Psychodrama and role-playing can be very useful under a skilled therapist because of their appeal to both imagination and emotion. Transactional analysis (TA) can be useful provided one does not get too involved in analyzing the games people play, or think of addiction as merely learned behavior that can be easily unlearned.

Because of the toxic action of alcohol on the brain, alcoholics may be less able to function than they appear. The result is that we may have unrealistic expectations of their performance, which can only mean frustration, a sense of failure, and lowered self-esteem for the patient and therapist. Cognitive and insight-oriented therapies may require more verbal mediation or abstract thinking than the patient can master; patients may resort to just repeating key words without inner growth. Behavioral and social-skill approaches may be more efficacious.

Just as no dosages were given when outlining medical management, no details of counseling will be attempted here for the same reason—that this is not a treatment manual. In any event, one does not become a trained counselor-therapist by reading a book any more than one becomes a surgeon by reading a medical treatise. Addiction counseling differs from other therapy; it demands knowledge and training from specialists. Alcoholics are usually skilled manipulators or con artists and have their own forms of rationalization. The counselor does well to listen rather than talk; in that sense the session should be client-centered even though it cannot be nondirective. The patient should never be allowed to dump all responsibility on the counselor, which many are prone to do. Transference and countertransference should be thoroughly understood; sexual attraction between therapist and client does occur, and a genuine interest must never be misinterpreted as a romantic interest. Lest the counselor become a codependent, he or she must be trained in termination techniques and the need to release rather than hold on to clients or allow them to hold on.

Hypnosis. In the past some have strongly advocated the use of hypnosis for the treatment of alcoholism. When used by a responsible professional, the technique has some value in diagnosis and as an adjunct to therapy. But its limitations are now recognized, chiefly because the effects do not last, being too artificial and superficially imposed in contrast to real growth from within. However, it is useful for diagnostic investigation of deep-seated problems while defenses are down and for promoting relaxation. Intravenous sodium pentothal is useful for the same two purposes and is not addictive when used in this way (Smith, Lemere, and Dunn, 1971).

Relaxation. Most patients have been anxious and tense, which inclines them to turn to chemicals to relax. Self-hypnosis can be taught for this purpose, individually or in groups. Therapeutic massage, records or tapes, deep-muscle relaxing exercises, biofeedback for tension control, transcutaneous nerve stimulators, progressive muscle relaxation, transcendental meditation (TM), and any drug-free means of promoting relaxation are to be encouraged.

Other Proposed Treatments

Nearly every possible approach known to human ingenuity has been proposed as a treatment for alcoholism at one time or another. Most have not stood the test of time. We have already noted the failure of LSD, anectine, Flagyl, and carbon dioxide, and can list others that have joined them in obscurity: lobotomy, electroconvulsive shock, spinal puncture, animal charcoal, salt, benzedrine, hormones such as ACTH and thyroid extract, and propranolol (Inderal).

A few have promise, or at least cannot be discarded without further testing. When *biofeedback* is used to control certain semiautomatic body functions, it gives some people a new sense of mastery over themselves instead of being at the mercy of forces beyond their control; they thus gain more control over the choice not to drink. It requires persistent effort and a skilled instructor but is worth pursuing. *Acupuncture* has been used in China for centuries; in terms of Western physiology, it may counteract addiction by stimulating neurotransmitters or endorphins. It is being credited with real success in treating addiction to alcohol, heroin, and cocaine.

A disputed question is whether alcoholics and street-drug addicts should be treated in the same facility. We say street drugs, because if we ask about prescription drugs the question is moot; most alcoholics also misuse prescription drugs. The problem is more sociocultural, as the two populations differ notably in attitudes and values. There is a tendency for each to look down on the other as inferior, or weird. Lifestyles are so different that there are serious problems in living together. A review of the literature indicates that the majority experience favors separate treatment. At least coordinated planning is called for, but alcoholism workers fear that even this may obscure the numerical preponderance of alcoholics and dilute their education and prevention campaigns.

Conclusion

Again we insist that no one treatment approach should be thought of to the exclusion of combining with others (Milkman and Shaffer, 1985). Whether from a desire for omnipotence or a lack of appreciation of how they can work together, many therapists seem afraid to complement their professional efforts with referral to Alcoholics Anonymous, while many members of AA seem unaware of their own long tradition of cooperation with non-AA so earnestly advocated in the writings of their cofounder, Bill W.

Those who report that no treatment is as good as "standard" treatment are no doubt referring to outmoded approaches with 10 to 15 percent recovery rates, perhaps unaware of newer methods that yield 70 to 90 percent success. Individual training and personalities of treatment staff might again be more important than differences in treatment modality.

Like patients with any chronic illness, addicts can be frustrating at times, and can relapse in discouraging ways. Psychotics who have been tranquilizing themselves with alcohol will erupt into bizarre symptoms. But the work can also be very gratifying. Years ago physicians commonly avoided treating alcoholics because they smelled up the office waiting room, didn't pay their bills, and got drunk again. Now a growing number of physicians say they enjoy treating alcoholics because they like to see patients get well and recover the glow of health and a zest for living.

Sources

Probably the best bibliographic help are the references cited in the various ongoing series listed at the head of our General Bibliography: *Advances in Alcohol and Substance Abuse;* Kissin and Begleiter, *Biology of Alcoholism;* Galanter, *Recent Developments in Alcoholism;* and Gibbins et al., *Research Advances in Alcohol and Drug Problems,* plus the ASAM/RSA journal *Alcoholism: Clinical and Experimental Research,* Part IV of Estes and Heinemann (eds.), *Alcoholism: Development, Consequences, and Interventions* (1986), contains ample references, as does Bean and Zinberg, *Dynamic Approaches to the Understanding and Treatment of Alcoholism* (1981). See also the works of S. Gitlow, M. M. Glatt, G. Strachan, Tarter and Sugerman, and S. Zinberg.

EDUCATION FOR PHYSICIANS

ASMA's *Principles of Addiction Medicine* (1994) is probably the best source for education of physicians—see Appendix. Project Cork at Dartmouth Medical School pioneered this subject. Entire issues of *Alcohol Health and Research World,* Fall 1983, 8(1) and 1994, 18(2), and "Alcoholism Education for Physicians and Medical Students: An Overview," *Alcohol Health and Research World,* Spring 1979, 3(3):2–9, all give ample references. The Addiction Research Foundation in Toronto produced a booklet by the Ontario Medical Association, *Diagnosis and Treatment of Alcoholism for Primary Care Physicians.* On AIDS, see the AMSAODD 1987 and 1988 listings in the General Bibliography, as well as those under "AIDS" (1988), and Siegel (1988). Interesting is Joseph J. Zuska, "Wounds Without Cause," *Bulletin of the American College of Surgeons,* October 1981, pp. 5–10.

TREATMENT OF OTHER DRUG ADDICTIONS

Lerner, W. D., and M. Barr (eds.), *Handbook of Hospital Based Substance Abuse Treatment.*

Levin, Jerome D., *Treatment of Alcoholism and Other Addictions.* Aronson, New York, 1987.

Lewis, Judith A., et al., *Substance Abuse Counseling: An Individualized Approach.*

Milkman, H. B., et al., *Treatment Choices for Alcoholism and Substance Abuse.*

Pita, Dianne D. *Addictions Counseling: A Practical Guide to Counseling People with Chemical and Other Addictions.*

Schuckit, Marc A., *Drug and Alcohol Abuse: A Clinical Guide to Diagnosis and Treatment.* 2d ed. Plenum, New York, 1984.

Wesson, D. R., and W. Ling, "Medications in the Treatment of Addictive Disease," *Journal of Psychoactive Drugs,* 1991, 23(4):365–85.

CHAPTER 16

Rehabilitation

J UST TO STOP drinking or taking drugs would be boring. The recovering person must develop a new life-style. What one does to stop using is less important than what one does to remain stopped—probably one reason some research suggests that all treatments without long-range rehabilitation work equally well. "Aftercare" is a misleading term; it should be "continuing care." For lasting results, treatment requires at least one year. The first twenty-one or twenty-eight days may be in a treatment center and the remaining eleven months on an outpatient basis, but we should never allow talk of twenty-eight-day treatment as if it were all over upon discharge. Given the chronic nature of the illness, it is wiser to think of the recovery process as lasting not one but two to three or even five years.

Freedom, Not Deprivation

"White knuckle sobriety" refers to people who are barely hanging on to abstinence but are not comfortable even clean and sober (DuWors, 1992). In contrast, truly recovered alcoholics move easily in a drinking society, serenely accepting the fact that others drink while they choose not to. Happy in their sobriety, these people do not consider themselves unfortunately deprived of the pleasures of drinking, but rather free of its compulsion and misery. Those who picture all recovered persons as pining for some way to use again successfully have not known the many who are delighted that all they have given up is hangovers and headaches, and have come to appreciate the joy of living and spiritual growth they might otherwise never have known (K. O'Connell, 1994).

Recovery Takes Time

All this does not occur automatically. Addiction is diffuse, encroaching upon every aspect of one's life. Even if intervention arrests the progression in its early or middle stages, many changes in life habits have occurred over a fair length of time. It may require a comparable length of time to reverse the changes. The modified Glatt chart in Chapter 6 lists in its ascending right half the many steps involved in full recovery. Admission of the problem and cessation of using, by whatever means, are only the beginning (see Wallen, 1993).

One must learn that addiction is an illness, see recovered persons functioning, discover that one is not alone or hopeless. Fears begin to diminish, physical appearance improves, sleep and meals start to become regular. A new hope dawns, and belief that a different life is possible generates the optimism known as the honeymoon or pink cloud stage. Thinking begins to clear and become realistic, as various adjustments are faced and self-discipline grows. A returning sense of self-esteem is bolstered by acceptance from others, including, perhaps, initial reconciliation with the family. Emotional stability is enhanced as one learns to trust and is trusted. The desire to escape passes, as the old rationalizations are unmasked and one accepts both oneself and a new way of life. Appreciation of real values and a rebirth of ideals may lead to a new interest in spiritual values.

Physical, Mental, Social

Figure 6, a chart by Dr. Margaret Mantell, adapted from Dr. Robert Gordon Bell, depicts three phases of recovery that occur over two to three years. The first year is predominantly physical recovery, which continues through three years. About halfway through the first year, emotional-psychological recovery gains in importance, and dominates the second year. Toward the end of the first year maturation and integration into full social living begin; they reach full bloom in the third year. There is, of course, much overlap and individual variation. Mantell generalizes that only 10 percent of total recovery takes place in the treatment center, 90 percent after returning to the community.

After inpatient treatment, the process may continue in recovery homes (halfway houses or more graduated aftercare transitional facilities called quarter or three-quarter houses), where regimen is gradually relaxed and more autonomy given. This supportive environment is more necessary when the patient has been a homeless drifter or otherwise leading an unstructured life. For others the family home may provide the support and stability needed. Scheduled return visits with a counselor or therapy group after discharge should be included in the package cost of treatment. Outpatient clinics and 12-Step meetings can provide invaluable guidance and serve as fixed navigational points as the new voyage through life gathers momentum. Planning life after discharge should begin early in treatment, not on the last day.

Not All Smooth Sailing

Note that the Mantell chart does not graph progress as a smooth upward line but realistically indicates occasional slumps and crisis periods. Those do not occur at exactly six months or one year of sobriety, for example, but tend to occur at five to seven months, or eleven to thirteen months, and so on. The recovering alcoholic becomes as restless as a caged lion, moody, depressed, or

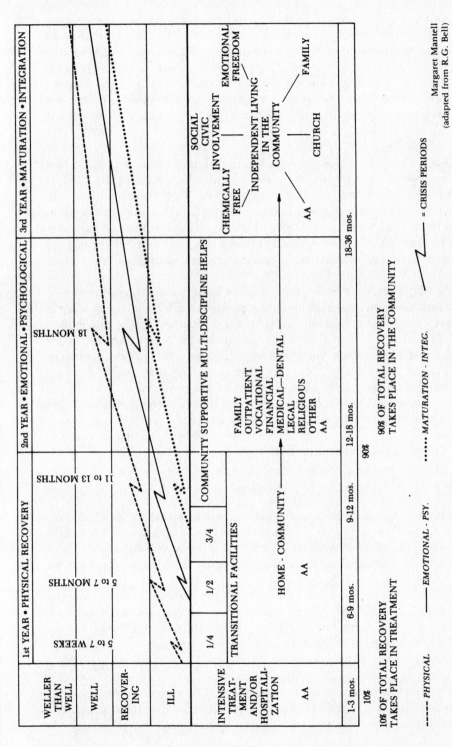

Figure 6 The Two- to Three-Year Recovery Process

grandiose. Sobriety may still be shaky, and there may even be a brief relapse, but this may just serve to confirm what is being heard in the group sessions about the need for total surrender and avoidance of compromise. The normal growth curve is never a smooth line, and occasional backsliding and plateaus are common. Too much attention to them could result in a self-fulfilling prophecy, but in general some knowledge of the problem by both counselor and patient eliminates the surprise factor and reassures that progress is normal.

"Weller than Well." These words in Figure 6 convey the notion that recovered persons not only get well but become better adjusted than before. This is somewhat controversial, but is not unique to Mantell; Pursch, Milam, and other authorities speak this way, and there seems to be scientific confirmation in the research of Mellor et al. (1986). The reason is that they must learn how to cope with life's stresses without the moderate use of drugs like alcohol available to others—just as a mild heart attack can teach good health practices conducive to a longer life.

Sensibly pursued, this is a much sounder ideal than the opposite: to hide from reality behind the illness and use it as an excuse for not coping. That is the point of a brief but forceful article entitled "Reality Can Be Uncomfortable" in the July 1971 *AA Grapevine,* reprinted in the November 1976 "classic" issue of that monthly. The article recounts cases where members refuse to take Steps 4 and 5 because it makes them uncomfortable, avoid 12th Step calls and even employment because they are "not comfortable around non-AAs," or otherwise keep themselves wrapped in the cocoon that is their idea of AA. Contrariwise, the article contends, learning to cope with life, people, and situations is vital to growth, which means accepting the challenges of life even though perhaps uncomfortable.

Physical

We have seen that there is considerable evidence now that the residual toxic effects of alcohol, especially on the brain as shown by brain wave studies, CAT scans, and psychological tests, persists two to five years after detoxification. Add the damage that, as we saw in Chapter 4, Section C, can occur to every other organ in the body. For instance, a computer fed eighteen tests of liver function will diagnose alcoholism 90 percent of the time even six months after detoxification. The "Physical Rehabilitation" section in Chapter 15 must be applied for a minimum of one year and probably much longer.

That should be with as little medication as possible and a maximum stress on good health habits (Myers, 1987). Exercise, recreation, relaxation exercises, and a balanced diet are far more useful than any chemical help. The effort should include not only strict avoidance of sleeping pills but also moderating excessive use of coffee and cigarettes. Moderation in these areas often makes sobriety easier because of a general sense of well-being. Even physicians sympathetic to Alcoholics Anonymous point to the irony of their using huge quantities of one drug while discussing avoidance of another; they laud the growing use of decaffeinated coffee and avoidance of smoking at AA meetings.

The above cautions do not rule out the continued use of medicines that a knowledgeable physician may prescribe for a recovered person's persistent or recurring medical problems. As in any chronic illness, continued contact with the physician is called for. The treatment center should make an informative referral back to the patient's own physician upon discharge. The doctor should understand the emotional and family aspects of living in recovery. Medications to prevent heart attacks, strokes, or chronic seizures; some non-addictive antidepressants; or medicine for diabetes and other metabolic or nutritional disorders may be necessary for the remainder of one's life and are not to be construed as inimical to sobriety (see R.S., 1981). On the other hand, there is no such thing as a nonaddictive pain pill, except possibly aspirin. A skilled physician can prescribe other means to cope with pain: nonsteroidal anti-inflammatory medicines, muscular relaxants, massage therapy, systematic relaxation, or self-hypnosis. If pain medication must be given, it should be carefully administered in hospital or by another person.

Marijuana. One caution cannot be put too strongly: Whatever one may feel about marijuana for others, it is very dangerous for recovered alcoholics. Experience confirms reports in the literature (see *Patient Care Magazine*, January 1975, for a summary) that even mild marijuana use can lull one's defenses and eventually lead to a relapse. The artificial euphoria may be considered a boon to others, but even mild unrealism is something the recovered alcoholic cannot afford. Marijuana use is usually accompanied by drinking, so the social setting is not conducive to sobriety. After use, "cotton mouth" or "the munchies" (hypoglycemia?) can be mistaken for a need for alcohol.

Mental

If addiction is not in the bottle but in the person, rehabilitation of mental and emotional states is vital. Positive attitudes, renewed self-esteem, and emotional stability must be built up if sobriety is to be permanent. Alcoholics must be satisfied that life without alcohol is preferable, with a conviction that they can stay sober, in spite of previous discouragement. Any notion of weak will must be shown false in view of their strength in getting a drink when they wanted one. But no pledges or promises or other added hurdles need be introduced.

It is not enough to spend the rest of one's life running away from alcohol and other drugs. Positive goals and a new life plan can be threatening in the early stages of recovery, but one could write out two lists: one of what alcohol had been doing to their lives, and one of what they would like for the future. The former might list damage to health, the cost of liquor, family disruption, loss of memory, morning depression, and the like. The second could list not only financial goals, but such things as hobbies, enjoyment of beauty, friends, fun—many cannot remember having fun without liquor. In many ways they have to learn to live all over again. In the case of the adolescent, it may mean learning for the first time, since the patient never had a normal adolescence. This may seem a gigantic task; it will have to be mollified by "one day at a time" realism.

Conflicts must be resolved and resentments removed, or relapse is inevitable. Escapism and self-deception diminish as one learns to stop playing games with oneself. Such growth is often achieved best in groups. The AA member may say, "Yes, you might do it on your own, but if you do it with us it will be fun." The discovery that one is not alone, that others have the same fears, is not only reassuring but can banish self-pity. Most good treatment centers have followup groups meeting regularly, and group sessions are a regular event in halfway houses. Those groups should include the spouse or the whole family.

One ingenious and successful means of followup is to have Al-Anon members, usually housewives with time at home, volunteer to make a friendly telephone call to discharged patients at regular intervals. This assures them that someone is interested, gives an opportunity to air minor problems, and nips major problems in the bud. It has the obvious advantage of costing nothing. Both AA and Al-Anon members might be encouraged to expand this novel form of Twelfth Step work. Other treatment centers phone the discharged patient every month for two years.

Grief. Much has been written about the necessity of "doing one's grief work" after the loss of a loved one—that is, to accept and work through a normal series of emotions instead of repressing those feelings with a show of bravery. Kellerman (1977), Bellwood (1975), and others have drawn an interesting parallel in a need for the recovering person to go through a similar process of grief work in accepting the losses attendant upon giving up some real or imagined conviviality, perhaps loss of health, job, family, memory, or moral respectability and sense of self-mastery. Failure to accept and express those feelings stems from false pride, which says "I should not feel this way" when in fact you do, or "I must act like my old self" when in fact you are not. If those feelings are vented with a skilled counselor or experienced 12-Step sponsor, they can then be understood and accepted. The past is truly forgiven if not entirely forgotten, and one begins a better life with hope. Kellerman notes a similar need for the family, especially the spouse.

Clinical Depression. Prolonged and continuous depression without any palpable cause, especially if accompanied by thoughts of suicide, is reason for seeking psychiatric help. This is not just the emotional flatness that most recovering persons experience when they discover that the honeymoon stage is over and they are back to day-to-day living. These latter should understand that grief over a true loss is a normal emotion and should get active in doing things, especially for others.

Sex After Sobriety. Recovery often means the emergence of problems connected with one's sex life, which need to be faced frankly. One problem is the feelings of guilt over any promiscuity during the drinking years; the principles pertinent to this problem are given in the last section of Chapter 19. Other problems stem from developments after sobriety. We noted in Chapter 4, Section C, that alcohol depresses sexuality, especially male, in several ways. That may have become unimportant as the addiction progressed to the point where the bottle took priority over all else. Recovery may bring a dramatic reversal. Feeling good again and looking better than they have for years, patients may experience a renewed interest in and from the opposite sex. The breakup of a previous marriage may not have led to any immediate sexual frustration while they were drinking, but now there can be strong resurgence of the sex drive.

This leads to three problems. One is readjustment of sexual relations with the spouse, if the marriage is still intact or if reconciliation has occurred. If the husband is the patient, the wife may be understandably slow to welcome his advances after years of hurt and revulsion. She may not even want him to touch her. It may take a long time to rekindle a close, delicate, loving sexual relationship. The needed patience is difficult for him, because he feels confident in his sobriety now and cannot appreciate her mistrust from having been burned so often. If the wife is the patient, the husband may have to overcome disillusionment in his once-idealized loved one. Or conversely, he may jeopardize her sobriety by remarking, "You were more fun in bed when you were drinking." Temporary pelvic insensitivity is common for women in early recovery, especially from cocaine addiction (K. O'Connell, 1994). In any case, we recommend frank discussion with a good counselor, by the couple and individually. There is also a wealth of literature on sexual adjustment available (see Lief and Schuster, 1988).

The single or divorced person in recovery faces two problems. One is promiscuity. The renewed interest in sex may result in a wild fling of sexual adventures. Regardless of one's moral code on this point, the emotional fluctuations and unstable interpersonal relations that this entails can be a serious obstacle to the maturity and psychological growth essential for a solid sobriety. If guilt over the moral aspect is added, relapse becomes even more likely. "First things first" suggests that staying sober must have top priority, and sexual activity should be postponed. For those who question the biological wisdom of this, the answer is that physicians who have treated celibates have testified unanimously for decades that there is no evidence of any physical detriment as a result of controlling the sex drive. Not all people experience a strong urge, and to them Dr. Jon Weinberg, in *Sex and Recovery* (1977, p. 24) sagely remarks, "If you are enjoying life without sex, don't feel something must be wrong with you. Not everybody likes apple pie either." Dr. Janet

Woititz (1981, p. 14) says that whereas before you had sex without affection, now you must learn to express affection without sex. This is mature love, not selfish exploitation.

The other problem of the unmarried person in recovery is the prospect of marriage. This, of course, may be a very laudable goal for the future, but if it comes too early it can be a disaster. Those involved are usually deaf to advice here, but counselors should make every effort to forestall an early marriage by warning against any romantic involvement for at least a year after recovery. Rebound marriages have a poor rate of success, and rebound from alcoholism is similar. Weinberg (1977, p. 32) echoes the experience of many AA members and all professionals. There are exceptions, but the problem is that everyone likes to believe they will be that rare exception. Here love can be not only blind but stupid.

Social

Under this heading we include all the aspects of rehabilitation involved in returning the recovered person to full life in the community: employment; housing; health, including teeth and eyeglasses or hearing aid; legal, including probation and parole as well as wage garnishments and divorce settlements; church affiliation; family, including reconciliation with children who have left the home; finances; recreation; education or retraining; and a host of others. A few general guidelines may be indicated.

First, easy does it. The above list can be overwhelming to the newly recovered. New skills must be learned, or old ones refurbished. Some may have to learn for the first time how to handle money, manage a checking account, shop and keep house, apply for a job. The transition to independent living must be paced to the degree of readiness and stage of recovery. One former bank vice president was advised to start as a bank janitor-custodian.

In the early stage patients will need a lot of help. One cannot apply for a job if one has no decent clothes to appear in and no means of transportation to get to the job interview. One may not know how to get public assistance or veterans' benefits, how to contact the Division of Vocational Rehabilitation, or what sheltered workshops and retraining opportunities are available. Continuum of care means that the system somehow provides those helps, in contrast to the case of one patient who left the treatment center alone on a bus that by incredible coincidence discharged him directly in front of his favorite old tavern.

Some education on the nature of alcoholism as a treatable illness and the nature of recovery may have to be conveyed to any or all of the people contacted in those efforts to help. One college fraternity held a kegger to celebrate the return of one of their fraternity brothers from alcoholism treatment! Judges, parole officers, employers or job interviewers, family, friends, former drinking pals, clergy, physicians, and others may not understand the need to avoid all alcohol and other psychoactive drugs, the impossibility of a return to social drinking, the time required for gradual recovery, the fact that declared sobriety means a better employment risk than hidden drinking. All must learn not to harp on the past but hope for the future. The married couple should agree never to bring up the past except in the presence of the counselor.

A part of the past that must be faced is the effects on the children from living in a dysfunctional home. To begin a new life after recovery as if the past never existed may sound fine, but the damage done to the personality development of the children must be rectified to the extent that is possible. Too often all the focus is on the recovered persons, and on the acceptance and support the children are supposed to give them in their new sobriety. That is merely continuing the role reversal that had been so damaging to the children all along. Parents are to accept and support children, not vice versa. In the educational phase of rehabilitation, we recommend incorporating Parent Effectiveness Training (PET) or membership in Parents Anonymous for child abusers.

Life in a Drinking Society. A crucial adjustment is learning how to conduct oneself at social gatherings, where drinking is a common feature. Our society does not make this easy, and there are always ignorant boors who will push drinks at the recovered alcoholic. One can begin by recalling that about 30 percent of American adults are nondrinkers and that nobody has to drink. Recovered alcoholics are more welcome at a party now that they don't get obnoxious. One should tell friends bluntly that alcohol is out; those who cannot understand or accept this are not worth keeping as friends anyhow. There should be no lame excuses about ulcers nor any explanation suggesting weakness or inferiority, but a simple "No, thank you"—which can indicate strength and independence. This comes with practice; during early sobriety it is difficult, and cocktail parties might better be avoided. For some, it is fun to stay sober and watch others make fools of themselves. As for being conspicuous, it is easy to rattle a few ice cubes in a highball glass full of ginger ale with nobody in the room aware of the difference. One should fix the drink oneself or observe its preparation, to prevent its being spiked. The only danger here is that an unknowing spouse or friends might worry that one is having a relapse. Eventually one may feel comfortable enough to serve alcoholic drinks at home if appropriate; the spouse must let the alcoholic decide when. All this is well presented in an article "My Trials as a Nondrinking Alcoholic" by a recovered alcoholic physician (Tabor, 1959).

Preparation to handle the pressure to drink should be a part of the final treatment stage with practice in the ways of *how* to refuse a drink gracefully, e.g., by actual role-playing sessions at the treatment center. Let another patient act the role of waiter, boss, escort, or friend offering a drink or drug; what do you say? Similarly, one should develop specific action plans for those times of the day or week that will be the most likely occasion for a drink: five o'clock closing time, end of a three-to-eleven shift, Saturday night. What will you do, where will you go, and how? Positive use of leisure time must be planned. A Hazelden pamphlet, *Now What Do I Do for Fun?* can be useful.

Relapse

Both patient and counselor may see relapse, always possible in any chronic illness, as failure. Rather, it can be the clincher argument that the patient really cannot take even one drink, hence the start of a long happy life of sobriety. Sometimes it is better not to push treatment too soon after a relapse. In any case, the type of alcoholism and treatment modality have to be reexamined (Daley, 1988, 1991; DuWors, 1992; Gossop, 1989). Coping skills training can reduce the severity of a relapse if one occurs. The work of Marlatt and Gordon (1985) uses behavioral conditioning and assertiveness training in a constructive way here, not to be confused with earlier futile attempts to condition recovered alcoholics to drink socially. A basic principle is to recognize different kinds of relapse.

Although we have stressed that analyzing why one drinks is largely a misleading therapy, causes for an actual or potential relapse can be profitably looked at. Thirst can be mistaken for a cue to drink, when body fluid is all that is needed. Hunger is a danger; here good nutrition and even the guidance of a dietitian may be helpful, and at least excessive sugar should be avoided. False notions about weak will, hopelessness, or social unacceptablity need to be corrected. Lack of attention from family does not mean less appreciation now that sobriety is taken for granted. We all like a pat on the back now and then, but it is childish to expect constant praise for just living. Sometimes the only prelude to a relapse seems to be that everything is going well. Is this a reason for drinking? Anger and loneliness must be understood as normal human experiences, not cues for a drink. The acronym HALT sums up four danger signals: Be on guard if one is Hungry, Angry, Lonely, or Tired.

The Dry Drunk

"Dry drunk" is an episode in which one may exhibit any or all of the feelings and behavior associated with intoxication although no alcohol is consumed. Formerly it implied grandiosity; currently it more often connotes moderate to severe depression. It commonly occurs after about six months or around the end of the first year of sobriety, but it can happen at any time. Shakes, insomnia, stiffness, headaches, and other flulike symptoms may accompany irritability, fatigue, depression, hunger, egocentrism, overreaction, unexplained sadness, aimless puttering or wandering, and a host of negative emotions. Sometimes the resemblance to actual intoxication is remarkable. A dry dream of getting drunk can be most vivid and terrifying. A "dry hangover" may follow.

Analysis of what leads up to a dry drunk reveals great similarity to the antecedents of relapse, but a caution against generalization and psychologizing is in order. "Stinking thinking" can indeed be a prelude, but the concepts of buildup and binge do not apply to all alcoholics, or not to all in the same way. At least the rationalizations are quite foreign to a comfortable sobriety and betray a lack of surrender or honesty of which the person may be unaware. Lurking indecision about commitment to a life of sobriety may be the basic cause, but a thousand factors can trigger the dry drunk. Resentments and self-centeredness are common causes.

Talking it over with a counselor or sponsor will usually help. Self-pity is countered by resisting the urge to remain alone. Getting busy, and especially helping others, has therapeutic value. But recreation and relaxation are also important. Going through the 12 Steps as if for the first time can evoke new light and incentives. Lastly, mood can improve through prayer and meditation on spiritual perspectives.

Sources

Most books dealing with alcoholism, particularly those concerned with treatment, include sections on rehabilitation. For example, see Denzin (1987a, 1987b), Ludwig (1987a, 1987b), K. O'Connell (1994), Twerski (1984), and Wallen (1993); Heinemann and DiJulio, "Assessment and Care of the Chronically Ill Alcoholic Person," in Estes and Heinemann (1986); and Strachan, *Practical Alcoholism Programming* (1971).

In the area of rehabilitation, much of the most valuable information is available in pamphlets, rather than in the technical literature. NCADI has put out several bibliographies that contain relevant materials, and two in particular are recommended: Part IV of NIAAA, *Alcoholism Treatment and Rehabilitation: Selected Abstracts,* and *Selected Publications on Rehabilitation Strategies for Alcohol Abusers.* NCADI has also published an excellent pamphlet by Ernest P. Noble entitled *Role of Halfway Houses in the Rehabilitation of Alcoholics.*

The Association of Halfway House Alcoholism Programs in St. Paul has published D. Fontaine, *Analysis of the Recovery Process;* T. Richards, *So You Want to Start a Halfway House for Alcoholics?;* M. Rudolph, *Therapeutic Intervention: Counseling in Post-Treatment Programs,* and *Standards for Halfway House Alcoholism Programs.* Hazelden has published D. Anderson, *The Joys and Sorrows of Sobriety;* J. Kellerman, *Grief: A Basic Reaction to Alcoholism* (1977); B. Kimball, *Aftercare: Blueprint for a Richer Life,* and *Counseling for Growth in a Halfway House for Women;* Bob W., *Transition from Treatment to A.A;* and many others. CompCare has published Janet Woititz, *Going Home: A Re-Entry Guide for the Newly Sober* (1981); Jon Weinberg, *Sex and Recovery* (1977); Muriel Zink, *Recovery: Turning Negatives into Positives;* and many others.

RELAPSE AND DRY DRUNK

The works of Terence Gorski and Merlene Miller (1986, 1987), and Merlene Miller et al. (1988) are important contributions, along with Chiauzzi (1991), Daley (1988, 1991), DuWors (1992), Ludwig (1987b), G. K. Litman et al. (1979), and the relapse prevention work of Marlatt and Gordon (1985). See also Pete M. Monti, *Treating Alcohol Dependence: A Coping Skills Training Guide* (1989); *Alcohol Health and Research World,* special issue "Recovery," Fall 1986, 11:(1); Alan Ogborne, "Evaluating Halfway Houses," in *Addictions,* 1976, 23:53–65; Jacquelyn Small and Sidney Wolf, "Beyond Abstinence," in *Alcohol Health and Research World,* 1978, 2(4):32–36; Jonathan Tabor, "My Trials as a Nondrinking Alcoholic" (1959); and Marc A. Schuckit, "The Identification and Management of Alcoholic and Depressive Problems," in *Drug Abuse and Alcoholism Review,* 1978, 1(4):1–8.

Vivid subjective accounts of these experiences have been provided by recovered and recovering alcoholics. Almost any issue of *AA Grapevine* will have at least one article dealing with such problems. The March and April 1976 issues contained a series of articles dealing with "slips" (returns to drinking after a period of abstinence), and depression. Two others are L. S., "That Thirteenth Step" on romantic involvement (February 1978); and M. McF., "Reality Can Be Uncomfortable" (July 1971, reprinted November 1976).

Pamphlets include Crewe, *A Look at Relapse;* Grimmet, *Barriers Against Recovery;* and Solberg, *The Dry-Drunk Syndrome,* all published by Hazelden. The following books also contain materials on the dry drunk: Blane, *The Personality of the Alcoholic* (1968); Meyer, *Off the Sauce* (1976); and two by Valles, *From Social Drinking to Alcoholism* (1969) and *How to Live with an Alcoholic* (1965).

CHAPTER 17

Alcoholics Anonymous and Other Twelve-Step Groups

S INCE ALCOHOLICS ANONYMOUS is numerically by far the most successful program of recovery from alcoholism, no one can claim a knowledge of the field without knowing what AA is and how it works. No physician would write a prescription and hand it to the patient remarking, "I don't know what this is or how it works; but take it, it will be good for you." No professional should recommend AA who has never attended AA meetings nor read "the big book," *Alcoholics Anonymous,* much less the mass of literature produced both by the fellowship and by scholars who have studied it. For all, a thorough study of AA can be most rewarding. The nonalcoholic founder of one famous treatment center is said to have taken off an entire year just to study AA.

Even longtime members sometimes betray a lack of familiarity with their own "official" literature, the AA Conference–approved books and pamphlets published by AA World Series, Inc., in New York, on which this chapter is based (along with close association with AA since 1942). Since each member and each group is different, one should both read AA literature and attend open meetings of several groups in diverse settings, to savor the variety while perceiving the basic uniformity of the program.

What Is AA?

Nobody can speak for AA. It speaks for itself. Two million success stories and the Twelve Steps that constitute the heart of the program speak more eloquently than any description. Further evidence is the fact that about sixty other problems are now being addressed by groups using the same Twelve Steps, for example Narcotics Anonymous (NA), Cocaine Anonymous (CA) and Marijuana Anonymous (MA).

Alcoholics Anonymous is a mutual-help group that combines many facets of good group therapy. But it is not therapy in any professional sense and has no official theory or model of alcoholism (Miller and Kurtz, 1994). It is universally available, meeting in 131 countries and listed in the telephone book of practically every city of any size in the world. One does not have to declare oneself an alcoholic, and there is no membership card. One is a member if one says so. One does not have to speak. Being anonymous, there are no member lists, so accurate statistical data are difficult to compile. Surveys by the organization every three years since 1968, however, have yielded considerable information about the group while protecting the anonymity of individual members.

AA is both a fellowship and a program. The program of Twelve Steps can be used successfully by those isolated from the group either by geography or by personal temperament. Yet the mutual support and fellowship are most important aspects, as depicted by Madsen in his excellent Chapter IX on AA in *The American Alcoholic* (1973) and summarized by Kurtz (1979) as "the shared honesty of mutual vulnerability openly acknowledged." Founded shortly after the repeal of Prohibition, it was careful to avoid any semblance of partisan involvement. Members often say, "If you want to drink, that's your business; if you want to stop, we can help." Alcohol is mentioned only once in the Twelve Steps; AA is a whole way of life. Although an intensely spiritual program, it is careful to avoid affiliation with any sect or religion. As its members describe themselves:

> Alcoholics Anonymous is a fellowship of men and women who share their experience, strength, and hope with each other that they may solve their common problem and help others to recover from alcoholism.
>
> The only requirement for membership is a desire to stop drinking. There are no dues or fees for AA membership; we are self-supporting through our own contributions. AA is not allied with any sect, denomination, politics, organization, or institution; does not wish to engage in any controversy; neither endorses nor opposes any causes. Our primary purpose is to stay sober and help other alcoholics to achieve sobriety.*

Perhaps the greatest contribution of AA is hope. Most alcoholics feel pretty hopeless, and the old moralistic and prohibitionistic approaches only accentuated that feeling. To see thousands of alcoholics recover and lead happy lives, and without great monetary cost, gave reason for hope to every alcoholic. Physicians and clergymen were at first chagrined and then delighted to see success where they had failed, and endorsed the program enthusiastically. Where each recovery seemed to some a miracle, the growth of AA itself without either promotion or money was to others a greater miracle.

A Bit of History

It all started when a New York stockbroker named Bill W., who had lost everything but discovered he could stay sober by trying to help other alcoholics, found himself alone and desperate in Akron, Ohio, on the eve of

* Copyright © and reprinted by permission of the AA Grapevine, Inc.

Mother's Day, 1935. He called a clergyman and asked to be put in touch with another alcoholic with whom he could talk. He was referred to Henrietta Seiberling of the rubber manufacturing family, who arranged a meeting the next day with Dr. Bob S., a "hopeless" alcoholic surgeon. The two talked for hours and agreed that they needed each other for the sake of their own sobriety. Dr. Bob had one relapse a few weeks later, and on June 10, 1935, began complete sobriety, which lasted until he died. Thus AA was born, though the anniversary is usually celebrated on the Fourth of July.

The Washingtonian movement in Baltimore in the early 1800s had helped some alcoholics with a religious approach but had soon destroyed itself by getting too involved with politics and prohibitionism. The Oxford groups (not the Oxford movement in England), started by the Protestant clergyman Frank Buchman early in this century, had tried a program of surrender, conversion, and confession, but their insistence on rigid "moral absolutes" made the groups repulsive to many, and they advocated prominence rather than anonymity. Bill W. was aware of those movements through his alcoholic friend Ebby T. and the Episcopal Reverend Sam Shoemaker, and Dr. Bob had attended Oxford group meetings. It was not until 1939 that AA entirely disengaged itself from the Oxford groups, which metamorphosed into Moral ReArmament (MRA). Bill W. was also influenced by his physician, William D. Silkworth, by the psychologist William James through his book *The Varieties of Religious Experience,* and by the great Swiss psychiatrist Carl Jung's observation that no profound change in the latter half of life takes place without a religious conversion. Dr. Bob and Bill W. were greatly aided by Sister Ignatia of St. Thomas Hospital in Akron (Darrah, 1992), and in 1940 the cofounders became very close friends with Father Edward Dowling, S.J., a St. Louis Jesuit priest who pointed out the remarkable similarity between the Twelve Steps of AA and the Spiritual Exercises of St. Ignatius Loyola, founder of the Jesuit order (Fitzgerald, 1995). This history is recounted in *Alcoholics Anonymous Comes of Age* (1957) and by Kurtz (1979).

But it should be made clear that the program of Alcoholics Anonymous was not borrowed from any of the earlier organizations. It grew out of the actual experiences of the founders and early members. The similarity with other movements is largely due to the basic psychological and spiritual soundness of what they have in common. That is why the Twelve Steps are not a prescriptive statement of what everyone should do but simply a record of what those particular people did: "We admitted . . . came to believe . . . made a decision . . ."—these experiences were formulated into twelve suggested steps in December 1938 and published in the book *Alcoholics Anonymous* in 1939, which has been added to several times since but never essentially changed. The source of AA's appeal was not its origins or its philosophy, but the fact that it worked.

Growth at first was slow. Only forty members were staying sober in the first two years, and a bare one hundred by the fourth anniversary. Brief articles in *Liberty* (Markey, 1939) and in *Collier's* (Anonymous, 1939) gave them some notice, but their rapid growth really began when Jack Alexander (1941) wrote an article in *The Saturday Evening Post* for March 1, 1941 (reprint available from AA). In 1944 a monthly, *The AA Grapevine*, commenced publication, and in 1953 the AA's *Twelve Steps and Twelve Traditions* (1953) set forth the workings and spirit of the group. The Twentieth Anniversary Convention at St. Louis in 1955 saw membership at about 200,000. Here the three legacies of recovery, unity, and service were turned over by its founders to an elected General Service Conference. By 1967 *The AA Way of Life* was published, and a large number of pamphlets were appearing. By then the movement, at first largely in the United States and Canada, had 20 percent of its membership overseas. The 1973 booklet *Came to Believe* expressed the wide range of individual members' spiritual views, smoothing the way for many doubters. In 1985 the Fiftieth Anniversary Convention was attended in Montreal by 48,000 people, and membership totaled more than 2.2 million by 1995.

The AA Program

One way to grasp quickly how AA works is to list the things it does *not* do, contrary to some assumptions. It does not solicit members, promote any religion or abstinence movement, provide social service such as housing or jobs or run shelters for battered spouses or children, run detox or any treatment services, follow up or try to control its members, claim to be a cureall or help with any other problem except excessive drinking, accept any money for services or contributions from outside sources, make medical or psychological diagnoses, prescribe or pay for treatment, engage in or sponsor research, affiliate with any other organization, hire professional field workers, or claim to be the only successful approach or that one must be an alcoholic to deal with the problem.

AA Is Not a Religion

AA is not a religion in the sense of any organized institution; unlike a religion, it has no prescribed creed of belief, no code of morals, no cult of worship. Traditions 6 and 10 explicitly rule out any affiliation with or endorsement of any religion. Kurtz (1979, 1991) points out that cofounder Bill W. was careful to avoid making it a religion and that the whole group did likewise right from the beginning. Chapter 4 of its "big book" is entitled "We Agnostics." God is always a Higher Power as the individual wishes to understand Him. The AA program does not favor a white man's God, for instance, but can apply equally well to the Great Spirit of our Native Americans. Where the custom has been to close a meeting by reciting the Our Father, nobody is obliged to join in. (When one Jewish member objected to the custom, another Jew retorted, "That prayer was composed by a Jew to teach other Jews how to pray.")

AA is very tactful in handling the skepticism of the agnostic or atheist and is careful not to impose any sectarian religion on anyone. But AA is an intensely spiritual program, God being mentioned explicitly six times in the Twelve Steps, and implicitly twice. Acceptance for some is not easy. There is no pressure, and each comes to understand in his own way, at his own pace. Psychologists and clergy have good reason to be wary of the old-time revival-meeting emotionalism, which was short-lived and superficial even when it was sincere. The AA program is both psychologically and spiritually sound. It does not feature ecstatic emotional experiences but is rather a sensible facing of the spiritual realities that are in all lives, even that of the avowed atheist (see Chapter 19).

How It Works

Dr. Bob and Bill W. did not succeed with anybody else for their first six months, but they noticed that as a result of their efforts they were staying sober themselves. AA members share their experience with anyone else seeking help with a drinking problem and offer the alcoholic an opportunity to develop a satisfying way of life free from alcohol. They sponsor new members and discuss their program at AA meetings, which may be either *open* to anyone or *closed* to all except members. Meetings are *speaker* meetings, in which members tell their stories; *discussion* meetings, which may center on either their experiences in recovery or some topic such as humility, faith, resentments, and so forth; *step* meetings, which explore in depth one of the Twelve Steps; or *study-group* meetings, which may take a chapter from one of the AA books.

The recital of personal history ("drunkalog") has many functions: It encourages newcomers to realize that no matter how bad they may seem, others have recovered who were worse off. It also serves as an emotional catharsis. It enables them to build self-respect by being accepted by the group. It teaches them to listen and respect others. Much practical wisdom is in these shared experiences. The sharing also fosters an emotional closeness among members. But the essence of the AA program is not the recitals; it lies in the serious study and personal application of the Twelve Steps. This is how Chapter 5 of the book *Alcoholics Anonymous* presents them:

> Our stories disclose in a general way what we used to be like, what happened, and what we are like now. If you have decided you want what we have and are willing to go to any length to get it—then you are ready to take certain steps.
>
> At some of these we balked. We thought we could find an easier, softer way. But we could not. With all the earnestness at our command, we beg of you to be fearless and thorough from the very start. Some of us have tried to hold on to our old ideas and the result was nil until we let go absolutely.

Remember that we deal with alcohol—cunning, baffling, powerful! Without help it is too much for us. But there is One who has all power—that One is God. May you find Him now!

Half measures availed us nothing. We stood at the turning point. We asked His protection and care with complete abandon.

Here are the steps we took, which are suggested as a program of recovery:

1. We admitted we were powerless over alcohol—that our lives had become unmanageable.
2. Came to believe that a Power greater than ourselves could restore us to sanity.
3. Made a decision to turn our will and our lives over to the care of God *as we understood Him.*
4. Made a searching and fearless moral inventory of ourselves.
5. Admitted to God, to ourselves, and to another human being the exact nature of our wrongs.
6. Were entirely ready to have God remove all these defects of character.
7. Humbly asked Him to remove our shortcomings.
8. Made a list of all persons we had harmed, and became willing to make amends to them all.
9. Made direct amends to such people wherever possible, except when to do so would injure them or others.
10. Continued to take personal inventory and when we were wrong promptly admitted it.
11. Sought through prayer and meditation to improve our conscious contact with God *as we understood Him,* praying only for knowledge of His will for us and the power to carry that out.
12. Having had a spiritual awakening as the result of these steps, we tried to carry this message to alcoholics and to practice these principles in all our affairs.

Many of us exclaimed, "What an order! I can't go through with it." Do not be discouraged. No one among us has been able to maintain anything like perfect adherence to these principles. We are not saints. The point is that we are willing to grow along spiritual lines. The principles we have set down are guides to progress. We claim spiritual progress rather than spiritual perfection.

Our description of the alcoholic, the chapter to the agnostic, and our personal adventures before and after make clear three pertinent ideas:

(a) That we were alcoholic and could not manage our own lives.
(b) That probably no human power could have relieved our alcoholism.
(c) That God could and would if He were sought.*

Why It Works

It is indeed quite an order. The fifth chapter continues with an analysis of selfishness and egocentricity that is a marvel of commonsense psychology. Reading the AA literature one is struck by the constant emphasis on humility, a favorite theme of cofounder Bill W. This is not to further beat down already discouraged alcoholics, but to inject some perspective into their self-esteem by an honest acceptance of limitations and acknowledgment of God rather than self as the ultimate source of assets. Pride, it seems, is the chief obstacle to sobriety as it is to progress in the spiritual life. Here psychology and spirituality meet in a common recognition of the need for dependence on a Higher Power, apart from any religious dogma (Peteet, 1993).

But simplicity of purpose, not psychological analysis, is the great strength of Alcoholics Anonymous. The fellowship concentrates on achieving and maintaining sobriety to the exclusion of other enterprises. Some criticize the use of clichés and simple-minded slogans, but the desperate alcoholic recovering from a foggy haze needs some simple hooks to grab on to, not complexity and subtlety. Moreover, simplicity tends to be a hallmark of greatness in art, philosophy, and science as well as in successful social movements. It is certainly no obstacle to being profound.

In keeping with this simplicity, we suggest that one reason why AA is so effective is that it applies the basic psychology of motivation. Lindworsky (1928) showed that there is no such thing as raw will power, that the key is not strength of resolution but keeping the motive in consciousness. Attendance at meetings and other contacts have the net effect of keeping the alcoholic always conscious of the danger of taking that first drink, and the need to nip in the bud any resentments or egotism that could lead to drinking. Add to this the whole psychology of surrender and the spiritual experience of turning one's life over to God as each understands Him, and you have a combination that is highly effective. The "Sources" at the end of this chapter indicate many more profound analyses, but this seems to put it in a nutshell.

Surrender, of course, demands humility, which is never easy for human pride. Focus is on staying sober, not analysis of why one drank. The self-examination is aimed at preventing relapse, not harping on the past. "One day at a time" is a motto that has a practical psychological value. One enormous boon is the discovery that one is not alone, that others have had the

* From *Alcoholics Anonymous* (Alcoholics Anonymous World Services, Inc., 1939), pp. 70–72, reprinted with permission.

same problems and discouragements. Sharing helps others, but the first benefit of Twelfth Step work is that it keeps oneself sober. For that reason members call it a selfish program, in that primacy is always given to maintaining one's own sobriety, even as a prior condition to helping others. That kind of enlightened selfishness naturally benefits everyone in the long run. Honesty, open-mindedness, and willingness are key words. The emphasis on personal responsibility is a healthy antidote to the current trend of blaming others and playing the victim—one is not guilty of being an alcoholic, but Steps 4, 8, 9, and 10 clearly demand acknowledging faulty behavior and making amends (Delbanco and Delbanco, 1995).

If there is a sense of grim earnestness in the members at times, it is because they know they are battling a "hard" drug: hard on the body, hard to overcome, hard on their lives, families, and friends. They know they need total surrender, total commitment, no half-measures. But along with that is a lighthearted good humor, a sense of friendliness and fellowship, dances and breakfasts and picnics where even complete strangers can relax and enjoy each other without fear that excessive drinking will spoil the fun.

The Three Legacies

Bill W. made three talks at the Twentieth Anniversary Convention in 1955, describing three legacies bequeathed to the membership. The talks constitute Chapter 2 of *Alcoholics Anonymous Comes of Age*. The first legacy is Recovery, focusing on personal survival. It is embodied largely in the Twelve Steps and in the book *Alcoholics Anonymous*. It may not have invented, but at least it recognized, assembled, and applied, some great psychological and spiritual principles.

Twelve Traditions. The second legacy is Unity, looking to the survival of AA as a whole. It is embodied principally in the following twelve traditions:

1. Our common welfare should come first; personal recovery depends upon AA unity.
2. For our group purpose there is but one ultimate authority—a loving God as He may express Himself in our group conscience. Our leaders are but trusted servants—they do not govern.
3. The only requirement for AA membership is a desire to stop drinking.
4. Each group should be autonomous, except in matters affecting other groups or AA as a whole.
5. Each group has but one primary purpose—to carry its message to the alcoholic who still suffers.
6. An AA group ought never to endorse, finance, or lend the AA name to any related facility or outside enterprise lest problems

of money, property, and prestige divert us from our primary purpose.

7. Every AA group ought to be fully self-supporting, declining outside contributions.

8. Alcoholics Anonymous should remain forever nonprofessional, but our service centers may employ special workers.

9. AA, as such, ought never to be organized; but we may create service boards or committees directly responsible to those they serve.

10. Alcoholics Anonymous has no opinion on outside issues; hence the AA name ought never to be drawn into public controversy.

11. Our public relations policy is based on attraction rather than promotion; we need always maintain personal anonymity at the level of press, radio, and films.

12. Anonymity is the spiritual foundation of all our traditions, ever reminding us to place principles above personalities.*

We shall comment briefly on only two features: poverty and anonymity. Voluntary poverty (Tradition 7) is a characteristic of AA that is striking in a materialistic age. By it they avoid accumulating any wealth, which might be a source of contention or create conflict of interest. Pride and ambition have little to feed on in AA. Authority is nonexistent. Leaders are but trusted servants—they do not govern; each group is autonomous except in matters affecting other groups or the whole (Traditions 2 and 4). The result (Tradition 9) is referred to by the members with loving humor as "the most unorganized organization in the world" but at least it presents no obstacles for the newcomer and no chance to build a power structure.

The anonymity implied by its name is another strong feature of the fellowship. Not intended to perpetuate the stigma of alcoholism, it has the great advantage of making membership no threat to the newcomer who might fear for his reputation. Anonymity protects the humility of its members, and protects the fellowship from the negative image that would arise if a well-known member relapses. A General Conference leaflet, *Understanding Anonymity,* based largely on writings of Bill W., lays out a balanced middle course between grandiosity, which might lead to relapse, and secrecy, which could prevent suffering alcoholics from receiving the message. In brief, Traditions 11 and 12 forbid self-identification with AA at the level of public communications media such as film, press, radio, or television, while allowing one to identify oneself as a recovered alcoholic. They forbid disclosure of the identity of another member outside the meeting but allow one to identify oneself as a member below the level of public media.

The third legacy is that of Service. Originally this meant service to AA itself, from making the coffee, to acting as a sponsor (Fitzgerald, 1995), to act-

---

* From *Alcoholics Anonymous* (1976), p. 564, reprinted with permission.

ing as an elected representative to the General Service Conference. More recently it has included the whole matter of serving other alcoholics who need help, not only in Twelfth Step work, which must remain forever nonprofessional according to Tradition 8, but also by the activity of AA members working professionally in the field. This latter situation has evolved gradually and sometimes painfully, but a clear tradition has emerged and is expressed in AA literature, especially *AA Guidelines for Members Employed in the Alcoholism Field* (1994), which again reveals the eminent common sense of the group conscience. This will be discussed further in Chapter 21.

AA Today

Over the years many changes have taken place, although the basic soundness and spiritual wisdom of the Twelve Steps have not changed. AA has come of age, professionalism has entered the field, those once in the honeymoon stage are now the entrenched old guard. That is inevitable, because AA is a living organism, not a corpse, and change is characteristic of living things. "There are no rules in AA, and God help anybody who breaks them"—as in any human group, there are always the liberals and conservatives, with resultant need for tolerance and a balance between the old and the new.

Change is also inevitable because each member is allowed to apply the steps as he or she sees fit: 2 million interpretations of a single program. Too often AA is stereotyped, by both professionals and its own members, on the basis of single or limited contacts. The wide variation among individuals and between groups must be stressed. Each member is unique, and one research study showed individuals in the same locality to vary on an important characteristic between zero and 86 percent. Another example is the fact that although some have had an ecstatic spiritual experience such as Bill W. had, most members have a gradual, less dramatic spiritual awakening, and many find the spiritual aspects difficult to accept at first.

The membership of AA today is younger, getting away from the old stereotype that one has to drink for a long time in order to be an alcoholic or that one must lose everything in order to hit bottom. The proportion of women in AA is steadily increasing, as the double standard lessens. There is more openness to working with professionals and to cooperation (but not affiliation) with other approaches to recovery (e.g., Brown, 1985). There is more awareness of the role of the family, and joint meetings with Al-Anon, the subject of our next chapter, are taking place.

Polyaddiction, especially among young members and women (now 78 percent of women twenty and under), has occasioned much controversy in AA, as evidenced by the fact that its pamphlet on the subject has been revised several times (see "Sources"). AA rightly insists that its effectiveness could be diluted if other drugs were allowed to obscure the sole purpose of AA and prevent newcomers from being able to identify with alcohol problems. Hence polydrug users are advised to focus on their alcoholism at AA meetings and to attend NA, CA, or PA if narcotics or cocaine or pills are their chief concern. However, older members forget that both Bill W. and Dr. Bob also had problems with other drugs. By Tradition 3 the only requirement for membership is a desire to stop drinking; no human being, including the cofounders, could join if they had to be free of all other problems. Mention of other drugs is now accepted and was even encouraged in one Conference-approved AA pamphlet (*The A.A. Member and Drug Abuse*, p. 16), so that members will learn how other psychoactive drugs can be a threat to their sobriety. A 1988 survey showed over 90 percent of groups warmly welcomed alcoholics with other addictions also.

Another touchy question is the matter of special-interest groups: physicians, nurses, airline pilots (Birds of a Feather), gays and lesbians, dually addicted, law enforcement personnel, Catholics (Calix), etc. In general, AA takes the position that anyone who needs help may use the Twelve Steps, as long as the Traditions are observed, specifically Tradition 4 granting autonomy to the groups as long as they do not affect other groups or AA as a whole. There is a letter from Bill W. extant which says that Calix, for example, is not against the Traditions of AA since it does not mean affiliation with or endorsement by AA, which would contravene Tradition 6. The danger is that any of these groups may become so engrossed in their own special interest that they lose sight of the purpose of AA. Thus one physician reports that his group just talked about problems of anonymity and how hard it is to be a doctor in AA, so that he had to attend mainstream AA meetings for his own growth and went to the physicians' group only to encourage newcomers.

Rate of Success

In addition to the tradition of anonymity, which means no member lists are kept, another reason it is hard to assess the success rate of AA with any accuracy is that today there is a tendency for alcoholics to utilize several approaches. Surveys show a surprisingly high percentage of members have been referred to AA by professionals, and a large number had combined AA with other helps. Thus many alcoholics need to break the habit-pattern and achieve some sobriety through other means first, and then find AA most helpful for long-term followup and a new way of life. Depending on criteria, success rates in AA have been put at 75 to 89 percent, after one relapse for about half of these. That is, the first year is the hardest, and about half relapse once; eventually a high percentage stay sober for five years or more. AA never claimed 100 percent success; the sheer numbers attest to the impact of the movement.

Not Perfect

AA has, of course, been criticized. Some of this may be due to professional jealousy, some to impatience with the nonscientific and unstructured nature of its operation, some to uneasiness with the spiritual, some to misunderstanding or ignorance. The Twelve Steps are not something to be read, but to be lived. Outside observers can hardly be expected to grasp them readily. Being human, the members themselves make it quite clear that their adherence to the program is not perfect. When cofounder Bill W. saw that some of the criticisms had foundation in fact, he urged in "Our Critics Can Be Our Benefactors" (*AA Grapevine,* April 1963) and elsewhere that they be taken with humility for what profit might be derived.

Some of the criticisms point to rigidity and literal-mindedness both in the interpretation of the steps and in the conducting of meetings. Since each member may interpret the steps at will, and the group conscience can decide how to conduct the meeting, theoretically such objections should not hold water. But in practice they sometimes have a point. Although AA never claimed to be the only means of recovery and explicitly rejects this position, some individual members talk as though that were the case. The same happens in regard to cooperation with the medical profession. There have always been close ties and much cooperation, from the days of Dr. Bob and Sister Ignatia, but individual members sometimes speak as if the opposite were true. It might be noted that the first two counselors were nonalcoholic women (Henrietta Seiberling and Sister Ignatia). Dogmatism and smugness are, of course, the direct opposite of the humility and tolerance advocated by the AA slogan "Live and let live." More important, they tend to drive into despair those who are not attracted to AA, presuming that if AA is the only way, then for them there is no hope.

Psychotherapists sometimes object that there is too much repression of emotion and not sufficient room for catharsis (they should attend some meetings!). That may be true for some individuals, but such a need is probably best handled by professional psychotherapy later and would be dangerous for amateurs. In general, alcoholics have led an undisciplined life and need some controls more than they need uninhibited expression. Some criticisms stem from the fact that psychotherapists get a distorted sampling, because they rarely see those who find a happy sobriety in AA and don't need therapy. Perhaps a more valid criticism is that AA prolongs dependence on the group for some and prevents their growth back into full involvement with society. Such institutionalized regression again is not intrinsic to the AA program, which is one of true growth. It may apply to some individuals, but we must recall that any chronic disease needs lifetime care, and some persons will always need more care than others. Good AA procedure balances the human need for belonging with individuality and freedom. Kasl (1992) has researched alcoholics who do not fit the AA mould. As for concentration on mere avoidance of drinking, alcohol is mentioned only in the first step, and the remaining steps have to do with total personality development. But some groups or individuals forget that sobriety is more than mere abstinence. *Twelve Steps and Twelve Traditions* (1953, pp. 116–20) speaks of "two-steppers"—members who seem to know only Steps 1 and 12 and ignore the demanding regime of Steps 2 through 11.

Some poor impressions of AA stem from inept referrals. One should prepare the prospect by careful explanation of AA (or Al-Anon), with special stress on anonymity and one's complete freedom in how they understand the Higher Power. Many find the coarse language offensive, so the counselor should explain that these people come from different backgrounds and are often just trying to show how rough it was for them. An appropriate sample of meetings should be given, with explanation of the choice between open and closed, stag, women-only, or mixed, nonsmoking, and special-interest groups. The sponsor plays an important role; the new member should select one carefully, matched to the client so there is at least some compatibility of age, occupation, or other common interest, and always be of the same sex (by an unwritten tradition). The counselor may suggest a temporary sponsor.

Sources

AA can be looked at from two perspectives. The first is from within AA, then how others see it. AA Conference-approved literature is obtainable locally at AA intergroup offices listed in most telephone directories, or from AA World Services (see Appendix) which will furnish a complete list. AA books are listed in the General Bibliography under *Alcoholics Anonymous*. Some consider *Twelve Steps and Twelve Traditions* (1953) the most useful.

AA pamphlets cover every phase of AA activity, and are too numerous to list here. We mention a few useful items; see also the items about cooperation with professionals listed in "Sources" for Chapter 21.

A Member's-Eye View of Alcoholics Anonymous (an excellent introduction)
The AA Group: How a Group Functions, How to Get One Started
44 Questions and Answers About the AA Program of Recovery from Alcoholism
Questions and Answers on Sponsorship
Understanding Anonymity

On dual addiction or polyaddiction, *Sedatives and the Alcoholic* (1953) was revised in 1964 as *Sedatives, Stimulants and the Alcoholic*, in 1974 and 1978 as *The A.A. Member and Drug Abuse*, and in 1984 as *The A.A. Member—Medications and Other Drugs*. See also Bill W., "Those Goof Balls," *AA Grapevine*, November 1945, and his "Problems Other than Alcohol," *AA Grapevine* February 1958 or AA reprint; "The Hurt That Shouldn't Be," *AA Grapevine*, October 1981, pp. 16–19; "AA and Drug Addicts," *AA Grapevine*, May 1984, pp. 6–17; "AA and Other Addictions," *AA Grapevine*, March 1986; and Edward J. Dowling, S.J., "AA Steps for the Underprivileged Non-AA," *AA Grapevine*, November, 1982, 21–23. James G. Jensen, *Another Look at Step One*, is a Hazelden pamphlet.

NON-AA SOURCES

It is important to see how AA is viewed from the outside (McCrady and Miller, 1993). Bishop and Pittman (1994) have compiled an extensive bibliography. Bradley (1988) gives copious references to the research that has been done, as do Tonigan and Hiller-Sturmhofel (1994). In addition to a wealth of pamphlet material from Hazelden, CompCare, NCADD, and others listed in the Appendix, we list a few items:

A., Lin, *Twelve Steps for Addicts*. Hazelden pamphlet.
Bean, Margaret, "Alcoholics Anonymous: Principles and Methods" (1975).
Blumberg, Leonard, "The Ideology of a Therapeutic Social Movement: Alcoholics Anonymous," *Journal of Studies on Alcohol*, 1977, 38:2122–43.
Bradley, Ann M., "Keep Coming Back" (1988).
C., Stewart, *A Reference Guide to the Big Book of A.A.* (1987).
Clinebell, Howard J., *Understanding and Counseling the Alcoholic* (1968), Chapter 5, "AA Our Greatest Resource."
Curlee, Joan, "How a Therapist Can Use Alcoholics Anonymous," *Annals of the New York Academy of Sciences*, 1974, 233:137–44.
Delehanty, Edward J., M.D., *The Therapeutic Value of the Twelve Steps of AA*, Utah Alcoholism Foundation, n.d. Hazelden reprint.
Fitzgerald, Robert, *The Soul of Sponsorship: The Friendship Between Bill W. and Father Ed Dowling, S.J.* (1995).
Gellman, I. P., *The Sober Alcoholic: An Organizational Analysis of Alcoholics Anonymous*.

Jones, K. J., "Sectarian Characteristics of Alcoholics Anonymous," *Sociology,* 1970, 4:181–95.

K., Ernie, *90 Meetings in Ninety Days* (1984).

Kurtz, Ernest, *Not-God: A History of Alcoholics Anonymous* (1979).

———, "Why A.A. Works: The Intellectual Significance of Alcoholics Anonymous" (1982).

Leach, Barry, "Does AA Really Work?" Chapter 11 in P. Bourne and R. Fox (eds.), *Alcoholism: Progress in Research and Treatment* (1973). Ample references.

Leach, Barry, and J. L. Norris, "Factors in the Development of Alcoholics Anonymous (AA)," in B. Kissin and H. Begleiter (eds.), *The Biology of Alcoholism* (1971–83), vol. 5, pp. 441–53.

Lee, John Park. "Alcoholics Anonymous as a Community Resource," *Social Work,* October 1960, 5:20–26. NCA reprint.

Madsen, William, *The American Alcoholic* (1973) Chapter IX, "AA: Birds of a Feather."

Mann, Marty, *New Primer on Alcoholism* (1972), Chapter 11; and *Marty Mann Answers Your Questions About Alcoholism,* Chapter 13.

Mantell, M. M., *Recovery for Women* (1995).

Maxwell, Milton A., "Alcoholics Anonymous: An Interpretation," in D. J. Pittman and C. R. Snyder (eds.), *Society, Culture and Drinking Patterns.* Wiley, New York, 1962.

———, *The A.A. Experience: A Close-up View for Professionals* (1984).

McCrady, Barbara S., and W. R. Miller (eds.), *Research on Alcoholics Anonymous* (1993).

Miller, W. R., and E. Kurtz, "Models of Alcoholism Used in Treatment" (1994).

Nace, Edgar P., "Alcoholics Anonymous," in J. Lowinson et al. (eds.), *A Comprehensive Textbook of Substance Abuse* (1992).

Norris, J. L., "Alcoholics Anonymous," in E. D. Whitney (ed.), *World Dialogue on Alcohol and Drug Dependence.*

———, "Alcoholics Anonymous and Other Self-Help Groups," in R. Tarter and A. Sugerman (eds.), *Alcoholism: Interdisciplinary Approaches to an Enduring Problem* (1976).

———, "The Role of A.A. in Rehabilitation," in Groupé, V. (ed.), *Alcoholism Rehabilitation* (1978).

P., Susan, *A Study Guide to the Big Book of Alcoholics Anonymous,* 2128 N. Fife, Tacoma, WA 98406.

Pittman, Bill, *AA: The Way It All Began* (1988).

Ripley, H. S., and Joan K. Jackson, "Therapeutic Factors in Alcoholics Anonymous" (1959).

Robertson, Nan, *Getting Better: Inside Alcoholics Anonymous* (1988).

Smith, Annette R. *Alcoholics Anonymous: A Social World Perspective* (1991).

Stewart, David, *Addicted and Free at the Same Time: A Study of Addiction and Fellowship* (1984), and *Thirst for Freedom* (1960), Chapter 7.

Strachan, J. George, *Alcoholism: Treatable Illness* (1968), Chapter 22; also treats relation of AA to public programs in *Practical Alcoholism Programming.*

Thomsen, Rob, *Bill W.* (1978), a biography.

Tiebout, Harry M., "Therapeutic Mechanism of Alcoholics Anonymous" *American Journal of Psychiatry* (1944); also "Alcoholics Anonymous: An Experiment of Nature" (1961).

Tonigan, J. S., and S. Hiller-Sturmhofel, "Alcoholics Anonymous: Who Benefits?" (1994).

Trice, Harrison M., "A Study of the Process of Affiliation with Alcoholics Anonymous" *Quarterly Journal of Studies on Alcohol,* 1957, 18:39–54; also his "Delabeling, Relabeling and Alcoholics Anonymous," *Social Problems,* 1970, 17:4; and "The Affiliation Motive and Readiness to Join Alcoholics Anonymous," *Quarterly Journal of Studies on Alcohol,* 1959, 20:313–20.

W., Bob, *Transition from Treatment to A.A.* Hazelden pamphelt, very useful.

Walker, Bill, *AA: The Way It Began* (1988).

Williams, J. M., et al., "Comparison of the Importance of Alcoholics Anonymous and Outpatient Counseling to Maintenance of Sobriety Among Alcohol Abusers," *Psychological Reports,* 1986, 48:803–6.

Willoughby, Alan, *The Alcohol Troubled Person* (1984), Chapter 7.

Wing, Nell, *Grateful to Have Been There* (1992).

Zinberg, N. E., "Alcoholics Anonymous and the Treatment and Prevention of Alcoholism," *Alcoholism: Clinical and Experimental Research,* 1977, 1:91–102.

CHAPTER 18

Al-Anon and Alateen

G RANTED THAT FUNDING for treatment of the alcoholic/addict is still inadequate, the family gets even less help. Here again, volunteers with
the AA philosophy fill the gap—this time in the form of offshoots of
the Alcoholics Anonymous program. It is totally unprofessional to attempt
counseling with spouse or family without a good working knowledge of Al-
Anon, yet it is not even mentioned in some job interviews.

Al-Anon is not just for wives. The alcoholic may or may not have
achieved sobriety and may or may not be in AA, may be still drinking or
sober, separated or divorced or dead—there are still residual emotional problems with which the family and those close to the alcoholic need help,
whether the alcoholic gets well or not. Nar-Anon is a parallel program for the
spouse or family of other addicts (not to be confused with NarcAnon, which
is not in the Twelve-Step tradition).

Origin. In the late 1930s, when Alcoholics Anonymous was beginning, close
relatives realized that they too needed help and sought solutions by following
the principles of AA. Al-Anon Family Groups incorporated in 1954 as a completely separate organization—the *AA Guidelines for Cooperation with Al-
Anon* spell out the relation. Founder Lois W., wife of Bill W., died in 1988.

Al-Anon is in more than ninety countries. Some 20,000 groups worldwide include 2,800 Alateen groups. Al-Anon has produced eight books, more
than forty pamphlets, and the monthly publication *The Forum,* as well as cooperating with the public media in the production of TV films, magazine articles, and other materials.

What Is Al-Anon?

Al-Anon is a fellowship of husbands, wives, other relatives, or friends of alcoholics who have banded together in a recovery program for people who
suffer because someone close to them drinks too much. At Al-Anon meetings
members learn, through mutual aid and loving interchange, that their own recovery is possible whether or not the drinker seeks help or even recognizes
that a drinking problem exists. Al-Anon groups are nonprofessional, nonde-
nominational, and self-supporting; they have no opinions on outside issues.
Anyone who feels his or her personal life is or has been deeply affected by a
problem drinker is eligible for Al-Anon membership.

The Al-Anon purpose is threefold: to offer comfort, hope, and friendship to the families of compulsive drinkers; to learn to grow spiritually by living the Twelve Steps; and to give understanding and encouragement to the alcoholic (see Al-Anon, *How Al-Anon Works,* 1995b).

What It Is Not

It is clear that the group does not have as its purpose to "reform" the alcoholic. Its members' primary purpose is to improve themselves and to work on their own defects. If the recovery of the alcoholic is hastened indirectly by changes observed in the member, that is a welcome by-product. But the image of Al-Anon as a group who sit around and complain about how much a spouse drinks or how badly they are treated is a stereotype that must be exploded at once. The new member is allowed to vent feelings on this subject early on, but soon the group kindly but firmly directs the conversation to what the new member should be doing about self-improvement. This is summarized in one version of the Serenity Prayer: "O God/Grant me the serenity to accept the people I cannot change/The courage to change the one I can change/And the wisdom to know it's me!"

How Al-Anon Works

Detachment—the First Step. In the first step members admit that they are powerless over alcohol, that they cannot control the excessive drinking of spouse, parent, or friend. After years of manipulating, nagging, worrying, and feeling guilty, this is as big a step as the admission is for the alcoholic. But the sense of relief when they move on to the second and third steps is equally great: They turn the matter over to a Higher Power as they understand Him, and then go about the business of correcting their own defects (Steps 4 through 10). We saw in Chapter 9 that for the most part the old psychological theories of alcoholic marriages put far too much stress on the predisposing personality of the spouse. Most of the spouse's apparent neuroticism is not the cause but the result of living with the problem, being obsessed with it, feeling guilty because surely the problem would not exist if only they could do the right thing or avoid doing the wrong thing. Recognizing in Step 1 that they cannot control the drinking means less guilt feeling in the Al-Anon member, but also, correspondingly, a recognition of the inability to do much about the drinker. They learn that their alcoholic is sick, not ungrateful or malicious. That is a relief, but it also shifts the focus from the alcoholic to learning how to manage their own lives properly. No longer can they blame the alcoholic's drinking for their own shortcomings.

As Al-Anon and Alateen members learn more about the illness of alcoholism, they stop fighting a lot of ghosts and come to grips with real issues. They learn that scolding or arguing does not help and only hurts both parties.

Most important, they learn that shielding the alcoholic, lying to the boss, paying bail or fine, and all forms of smother love only encourage the alcoholic behavior. Letting alcoholics feel the full responsibility for their actions previously seemed cruel, but it is now seen as kindness, because it hastens that moment of truth that is the beginning of recovery. Detachment is not cold and selfish but a form of the "tough love" that has proved so beneficial in occupational programs and other interventions. Members detach from the problem, not the person.

Denial of alcoholism plays a big role in the family, as it does in the thinking of the alcoholic. The group helps to penetrate denial, because they can share insights. For the spouse the denial is more likely to be interwoven with self-pity. Again the group can often work more effectively on the "poor me" syndrome than an individual therapist can. Resentments and blaming the alcoholic need to be aired, and the group is able to put those feelings in an objective light, because they have all been through them. The fact that they are not alcoholic has been used subconsciously to mean that all the family troubles stem from the drinking. Although that may be true to a great extent, the picture has become distorted. Chaos results when the most disorganized member, the alcoholic, runs the family, who are Enablers, as explained in the many writings of Joseph L. Kellerman.

Spiritual. Like AA, Al-Anon is compatible with all religions and offends none. It is a spiritual program that allows each to conceive of God in his or her own way, careful not to affiliate with any sect or denomination. Skeptics and agnostics are accepted and allowed to work out their own programs as they see fit. Tolerance and good humor are evident at meetings and in the social events the groups often sponsor jointly with AA.

Sharing Is Beneficial. The fellowship of Al-Anon does two things: (1) It lets people know they are not alone, that others have the same fears and frustrations and have made the same mistakes. (2) It gives the opportunity to get involved in helping others, a source of personal satisfaction as well as a distraction from one's own troubles. The warmth and genuine friendship stem from the sense of mutual understanding, after years of thinking that nobody could possibly know what the family member was going through. Alcoholics can anesthetize themselves to much of the misery simply by drinking and might find at least superficial companionship in their drinking buddies. The spouse or child of the alcoholic lacks both of those cushions. Joining Al-Anon or Alateen does not provide the anesthesia, but it does give a much deeper companionship.

The new member says, "My case is different from any of yours because my husband says if he weren't married to me, he wouldn't need to drink." Someone replies, "That's the cop-out every one of us has used." The new member raises her head and sees members nodding in agreement all around the table, some with soft smiles of reassurance. She is not alone.

Differences from AA

Al-Anon and Alateen use the same Twelve Steps as Alcoholics Anonymous but use them differently, as we saw in describing Step 1. There are more daytime meetings and more attention to such arrangements as babysitting. Anonymity is a more sensitive issue, and there are fewer open meetings. That is understandable. "The whole town knew I was a drunk," says many an alcoholic. "I don't care who knows I'm happy to be a member of AA." But the spouse says, "If I am identified as Al-Anon, that could hurt my marriage partner's business or career." Visitors at open meetings are well advised not to bring notebooks or cameras and to be very discreet about even the semblance of violating anonymity.

A special problem for Al-Anon is the detachment called for in Step 1 (Reddy, 1978). After years of feeling responsible for the alcoholic's drinking, it may be as difficult to break this habit as it is for the alcoholic to stop drinking. By first admitting in Step 1 their own powerlessness to control the alcoholic, they are able to turn the matter over to God (Step 3) and learn to live their own lives. A delicate question is whether Al-Anon sometimes prolongs the detachment of the first step to the point of missing the chance for an intervention with the alcoholic, which might get him or her into treatment. Here one must balance a respect for the traditional emphasis in Al-Anon on that first step against what we now know about the success rates of forced treatment. We repeat, this is a delicate issue, to be raised only when the surrender is complete, detachment has been achieved, and the false guilt problems have been well worked through. For example, Jane learned that to detach is not to ignore and that Step 1 does not mean she must let her husband drink himself to death. When she finally arranged an intervention, he went immediately into treatment.

The Al-Anon philosophy can apply in a wide variety of situations. Attendance at meetings may be helpful while the alcoholic is still drinking; during the early days of recovery; as the period of sobriety lengthens even into years; if the alcoholic is no longer in the home; and if the spouse is a man. The point is to recognize that they need help as much as does the alcoholic. An increasing number of parents of alcoholics are finding help in Al-Anon, especially with problems of stigma and false guilt about the alcoholism of their offspring. In Chapter 10 we saw that ACoA and Al-Anon have similar functions and are compatible.

Problems After Recovery. The last section of Chapter 9 detailed the family problems that arise in Jackson's Stage 7, after recovery and reunion. Although one may be a member of Al-Anon whether the alcoholic is in AA or not, the following advice applies especially if the alcoholic is an AA member:

The Al-Anon member should be willing to cooperate with the alcoholic's efforts to get and maintain sobriety in AA but should not interfere or advise. Alcoholics have a better chance of success when the family leaves them free to work out their own problems. Overcoming the obsession with drink requires an equally strong drive toward involvement with something positive like Alcoholics Anonymous, so one must accept graciously the need for spending much time at meetings and in doing Twelfth Step work helping others. When the alcoholic is busy with AA, one can cure the lonely, left-out feeling by becoming active in Al-Anon. Sometimes the AA member, elated with the achievement of sobriety, may assume a superior attitude. That is a natural reaction from former inferiority feelings; AA is a spiritual program, and as one grows in humility this attitude will moderate. We must have patience, and then more patience. Sometimes it is harder to tolerate petty daily irritations than it was to deal with the big problem of alcoholism. So don't be discouraged if progress is slow. Some alcoholics are sicker than others and take longer to get well (see Al-Anon, *From Survival to Recovery*, 1995a).

Al-Anon warns its members not to expect immediate personal readjustment, as the distorted relationships that resulted from the drinking will still leave many personal problems to be ironed out. As Al-Anons share their experiences, strength, and hope, they help each other to cope with possible relapses and remind each other that AA has a long history of success with cases that seemed hopeless.

Husbands of alcoholic wives seem to have special problems, which are only now beginning to be studied. It has long been known that they are far more prone to divorce their wives, whereas the wife of an alcoholic husband will tend to hang on to the marriage. How much of this is feminine loyalty and how much is sheer economic dependence is not known. Denial seems stronger in the husband. Perhaps the male ego still holds him to the role of protector and head of the household. His wife's alcoholism is an affront to his management ability and pride of leadership. Perhaps chivalry prevents him from admitting that the lady he vowed to love and cherish is an alcoholic. While the wife of the alcoholic husband finds sympathy from family, friends, and the clergy, the husband of the alcoholic wife too often out of pride refuses to discuss his secret with anyone. Without the help of Al-Anon the resentments build up until he simply packs up and leaves. If the alcoholic wife is also a career woman, the competition and overlapping of roles may make the situation extremely complex.

"I don't need Al-Anon, I have the Twelve Steps in AA" is a fallacy. One may need AA for his or her own sobriety, and Al-Anon for the marriage. *Dual Members,* formerly *Al-Anon Spoken Here* or *Double Winners,* is an Al-Anon leaflet addressed to those who have reason to belong to both: recovering alcoholics who are also married or close to an alcoholic. Even the person who is working the AA program well can learn how to take a different inventory (Step 4) as an Al-Anon spouse or family member rather than as an alcoholic. Release or "detachment with love" can eliminate a lot of marital friction. The dual members often say that in AA they learned how to accept themselves, and in Al-Anon they learned how to accept the spouse.

Alateen

Alateen started in 1957 when Bob, the seventeen-year-old son of an alcoholic, hoped to find the serenity his mother found in Al-Anon and his father found in AA. He contacted five other teenagers with alcoholic parents. They chose the name Alateen and became a component of Al-Anon. Although both groups began with families, the fellowship now extends to anyone who suffers because of someone close. In some cities there are special groups of Ala-tots for children younger than teenage, who often prefer to be called Preteens.

The Alateen program uses the same Twelve Steps and much of the literature of Al-Anon but has also developed its own traditions and materials. Usually the sponsor of an Alateen group is a member of Al-Anon who helps the Alateen leader arrange the time and place of the meeting and sometimes helps conduct it. This sponsorship is necessary to ensure continuity (teenagers soon outgrow this period) and to lend adult status to meeting arrangements and permissions to be out at night. But the Alateen group runs its own meetings and develops its own leadership. *Meetings at school* can have the advantages of not having to be out at night, not requiring transportation to another site, and not antagonizing the alcoholic parent. Anonymity is protected, as nobody need know whether the child is using the activity period for debate, orchestra, or whatever.

Alateen helps its members to acknowledge that the feelings and behaviors described in Chapter 10 are mere escapes and to take responsibility for their own lives regardless of whether the alcoholic parent stops drinking or not. Sharing all this in Alateen helps children to understand and handle those disturbing emotions. It must be emphasized that Alateens do not criticize the alcoholic's behavior but learn to live less affected by it. They learn that they are not responsible for their family situation, and that they are not crazy, in spite of having been told that by their alcoholic parent. Perhaps most important, they come in thinking they must be the only ones who have these problems and discover that they are not alone, that there are thousands of other children in very similar circumstances.

Referral to Al-Anon and Alateen

As with referrals to AA, merely giving someone a phone number of Al-Anon is not enough. Referral should be based on a good understanding of the Al-Anon program, awareness of different groups and their characteristics, the mechanism of sponsorship, and with some preparation of the client through prior explanation and reading of the Al-Anon literature. If the spouse is already in therapy, the professional can use Al-Anon as supportive or adjunctive therapy and long-term followup. Clergy, skilled alcoholism counselors, and, surprisingly, even members of AA working professionally in the field sometimes neglect to use Al-Anon as a resource. Occupational alcoholism programs in business and industry now see the value of engaging the spouse in Al-Anon, both for the spouse's own sake and for the added understanding support it gives the alcoholic. Al-Anon is prepared to furnish speakers and otherwise cooperate with health agencies, recovery centers, and institutions, making it a valuable adjunct without adding to budget.

Alateen referrals take special care. Teenagers need to be told that it is free, that it is strictly anonymous, and that attendance is not a sign of disloyalty to their parents. Reassurance that it is okay to have an alcoholic parent is coupled with the idea that it is not okay to do nothing about it. All adolescents have troubles and doubts, so others can understand and help. The child is better off knowing that alcoholism is the problem, rather than remaining baffled by the unknown and risking greater danger of alcoholism for himself or herself later. Referral must have the explicit permission of the child before contact is made with a sponsor, either Al-Anon or Alateen. Rather than drive newcomers to a meeting, it is better to take them on the bus, if that is the way they will be going to meetings. Although not necessary for participation in Alateen, if the nonalcoholic parent can be referred to Al-Anon, so much the better.

Sources

The primary source here is the Al-Anon and Alateen Conference–approved literature, available locally from the groups or from Al-Anon Family Group Headquarters, P.O. Box 862, Midtown Station, New York 10018-0862. The writing of this chapter relied greatly on this literature. Al-Anon books are listed in the General Bibliography. Pamphlets and leaflets, some addressed to the new inquirer and some to those who wish to know more about how to form or sponsor groups, explain every phase of Al-Anon and Alateen activity. A few of the many titles available are listed here:

Al-Anon and Professionals (for Al-Anons working in the field, formerly *Working as, for, or with Professionals*).

Al-Anon Speaks to You, The Professional.

Al-Anon Speaks Out, a periodical mailed to professionals on request.

Blueprint for Progress (Al-Anon Step 4 Inventory); see also Hazelden Foundation, *Guide to the Fourth Step Inventory for the Spouse*).

Homeward Bound (for relatives of alcoholics returning from treatment).

A Teacher Finds Guidance in Al-Anon.

(For men) *Men in Al-Anon; Al-Anon Is for Men; My Wife Drinks Too Much;* and *"What's Next?" Asks the Husband of an Alcoholic.*

(For parents) *To the Mother and Father of an Alcoholic;* and *How Can I Help My Children?*

(For Alateens) *A Guide for Sponsors of Alateen Groups; Twelve Steps and Twelve Traditions for Alateen; Moving On! From Alateen to Al-Anon;* and a periodical, *Alateen Talk.*

CHAPTER 19

Spiritual and Moral
Aspects

ADDICTION HAS BEEN DESCRIBED as an illness: physical, mental-emotional, and spiritual. But few have analyzed the precise nature of the spiritual illness (W. R. Miller, 1990). One is tempted to say "Why all this God stuff? Why drag religion into it?"

One can get fellowship in a tavern, but not sobriety (see Clinebell, 1995). One national authority says that relapse is almost invariably tied to lack of spiritual growth, and another says that spirituality is our number one means of coping with stress. A three-year study of 441 patients called the spiritual "the most neglected part of therapy" (*NIAAA Info*, April 1, 1983, p. 2), and a recent research study reported that 91 percent of patients said their spiritual needs were not met in treatment programs. Those are hard data, facts of human experience which as scientific psychologists we cannot ignore. This chapter will analyze the spiritual needs of alcoholics as they describe themselves. This is not theory, but the experience of 2.2 million people. The founders of Alcoholics Anonymous found no lasting serenity until they came to believe that no human power is adequate to the alcoholic's problems, and that applies to other addictions as well.

The counselor may or may not consider spiritual values important; the question is how the client feels, and how to respect the faith of patients and to use it to best advantage. Gerald May (1989, 1991) is a physician who explores the relations between addiction and spirituality. The counselor must look at the client's needs and at least understand them well enough to make a good referral (T. S. Baker, 1994).

Role of the Churches

We saw in Chapter 17 that AA is not a religion, that one must distinguish between spiritual and religious. In the realm of organized religion we do note some remarkable changes in church policy and activity during the past few decades. The image of the church was formerly associated with the moralistic crusading of the Prohibition era, which only provided the alcoholic with an excuse to drink again. We list briefly some of the contributions the churches are making.

The church can be a strong influence in changing public attitudes. Instead of the hypocrisy in former condemnations of all drinking, many churches are now expressing genuine concern over excessive drinking and are promoting reasonable guidelines for alcohol use (for example, those developed by the Episcopal Church). Alcoholism is recognized as an illness, e.g., by the United Presbyterian Church in 1946 (Apthorp, 1990) and by the Vatican in 1972 and 1992 (Pontifical Council, 1992). Positive spiritual values are being substituted for feelings of guilt and discouragement. Cooperation with the professional agencies is encouraged. Strong support is given to AA, and the clergy are learning to use Al-Anon as a spiritual resource in their family counseling. Some churches are including educative tidbits of information about alcohol and other drugs in their parish bulletins or other publications. Most important, instead of leaving the problem to treatment centers, individual church members are beginning to understand and help the alcoholic within the parish community (Fuad, 1992).

Self-description Reveals Needs

The *spiritual* is our capacity to relate to the Infinite. The material or physical is always limited or finite, measurable or quantifiable; a light can be too bright, or a sound too loud. The spiritual transcends matter, goes beyond what can be weighed or measured, gives meaning to life in terms of ultimate goals. It enables us to relate to the Eternal, to Infinite Beauty, Goodness, and Intelligibility with no limits—to reach beyond the farthest stars, to dream the impossible dream. Spiritual values are beyond the monetary and sensual; hence spiritual love relates to one as a *person*, as opposed to using another as a *thing*.

Spiritual dis-ease means being dysfunctional, ill-at-ease in the presence of the Creator. It is important to recognize that AA is not the only or necessary way to approach the spiritual aspects of this problem. Rather than any program, we shall examine spiritual needs reported by alcoholics. Figure 7 charts the progression of alcoholism as a spiritual disease, and the spiritual aspects of recovery. A similar pattern occurs in those addicted to other drugs, but this chart reflects forty-five years of counseling alcoholics (Royce, 1995).

Patients find it helpful to follow the chart (pp. 290–91), starting at the upper left corner.

- Alcohol in the brain sedates one's scale of values, so we get confused as to what is more important than what. Gradually we grow indifferent—God isn't really that important anyway. Alcohol impairs the ability of the mind to think and feel right about God. It is rather hard to pray when you are drunk or suffering from a hangover.
- From this follows grandiosity, pride. Chapter 5 in the AA big book describes how we try to run the whole show, trying to play God. Perfectionism becomes the bane of many alcoholics.

- Intolerance of others grows, since others are imperfect. We argue with everybody about every little point—on which we are always right, of course.
- The alcoholic's religion is starting to get sick: rigid, arrogant, unrealistic, mechanical, shallow. Alcohol has anesthetized his or her spiritual values. Alcoholics become disenchanted with their childish ideas of God. If one has distorted ideas of God or feelings toward God, one cannot believe or trust, and hence can never love, our Higher Power. The trouble is not with God, but with our inadequate and childish concepts of Him—"God as we *don't* understand Him," if you will (Royce, 1994). The image of God as a cruel tyrant who won't let us have any fun (like the mother who won't let the three-year-old play with the nice sharp butcher knife), or a faraway abstract principle, or an old graybeard, a male instead of the purely spiritual Source of all perfections female and male, or an egotistical pipsqueak that has to be adored every Sunday to gratify his Ego.
- There is a loss of interest in life, which becomes a big blah. The result is frequent bouts with "the blues."
- With things going this way, there are usually feelings of guilt. Anger at God is just one more projection of blame on others. There is a tendency to blame the clergy or nuns, the church, or even God. There is a feeling of guilt, not because God is unforgiving and cruel, but because alcohol has blinded the alcoholic to God's infinite mercy and kindness. He or she is not "at ease" with God.
- Although they don't realize it at the time, looking back, many alcoholics say that the first mark of progression in their spiritual disease was stopping daily prayer. They may continue to go to church, out of habit or pretense.
- There is a sense of being "nobody"—alienated, estranged from friends, self, and God. No wonder the drinking alcoholic feels lonely!
- Alcoholics exhibit a certain degree of immaturity, once thought to be the cause of alcoholism and now recognized as an effect. They show irresponsibility—alcohol is a "don't-give-a-damn" drug.
- Life begins to become meaningless: "Who cares? Have another drink!"
- But since alcoholics are basically good people, not morally depraved no-goodnicks, there is a sneaking anxiety underneath this bravado: vague, indefinable fears that all is not well.
- The anxiety creates resentments: they are hostile at the very mention of religion, which reminds them of their responsibilities. They justify, rationalize, defend, get angry—a sure sign they have a problem. Their professed atheism *may* be just shame and guilt.
- They also report moral deterioration: they become dishonest, selfish, perhaps sexually promiscuous, although not all are, and it is a mistake to assume this. The moral deterioration was once thought to be the cause of alcoholism. We now know that it is largely the result of the addiction, as alcohol has anesthetized the users' sense of values.

Figure 7 Alcoholism as a SPIRITUAL Dis-ease: Progression and Recovery

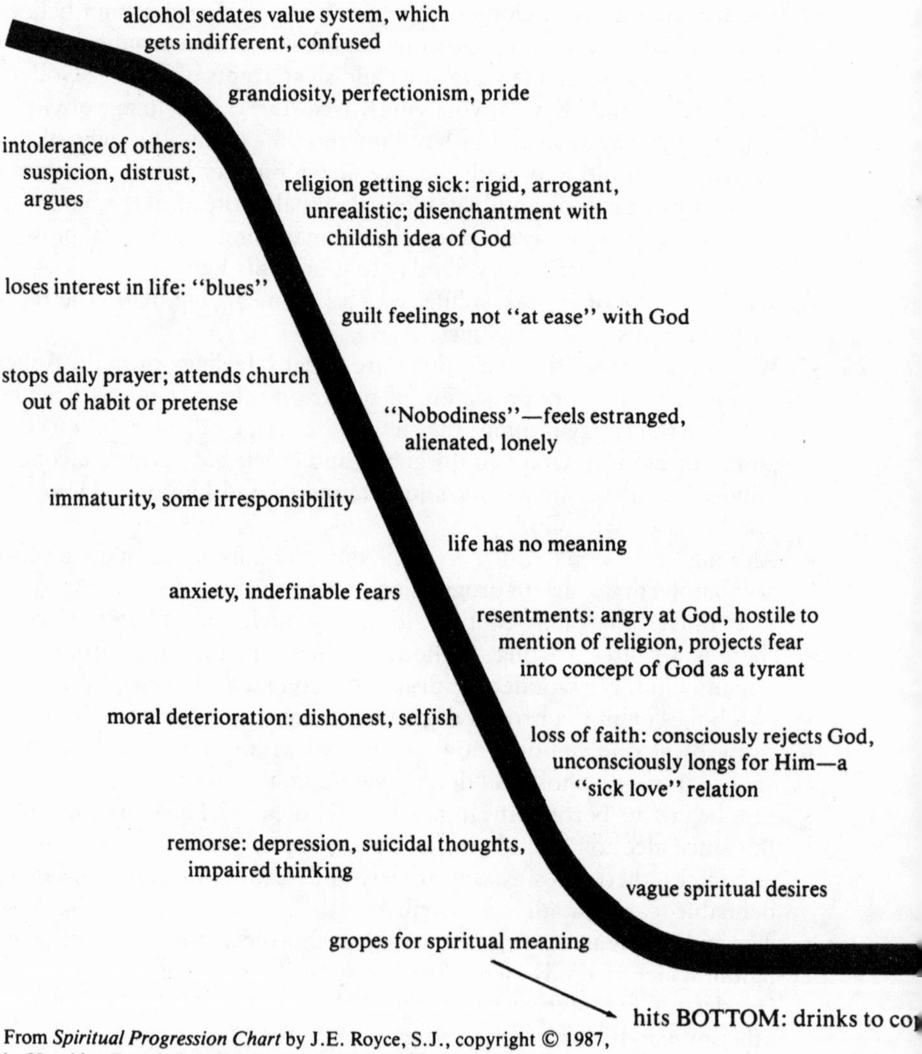
alcohol sedates value system, which gets indifferent, confused
grandiosity, perfectionism, pride
intolerance of others: suspicion, distrust, argues
religion getting sick: rigid, arrogant, unrealistic; disenchantment with childish idea of God
loses interest in life: "blues"
guilt feelings, not "at ease" with God
stops daily prayer; attends church out of habit or pretense
"Nobodiness"—feels estranged, alienated, lonely
immaturity, some irresponsibility
life has no meaning
anxiety, indefinable fears
resentments: angry at God, hostile to mention of religion, projects fear into concept of God as a tyrant
moral deterioration: dishonest, selfish
loss of faith: consciously rejects God, unconsciously longs for Him—a "sick love" relation
remorse: depression, suicidal thoughts, impaired thinking
vague spiritual desires
gropes for spiritual meaning
hits BOTTOM: drinks to co

From *Spiritual Progression Chart* by J.E. Royce, S.J., copyright © 1987, by Hazelden Foundation, Center City, MN. Reprinted by permission.

"weller than well"—higher levels than
believed possible

unselfish: goes out to others because
God loves them

deeper relation
to God as a
loving God

growth in proper concept of God

prayer and meditation

Serenity, peace of soul, joy

increased tolerance
of others

Gratitude

appreciation of spiritual
values

rebirth of ideals

courage, optimism—
new Freedom

promptly admits when wrong

Honesty: make amends

return of self-esteem (God not a
rescuer)

false ego deflated

Humbly asks God to remove
shortcomings

Reconciliation: personal relationship
"at ease" with God (more than just
"dumping garbage")

Forgiveness: not "why did I?" but
"forgive me"

appreciates possibility of new way
of life

Patience: "one day at a time"

Conversion: "let go and let God"

Trust: "Thy will be done"

• second bottom: "existential crisis"

acceptance (surrender—Tiebout)

thirst for God examined (hard struggle
for some)

pe dawns: can be restored to sanity

vague notion of Higher Power

new Faith: "Came to believe"

in spiritual fog

honest desire for help

• admission (compliance—Tiebout)

h problems of drinking

- All this involves some loss of faith, although it varies greatly with the individual. Rarely is faith gone entirely.

The alcoholic, perhaps more than others, is a God-seeker. This is congruent with the facts in chapter 8 that most alcoholics do not drink to sedate psychological problems, but for the lift, the glow, the positive effects of alcohol—not looking for sedation so much as for solace, trying to satisfy the hunger of the heart. Not that the world is too much for them, but that it is not enough. It may be that they are seeking to find in alcohol the answer to spiritual needs not met in our materialistic culture. They complain of spiritual hunger or spiritual bankruptcy. One alcoholic said that human nature has a "God-shaped hole" in it—a vacuum that only God can fill. Whether they know it or not, in their perfectionism they want nothing less than the Infinite. Bill W. said that alcoholics "seek God in a bottle."

Alcoholics tend to both feel rejected and to be rejecting. Their love affair with God is certainly sick in this way: Consciously they reject God, even though unconsciously they are longing for Him. One alcoholic said, "I don't believe in God, but I pray to Him a lot."

- There is a vague groping for the spiritual meaning of life. Even professed atheists have vague spiritual desires.

Hitting Bottom. In this state of impaired thinking, guilt feelings, remorse, discouragement, depression, even suicidal thoughts inevitably follow. The alcoholics have reached bottom. The depression they feel might be compared to the dark night of the soul described by the mystics: The cup must be emptied of all that is material before it can be filled with God. Hitting bottom really means acceptance of the fact that one is powerless over alcohol, that one's life has become unmanageable.

Spiritual Recovery

We come now to the righthand or "up" side of the chart. Note that this side of the chart has more on it than the down side—spiritual recovery is very rich.

A recent study reported that 60 percent of one group said they were atheists while drinking, but all believe in God now that they are sober for a while. It is important that organized religion not look on AA as competition, but as complementary. Many alcoholics who have wandered far from the religion of their childhood need to grope their way back to God out of the alcoholic fog by means of some vague notion of a "Higher Power," and to force more formalized concepts of religion on them too soon may just drive them away.

- Hitting bottom means admitting our powerlessness. This is so hard on our ego that the admission may be just a superficial compliance.

- At first there may be just an honest desire for help. With a new faith, they "came to believe" that there is hope, that they can be restored to sanity. The great psychiatrist Carl Jung felt that alcoholics are unconsciously seeking God and will never find lasting and comfortable sobriety until they find God.

The big reason this is a hard struggle for some is those false images of God from childhood we spoke of earlier. If we are going to let God be our new Manager for lives that have become unmanageable, we have to know Him correctly. Just common sense tells us that the Creator must have Infinite Goodness and mercy, yet we don't give God credit for the decency we would expect from a stranger. The proof is how all this changes when one stops drinking. Like the parents who are seen quite differently after their adolescent children mature, God improves greatly when we get sober!

- Admission gradually becomes acceptance, a preferable term to Tiebout's *surrender.* Here we have a true conversion, a radical personality change, which enables one to "let go and let God." After years of being unable to trust anybody or anything, the alcoholic can now say "Thy will be done."
- Many will face a "second bottom" later on in sobriety, when the residual brain toxicity has subsided enough to allow them to face an existential crisis. (For most, this probably occurs later than indicated on the chart.) Abstinence alone may not bring a lasting state of peace. New anxiety arises as they begin to face the larger issues of life, ignored during the first crisis of freeing themselves from the addiction by learning just to avoid that first drink one day at a time. "Now that I'm no longer a drunk, who am I?" "What do I really value in life?" Also, AA Steps 8, 9, and 10 may force them to see that growing up means they have to face responsibility, which makes them uncomfortable.
- Hence the need for patience. They must learn to take up these new tasks one day at a time. That is why some AA's define time as God's way of seeing to it that everything doesn't happen at once.
- We now come to realize the true answer to guilt is God's forgiveness, not analyzing why we did something to explain it away but accepting the fact that we are imperfect human beings. Psychology is good to get rid of false or unrealistic guilt, but it can make you feel guilty about feeling guilty. Real guilt can be relieved only by the infinite mercy of God. Since God is infinite, you can't possibly commit sins bigger than God's infinite forgiveness.

And forgiveness is more than just "dumping garbage." We recognize the psychological value of catharsis, but reconciliation involves more than that. True healing means reestablishing a personal relationship, eliminating the spiritual dis-ease, getting "at ease" with God again. There is a lot of practical psychology in the Twelve Steps—Step 5 does not allow one to confess to God solely in the secrecy of the heart. Rather, it calls for one to do so out loud to another human being—reality therapy or authentic encounter, if you will. That is why Step 5 is more important than Step 4, the moral inventory. One person said, "I learned more about myself from having to say it out loud to you than I did writing out the Fourth Step." Incidentally, the big book *Alcoholics Anonymous* (1939, p. 86; 3d ed., 1976, p. 74) says it is quite permissible and even recommended to do a fifth step in confession if called for by whatever religion one may happen to belong to.

- Being entirely ready for God to remove our shortcomings, as the AA 6th Step suggests, we can then in Step 7 humbly ask God to remove them. But *humbly* implies deflating our false ego. Perfectionism and grandiosity are classic alcoholic symptoms and the source of many problems (Ackerman, 1989; Adderholt-Elliott, 1989; Kurtz and Ketcham, 1992). Perfectionism stems from pride, an inability to accept our own limitedness. Pride and humility appear often in the writings of Bill W. Humility is the remedy, but humility is much misunderstood. It is simply truth, and the truth is not that you are no good, just that you are not perfect—*Not-God*, in the felicitous title of that most scholarly history of AA by Kurtz (1979, 1991): the story of 2 million people who discovered they are not God. Humility gives a sense of ease with ourselves, others, and God; we are no longer spiritually diseased—satisfaction guaranteed or your ego back!
- The result of true humility is not a beating down of the person, but a return to a correct self-esteem, dropping the façade we tried to maintain and drank to avoid admitting. Slavery to the bottle gives way to a new sense of freedom; the power of choice is restored: with God's help, I can choose NOT to drink (Peteet, 1993). Paradoxically, acceptance of our own imperfection can become humility rather than humiliation—a relief rather than a burden: "Thank God, I don't have to do it all alone any more!" For this reason we object to the current phrase "self-help" programs. The whole burden of Chapter 5 of the big book *Alcoholics Anonymous* is that reliance on self is exactly what got us in trouble, and the answer is to stop playing God. They are really *God*-help programs, not self-help; those who find that objectionable can say *Twelve-Step* or *group-support* programs.

As for those psychologists who think that dependence on God is neurotic escape, if God is the Supreme Reality then it is the atheist who is escaping. The spiritual is a major portion of the universe, which it is unscientific to ignore. Admission of dependence on God need not be taken as neurotic or demeaning, any more than our dependence on oxygen. One suggestion to a patient struggling with the notion of Higher Power: "Think of whatever it is that enables you to breathe." Some people talk as if dependence on a psychotherapist is all right, but not dependence on the Creator.

On the other hand, this does not mean an immature escaping from responsibility. It is good theology that God helps those who help themselves; God is a good Al-Anon, not an Enabler or Rescuer. The expression heard around AA meetings, "turn it over to God," is not what Step 3 says. "To turn our will and our lives over to the *care* of God" means that we still have to do it, but under God's loving care, not sitting back and leaving it to God. And "One day at a time" refers to not taking that first drink—not that one does not buy fire insurance until twenty-four hours before the house burns down.

- Real humility is required by AA Steps 8 and 9, which bring a return to honesty by making amends where appropriate, and by Step 10, which says that when wrong we promptly admitted it. As we grow spiritually, pride, perfectionism, and grandiosity are replaced with a genuine humility, which makes the person more attractive to others because comfortable with self.
- The new freedom these steps bring generates a rebirth of ideals, a courage and an optimism not felt in years.
- Appreciation of spiritual values is growing, as shown in our increased tolerance of others and in our gratitude. AA members often introduce themselves as grateful alcoholics. Presumably they have a God to thank.
- They exhibit a serenity, a peace of soul, and a joy they could not have imagined a few years earlier. (Their *Serenity Prayer* was composed in 1934 by Reinhold Niebuhr; AA adopted the first part in 1942.) They find that sobriety is more than just abstinence. Spirituality becomes the number one means of coping with stress. Lasting and joyous sobriety seems inevitably to involve growth in the spiritual life. That is why in Step 11 the AA founders "sought through prayer and meditation to increase our conscious contact with God as we understood Him" and their whole lives began to change. By conscious contact with God in prayer one grows in knowledge of a loving God, not one to be feared. Meditation is just thinking quietly in God's presence about some saying or truth or passage from the AA big book or whatever, and then talking it over with God and trying to see it from God's perspective, which is that of eternity. Prayer is conversation with God, and conversation is a two-way street. We don't pray to inform God, who already knows everything. We pray to dispose ourselves to receive what God sends.

"Praying *only* for knowledge of His will for us and the power to carry that out," as Step 11 bids, our lives become simpler and set in the path of spiritual *progress*, not perfection. One proof, even a test of this, is that relations with others improve. One becomes unselfish when one begins to love others because God loves them and wants us to, not because they are pretty or handsome or rich or fun. Spiritual values have replaced material values.

- As indicated at the top of the chart, where the heavy line ends up higher than it starts on the down side, they become "weller than well"—better than they were before their illness, or than they would have been had they not found AA. Research seems to confirm this notion (Mellor, 1986). The first time one hears people say "I'm glad I'm an alcoholic" is shocking until they go on to explain that if they weren't alcoholic, they would never have joined AA and learned how much God loves them and how much they love God. Recovering persons develop a deeper relationship with God, now seen as a loving God rather than a cruel tyrant. After years of tension, anxiety, and guilt, the kind of psychological growth and deep personality change necessary for successful rehabilitation is often and perhaps only achieved by letting God seep slowly and quietly into the thirsty soul of the alcoholic.

Addiction and Responsibility

Probably the most sensitive aspect of the problems arising from the overuse of drugs is the area of moral responsibility. How guilty should one feel—if at all—for the drinking, for the subsequent behavior, even for being an alcoholic? There is an understandable reluctance even to mention these issues, both because of bitter emotional controversies that surrounded Prohibition and because the recovering addict is already burdened with unnecessary guilt feelings to which we do not wish to add. But a mature look demands that we consider the moral side, if only for the sake of completeness. We are asking hard questions, to which there are no easy answers. Andrews (1987, Chapter 2) gives an excellent review of the dramatic shift in modern psychology away from sterile science toward a value-centered approach, and applies this (Chapter 12) to the addiction field. Dr. John C. Ford, the Jesuit moral theologian who was one of the earliest to write professionally about this aspect of alcoholism, once wrote an article, "Clerical Attitudes on Alcohol" (1955) with the delightful subtitle "—Most of Them Wrong." He talks about clergy attitudes that are Unformed (immature, confused), Uninformed (ignorant), Misinformed (erroneous, myths), Deformed (extremes on either side of the drinking question—either it's *the* moral issue, or it's no moral issue at all), and Reformed (holier than thou, hard to live with).

In former days alcoholism was a sin and fell into the province of the clergy. Today most have gone beyond the preachy, moralizing tone of the mission flop houses, when men made a "nosedive" sham conversion just to get a free meal. Pledges, promises, and pious resolves not backed by sound remedial approaches have been found to be equally ineffective. When alcoholism became a civil crime, it was handled by the police, courts, and jail—the "drunk tank." But the model Uniform Alcoholism and Intoxication Treatment Act requires that the alcoholic be taken to treatment rather than punished (see next chapter). The person is not bad, but sick. We do not talk about "reformed" but "recovered," and say "relapse," not "recidivism."

Nature of Addiction

As necessary groundwork for addressing the moral issues, we first have to review from Chapter 8 the kind of a disease addiction is. The usual answer is

"Physical, mental, and spiritual." Addiction is neither weak-willed moral depravity nor usually the symptom of a psychiatric conflict, but rather a pathology in its own right: a compulsion rooted in the whole complex of mental and biological changes already referred to.

This means that in asking questions of moral responsibility we must clearly distinguish among *drinking, drunkenness,* and *alcoholism.* Obvious as the distinctions are, they are constantly ignored in moral discussions, with resulting disastrous confusion. For instance, to oppose moderate drinking by asking "Would you advocate moderate gluttony?" misses the point that gluttony of its very nature is immoderate. Similarly, "moderate adultery" makes no sense. Food, drink, and sex in marriage are all good; their abuse is immoral; and eating disorders, alcoholism, and sexual perversion are sick behavior.

Drink Versus Abstinence

This, of course, is the area where American churches have disagreed widely and even bitterly. Even when they agreed about drunkenness (abuse or overuse or misuse), they differed on drinking (use). The battle went on for more than a century. The intent here is not to dictate anyone's morals but to promote thinking objectively and in terms of moral principles, instead of emotion or blind loyalty to a tradition. We might even swing the pendulum back toward the middle, which could possibly prevent some alcoholism in the light of research by Ullman (1953) and Jackson and Connor (1953b) showing one common factor in a lot of cases was confused or ambivalent attitudes about drinking and drunkenness at the time one took the first drink in his life. As we saw in Chapter 3, the T in WCTU did not mean temperance but abstinence, causing one authority to remark that the "identification of total abstinence with the Christian Ethic was the basic fallacy of the temperance movement."

H. L. Mencken once defined Puritanism as "the haunting fear that somewhere, someone might be having fun" and St. Paul seems to express the same thought (I Timothy, 4:1–2). Extreme Puritanism would make anything pleasurable a sin—which makes God out to be a fool, since God made sunsets and flowers beautiful, and food enjoyable. Most of us would be undernourished if food didn't taste good, and it would be a dreary world without flowers or sunsets. Because they confuse use and abuse, people wonder if there is something wrong with alcohol, or with God, or even with themselves.

There seems to be neither historical nor theological basis for the total abstinence movement, since historically we saw in Chapter 3 that the Jews, Christ, and the founders of the major Protestant denominations all drank. Although drunkenness is condemned in both the Old and New Testaments, there is no condemnation of drinking in either. The wedding at Cana and the Last Supper are not isolated incidents in Christ's life, but reflect the ordinary life-style of His day, as seen in the customs of Orthodox Jews down to this time.

Hewitt (1980) of Southeastern Baptist Seminary exemplifies the common teaching of scripture scholars that there is no biblical justification for using grape juice rather than wine in the sacrament, and it was wine that Christ used when He instituted it. The same Hebrew and Greek word is used for the wine that made Noah drunk as that which Isaiah (25:6–10) considers a special sign of God's favor for His chosen people ("Pure, choice wines") and the Psalmist praises as "wine that gladdens the heart of man." From a scientific standpoint, grape juice was physically impossible in a semitropical climate with no preservatives, no modern sealing techniques, and no refrigeration—with yeasts in the air and on the skin of the grapes, the natural fermentation process inevitably yields wine.

We conclude that drinking itself (for the nonalcoholic) is not wrong. The Judeo-Christian tradition, which sees drink as "lawful but not expedient," makes total abstinence a matter of ascetic counsel rather than moral precept. Our point here is simply that drinking is not alcoholism; it is not even drunkenness. Use of alcohol is one thing, excessive use is something else.

Drunkenness versus Temperance

Whatever disagreements there are about use, most agree about misuse. Although the Jewish, Roman Catholic, Orthodox, Episcopal, and Lutheran traditions generally allow moderate drinking for those who can do so, it is simply incorrect to accuse them of condoning drunkenness. Temperance is an accepted Judeo-Christian virtue.

In this section we are talking about drunkenness in nonalcoholics; the case of the alcoholic/addict is special and will come later. Ethically, it seems clear that to deprive oneself *deliberately* of one's rationality and self-control by a chemical is an abuse. And if it is the design of nature that human beings have the ability to exercise rational control, then drunkenness is obviously contrary to the intent of the Author of nature and therefore morally wrong.

Short of severe loss of the exercise of rational control, to be slightly drunk or high has some moral implications, too. For one thing, lesser degrees do not excuse one from all guilt. Second, there is the danger of going further once one starts, because control and inhibitions are dulled. Third, short of being drunk, one can be just relaxed enough so that poor reaction time or perceptual judgment might kill someone in an auto accident.

Alcoholism/Addiction

We have already made the distinction between choosing to drink and choosing to be an alcoholic. Nobody chooses to be an alcoholic or addict, any more than one chooses to be a diabetic. Half the children of alcoholics become alcoholics in spite of firmly resolving not to. In this sense alcoholism is not a moral problem, and there is no question of responsibility or guilt here. We shall return to this distinction in the next section when dealing with controlled drinking by alcoholics.

Freedom over Drinking/Using. But are alcoholics, when sober, free in the choice to drink, and in control over getting drunk? Here we have a paradox. There is least responsibility in the precise area where there was once the most moralizing: excessive drinking by the alcoholic. Hence the importance of applying the concept delineated above of an obsessive-compulsive habit, an addiction with powerful psychological and physiological dynamics that greatly diminish one's ability to control behavior.

If it were merely a matter of sin, we would say, "Use your will power." They have tried that, only to find that they are powerless and life has become unmanageable. An old adage says, "A drunk could quit if he would, an alcoholic would quit if he could." Will power is not the issue here. Clergymen have drunk themselves to death while clinging to the old idea that they could lick the problem if they just prayed more and tried harder.

Rather, we must apply what we know of the nature of the illness. Of its very nature, habit diminishes freedom. If we are powerfully disposed through habit to act in a certain way, then we are not as free to choose the opposite as we would be without the habit. Choice means selection between alternatives, and to the extent that we are unable to consider alternatives fully or see them clearly, our free choice is limited. Now habit is unconscious; what is conscious is habitual behavior or action. Therefore the full force of habit does not appear in consciousness and hence cannot enter into any clear deliberation between alternatives. Habit does its work in subtle, unconscious ways, which render choice exceedingly difficult. Moreover, addiction has physiological components, and nobody is aware of their cellular or hormonal state. This further restricts the conscious deliberation that is essential for full freedom of choice.

All this means is that an alcoholic is less free, and hence less responsible for drinking and getting drunk, than one who is not addicted. We must further distinguish between before recovery and after recovery.

Before Recovery. If addiction is an illness, then it seems we should apply the same reasoning we use in other illnesses, namely the concept of *diminished* responsibility. We say with perfect understanding, "Joe's sick today; don't pay any attention if he's a bit grouchy." We do not tell a tubercular patient not to cough, a starving man to just use will power. The Reverend John P. Cunningham, longtime director of the National Clergy Conference on Alcoholism, rightly asks whether those persons are capable of making a responsible moral decision who have been living for years with an overwhelming need for a chemical and in constant fear of the pain its deprivation would entail, hopelessly frustrated by their inability to control it, unaware of the deterioration it has caused until too late to turn back, convinced that they are worthless, suspicious of others, alienated from everybody, including God. For such a person the ordinary concepts of guilt and responsibility may not apply at all, or only to a limited extent.

A further question is whether the disease concept absolves one of *all* moral responsibility. A diabetic must still take insulin and follow a diet, and a cancer patient may still have to choose to undergo surgery. To the extent one is able, one may have some obligation to get help for overcoming the illness. In light of the foregoing discussion on diminished freedom, an alcoholic before recovery should not be faced with a choice to stop drinking, only to accept help.

But alcoholics live in an alcoholic fog much of the time, and even in their sober periods their thinking is distorted by denial and rationalization. Cancer patients may find it as difficult to undergo surgery as alcoholics do to go into treatment. But there is nothing about cancer that makes it attractive for cancer victims to continue it, whereas the vicious circle of alcoholism causes alcoholics to feel a strong if not uncontrollable urge to imbibe the very cause of their ills. Hence their responsibility is greatly diminished, and it may devolve more on others who are in a position to confront alcoholics effectively with the tough love intervention discussed in Chapter 14.

After Recovery. The aim of treatment is to restore freedom of choice. Some say that an alcoholic is not free to take or not take the first drink. The sobriety of 2 million AA members and many other recovered alcoholics shows that at least with God's grace and the help of the fellowship or some other means, they can successfully choose not to drink. This varies with the type and degree of their disease. It is true that for recovered alcoholics the choice is much harder, the temptation much stronger, so they are less free. But we all struggle with temptations of various strengths: sex, stealing, whatever. The alcoholics' compulsion (perhaps not craving) may seem almost insuperable at times, and certainly their guilt is far less than if they did not have the enduring habitual disposition. But they do have some freedom and therefore some moral responsibility for taking the means or getting the help to avoid that first drink.

A true alcoholic probably has no free choice over whether he takes a third drink. By the time he has two in him he is not free to choose. That is because the direct absorption of alcohol into the bloodstream can quickly affect the brain centers that mediate control and judgment as to whether he ought to have another one. In that sense he should be treated as a sick person and not as a criminal.

Controlled Drinking by Alcoholics

In saying that alcoholics have some choice over taking the first drink, and none over taking the third, the second drink was omitted. This is a gray area; there is some responsibility, in some cases, maybe. The very nature of the illness is some loss of control, some degree of psychological and/or physiological dependence whereby the alcoholic drinks not because he wants to but because he needs to. The advice to "drink like a lady" ignores the basic psychology and physiology of addiction. Whatever other choices she might have, that is precisely the one thing she *cannot* do.

The concept of alcoholism as a compulsive addiction raises questions of professional ethics about attempts at controlled or moderate drinking for alcoholics. For both psychological and physiological reasons, the safe choice is to avoid drinking. Behavior modification can help them choose not to drink, but it is vapid to "choose" to change the nature of alcoholism.

A Paradox. In controversies over conditioning alcoholics to drink, Mark and Linda Sobell, psychologists who are well known for their advocacy of conditioning alcoholics to drink socially, paradoxically defend free choice, or at least repudiate the old "weak will" theory, and to that extent are in agreement with AA. The answer may lie in the difference between surrender and compliance. The choice not to drink (so neglected in talk about responsible drinking) is *conscious*. But this may be merely superficial compliance if the alcoholic *unconsciously* refuses to accept a life of total abstinence—that is, if there is no surrender. He makes promises in all sincerity, but fails again and again. Why?

He is not powerless over the choice about drinking, but about being an alcoholic. One can choose to eat candy or not to eat candy, but one has no choice about being a diabetic. That is an object not of choice but of feeling. Surrender here is not defeat but acceptance of reality. An alcoholic does not give up the power of choosing to drink or not to drink but accepts the fact that he has no choice over whether he is an alcoholic whose very nature involves not being able to drink socially.

The emotional aspects of AA have a most important psychological function, since surrender is at the feeling level rather than at the level of reason. Compliance at the conscious level without surrender at the feeling and unconscious levels not only has the alcoholic divided against himself, but the superficial compliance actually blocks the surrender. In contrast, surrender or acceptance leads not to a sense of crushing defeat but to a sense of freedom, of completeness, serenity, and honesty, because now the alcoholic's conscious and unconscious are in harmony. Analysis of the reasons why one drank cost thousands of dollars in psychiatrist's fees and did not buy sobriety. Being a member helps one *feel* good about choosing not to drink. Now one can identify with the speaker at an AA meeting—and feel at home.

Consequences

A very large area of moral responsibility has to do with the consequences of our choice. Here ethics gives a basic principle: One is responsible only to the extent that one knows *at the time* of the choice what the consequences are, and deliberately chooses a course of events *then* under his or her control. For this reason *blackout* is not a defense for criminal actions, because the question is not whether the person remembers later, but how much conscious control one had at the time of the act. This of course is often very difficult to determine.

The time factor is important, because many recovered people suffer needless guilt feelings over consequences they now see through sober eyes. They must not judge themselves in the light of their present knowledge, but according to what they knew at the time. For example, the recovering alcoholic woman who reads about the fetal alcohol syndrome feels guilty about having risked deformity for her baby. She ought to judge in light of her ignorance at the time she was pregnant, not her present knowledge. (What she now knows should govern her choice of whether to drink in future pregnancies.)

But suppose a man, cold sober and fully conscious, knows for certain that if he goes into this bar or tavern with these companions on Friday and has even one beer, he will end up drinking and gambling away his week's paycheck, will come home drunk and beat up his wife, and his children will have no food next week. Suppose that in light of this knowledge he deliberately chooses to have the beer regardless of the consequences. Would just the fact that he is an alcoholic automatically acquit him of all responsibility?

We have painted the extreme case to make the point; in real life it may be more gray and fuzzy. Thus, in this case, the degree of responsibility will vary with the severity and type of alcoholism, the length and quality of sobriety since last drinking, the influence of companions, one's physical condition, including fatigue, and other factors. For a woman alcoholic the menstrual period can vary her reaction to alcohol and her actual blood alcohol level, to say nothing of her emotional sensitivity. Note that the question is not whether the man in our foregoing example is free to choose at the time he comes home and beats up his wife. It is his conscious control at the time he makes the choice to drink that determines his degree of guilt.

All this must be kept in mind when attempting to assess guilt for the consequences of one's drinking. One is not a bad person, but one may have done some bad things. We must distinguish between true responsibility and irrational feelings. If one has done something wrong and knew at the time it was wrong, to feel responsible is not neurotic but realistic. On the other hand, it is irrational to feel guilty if the act was not really wrong, or if one did not know at the time that it was wrong, of if it could not have been avoided, or if one has every reason to believe that it has long since been forgiven. Those are baseless guilt feelings, a frequent symptom of neurosis. The spouse or children may have special problems of false guilt. They often feel it must be their fault that the alcoholic drinks. Al-Anon and Alateen can help them detach from those feelings and to know they are not responsible.

Psychologists and psychiatrists sometimes reject the whole notion of guilt, because they deal with so many patients obsessed with neurotic guilt feelings over past deeds for which they were not really responsible and therefore should not feel guilt. The answer is not to attack the notion of guilt but rather the neuroticism (see Kurtz, *Shame and Guilt,* 1981).

Again, we must distinguish regret from guilt. If I accidentally kill a little girl who ran in front of my car with no neglect on my part, I naturally regret the fact. But I am not guilty of her death. Likewise, the desire to make amends must not be confused with guilt. Even though one was not culpable, one may still want to try to make up for the effects of one's drinking.

The question of whether intoxication is an excuse comprises a complex portion of criminal law. It is important to note that the new Uniform Act explicitly disclaims any change in criminal law. It affects only the simple act of being drunk in public, as exhibiting a symptom of the disease of alcoholism. One is still just as liable legally for anything else as he was before passage of the Uniform Act. So it is legal to jail the alcoholic drunk driver even though "ill," and likewise the alcoholic rapist or murderer. That is true morally as well as legally. The consequences, to the extent they were foreseen and controllable, are still our responsibility. AA Steps 8 and 9 "made a list . . . made amends . . ." imply some responsibility. Let us mention some specific instances.

Driving. One need not be legally drunk to kill somebody with an automobile. Nor must one be an alcoholic. There could be some moral responsibility every time anyone turns the ignition key in a potentially lethal weapon with even small amounts of blood alcohol. Research has shown some impairment at blood alcohol levels well below the legal limit (see Chapter 4, Section B, "What Is Safe?"). Science and ethics can combine forces here.

Assault. Assault and battery do not always result in death, but alcohol and other drugs are involved in over 70 percent of American homicides, and most homicides among Native Americans. This may diminish responsibility for the act but also may shift the focus to responsibility for doing something about the drinking problem. One massive brute of a man never touches a drop because he is afraid that if he ever drinks he will kill somebody—and with reason. Few people have this degree of insight.

Sex. Alcohol is no aphrodisiac, but it can result in illegitimate pregnancy because inhibitions are lowered and judgment is impaired. A 1985 study showed over 70 percent of teenagers have their first sexual encounter under the influence of alcohol, with terrifying implications for the spread of AIDS.

Harm to Body. When students are asked to list the moral implications of drinking or drugging, the most frequent answers involve damage to the body and damage to one's self-respect. This is, of course, usually unforeseen, but it is interesting that self-destruction—suicide—is against the law in most jurisdictions.

Family, Employees, or Employers. The consequences of excessive drinking and drug use on others are rarely seen from the viewpoint of moral responsibility and ethical principles. If the spouse tries to present such consequences objectively, it still often sounds like nagging. When the client does state guilt feelings about harm to family and others, it could be more productive if the counselor reflected those feelings in a nondirective way rather than dismiss them too hastily.

Property Destruction. Not only personal injury but millions of dollars in damage is done each year through alcohol and other drug-related accidents: auto and home, boat, fire, private planes, and so on. Passing bad checks might be included here, when the question of amends or restitution is discussed.

A special case that nobody talks about is vandalism. The destruction, which might involve whole city blocks, is rarely done by those who are clean and sober. Who pays? Not the rioters. Should they? These questions need to be asked.

Liability for Actions of Others. An interesting recent development is the question of responsibility for the intoxication and subsequent offenses of people other than oneself. Liquor and tobacco companies are being sued for FAS damage and other consequences of consuming their products. Regardless of lawsuits, what is the moral responsibility of the host or hostess, bartender, or clerk in a liquor store, supplier, manufacturer, and especially the advertiser who makes it so attractive?

Another area of influence on others is the whole question of responsibility for alcohol education: in schools, in the professions (especially medicine), in the public media, in business and industry (promulgation versus burying of company policy on alcoholism). Irresponsible advertising is condoned by society and is not just the responsibility of the advertiser. In this connection, there is the interesting question of what responsibility, if any, we as a nation of consumers and advertisers have for perpetuating the "pill for every ill" mentality (see Ford, 1959).

Much as we applaud the saving of young lives by the contract between parents and their children advocated by Students Against Drunk Driving (SADD), the question remains whether it leaves parents liable for the implied permission to drink heavily as long as one does not drive home intoxicated. Can we ignore the assaults, broken friendships, unwanted pregnancies, harm to health, danger of becoming addicted, vandalism, and other consequences of excessive drinking? The same can be said of friends in the Designated Driver programs.

Some advocate that a pledge be made, usually at confirmation, not to drink until one is twenty-one. Certainly it should not be forced, even through moral pressure. But if voluntary and with full awareness of the fact that it is not a moral issue unless one intends so to bind oneself, a pledge can be useful, because it defers drinking to a more mature stage of development.

Next, is there some responsibility in our social agencies for prolonging the abuses of the term disease? The medical detoxification center becomes just an expensive, if more humane, substitute for the drunk tank, unless the revolving-door alcoholic is gotten into long-term treatment. We know now that forced treatment can work. Maybe the best help we might give a chronic repeater would be to refuse treatment, so that the notion of responsibility for doing something about his *illness* (not his drinking) might eventually penetrate through the alcoholic fog.

Contraction of Habit. Lastly, there is the extremely tricky question of to what extent one might be responsible for contracting or enhancing one's habitual addiction to the drug alcohol. It is possible that in some subtle and subconscious ways one chooses to neglect facing the danger of addiction. Rather than blame the doctors, AAs admit that they manipulated their physicians for pills and lied to them about their drinking. How often do we hear "It's not *that* bad yet"? The problem here is that it is in the nature of alcohol to make things seem "not that bad."

No Pat Answers. Throughout these last sections we have raised more questions than we have given answers. Responsibility cannot be imposed or legislated. Ethics can only indicate principles and try to raise the right questions. The result may be a growing sense of responsibility throughout the profession and an awareness that more sensitive counseling is needed in these areas.

Sources

The only periodical devoted to this subject is *Journal of Ministry in Addiction and Recovery,* 1994– . Berg (1993) has an extensive bibliography. Regarding spirituality, we divide our sources into those dealing primarily with the spiritual, independently of organized religion (including a subsection on the atheist), and those dealing with church and clergy.

ADDICTION AS A SPIRITUAL ILLNESS

Anonymous, "Search for Spiritual Experience," *AA Grapevine,* April 1978, pp. 2–16.

Baker, Thomas S., *Understanding the Spiritual Nature of Addiction* (1994).

Bowden, Julie, and H. Gravitz, *Genesis: Spirituality in Recovery from Childhood Traumas* (1988).

Carol, Gail, *Alcoholics in Recovery* (1991).

Clinebell, Howard, *Counseling for Spiritually Empowered Wholeness* (1995).

Fichter, Joseph H., "Spirituality, Religiosity, and Alcoholism" (1977).

Fishel, Ruth, *The Journey Within: A Spiritual Path to Recovery.* Health Communications, Deerfield Beach, FL, 1988.

Johnson, Vernon, "The Dynamics of Forgiveness," in *I'll Quit Tomorrow* (1980), pp. 114–25.

Kurtz, Ernest, and K. Ketcham, *The Spirituality of Imperfection* (1992).

Larsen, Earnie, *Stage II Relationships: Love Beyond Addiction.* Harper & Row, New York, 1987.

Marsh, Rev. Jack, *You Can Help the Alcoholic* (1983).

Martin, Fr. Joseph, *Some Personal Comments on the 12 Steps of AA.* Kelly Productions, Aberdeen, MD, 1986.

May, Gerald G., *Addiction and Grace* (1989).

———, *The Awakened Heart: Living Beyond Addiction* (1991)

Mehl, Duane, *You and the Alcoholic in Your Home.* Augsburg, Minneapolis, 1981.

Peteet, John R., "A Closer Look at the Role of a Spiritual Approach in Addictions Treatment" (1993).

Royce, James E., "Alcohol and Other Drug Dependencies" (1985a).

———, "What Do You Mean, *Spiritual* Illness?" *Alcoholism and Addiction,* January–February 1985, p. 28.

———, "Christianity: An Alternative Tradition" (1994).

———, "The Effects of Alcoholism and Recovery on Spirituality" (1995).

"Search for Spiritual Experience," *AA Grapevine,* April 1978, 2–16. Six brief articles on alcoholism and the need for spiritual experience. The April issue often has articles on the spiritual.

Tyrrell, Bernard J., *Christotherapy: Healing Through Enlightenment* (1975); *Christotherapy II* (1982).

Wenger, Samuel A., "This Higher Power Business," *Alcoholism: The National Magazine,* December 1981, pp. 31–33.

Whitfield, Charles L., *Alcoholism, Other Drug Problems and Spirituality.* Resource Group, Baltimore, n.d.

Some useful pamphlets are *Clergy Ask About Alcoholics Anonymous,* from AA World Services, Inc.; Grateful Members, *The Twelve Steps for Everyone . . . Who Really Wants Them,* and R. Hamel, *A Good First Step,* both CompCare paperbacks; Jeanne E., *Women and Spirituality: Guide to the Fourth Step Inventory,* and *A New Fourth Step Guide,* plus Reverend Suzanne Smith, *Working the Steps* (1977), all three from Hazelden. For the spouse or family there are *Blueprints for Progress: Al-Anon's Fourth Step Inventory,* from Al-Anon; and *Guide to the Fourth Step Inventory for the Spouse,* from Hazelden.

Regarding the atheist, a Hazelden pamphlet by Jon Weinberg, *AA: An Interpretation for the Nonbeliever,* and Chapter 4, "We Agnostics," in the book *Alcoholics Anonymous,* speak directly to the issue, as do parts of the AA pamphlets *Do You Think You're Different?* and *Clergy Ask About Alcoholics Anonymous.* The AA booklet *Came to Believe* (1973) shows how broadly the Higher Power can be taken, as does an article by an atheist, "Sober for Thirty Years," *AA Grapevine,* November 1976, p. 2. *Your God Is Too Small* by Phillips is a Macmillan paperback that is relevant, as are parts of the six articles in *AA Grapevine,* April 1978, pp. 2–16, and parts of *The Twelve Steps for Everyone . . . ,* a CompCare paperback.

RELIGION AND ALCOHOLISM

Apthorp, Stephen P., *Alcohol and Substance Abuse: A Clergy Handbook* (1990).
Cairns, T. H., *Preparing Your Church for Ministry to Alcoholics and Their Families* (1986).
Clinebell, Howard J., "Philosophical-Religious Factors in the Etiology and Treatment of Alcoholism" (1963).
———, *Understanding and Counseling the Alcoholic Through Religion and Psychology* (1968).
Conley, Paul, and Andrew Sorenson, *The Staggering Steeple* (1971).
DeJong, Rev. Alexander C., *Hope and Help for the Alcoholic.* Tyndale House, Wheaton, IL, 1982.
Fuad, Margaret, *Alcohol and the Church* (1992).
John, Harrison W., "The Church and Alcoholism: A Growing Involvement," *Alcohol Health and Research World,* Summer 1977, 2–10.
Keller, Rev. John E., *Ministering to Alcoholics* (1966) and *Let Go, Let God* (1988).
Kellerman, Rev. Joseph L., "Pastoral Care in Alcoholism" (1974).
———, *Alcoholism: A Guide for Ministers and Other Church Leaders* (1980).
Lincoln Council on Alcoholism and Drugs, *Parishioner's Assistance Program.* Lincoln, NE, 1976, a program package.
Lum, Doman, "The Church and the Prevention of Alcoholism," *Journal of Religion and Health,* 1970, 9:138–61.
Marsh, Jack, *You Can Help the Alcoholic* (1983).
Pontifical Council for Pastoral Assistance to Health Care Workers, *Drugs and Alcoholism Against Life* (1992).
Proceedings of the Symposium on the Role of the Christian Churches in the Recovery of the Alcoholic. DePaul Rehabilitation Hospital, Milwaukee, n.d.
Royce, James E., "Alcohol and Other Drugs in Spiritual Formation" (1987).
———, "Sin or Solace? Religious Views on Alcohol and Alcoholism," *Journal of Drug Issues,* Winter 1985, 15(1):51–62. Also in T. D. Watts (ed.), *Social Thought on Alcoholism.* Krieger Publishing, Malabar, FL, 1986, pp. 53–66.
Schneider, Karl A., *Alcoholism and Addiction* (1976), for parish use, and *Stumbling Blocks or Stepping Stones,* NCA, 1977, for clergy.
Shipp, Thomas J., *Helping the Alcoholic and His Family.* Prentice-Hall, Englewood Cliffs, NJ, 1963.
Taylor, G. Aiken, *A Sober Faith: Religion and Alcoholics Anonymous,* Macmillan, New York, 1953.
Two NCA pamphlets: Joseph Kellerman, *Alcoholism: A Guide for Ministers and Other Church Leaders* (1980), and John Parks Lee, *The Church's Ministry to the Alcoholic.*

U.S. Navy, *Navy Alcoholism Prevention Program, The Chaplain's Role.* Bureau of
Naval Personnel booklet.

MORAL RESPONSIBILITY

Very little was formerly written on this topic, except by John C. Ford, S.J. A recent
very valuable contribution has been Lewis M. Andrews, *To Thine Own Self Be True:
The Rebirth of Values in the New Ethical Therapy,* Chapter 2, "What Is Ethical Therapy?" and Chapter 12, "Beyond Addiction." In Royce, *Personality and Mental
Health,* rev. ed., 1964, pp. 249–57, the principles are laid down regarding persons
with mental disorders, but applications to alcohol problems are difficult. We list a few
items.

Becker, Arthur H., *Guilt: Curse or Blessing?* Augsburg, Minneapolis, 1977.
Bissell, LeClair, and J. E. Royce, *Ethics for Addiction Professionals.* rev. ed. (1994).
Finkelstein, N., et al., "Alcoholic Mothers and Guilt: Issues for Caregivers," *Alcohol
    Health and Research World,* Fall 1981, 45–49.
Ford, John C., *Depth Psychology, Morality, and Alcoholism* (1951).
————, "Clerical Attitudes on Alcohol—Most of Them Wrong" (1955), reprinted as
    NCA pamphlet.
————, "Chemical Comfort and Christian Virtue" (1959).
Gallagher, Joseph P., *Pleasure Is God's Invention.* Hazelden booklet.
Hewitt, T. Furman, *A Biblical Perspective on the Use and Abuse of Alcohol and Other
    Drugs* (1980).
Kurtz, Ernest, *Shame and Guilt* (1981).
Tiebout, Harry M., "Surrender Versus Compliance in Therapy with Special Reference
    to Alcoholism" (1953), reprinted as NCA pamphlet.

CHAPTER 20

Drugs and the Law

L IKE MANY OTHER CHAPTERS in this volume, this one could be an entire book. We can only point out some of the chief relations between law and the use or misuse of alcohol, and cannot begin to cover the ramifications of illegal drugs, although many of the same principles apply. (The Anti-Drug Abuse Act of 1988 includes alcohol, except where the word "illegal" appears.) The American Bar Association in July 1985 passed a resolution recommending action on seventeen points, many of them discussed in this chapter. Laws differ from state to state; those actually working in the field must become familiar with statutory law as it applies locally. Moreover, new legal precedents are constantly being set in this rapidly developing field, so today's ruling may be reversed by tomorrow's decision or a change in the law. The prudence of obtaining legal counsel is obvious.

On the other hand, both judges and attorneys in presentence investigations or diversion proceedings are turning now to addiction professionals for their expertise. Alcohol and other drug use may have legal implications for both civil and criminal cases. They may include liability from serving drinks to intoxicated persons, job discrimination, legal regulation of liquor sales, traffic violations, and the Uniform Act aimed at diverting the alcoholic from punishment to treatment.

Liability

"Dram Shop" laws mean that one can be held liable for death, automobile crashes, and other damages that result if alcoholic beverages are furnished to apparently intoxicated persons in conditions involving a reasonably foreseeable risk of harm to others. That includes not only bars, restaurants, liquor stores, and the company giving an office party but also to the host or hostess in a private home. Some jurisdictions require a certain number of hours of training in server liability for bartenders and those who serve. Such laws are not a total answer to these problems but are increasingly being invoked. As a result many corporations now serve only nonalcoholic beverages at their Christmas parties.

Many states have very specific statutes that forbid allowing or furnishing alcoholic beverages to minors. Some states exempt parents serving alcohol to their own children within the home, but others do not. In either case the parent or other adult may be liable for both civil and criminal charges arising from subsequent actions of the minor, including assault and traffic violations. In another area, one clergyman was sued over a suicide because he failed to refer to an alcoholism agency.

Discrimination

Section 503 of the Vocational Rehabilitation Act on affirmative action regarding employment of handicapped persons, and Section 504 on equal opportunity, clearly included alcoholics and drug addicts among those so protected against discrimination. In 1978 the act itself was so amended. Addiction is not a crime or a moral flaw, but a treatable illness, which should not in itself be reason for discrimination against a person otherwise qualified. The alcoholic is never cured in the sense of ability to return to social drinking, but neither is the amputee cured.

The key word is *qualified,* for there is no intent to guarantee jobs for the unqualified or the unemployable. Those whose dependency on alcohol or other drugs interferes with acceptable behavior or normal job performance can be terminated according to the same standards as any other employee. On the other hand, rehabilitation is not a condition for receiving education or service, since in many cases such benefits are designed precisely to rehabilitate. And the distinction between equal opportunity or nondiscrimination in Section 504 and affirmative action in Section 503 must be observed. Thus addiction is not an entitlement to benefits, which would amount to the government's becoming an Enabler.

Mandatory testing for alcohol and other drugs is a very complex issue. Test results can be misused to discriminate unfairly. But in a year and a half thirty-three people were killed in sixty railroad accidents in which one or more employees tested positive, and nine people were killed in one plane crash where the pilot tested positive for cocaine. Balance must be kept between the rights of individuals and threats to public safety (as in the transportation industry). At least there must be reasonable cause for testing an individual or subgroup, strict control of the sample, confidential guarding of results, respect for privacy, rehabilitation rather than termination for those who have a problem, always a second test of a different type to prevent false positives, and a personal assessment by an addictions professional, since even a reliable test shows only use, not addiction or even abuse (see Bissell and Royce, 1994, pp. 33–36).

Regulation of Sale

It was noted in Chapter 12 that some researchers advocate prevention of alcoholism by reduction in overall per capita consumption, and we suggested that this lognormal curve theory is not incompatible in practice with a bimodal theory of high-risk population. This is a complex issue. In an effort toward an objective view, we shall simply condense the relevant section in the

National Institute on Alcohol Abuse and Alcoholism's (NIAAA) second special report to Congress entitled *Alcohol and Health: New Knowledge* (1974, pp. 154–63):

> Liquor control laws have their roots in antiquity, and the development of variations in the means and methods of control can be traced through various stages of civilization to modern times. Laws and organizations exist in all developed nations and states, and in most underdeveloped nations of the world.... The United States, on the other hand, has not had a national policy on the manufacture and sale of alcoholic beverages since 1933. There are federal statutes governing the export and import of alcoholic beverages, but each state has full and complete authority over the manufacture, distribution, and sale of alcoholic beverages within its borders.
>
> While broad generalizations should not be hastily formulated from one experiment, the experience with Prohibition clearly suggests that social policies which conflict with widely accepted societal practices and mores are, if not doomed to failure, potentially dysfunctional to societal institutions, including the broad area of law and justice.... It must be recognized also that societal customs that are deeply embedded in and part of accepted behavior patterns are not easily subject to change, certainly not in the short run, as was attempted through Prohibition....
>
> ### Attempts at Control
> Licensing, limiting the number of licenses, and monopoly control of off-premise sales are negative controls, as are all or nearly all of the controls established for the industry. Other types of controls include hours of sale, age of purchasers, separation of licenses for on-premise and off-premise sales, prohibitions against "tied house" arrangements, minimum pricing, and limitations on advertising.
>
> ### Prices, Locations, Hours, and Eligibility
> One form of control is to regulate prices. Another widespread form of control prohibits the sale of alcoholic beverages within a specified distance of certain public and private institutions. In addition, most states allow local zoning restrictions to prevail in the issuance of most types of new retail licenses. Because of the presumed relation between hours of availability and levels of consumption, all fifty states have some restrictions on times of sale at retail or permit local governments to establish opening and closing hours....
>
> Most states prohibit the sale of beverage alcohol to specified classes of people. Sales to minors are the most obvious example. But there are also restrictions on sales to insane or interdicted persons, persons of ill repute, and intoxicated persons. Some states have ban-

ished the two-for-one "happy hour" which encourages heavy drinking before driving home from work.

Enforcement of some of these restrictions is obviously difficult. But the Ledermann hypothesis on the relation between availability of alcohol and incidence of alcoholism, as discussed under "The Agent" in Chapter 12, seems to
have real validity as one factor in the total picture.

Legal drinking age is one law that has been thoroughly researched, one
reason why the federal government forced the states to adopt a uniform minimum age of twenty-one. Controlled research showed that when states lowered their drinking age deaths went up, and when they raised the age deaths
went down by as much as 31 to 44 percent—see "Sources" for ample documentation. The Wine Institute concurred (*The Alcoholism Report,* May 17,
1984, p. 2). An important argument for uniformity was that variation in state
laws prompted young people to cross state lines to obtain alcoholic beverages, resulting in "blood alley" highways, which contributed to alcohol-
related traffic accidents as the leading cause of death among youth (O'Malley
and Wagenaar, 1991; Valle, 1986; Wagenaar, 1983, 1993).

Traffic Laws

It should be noted that most states outlaw impairment in driving whether it
be from alcohol or other drugs—illegal, prescription, or even over-the-
counter drugs. Many laws apply to bicycles and even to pedestrians.

In Chapter 4, Section B, we described briefly the effect of alcohol on driving, the increased impairment at higher levels of blood alcohol content
(BAC), and the use of chemical tests of breath alcohol in arrests for driving an
automobile while intoxicated (DWI or DUI), which were shown to be valid
measures of impairment because alcohol in the breath is in direct and fixed
ratio to alcohol in the blood. The breath test is more accessible than samples
from sweat, urine, or the blood itself, being easily obtainable by having the
subject blow hard enough to get alveolar or deep-lung air. Many devices have
been developed, varying in cost per use, accuracy, ease of use, and portability:
Breathalyzer, Intoximeter, Alcotester, Alcometer, Sober-meter, and others.
Some statutes allow the suspect to obtain blood or urine tests, but not to use
delaying tactics so as to allow the blood alcohol level to fall.

The devices are always set to favor the accused and are specific to alcohol
(not reactive to onions or garlic, as sometimes claimed). It is true that alcohol
in the breath from mouthwash or cold medicine containing high amounts of
alcohol can affect it, but that does not discredit the test if deep alveolar air is
obtained. One study has shown breath tests to be admissible as evidence in
courts of appeal for all states, and another study for 550 decisions in forty-
four states (Donigan, 1966). Use of the test is not a violation of secrecy, since
the driver enters into no confidential relationship with the arresting officer.
Blood level is a public fact, like one's fingerprint. Lastly, an implied consent

law involves no violation of human rights, since the granting of a license is a privilege granted under whatever conditions the voters wish to impose and freely entered into when the driver obtained a license.

It must be noted that in addition to observed erratic driving, the arresting officer has other tests, used long before chemical tests of BAC were developed. They include walking a chalk line, touching the nose with the index finger while the eyes are closed, and other harmless exercises. Most impressive now is a videotape of the driver's behavior at the time of arrest, which, when played later for a jury, belies the well-dressed appearance and decorum of the defendant in court. In 1985 the U.S. Department of Transportation (DOT HS 806-512) urged use of the Horizontal Gaze Nystagmus Test, which refers to a jerking of the eyes as they gaze to the side; it is also useful because a noticeable disparity between a low BAL and high nystagmus may indicate use of other drugs, such as marijuana, which the Breathalyzer does not reveal.

However, the disparaging tactics of defense lawyers still make it difficult to obtain convictions in some places. Addiction professionals should remember that ours is an adversary system characterized by two sides working zealously to provide a distorted and partisan view, seeking not truth but victory. So BAC levels can be made to seem an unreliable indication of impairment for a variety of reasons, such as problems of calibration, security of samples, confusion between volume and weight, temperature variations, and especially individual differences. Although these may confuse the jury, the tests are basically valid (*JAMA*, June 28, 1985, 253[24]:3509–17).

Jail or Treatment? Research was cited in Chapter 4, Section B, which suggests that our American laws are too lenient in the level of BAC allowed before a driver is considered unsafe. "Drinking and driving" rather than "drunk driving" was suggested, because the more stringent laws in other countries seem to reflect more accurately than our own the real dangers of impairment and the consequent risk of accidents, especially fatal accidents. Many countries have very severe penalties, such as deprivation of the driver's license for life after a second conviction (at 0.05 percent BAC), mandatory jail sentences to be served on weekends if one must work, and even execution (Bulgaria and El Salvador). Unfortunately, in America the net effect of tougher penalties has been merely to make juries more lenient, reluctant to inflict the severer punishment. That in turn encourages the arresting officer to settle for a lesser charge, like reckless driving, because he knows there is a better chance of conviction. Mandatory severe sentences also result in more plea bargaining, where the role of alcohol gets obscured, and clog the courts as more defendants demand jury trials.

Most of the drivers in fatal accidents had a BAC well above the level designated legally as safe, and many had a history of previous alcohol-related offenses. This latter fact points to the need for diversion into some corrective course of action rather than merely imposing a fine or jail sentence or revocation of driving license, all of which have proved quite ineffective. Our sad experience with stringent laws and scare slogans suggests that a new approach is called for.

Instead of jail, drunk drivers today are being sent by many courts to attend Alcohol Information Schools (AIS), where they learn about the effects of alcohol on driving and other behaviors as well as about alcoholism. That may be enough for a few; if the instructor is a skilled alcoholism specialist, some discover that they have a drinking problem and choose treatment. For others the court may force a choice of jail or treatment, which may include monitored doses of Antabuse, mandatory attendance at AA meetings for two years, or some combination of inpatient and outpatient approaches. Some few states have a *deferred-prosecution* law whereby the accused can go directly into treatment without entering the criminal justice system at all. A preliminary report from one state (Washington) shows a recidivism rate of only 4 percent out of two thousand cases handled in this manner but admits that the time period for some was rather short. Jail is rarely if ever a deterrent, whereas forced treatment can be 80 percent effective. This preliminary report, if further verified, would mean that the chances a defendant will drink and drive again are almost 100 percent after jail, but only 20 percent if forced into treatment. Judges and attorneys are learning that alcohol education and treatment can save lives more effectively than jail, whereas leniency can actually kill an alcoholic defendant by failing to stop the progression of a terminal illness. An attorney has an ethical obligation to act in the best interest of the client.

A very effective measure in at least two states, Massachusetts and Washington, has been to mandate as part of the sentence that the convicted person meet with a volunteer panel of victims of drinking drivers. The victims are cautioned that it is counterproductive to be accusatory, vindictive, or bitter; they simply tell how their lives have been affected by the accident, whether it crippled them for life or killed a dear one. Results are reported to be dramatic.

The Uniform Act

History. Public intoxication was first made a criminal offense in England by a 1606 statute. It was carried over to the colonies and continued in all jurisdictions in the United States until 1966, when the legal status of public intoxication changed dramatically. That year two different U.S. district courts of appeal (in *Driver* v. *Hinnant* and *Easter* v. *District of Columbia*) ruled that an alcoholic cannot be jailed for being drunk in public. The two principal issues were whether the alcoholic is capable of criminal intent or *mens rea* in such behavior, and whether it is cruel and unusual punishment and therefore unconstitutional to jail a person for exhibiting the symptoms of a disease. In June 1968 the U.S. Supreme Court in *Powell* v. *Texas* gave a 5–4 decision which, although it did not reverse Powell's conviction, confirmed much of the reasoning of the appeals courts. Disagreement among the nine justices centered largely on problems of evidence and whether the practical issue should be left to the states, but a majority accepted the term "disease" and the involuntary nature of the alcoholic's public intoxication.

Court decisions about whether alcoholism could be used as a defense in other criminal actions continued to be conflicting, but a consensus emerged that alcoholism itself is involuntary. Finally, in August 1971 the National Conference of Commissioners on Uniform State Laws, comprising representatives of the governors of each state, adopted the *Uniform Alcoholism and Intoxication Treatment Act.* This has been enacted in some form by about thirty-five states, the State of Washington having been the first (but Maryland the first to implement it). Although varying in how closely they follow the model, the general thrust of the state laws is to take alcoholism out of the drunk tank and the criminal justice system, making the alcoholic not a criminal but a sick person.

Scope. None of the preceding items in this chapter is touched by the Uniform Act, which only removes the act of being drunk in public from the criminal code and makes alcoholism a matter for treatment instead of punishment. Section 19 of the act explicitly says that it does not apply to such questions as drunk driving or the sale of liquor. The intricate question of using intoxication as a defense in criminal cases is left intact. That is important, because the public has sometimes misunderstood the Uniform Act as allowing one to commit any crime and then use the illness of alcoholism as an excuse. The alcoholic can still be arrested on charges of disorderly conduct, assault, murder, rape, DWI, and so on, and the court must decide to what degree responsibility was diminished by alcoholism.

Implementation. It would be naïve to infer that mere passage of laws has solved the problems of alcoholism. For one thing, such laws affect principally the vagrant or homeless, at most perhaps 3 to 5 percent of all alcoholics. Second, merely decriminalizing public drunkenness does not create an adequate system of treatment and rehabilitation or guarantee its use by those who need it. Some states passed the law but have been woefully negligent in funding adequate treatment facilities to implement it. Some thorny attendant problems include the following: applicable definitions, voluntary and involuntary commitment, confidentiality of records, adequate continuum of care, individualized treatment plans, police and civilian transportation from public places to detoxification or treatment centers, and training of personnel competent in alcoholism. Each problem is provided for in the Uniform Act. None is simple.

It is interesting that the act defines treatment broadly to include a wide range of types and kinds of services, indicating that there is no single or uniform method of treatment that will be effective for all alcoholics. Section 5(15) of the Uniform Act reflects the provision of the Hughes Act that a general hospital can be denied federal funds for discriminating against alcoholics.

The main concern is whether the act is achieving its declared end of getting alcoholics into treatment. Because of our strong tradition of safeguarding human rights, Section 14 on involuntary commitment is so cumbersome as to be almost impossible to enforce. Sometimes the mere threat of involuntary commitment is enough to motivate someone into treatment. As the Uniform Act is adopted by each state legislature in a different form and interpreted differently by the courts in various jurisdictions, we cannot give a final or universal version of the act in practice. The entire model act is printed with running comments in the first NIAAA special report to Congress, *Alcohol and Health* (1971), as Appendix A, and Chapter 7 (pp. 85–97) gives the history.

Sources

In a book entitled *Alcoholism and the Law,* Grad and his co-authors (1971) have dealt in a general way with the legal aspects of alcohol use and of alcoholism. Another source of general information is the NCALI bibliography, "Selected Publications on Legal Aspects of Alcohol Use and Abuse." Evans (1983) is for attorneys and other professionals. Chapters 13–17, Part IV, of Ewing and Rouse, *Drinking: Alcohol in American Society* (1977), pp. 219–38, are well documented and very relevant.

Regarding *server responsibility,* there are ten articles with references in the special focus issue of *Alcohol Health and Research World,* Summer 1986, 10(4). Other useful sources are the National Highway Traffic Safety Administration (NHTSA) of the U.S. Department of Transportation, the American Automobile Association (AAA), the National Safety Council, the National Council on Alcoholism, and the Alcohol Research Center of the University of California at Los Angeles (UCLA).

Taxation and *regulation of sale* research is reported in Casement (1987), Cook (1984), Gerstein (1984), Moore and Gerstein (1981), and Olson and Gerstein (1986). Medicine in the Public Interest, Inc. (1979), has published an abridged version of its two-volume study for NIAAA on the effects of various types of governmental action on the prevalence of problems associated with the use of alcohol (Matlins, 1976). The Addiction Research Foundation of Toronto, Canada, has many publications; for example, Single and Storm (1985), and an article by R. E. Popham and others, "The Prevention of Alcoholism: Epidemiological Studies of the Effects of Government Measures," *British Journal of Addiction,* 1975, 70:1125–44, which examines in a world context the effects of the taxation of beverage alcohol.

Regarding *alcohol and traffic,* Crandell, *Effective Outpatient Treatment for Alcohol Abusers and Drinking Drivers* (1988); Jacobs, *Drunk Driving: An American Dilemma* (1989); Laurence et al., *Social Control of the Drinking Driver* (1988); Ross, *Confronting Drunk Driving* (1992); and Valle, *Drunk Driving in America: Strategies and Approaches to Treatment* (1986) are more recent, but still useful are Finch, *Psychiatric and Legal Aspects of Automobile Fatalities* (1970); J. D. Havard (1975); Israelstam and Lambert, *Alcohol, Drugs, and Traffic Safety* (1975); Perrine, *Alcohol, Drugs and Driving* (1974), especially the section by Driessen and Bryk; and Chapter 6, "Alcohol and Highway Traffic Safety," pp. 97–110 in the NIAAA Second Special Report to Congress, *Alcohol and Health: New Knowledge* (1974). Resource materials can be obtained from the agencies listed above under *server responsibility.*

Most of the research on the effect of *lowering the drinking age* has dealt with drinking and driving, for example, O'Malley and Wagenaar (1991); Wagenaar (1983, 1993); Whitehead, *Alcohol and Young Drivers* (1977); A. F. Williams, "Raising the Legal Purchase Age in the United States: Its Effects on Fatal Motor Vehicle Crashes," *Alcohol, Drugs, and Driving,* April–June 1986, 2(2):1–12; R. L. Douglass, "The Consequences of Lower Legal Drinking Ages on Alcohol-related Crash Involvement of Young People," *Report on Alcohol,* Fall 1976, 19:13–19; an article that deals more broadly with the implications is R. G. Smart and M. Goodstadt, "Effects of Reducing the Legal Alcohol-purchasing Age on Drinking and Drinking Problems," *JSA,* 1977, 38:1313–23. See also "Sources" for our Chapter 12.

Among the few articles relating actual experience with the Uniform Act is L. R. Daggett and E. J. Rolde, "Decriminalization of Public Drunkenness: The Response of Suburban Police," *Archives of General Psychiatry,* 1977, 34:937–41. See also the writers listed under "Skid Road Alcoholics" in the "Sources" at the end of Chapter 11.

CHAPTER 21

The New Profession

THE BIRCH AND DAVIS REPORT (1986) and a needs assessment of EAP programs in 1986 both ranked a need for professional ethics as the top priority for addiction workers. When time-honored professions like medicine and law are having problems with their public image, this new field has a serious duty to itself to build a strong tradition of professionalism in the best sense.

Since the first Yale Plan Clinic in 1944, recovered alcoholics have been a part of most treatment teams, whether or not they belonged to a profession or had a college degree. Moreover, members of AA were helping thousands of suffering alcoholics to recover through their Twelfth Step work both before and after treatment centers were established. The understanding and empathy those workers gained from their own experience as alcoholics have long been recognized as valuable contributors to the recovery process.

Human nature being what it is, the picture has not always been one of serene cooperation between degreed professionals and nondegreed workers. Events of the past few decades have occasioned difficulties for both, as rapid developments brought changes for which neither side was prepared. The story is well told in Staub and Kent (1973).

The chagrin of mental health professionals at the fact that AA was succeeding where traditional psychiatric approaches had failed is understandable. The Krystal-Moore (1963) debate found other psychiatrists agreeing with Moore that the recovered alcoholic, degreed or not, has an important role to play (Lemere, 1964). But the psychiatrist, psychologist, or psychiatric social worker with little specialized knowledge or training in alcoholism found it difficult to relate to the alcoholism community or to abandon traditional methods.

On the other hand, members of AA themselves have come to recognize that mere experience as a recovering alcoholic does not automatically qualify one to work professionally in the treatment field. Not only were the degreed professionals reluctant to accept them, but they had problems stemming from their own lack of training and limited knowledge.

A New Profession

The senior author is a degreed professional who, for many decades, has been very close to AA and in an advantageous position to observe all this from both sides, as cochairman of the Washington State committee on norms for the certification of alcoholism workers and later as a member of the NIAAA-Littlejohn Board for the same purpose. Each group began as two mutually suspicious camps: the professional clinging to his degree even though he might not know an alcoholic from an alligator, and the recovered alcoholic smug in his private knowledge and unaware of his lack of other qualifications. Both quickly dropped their defenses and reached a consensus that *both* were wrong, that both the degreed professional and the recovered alcoholic need training and knowledge that their respective prior experiences do not guarantee them.

A new profession is emerging, based on knowledge and competence rather than on degree. For this reason the term *paraprofessional* is inappropriate and should be dropped. Moreover, the old dichotomy between degreed professional and recovered alcoholic is disappearing as more and more degreed professionals identify themselves as being also recovered.

What Is a Profession?

The best corrective for an image of "amateurs, sick people helping sick people," is a profession with integrity and respect. As a new profession, addiction workers have a responsibility to both themselves and their patients to develop a tradition. What are the characteristics of a profession?

Service. Contrary to the myth that professionals are interested only in money rather than in helping sick addicts, the very difference between a business and a profession is that a business is frankly aimed at making money whereas a profession is primarily aimed at service. One does not work for a boss or for dollars, but in a true sense for the client or patient.

Self-regulation. A prominent characteristic of a profession is that it is supposed to be self-regulating, rather than policed from the outside. Most professions have an ethics committee or conduct review board. Members of the profession take responsibility for the conduct of other members. That is not "tattling" but professional integrity. It includes intervention to get a colleague into treatment for alcoholism or other drug misuse, or honesty in recommendations for employment rather than covering up for an incompetent person who may harm patients. This also implies responsibility of a prospective employer to check with previous employers or trainers.

Code of Ethics. It is a mark of a profession to develop its own code of ethics, and many addiction counselor associations have done so. They are all similar, as exemplified in the topics covered by one code (NAADAC, 1987):

1. *Nondiscrimination*
2. *Responsibility* for objectivity, integrity, high standards

3. *Competence,* including ongoing education, reporting of unethical conduct, accepting one's limitations, helping impaired professionals
4. *Legal and moral standards,* including care in endorsing services or products
5. *Public statements* must be cautious and professional, including responsible reporting and training practices.
6. *Publications credit* should be properly attributed.
7. *Client welfare* should be primary; conflict of interest, exploitation of the patient, divulging information without informed consent, and failure to collaborate with other professionals must be avoided.
8. *Confidentiality* must be respected and records safeguarded.
9. *Client relationship* must not be jeopardized or abused in any way, including sexually.
10. *Interprofessional relationships* must recognize rights of patients and other professionals.
11. *Remuneration* arrangements should be in accord with professional standards, which forbid fee-splitting, kickbacks, and gifts.
12. *Societal obligations* require that one adopt both a personal and a professional stance in civic and personal conduct, legislative and public policy, which promotes the welfare of patients and all human beings.

Wordings may vary in other codes, and discussion could be lengthy. All codes demand acceptance of personal limitations by not attempting services that are beyond one's training or competence. See the section on "Objectivity" in Chapter 14. Professional responsibility requires that one always distinguish clearly between any public statements or actions as an individual and as a representative of one's organization. Private and professional roles must be kept cleanly separate, which means not socializing with clients or accepting personal gifts from them while in therapy or shortly thereafter.

"Helping the client to help himself" discourages fostering, perhaps unconsciously, a patient's dependence, which may be flattering to the counselor but stunts the growth of the patient. For that reason counselors must be trained in how to handle separation anxiety and terminate the relationship gracefully. All codes forbid exploitation of the patient for the counselor's own financial, sexual, or other personal needs. A romantic inclination on the part of either patient or therapist really reflects a cry for help from an emotionally confused person, which the inexperienced counselor can mistake for love. Personnel policy and training manuals should include a section on transference and countertransference. Consultation, and usually a switch to another counselor, are necessary to prevent needless hurt for both parties and possible court action.

Confidentiality. The ethics of professional secrecy can bring up a host of complicated issues. The basic principle is that private information divulged by patients in the course of treatment may never be used or repeated in any way that can be identified with the patient. This clause allows for generalized statements or research without risking harm to any individual's reputation. One may not make available any information without first obtaining their written consent (while rational and sober), unless there is clear and imminent danger of serious harm to them or a third party by not doing so. Professional consultation in a difficult case is allowed, but in that case the consultant is equally bound to secrecy. One may not share private information with a colleague or one's spouse, no matter how trusted.

The new profession has a serious task here. Members of the medical profession occasionally violate their tradition of confidentiality through human weakness, but at least they have a tradition to violate; the alcoholism profession sorely needs to build a tradition to counteract the current laxity that prompted special federal regulations. One treatment center was sued because a counselor thought it too much trouble to get a signed release before giving information to the patient's EAP. What you learn as a result of a colleague's carelessness in this regard must still be treated by you as confidential. A secretary must be instructed about secrecy of records and correspondence. Volunteers have restricted access to files but must be informed that even seeing which people come in is private information.

"Privileged communication" refers to the right to have evidence withheld in court. The privilege is that of the client, not of the professional. Nevertheless, the law is always tied to a particular profession, and so far there is almost no legislation for addiction workers comparable to that for physicians, attorneys, and the clergy. Hence a court may order disclosure of their confidential information or files. There is likewise little provision covering liability for disclosure by other members of a group therapy session, but the group leader is well advised to spell out an explicit obligation of secrecy to all.

DHHS has issued detailed regulations covering the handling of records by all individuals and programs that receive any form of federal support, direct or indirect, relating to alcohol or other drug abuse (see Blume, 1987). They are stricter than the usual rules of confidentiality. For instance, the mere fact that a person is or is not a patient in a general hospital is a matter of public knowledge, but in an alcohol or other drug facility it may not be revealed, because the very fact of the person's presence there is a diagnosis. The usual signed consent for disclosure of information to other agencies or professionals will not suffice; it must specify to whom the disclosure will be made and other details. The redisclosure of this authorized information to another agency without explicit consent is forbidden.

Education and Experience

This new profession requires specialized knowledge of addiction and training specific to treatment of the illness, regardless of traditional degrees or the experience of recovery. The time is past when mere on-the-job training or attendance at short summer institutes can be considered professional education.

Increasingly tied to a degree, certificate programs now tend to require at least two years. That may mean sacrifice for both worker and agency, but one does not become a surgeon without going to medical school. The good of the patient demands a competence that cannot be guaranteed by instant expertise.

Education

A professional is an educated person. A technician can fix your electric toaster, but an electrical engineer knows the principles behind its working. More important, truly educated people know more than just their own field; they have a broad, humanistic knowledge of its history and values. Certainly included is a knowledge of the ethics of counseling, yet this is often the most neglected part of training. As in many professions, the national norms require continuing education as a condition for recertification. It is arrogant and totally unprofessional to assume that once a degree or certificate is obtained, further learning is unnecessary.

All need courses taught by addiction specialists rather than standard curricula taught by professors, otherwise highly qualified, who have no real expertise in the field. A mix of recovered alcoholics and nonalcoholic students provides lively exchanges in and out of the classroom, wherein both learn from each other. Competence in both alcohol and other drugs is mandated by the facts of polyaddiction.

For the professional who happens not to be in recovery, other elements of education are necessary or appropriate. It is essential to attend meetings of various AA, NA, and Al-Anon groups, to get a feel for the variety of styles and people involved (see Grutchfield, 1979). Professionals who feel embarrassed at being seen going to an open AA meeting should consider whether or not their attitudes disqualify them from working in the field. Some trainers have their nonalcoholic students abstain from all alcohol for a month or two just to heighten sensitivity and develop empathy for how a recovering alcoholic feels. They may give any or no reason for not drinking, except that they are not to say they are in any kind of training or experiment.

Certification

Starting at the grassroots level, a movement has spread through most states toward the development of professional standards for addiction workers and development of the means for certifying that one has met those standards. Professional status should be granted for many reasons, including these:

1. Protection of the patient. This is primary. Quality of service requires that we take the means to see that treatment is not bungled.
2. Protection of the worker. If one is to gain recognition and dignity as a professional, compete for insurance or other third-party payment, be defended in malpractice suits, fit into a career ladder of promotion or have

job stability, and be able to move with equal status to a new agency, especially when moving to another state, there must be national credentialing with reciprocity between states.

3. Protection of the profession itself. To have confidentiality protected by privilege of communication, to have credibility when testifying in court as an expert witness, to build up a tradition of professional ethics, to gain respect from other professions and agencies, this new profession must have a legally acceptable identity.

A license is granted by law; a certificate by the profession. The Birch & Davis Report (1986) amplified norms and suggested procedures. Coalitions continue to develop standards on training, certification, credentialing, and reciprocity consortia. Along with some turfdom struggles, a serious problem has been to maintain the delicate balance between rights of individual states and the need for uniformity (both for reciprocity between states and to assure a minimum of high quality).

Consideration has been given (through certification by prior practice or "grandfather clause") of those already working in the field, whether degreed or not, who are truly competent. But it is not to the advantage of either the worker or the patient to retain workers who are not suitable. Concern has been primarily about counselors, but it should be evident that information, education, community organization, administration, and other activities also require accurate knowledge and proven ability.

Examination. Measuring competency by actual examination, rather than by merely evaluating experience and degrees or training records, is an extremely difficult task. There is no perfect way to assess how well a person will function on the job or even to measure the breadth and correctness of one's knowledge about addiction. More difficult or impossible to measure are the most important qualities: the warm empathy, compassionate understanding, communication skills, personal integrity, and generous dedication that create good relations between patient and counselor.

Length of Sobriety. It is commonly agreed that a recovered person should be clean and sober for a certain period of time before attempting to work in the field, for many reasons. One is the worker's own protection, lest the stress of dealing with troubled persons precipitate a relapse. It is also for the sake of the patients, who need a model of stable and comfortable sobriety as part of their own recovery. Again, the profession itself is harmed if a worker starts too soon, either creating a poor impression on members of other professions or risking the bad example of a relapse. Even when not permanent, residual toxicity in the brain may require up to two or three years to disappear entirely. But a substantial reason, often overlooked, is that a newly recovering person is emotionally too close to his or her own case and tends to see all patients in the light of subjective personal experience. It takes time, regardless of intelligence or quality of sobriety, to mature emotionally after recovery to the point where one can diagnose and treat with professional objectivity unspoiled by personal involvement.

There is also common agreement that quality of sobriety cannot be measured in months or years. Some are more ready after a year or two than others are after ten. But a consensus based on the accumulated experience of administrators and trainers throughout the country is confirmed by the *AA Guidelines* (1994), namely three to five years of sobriety. An applicant's inability to see the need for a certain duration of sobriety is itself an indication that one is not ready.

A new problem is codependency. Although the AA birthday may not be a fully valid measure, at least it is usually clear-cut. But how do we measure a codependent's readiness? Two years in Al-Anon or ACoA? Not fair, some say, and rightly so. Some scales based on the characteristics described in Chapter 10 are being developed, which may prove valid.

The Addictions Worker

Staub and Kent (1973) and Valle (1979) have many excellent chapters discussing the various problems faced by the nondegreed professional in the addictions field, especially if also in recovery. Some of the problems stem from the attitudes of the degreed professionals, some from personnel boards and other bureaucratic structures outside the field, some from punitive attitudes lingering from the old prohibition-temperance movement, and some from the disadvantages intrinsic to the very fact of being a recovered person. The result is often a dead-end job with no hope of advancement. On the part of degreed persons, the following faults have been cited: assuming inferiority and even deterioration in all recovered persons, fostering a caste system with inequity in salaries and promotion, problems in communication and cooperation, and the unreasonable expectation that every member live up to the ideals of AA in the highest degree.

On the other side, no less a friend of AA than Marty Mann (1973, p. 7) points out that using mere length of sobriety in AA is not a valid criterion of suitability for counseling, as some who have passed the minimum years still retain a tunnel vision that makes them too inflexible to adjust in a cooperative venture. Some are defensive about their lack of a degree. Those whose very real contributions are recognized sometimes become proud and look with disdain on all degrees and professional approaches. Some cannot cooperate well with degreed professionals or nonalcoholics because they cannot break out of their inner circle of shared experience.

"Only an alcoholic can help an alcoholic" is still being mouthed by some, in spite of the official disclaimer from AA mentioned earlier. The truth is probably that a balance of recovered alcoholics and nonalcoholics is the best staffing policy. There is always the tendency for the recovered person to ignore methods of treatment appropriate for a given patient, other than the particular modality through which the counselor achieved sobriety. Such loyalty is understandable, but it shows professional immaturity and impedes correct diagnosis of other types. There is also a tendency for the recovered counselor to focus too exclusively on the patient, to the neglect of the spouse and family.

Counselors rightly insist that a role model should be clean and sober. There is a growing trend in the field nationally to deplore those who continue to smoke when nicotine is now recognized as a highly addictive drug—to say nothing of the severe health hazards it entails.

Cooperation But Not Affiliation

Forbidden by its traditions to affiliate with any other cause or group, AA has always cooperated with the medical profession, labor–management programs, the armed services, chaplains, and various institutions. It also cooperates with professional training programs. Most gratifying is the trend reported in the periodic surveys of its membership wherein AA reports that an increasingly high percentage of newcomers are being referred to AA by professionals outside the fellowship. This suggests that things have come a long way since the early days of AA, founded soon after the repeal of Prohibition, when recovered alcoholics were looked upon with suspicion and skepticism.

Two Roles. Some AA members employed in the field experience conflict between their professional role and their membership in AA. This can be due to jealousy or misguided attitudes on the part of other members, who, for example, accuse them of taking money for doing Twelfth Step work. Aside from the danger of imputing motives to another human being, there is the fact that if all doctors and nurses yielded to the accusation of profiteering off the misfortune of others there would be no hospitals or surgeries. Such misunderstandings led some AAs to reject the term *two hats* when referring to members who pursued the two roles of AA Twelfth Step work and paid employment in the field. Regardless of the term, the practicalities of delineating the two roles have been worked out with admirable common sense in the *AA Guidelines for Members Employed in the Field* and by Al-Anon (with some added insights) in a comparable publication, *Al-Anon and Professionals*. These two guides are a "must" for all members working in the field or those who wish to discuss the matter.

Tradition 8 of AA says "Alcoholics Anonymous should remain forever nonprofessional," but it does not say that members cannot be professionals. Dr. Bob was the first to wear both hats, and his cofounder, Bill W., has written extensively about cooperation with the professionals and the great contributions that members can make both as professionals and as AA members. For a brief time members employed in the field were excluded from holding office in AA, but that has been reversed in the current *AA Guidelines* (1994,

p. 1). Significantly, this reversal is not an innovation but a return to the original tradition, which was temporarily interrupted by that exclusion.

Note that the term "AA *counselor*" is not used, because that would be contrary to the AA tradition of nonaffiliation. A person may happen to be a member of AA and also a counselor, but he or she does not speak for AA and was not hired with that as a credential. The counselor should not act as an AA sponsor for one's own professional client. It is usually felt that AA meetings within an institution should not be organized or run by AA members on staff, to avoid confusion of roles in the minds of both patients and staff. But local circumstances and the group conscience will have to determine this. When those who happen to be psychologists, clergymen, or other professionals attend meetings as members, they go for their own sobriety and spiritual growth—not to counsel others. As long as the two roles are kept distinct, there should be no problems (Bissell and Royce, 1994). Some confuse the AA tradition on anonymity with the ethics of confidentiality discussed earlier in this chapter. They are different, but with some overlap.

AA Conference-approved literature, much of it using the writings of Bill W. and all of it reflecting the group conscience of the entire fellowship, contains excellent discussions of these matters, including frank admission of fault on the part of AA members. In addition to the *Guidelines* cited above, see the last section of "Sources" for this chapter, and especially pages 7 and 8 of *How AA Members Cooperate with Other Community Efforts to Help Alcoholics,* where members are urged in strong terms to maintain humility with regard to AA and respect for the genuine contributions of other approaches.

In an article on "Pride" in *AA Grapevine* (April 1976, p. 33), Bill W. is quoted as stressing a middle course between the "bog of guilt" on the one hand and pride on the other. A similar middle course appears in the AA leaflet *Understanding Anonymity,* which strikes a nice balance between public exposure and being so anonymous that one fails to help others or spread the message.

Court Programs. Another publication containing suggestions born of long experience is the *AA Guidelines on Cooperating with Court, ASAP, and Similar Programs* (1993). Without violating their tradition against affiliation, for more than forty years AA members have been cooperating with courts, correctional facilities, and more recently safe driving programs. That may take the form of Twelfth Step work or may occur as part of their duties while employed in the field, or simply through having the secretary sign a form which people who have been arrested can bring to the judge as evidence that they have fulfilled their court-ordered attendance at AA meetings.

This latter practice, at first questioned by some members, is now recognized as a valuable means of carrying the AA message to many who would not otherwise have been exposed to it. Granted that eventually one must want sobriety for oneself, most members admit that they were originally forced into AA—if not by a court, then by employer, family, doctor, counselor, or one's own inner suffering. As the *Guidelines* (p. 4) say, "We are not concerned about who or what first sends the alcoholic to us, or how. *Our* responsibility is to show AA as such an attractive way of life that all newcomers who need it soon want it." There is no affiliation of the group with the court (p. 5). Various suggestions are made as to how the secretary *after* the meeting may sign a slip or issue an envelope that the individual mails to the court with his own name and address. There is obviously no violation of anonymity here, because it is not at the level of public media, but most importantly because it is the individual offender himself who attests to the court his attendance at a meeting. The secretary merely complies with his request. AA has also published a four-page leaflet "Information on Alcoholics Anonymous for Anyone Sent to AA, and for Administrators of Court Programs and Other Referring Agencies," which contains many of these guidelines.

Speaking at Non-AA Meetings is the title of an AA Conference-approved pamphlet for members going out to schools, other institutions, service groups, and the general public. It contains excellent and detailed suggestions as to topics, approach, and available literature. One caution is against giving a "drunkalog" or personal-history talk that a member might give at an AA meeting (p. 6). The audience often finds it hard to identify with this and may even feel aversion rather than attraction. However, the pamphlet goes on to say that members may find it helpful to relate incidents from their own history to illustrate a point.

AA and Pills. AA rightly takes a strong stand against substituting one addictive drug for another. But overenthusiasm has trapped some AA members into incautious statements about pills that are not substitute addictions and may be medically necessary for a recovering alcoholic. Thus one sometimes hears horror stories about advice to a heart patient not to take digitalis, a diabetic not to take oral insulin, an epileptic not to take Dilantin, or a psychotic not to take lithium. This is not only practicing medicine without a license, it can amount to murder. The same applies to Antabuse, which is not a substitute addiction and may be life-saving for some alcoholics. AA has never approved this kind of advice, and in fact strongly disapproves (see R.S., 1981).

Staff Burnout Syndrome

The health of the patients will hardly rise above that of the staff. Good morale, open communication, and general physical and mental health of all staff members is important to any treatment process. A major problem that workers, and especially administrators, are beginning to face is the high burnout rate among addiction workers. They enter the field with great idealism and high expectations, work for a while with enthusiastic dedication, then leave with disillusionment or broken health. The staff may resemble a dysfunctional family, with its denial of the problem or inertia in doing any-thing about it.

Many factors may affect staff morale: low percentage of success, negative and pessimistic attitudes toward alcoholics/addicts, denial and poor motiva-tion on the part of patients, fragmentation and lack of continuity in treatment services, conflicting objectives of boards and staff. Other factors might be the slowness of the credentialing process, the impossibility of keeping up with the ever spreading delta of research data, and the uncertainty of federal or state funding.

Other reasons may be more specific to the high turnover rate: unrealistic ideals; emotional immaturity; lack of solid sobriety; frustration at the in-equity of salary and career opportunities for nondegreed professionals; bu-reaucratic structures and endless paperwork, which hamper efficient contact with actual clients; boards and administrators who lack understanding; too subjective an involvement with clients, which leads to dejection when one of them relapses; inability to let go of patients, due perhaps to lack of training in termination techniques; and the stress that is inevitable in human services.

Staff burnout takes many forms. It may manifest itself in psychosomatic illness and various behavioral symptoms. In the context of all the factors enu-merated above, the main cause seems to be overcommitment or too-intense dedication. Thinking only of one's work to the neglect of family or other out-side interests while spending all one's time and conversation with fellow staff members and patients may seem very noble and dedicated. But it is a trap that can lead to disaster. Frustration, feelings of not being appreciated, resentment against supervisors, retreat into routine and cheerless performance of duty, use of tranquilizers or sleeping pills, sexual involvement with staff or clients, and other serious consequences can ruin the career of a generous and dedi-cated worker (see "Sources" under "Burnout").

Prevention. The most obvious preventive measure is that staff take adequate vacations. The administrator should insist that the workers get out of the city or state, or at least forbid them to have any contact with the facility or pa-tients. We agree with the warning of Freudenberger and Richelson (1980, p. 17) against sending them to marathon encounters, and with the other sug-gested means of prevention: careful screening, rotation of assignments, send-ing them away for workshops, physical exercise, limiting patient loads, encouraging a hobby or recreation, opportunity to share problems with su-pervisor or trusted staff member. But there is no substitute for full vacation away from the facility. Probably the second most important item is to accept one's limitations, to realize that no one person can do it all and no one ap-proach is fitting for every patient. Dedication does not mean taking full re-sponsibility for the client, nor making oneself available twenty-four hours a day. Al-Anon, whether in staff or other meetings, can be a preventive by help-ing counselors to "detach with love" and avoid being an Enabler.

Epilogue

We have said little about advances in education in the medical and other professions, where there has been much progress. Inclusion of a section on addiction in the examination for licensing as a physician serves notice to medical schools that this must be part of the regular curriculum. ASAM certifies for the specialty of addiction medicine. Attorneys, judges, and correctional workers are becoming aware of addiction training needs, as are social workers, psychologists, and others in the helping professions. Nurses have generally been ahead of most others.

All this could mean better understanding and greater cooperation by all concerned. Mutual respect and open-mindedness seem to be replacing the older defensive attitudes among the professions. In spite of human imperfection, the net result will be more help for the object of all this buzz of activity, the alcoholic/addict.

Sources

Journals such as *The Counselor* (NAADAC) and *Professional Counselor,* along with *Alcoholism and Addiction* magazine and the *U.S. Journal of Alcohol and Drug Dependence,* contain frequent articles on professionalism for this field.

Alley, Sam, and Judith Blanton (eds.), *Paraprofessionals in Mental Health: An Annotated Bibliography 1966 to 1977.* Section on "Alcohol." Social Action Research Center, Berkeley, CA, 1978, pp. 224–30.

Birch & Davis Associates, Inc., *Development of Model Professional Standards for Counselor Credentialing* (1986), or NIAAA, 1984.

Borreliz, M., and P. H. Deleon, "Malpractice: Professional Liability and the Law," *Professional Psychology,* 1978, 9(3):467–77.

Corrigan, Eileen M., and Sandra C. Anderson, "Training for Treatment of Alcoholism in Women," *Social Casework,* 1978, 59:42–50.

Curlee, Joan, "How a Therapist Can Use Alcoholics Anonymous," *Annals of the New York Academy of Sciences,* 1974, 233:137–43.

Finkelstein, Ann B., and John J. Bosley, *Alcoholism Training in the United States: A Summary Report of Thirty-nine Programs.* National Center for Alcohol Education booklet.

Grutchfield, Lee, "What AA Meetings Taught a Non-AA Counselor" (1979).

Keller, Mark, "Multidisciplinary Perspectives on Alcoholism and the Need for Integration: An Historical and Prospective Note" (1975a).

Kilty, Keith M., "Attitudes Toward Alcohol and Alcoholism Among Professionals and Nonprofessionals," *Journal of Studies on Alcohol,* 1975, 36:327–47.

Krimmel, Herman. *Alcoholism: Challenge for Social Work Education.* Council on Social Work Education, New York, 1971.

Krystal, H., and R. A. Moore, "Who Is Qualified to Treat the Alcoholic?" (1963).

Lemere, Frederick, "Who Is Qualified to Treat the Alcoholic? Comment on the Krystal–Moore Discussion," (1964).

Littlejohn Associates, *Proposed National Standard for Alcoholism Counselors: Final Report* (1974).

Mann, Marty, "Attitude: Key to Successful Treatment" (1973).

Norris, John L. "What AA Can Offer Professional Schools and What It Cannot" (1971).

R.S., "Pill Consciousness" (1981).

Staub, George, and Leona Kent (eds.), *The Para-Professional in the Treatment of Alcoholism: A New Profession* (1973).

Valle, S., *Alcoholism Counseling: Issues for an Emerging Profession* (1979).

Wright, R. H., "What to Do Until the Malpractice Lawyer Comes: A Survivor's Manual," *American Psychologist*, 1981, 36(12):1535–41.

BURNOUT

Blankman, B., and B. Anderson, "Peer Assistance for Counselors," *The Counselor*, November–December 1986, pp. 8–9.

Freudenberger, Herbert J., and G. Richelson, *Burn-out: The High Cost of High Achievement* (1980). See also *The Staff Burn-out Syndrome*. Drug Abuse Council, Washington, DC pamphlet.

Gottheil, Edward, "Poor Morale in Treatment Personnel," *Alcohol Health and Research World*, Spring 1975, pp. 20–25.

Maslach, Christina, *Burnout: The Cost of Caring* (1982).

O'Connell, K. R., "The Clinical Staff of an Alcohol and Drug Treatment Program as an Alcoholic Family," *The Counselor*, September–October 1986, pp. 4–5.

Pines, A. M., et al., *Burnout: From Tedium to Personal Growth* (1982).

Powell, David J., "Clinical Supervision: The Missing Puzzle Piece," *The Counselor*, 1988, 6(3):2–22.

Valle, Stephen K., "Burnout: Occupational Hazard for Counselors," *Alcohol Health and Research World*, Spring 1979, 3(3):10–14.

ETHICS, CONFIDENTIALITY

Andrews, L. M. *To Thine Own Self Be True: The Rebirth of Values in the New Ethical Therapy* (1987).

Bissell, LeClair, and J. E. Royce, *Ethics for Addiction Professionals* (1994).

Blume, Sheila B., *Confidentiality of Medical Records in Alcohol-related Problems*. NCA pamphlet.

Gazda, George M., *Group Counseling: A Developmental Approach*. 2d ed. Allyn & Bacon, Boston, 1978. Chapter 10, "Guidelines for Ethical Practice in Group Counseling and Related Group Work" reports survey of twenty professional associations who shared codes of ethics; Chapter 12 is "Controversial Issues in Small Group Work—With an Emphasis on Encounter Groups."

Gill, James J., Francis J. Braceland, et al., "Ethics and Psychiatry," *Psychiatric Annals*, February 1979, 9(2), entire issue.

Hannah, G. T., et al. (eds.), *Preservation of Client Rights*. Free Press, New York, 1982.

Hare-Mustin, Rachel T., et al., "Rights of Clients, Responsibilities of Therapists," *American Psychologist*, 1979, 34:3–16. Ample references.

U.S. Department of Health and Human Services, "Confidentiality of Alcohol and Drug Abuse Records," *Federal Register*, June 9, 1987, 52(110), Part II. Title 42, Code of Federal Regulations (42 CFR), Part 2.

White, William L., *Critical Incidents: Ethical Issues in Substance Abuse Prevention and Treatment* (1993).

COOPERATION WITH ALCOHOLICS ANONYMOUS

AA Grapevine, October 1963 and September 1974 issues.
AA Guidelines for Members Employed in the Field.
About A.A. (free newsletter for professionals).
Alcoholics Anonymous and the Medical Profession.
Alcoholics Anonymous Comes of Age.
How AA Members Cooperate with Other Community Efforts to Help Alcoholics.
If You are a Professional, AA Wants to Work with You.
Let's Be Friendly with Our Friends.
Three Talks to Medical Societies, by Bill W.

Appendix

Sources for Literature on Alcoholism
and Other Addictions

Much valuable material is available in pamphlet form rather than in hardback books. The asterisk indicates a source for some free materials.

Addiction Research Foundation (ARF)
33 Russell St.
Toronto, Ont. M5S 2S1

Adult Children of Alcoholics
(ACoA)
P.O. Box 3216
Torrance, CA 90510
310-534-1815
COA 1-800-359-2623

African-American Family Services
2616 Nicollet Ave., South
Minneapolis, MN 55407
612-871-7878

Al-Anon Family Group Headquarters,
Inc.
(Al-Anon and Alateen)
Box 862, Midtown Sta.
New York, NY 10018-0862
1-800-356-9996

Alcohol and Drug Problems
Association (ADPA)
1555 Wilson Blvd., #300
Arlington, VA 22209
703-875-8684

Alcoholics Anonymous World
Services
475 Riverside Dr.
New York, NY 10115
212-870-3400

American Council for Drug Education
136 E. 64th St.
New York, NY 10021-7360

American Society of Addiction
Medicine (ASAM)
4601 North Park Ave. # 101
Chevy Chase, MD 20815
301-656-3920

Association of Halfway House
Alcoholism Programs of N.
America (AHHAP)
786 E. 7th St.
St. Paul, MN 55106
612-771-0933

The Bottom Line
American Business Men's
Foundation
1120 E. Oakland
Lansing, MI 48906

CANSA International
(National Chemical Dependency
Nurses Association)
303 W. Katella Ave., # 202
Orange, CA 92667

* Center for Substance Abuse
Prevention (CSAP)
5600 Fishers Lane, Rockwall II
Bldg.
Rockville, MD 20857
CSAP hotline 1-800-662-HELP

Community Anti-Drug Coalitions of
America
701 N. Fairfax St.
Alexandria, VA 22314-2045
1-800-542-2322

Community Intervention
529 S. 7th St. #570
Minneapolis, MN 55415

CompCare Publications are now
  obtainable from Hazelden

Employee Assistance Professionals
  Association (EAPA, formerly
  ALMACA)
2101 Wilson Blvd. #500
Arlington, VA 22201-3062
703-522-6272

Hazelden Publications
Box 176
Center City, MN 55012-0176
1-800-328-0098

Health Communications, Inc.
3201 S.W. 15th St.
Deerfield Beach, FL 33442
1-800-851-9100

JACS (Jewish alcoholics, etc.)
197 East Broadway
New York, NY 10002
212-473-4747

Johnson Institute
7205 Ohms Lane
Minneapolis, MN 55439-2159
1-800-231-5165

*Join Together
441 Stuart St. 6th floor
Boston, MA 02116
617-437-1500

*Kemper Insurance Companies
Public Affairs Dept.
Long Grove, IL 60049

Learning Publications, Inc.
5351 Gulf Dr.
Holmes Beach, FL 34217

*MADD (Mothers Against Drunk
Driving)
511 E. John Carpenter Frwy.
  # 700
Irving, TX 75062-8187
214-744-MADD

Mitchell Press Ltd.
P.O. Box 6000
Vancouver, BC, Canada V6B 4B9

Nar-Anon Family Groups
P.O. Box 2562
Palos Verdes Peninsula, CA 90274
213-547-5800

Narcotics Anonymous (NA)
P.O. Box 9999
Van Nuys, CA 91409
818-780-3951

National Association for Children
  of Alcoholics (NACoA)
11426 Rockville Pike, # 100
Rockville, MD 20852
301/468-0985

National Association for Native
  American Children of Alcoholics
  (NANACoA)
P.O. Box 18736
Seattle, WA 98118
206-467-7686

National Association of Alcoholism and
  Drug Abuse Counselors (NAADAC)
1911 N. Fort Meyer Dr. #900
Arlington, VA 22209
1-800-548-0497

National Black Alcoholism/Addictions
  Council
1629 K St., NW
Washington, DC 20006
202-296-2696

National Catholic Council on
  Alcoholism
1550 Hendrickson St.
Brooklyn, NY 11234
718-951-7177

*National Clearinghouse for Alcohol
and Drug Information (NCADI)
P.O. Box 2345
Rockville, MD 20847-2345
1-800-729-6686

National Cocaine Hotline
1-800-COCAINE

*National Council on Alcoholism and
    Drug Dependence (NCADD)
12 W. 21st St.
New York, NY 10010
1-800-NCA-CALL

*National Institute on Alcohol Abuse
    and Alcoholism (NIAAA)
6000 Executive Blvd.
Rockville, MD 20892-7003
301-443-3860

*National Institute on Drug Abuse
    (NIDA)
11400 Rockville Pike
Rockville, MD 20852
301-443-1124

National Nurses Society on Addictions
    (NNSA)
5700 Old Orchard Rd.
Skokie, IL 60077
708-966-5010

*National Safety Council
1121 Spring Lake Dr.
Itasca, IL 60143
1-800-285-1121

Perrin & Treggett, Inc.
P.O. Box 190
East Rutherford, NJ 07070

PRIDE (Parents' Institute for Drug
    Education)
50 Hurt Plaza, #210
Atlanta, GA 30303
404-577-4500

Project Cork Resource Center
Dartmouth Medical School
Hanover, NH 03755

Recovered Alcoholic Clergy Association
    (RACA)
5615 Midnight Pass Rd., Siesta Key
Sarasota, FL 54242
813-349-5616

Rutgers Center of Alcohol Studies-
    Publications
P.O. Box 969
Piscataway, NJ 08854-969
201-932-4442

Christopher D. Smithers Foundation
P.O. Box 67
Oyster Bay Rd.
Mill Neck, NY 11765

Substance Abuse Librarians and
    Information Specialists (SALIS)
P.O. Box 9513
Berkeley, CA 94709-0513
415-642-5208

Tough Love
1-800-333-1069

Wisconsin Clearinghouse
P.O. Box 1468 (1245 E. Washington
    Ave.)
Madison, WI 53701

Women for Sobriety, Inc.
P.O. Box 618
Quakertown, PA 18951
1-800-333-1606

General Bibliography

See notes in "Sources" at end of Chapter One.

SERIES

Advances in Alcohol and Substance Abuse. Haworth, New York, 1981– .

Alcohol and Health: Special Report to the U.S. Congress. National Institute on Alcohol Abuse and Alcoholism (NIAAA), DEW/DHHS, Washington, DC. First, 1971 (o.p., reprinted by Scribner's, New York); Second, 1974; Third, 1978; Fourth, 1981; Fifth, 1983; Sixth, 1987; Seventh, 1990; Eighth, 1994. (Note that these are not successive editions but distinct books.)

Annual Review of Addictions Research and Treatment, Pergamon Press, New York, 1991– .

Galanter, Marc (ed., AMSA/ASAM/RSA), *Recent Developments in Alcoholism.* Plenum, New York, vols. 1–5, 1983– .

Gibbins, R. J., Yedy Israel, et al. (eds.), *Research Advances in Alcohol and Drug Problems.* Plenum, New York, vols. 1–9, 1976– .

Kissin, Benjamin, Henri Begleiter, et al. (eds.), *Biology of Alcoholism.* Plenum, New York, vols. 1–7, 1971– .

Seixas, Frank, Marc Galanter, et al. (eds.), *Currents in Alcoholism.* Grune & Stratton, New York, vols. 1–8, 1976– .

JOURNALS

Addiction and Recovery. Was *Alcoholism: The National Magazine,* 1980–85; *Alcoholism and Addiction,* 1985–89.

The Addiction Letter.

Addictive Behaviors: An International Journal.

Alcohol.

Alcohol and Alcoholism.

*Alcohol Health and Research World. Quarterly, National Institute on Alcohol Abuse and Alcoholism, DEW/DHHS, Washington, DC. Spring 1973– (experimental issues preceded regular volume numbering in 1976).

*Alcoholism: Clinical and Experimental Research (ASAM/RSA).

The Alcoholism Report.

Alcoholism Treatment Quarterly.

American Journal of Drug and Alcohol Abuse.

*British Journal of Addiction. Was *British Journal of Inebriety.*

The Counselor (NAADAC).

DATA: Digest of Alcoholism Theory and Application.

Drug Abuse and Alcoholism Review.

The Drug Abuse Report.

Drug Abuse Update.

Drug and Alcohol Dependence: An International Journal of Biomedical and Psychosocial Approaches.

The International Journal of the Addictions.

* Indicates the most important scientific journals.

The Journal (Addiction Research Foundation, Toronto).

Journal of Addictive Diseases, the official journal of the American Society of Addictive Medicine (ASAM).

Journal of Alcohol and Drug Education. 1972– . Was *Journal of Alcohol Education, 1967–71.*

Journal of Chemical Dependency Treatment, 1987– .

Journal of Drug Education.

Journal of Drug Issues. Each quarterly issue deals with a specific topic, e.g., Winter 1985 (vol. 15, no. 1) is on "Social Thought on Alcoholism."

Journal of Ministry in Addiction and Recovery, 1994– .

Journal of Psychoactive Drugs.

*Journal of Studies on Alcohol (JSA), 1975– , monthly; was *Quarterly Journal (QJSA)* through 1974.

Journal of Substance Abuse Treatment.

Prevention Pipeline.

Professional Counselor.

Psychology of Addictive Behaviors. Was *Bulletin of the Society of Psychologists in Addictive Behaviors.*

Substance Abuse.

Substance Abuse Report.

U.S. Journal of Drug and Alcohol Dependence.

BOOKS AND ARTICLES

N.B. The *Quarterly Journal of Studies on Alcohol* is abbreviated as *QJSA;* in 1975 it became a monthly, the *Journal of Studies on Alcohol (JSA).* See the Appendix above for NCADD, NCADI, etc. The *Journal of the American Medical Association* is *JAMA.*

Abel, E. L., *Marijuana, the First Twelve Thousand Years.* Plenum, New York, 1980.

——, *Fetal Alcohol Syndrome and Fetal Alcohol Effects.* Plenum, New York, 1984.

——, *Psychoactive Drugs and Sex.* Plenum, New York, 1985.

——, *Fetal Alcohol Syndrome: An Annotated Bibliography.* Praeger, New York, 1986.

Ables, Billie S., "A Note on the Treatment of Adolescents Who Use Drugs," *Journal of Psychedelic Drugs,* 1977, 9:127–31.

Abrams, R. C., and G. Alexopoulos, "Substance Abuse in the Elderly: Alcohol and Prescription Drugs," *Hospital and Community Psychiatry,* 1987, 38:1285–88.

Ackerman, Robert J., *Children of Alcoholics: A Guidebook for Educators, Therapists, and Parents.* 2d ed. Learning Publications, Oshtemo, MI, 1983.

——, *Growing in the Shadow.* Health Communications, Deerfield Beach, FL, 1986.

——, *Perfect Daughters: Adult Daughters of Alcoholics.* Human Services Institute, Bradenton, FL, 1989.

Adderholt-Elliott, M., *Perfectionism: What's Bad About Being Too Good?* Johnson Institute, Minneapolis, Bradenton, FL; 1989.

"AIDS," *Advances in Alcohol and Substance Abuse.* Summer 1988, vol. 7, no. 4.

Al-Anon, *Alateen: Hope for the Children of Alcoholics.* Al-Anon Family Group Headquarters, New York, 1973.

——, *Al-Anon Faces Alcoholism.* Rev. ed. Al-Anon Family Group Headquarters, Inc., New York, 1975.

——, *Dilemma of the Alcoholic Marriage.* 4th ed. Al-Anon Family Group Headquarters, New York, 1977.

——, *Al-Anon Family Groups.* Rev. ed. Al-Anon Family Group Headquarters, New York, 1978. Formerly *Living with An Alcoholic.*

————, *Twelve Steps and Twelve Traditions for Al-Anon.* Al-Anon Family Group Headquarters, New York, 1981.

————, *First Steps: Al-Anon . . . 35 Years of Beginnings.* Al-Anon Family Group Headquarters, New York, 1986.

————, *From Survival to Recovery.* Al-Anon Family Group Headquarters, New York, 1995a.

————, *How Al-Anon Works: For families and friends of alcoholics.* Al-Anon Family Group Headquarters, New York, 1995b.

————, *Twelve Steps and Twelve Traditions for Alateen.* Al-Anon Family Group Headquarters, New York, n.d.

Alcoholics Anonymous, *Twelve Steps and Twelve Traditions.* Alcoholics Anonymous World Services, New York, 1953.

————, *Alcoholics Anonymous Comes of Age: A Brief History of AA.* Alcoholics Anonymous World Services, New York, 1957.

————, *The AA Way of Life (As Bill Sees It).* Alcoholics Anonymous World Services, New York, 1967.

————, *Came to Believe.* Alcoholics Anonymous World Services, New York, 1973.

————, *Living Sober.* Alcoholics Anonymous World Services, New York, 1975.

————, *Alcoholics Anonymous: The Story of How Many Thousands of Men and Women Have Recovered from Alcoholism.* 3d ed. Alcoholics Anonymous World Services, New York, 1976 (orig. pub. 1939).

————, *Dr. Bob and the Good Oldtimers.* Alcoholics Anonymous World Services, New York, 1980.

————, *Pass It On: The Story of Bill Wilson and How the A.A. Message Reached the World.* Alcoholics Anonymous World Services, New York, 1984.

————, *AA Guidelines on Cooperating with Court, ASAP, and Similiar Programs.* Alcoholics Anonymous World Services, New York, 1993.

————, *AA Guidelines for Members Employed in the Alcoholism Field.* Rev. ed., Alcoholics Anonymous World Services, New York, 1994.

Alexander, Bruce K., *Peaceful Measures: Canada's Way Out of the "War on Drugs."* University of Toronto Press, Toronto, 1990.

Alexander, Jack, "Alcoholics Anonymous: Freed Slaves of Drink, Now They Free Others," *Saturday Evening Post,* March 1, 1941, 213:9–11ff.

Alibrandi, Tom, *The Young Alcoholics.* CompCare, Minneapolis, 1977.

Alling, C., et al., *Alcohol, Cell Membranes and Signal Transduction in Brain.* Plenum, New York, 1994.

Alterman, Arthur I., *Substance Abuse and Psychopathology.* Plenum, New York, 1985.

Altman, Marjorie, and Ruth Crocker (eds.)., *Social Groupwork and Alcoholism.* Haworth, New York, 1982.

AMSAODD/NCA (American Medical Society on Alcoholism and Other Drug Dependencies), *Acquired Immune Deficiency Syndrome and Chemical Dependency.* U.S. Department of Health and Human Services, DHHS Publ. No. (ADM) 87-1513, Washington, DC, 1987.

————, *Guidelines for Facilities on AIDS.* NCA, New York, 1988.

American Psychiatric Association, "Megavitamin and Orthomolecular Therapy in Psychiatry," *Nutrition Review,* 1974, 32 (supp.):44–47.

————, *Diagnostic and Statistical Manual of Mental Disorders,* Fourth Edition (*DSM-IV*), American Psychiatric Association, Washington, DC, 1994.

Anderson, Daniel J., *A History of Our Confused Attitudes Toward Beverage Alcohol.* Hazelden, Center City, MN, 1967.

————, *The Psychopathology of Denial.* Hazelden, Center City, MN, 1981.

Andreasen, Nancy, *The Broken Brain.* Harper & Row, San Francisco, 1985.

Andrews, Lewis M., *To Thine Own Self Be True: The Rebirth of Values in the New Ethical Therapy,* Chapter 12, "Beyond Addiction," pp. 144–56. Anchor Press/Doubleday, Garden City, NY, 1987.

Anonymous, "Where Good Drinkers Go," *Collier's,* September 1939, 104:14–15.

Apthorp, Stephen P., *Alcohol and Substance Abuse: A Clergy Handbook.* 2d ed. Morehouse–Barlow, Wilton,CT, 1990.

Armor, David, J., *Alcoholism and Treatment.* Rand Corporation, Santa Monica, CA, 1976.

Asher, Ramona M., *Women with Alcoholic Husbands: Ambivalence and the Trap of Codependency.* University of North Carolina Press, Chapel Hill, 1992.

Ashley, Mary Jane, and J. G. Rankin, "Hazardous Alcohol Consumption and Diseases of the Circulatory System," *JSA,* 1980, 41(11): 1040–70.

Ashley, Mary Jane, et al., "Skid Row Alcoholism: A Distinct Socio-Medical Entity," *Archives of Internal Medicine,* 1976, 136:272–78.

Atkinson, Roland M., *Alcohol and Drug Abuse in Old Age.* American Psychiatric Association, Washington, DC, 1984.

Austin, G. A., *Perspectives on the History of Psychoactive Substance Use.* NIDA Research Issues no. 24. U.S. Department of Health, Education, and Welfare, Washington, DC, 1978.

———, *Alcohol in Western Society from Antiquity to 1800: A Chronological History.* ABC Clio Information Services, Santa Barbara, CA, 1985.

Babor, Thomas F. (ed.), *Alcohol and Culture: Comparative Perspectives from Europe and America.* Annals of the New York Academy of Sciences, vol. 272, 1986.

Bacon, Selden D., "The Process of Addiction to Alcohol: Social Aspects," *QJSA,* 1973, 34:1–27.

———, "Concepts," in William Filstead, Jean Rossi, and Mark Keller (eds.), *Alcohol and Alcohol Problems: New Thinking and New Directions.* Ballinger Publishing, Cambridge, MA, 1976, pp. 57–134.

———, "On the Prevention of Alcohol Problems and Alcoholism," *JSA,* 1978, 39:1125–47.

Bahr, H. M., *Skid Row: An Introduction to Disaffiliation.* Oxford University Press, New York, 1973.

Baker, Joan K., "Alcoholism and the American Indian," in Nada J. Estes and Edith Heinemann (eds.), *Alcoholism: Development, Consequences, and Interventions.* Mosby, St. Louis, 1986.

Baker, Thomas S., *Understanding the Spiritual Nature of Addiction.* Behavioral Health Care Press, Alexandria, VA, 1994.

Bard, Bernard, "The Shameful Truth and Consequences of School Drug Programs," *Parents' Magazine,* 1974, 49(9):40–52.

Barnard, Charles P., *Families, Alcoholism and Therapy.* Charles C Thomas, Springfield, IL, 1981.

Barnes, Grace M., "The Development of Adolescent Drinking Behavior: An Evaluative Review of the Impact of the Socialization Process Within the Family," *Adolescence,* 1977, 12:571–91.

———, *Alcohol and Youth: A Comprehensive Bibliography.* Greenwood Press, Westport, CT, 1982.

Barnes, Grace M., et al., *Alcohol and the Elderly: A Comprehensive Bibliography.* Greenwood Press, Westport, CT, 1980.

Bateson, Gregory, *Steps to an Ecology of Mind.* Chandler, San Francisco, 1972.

Bean, M., "Alcoholics Anonymous: Principles and Methods," *Psychiatric Annals,* 1975, vol. 5, nos. 2 and 3.

Bean, M., and N. Zinberg (eds.), *Dynamic Approaches to the Understanding and Treatment of Alcoholism.* Free Press, New York, 1981.

Bean-Bayog, M., "Alcohol and Drug Abuse: Alcoholism as a Cause of Psychopathology," *Hospital and Community Psychiatry,* 1988, 39:352–54.

Beard, J. D., and D. H. Knott, "Fluid and Electrolyte Balance During Acute Withdrawal in Chronic Alcoholic Patients," *JAMA,* 1969, 204:133–37.

Beasley, Joseph D., *Wrong Diagnosis, Wrong Treatment: The Plight of the Alcoholic in America.* Creative Informatics, Durant, OK 74702-1607, 1987.

Beauchamp, Dan E., *Beyond Alcoholism: Alcohol and Public Health Policy.* Temple University Press, Philadelphia, 1980.

Becker, Charles E.; R. L. Roe; and R. A. Scott, *Alcohol as a Drug: A Curriculum on Pharmacology, Neurology and Toxicology.* Williams & Wilkins, Baltimore, 1974.

Beckman, L. J., "Women Alcoholics: A Review of Social and Psychological Studies," *QJSA,* 1975, 36:797–824.

Begleiter, Henri (ed.), *Biological Effects of Alcohol.* Plenum, New York, 1980.

Begleiter, H., et al., "Event-related Brain Potentials in Boys at Risk of Alcoholism," *Science,* September 28, 1984, 225:1493–96.

Bell, Peter, and J. Evans, *Counseling the Black Client: Alcohol Use and Abuse in Black America.* Hazelden, Center City, MN, 1984.

Bell, Robert G., *Escape from Addiction.* McGraw-Hill, New York, 1970.

Bellwood, Lester R., "Grief Work in Alcoholism Treatment," *Alcohol Health and Research World,* Spring 1975, pp. 8–11.

Bennett, A. E., *Alcoholism and the Brain.* Stratton Intercontinental Medical Book Corp., New York, 1977.

Bennion, Lynn J., and Ting-Kai Li, "Alcohol Metabolism in American Indians and Whites: Lack of Racial Differences in Metabolic Rate and Liver Alcohol Dehydrogenase," *New England Journal of Medicine,* 1976, 294:9–13.

Bepko, Claudia, and Jo Ann Krestan, *The Responsibility Trap: A Blueprint for Treating the Alcoholic Family.* Free Press, New York, 1985.

Berg, Stephen L. (ed.), *Alcoholism and Pastoral Ministry.* Guest House, Lake Orion, MI, 1989.

——, *Spirituality and Addiction: A Bibliography.* Bishop of Books, Wheeling, WV, 1993.

Berne, Eric, *Games People Play.* Grove Press, New York, 1967.

——, *Transactional Analysis in Psychotherapy.* Grove Press, New York, 1961.

Berry, Ralph E., and James P. Boland, *The Economic Cost of Alcohol Abuse.* Free Press, New York, 1977.

Beschner, G. M., and A. S. Friedman, *Teen Drug Use.* D. C. Heath, Lexington, MA, 1986.

Besharov, Douglas J., *When Drug Addicts Have Children: Reorienting Child Welfare's Response.* Child Welfare League of America, Washington, DC, 1994.

Bickerton, Yvonne J., and Roberta V. Sanders, "Ethnic Preferences in Alcoholism Treatment: The Case of Hawaii," *Annals of the New York Academy of Sciences,* 1976, 273:653–58.

Birch & Davis Associates, Inc., *Development of Model Professional Standards for Alcoholism Counselor Credentialing.* NAADAC, Arlington, VA, 1986.

Bishop, Charles, and Bill Pittman, *To Be Continued: The Alcoholics Anonymous World Bibliography: 1939–1994.* Bishop of Books, Wheeling, WV, 1994.

Bissell, LeClair, and P. Haberman, *Alcoholism in the Professions.* Oxford University Press, New York, 1984.

Bissell, LeClair, and J. E. Royce, *Ethics for Addiction Professionals.* Rev. ed. Hazelden, Center City, MN, 1994.

Bissell, LeClair, and Jane K. Skorina, "One Hundred Alcoholic Women in Medicine," *JAMA,* June 5, 1987, 257(21):2939–44.

Black, Claudia, "Innocent Bystanders at Risk: The Children of Alcoholics," *Alcoholism: The National Magazine,* January–February 1981, 1(3):22–26.

———, *It Will Never Happen to Me.* MAC, Denver 80207, 1982.

———, *My Daddy Loves Me, My Daddy Has a Disease.* MAC, Denver 80207, 1982.

———, *Repeat After Me.* MAC, Denver 80207, 1985.

———, *The Stamp Game.* MAC, Denver 80207, 1985.

———, *Double Duty: Dual Dynamics Within the Chemically Dependent Home.* Ballantine Books, New York, 1990.

Blaine, Allan (ed.), *Alcoholism and the Jewish Community.* Federation of Jewish Philanthropies, New York, 1981.

Blane, Howard T., *The Personality of the Alcoholic.* Harper, New York, 1968.

Blane, Howard T., and K. E. Leonard (eds.), *Psychological Theories of Drinking and Alcoholism.* Guilford, New York, 1987.

Blane, Howard T., and Linda E. Hewitt, *Alcohol and Youth: An Analysis of the Literature, 1960–1975.* National Institute on Alcohol Abuse and Alcoholism, Rockville, MD., 1977 (U.S. Department of Commerce, National Technical Information Service, PB-268 698).

Blum, Kenneth, *Handbook of Abusable Drugs.* Gardner Press, New York, 1984.

Blum, Kenneth, and J. E. Payne, *Alcohol and the Addictive Brain: New Hope for Alcoholics from Biogenetic Research.* Free Press, New York, 1991.

Blum, Kenneth, and Helga Topel, "Opioid Peptides and Alcoholism: Genetic Deficiency and Chemical Management," *Functional Neurology,* January–March 1986, 1(1):71–83.

Blumberg, Leonard U.; Thomas E. Shipley; and Stephen F. Barsky, *Liquor and Poverty: Skid Row as a Human Condition.* Rutgers Center of Alcohol Studies, New Brunswick, NJ, 1978. Monograph 13.

Blume, Sheila B., "Iatrogenic Alcoholism," *QJSA,* 1973, 34:1348–52.

———, *Alcohol/Drug Dependent Women.* Johnson Institute, Minneapolis, 1986.

———, *Confidentiality of Patient Records in Alcoholism and Drug Treatment Programs.* National Council on Alcoholism, New York, 1987.

Bohman, M., et al., "Marital Inheritance of Alcohol Abuse: Cross Fostering Analysis of Adopted Women," *Archives of General Psychiatry,* 1981, 38:965–69.

Booth, Leo. *When God Becomes a Drug: Breaking the Chains of Religious Addiction and Abuse.* Jeremy Tarcher, Los Angeles, 1992.

Borkenstein, R. F., et al., *The Role of the Drinking Driver in Traffic Accidents.* Indiana University, Department of Police Administration, Bloomington, 1964.

Botkin, Gilbert J., "Prevention Report: Early Intervention is Effective," *Alcoholism and Substance Abuse Weekly,* 1995, 7(16):4.

Bourne, P. G. "Alcoholism in the Urban Negro Population," in P. G. Bourne and R. Fox (eds.), *Alcoholism: Progress in Research and Treatment.* Academic Press, New York, 1973, pp. 211–26.

Bourne, P. G., and R. Fox (eds.), *Alcoholism: Progress in Research and Treatment.* Academic Press, New York, 1973.

Bowden, Julie, and H. Gravitz, *Genesis: Spirituality in Recovery from Childhood Traumas.* Deerfield Beach, FL: Health Communications, 1988.

Bowen, Murray, "Alcoholism as Viewed Through Family Systems Theory and Family Psychotherapy," *Annals of the New York Academy of Sciences,* 1974, 233:115–222.

Bradley, Ann M., "Keep Coming Back: The Case for a Valuation of Alcoholics Anonymous, *Alcohol Health and Research World,* 1988, 12(3):192–99.

Brain, Paul F. (ed.), *Alcohol and Aggression.* Crown Helm, Dover, NH 03820, 1985.

Brecher, Edward (ed.), *Licit and Illicit Drugs.* Little, Brown & Co. for Consumer Reports, Boston, 1972.

Breed, Warren, "Study Criticizes Portrayal of Drinking on TV," *NIAAA Information and Feature Service,* Washington, DC, May 31, 1978, p. 2.

Brisbane, Frances L., and M. Womble (eds.), *Treatment of Black Alcoholics.* Haworth, New York, 1985.

Brook, Judith S., et al. (eds.), *Alcohol and Substance Abuse in Adolescence.* Haworth, New York, 1985.

Brown, Stephanie, *Treating the Alcoholic: A Developmental Model of Recovery.* Wiley, New York, 1985.

Bruel, L., "Fight Against Chronic Alcoholism: Intravenous Injections of 30% Alcohol," *Echo Medical du Nord,* 1939, 10:497–501.

Bruel, L., and R. LeCoq, "La prevention des accidents operatoires chez les ethyliques," *Concours Medical,* 1947, 69:2172–75.

Brunswick, Ann F., and Carol Tarica, "Drinking and Health: A Study of Urban Black Adolescents," *Addictive Diseases,* 1974, 1:21–42.

Burch, George F., and Thomas D. Giles, "Alcoholic Cardiomyopathy: Concept of the Disease and Its Treatment," *American Journal of Medicine,* 1971, 50:141–45.

Busse, S.; C. T. Malloy; and C. E. Weise, *Disulfiram in the Treatment of Alcoholism: A Bibliography.* Addiction Research Foundation, Toronto, Canada, 1979.

Butler, B., *Alcohol and Drugs in the Workplace.* Butterworth-Heinemann, Newton, MA, 1993.

C., Stewart, *A Reference Guide to the Big Book of Alcoholics Anonymous.* Recovery Press, Box 19762, Seattle, WA 98109, 1987.

Caddy, G. R., "Abstinence and Controlled Drinking," in J. Newman (ed.), *Time for Change in Alcoholism Treatment: Traditional and Emerging Concepts.* University of Pittsburgh Press, Pittsburgh, 1979.

Cahalan, Don, "Drinking Practices and Problems: Research Perspectives in Remedial Measures," *Public Affairs Report,* 1973, 14(2):1–6.

———, *Understanding America's Drinking Problem: How to Combat the Hazards of Alcohol.* Jossey-Bass, San Francisco, 1987.

———, *An Ounce of Prevention.* Jossey-Bass, San Francisco, 1991.

Cahalan, Don; I. H. Cissin; and H. M. Crossley, *American Drinking Practices: A National Study of Drinking Behavior and Attitudes.* Rutgers Center of Alcohol Studies, New Brunswick, NJ, 1969. Monongraph 6.

Cain, Arthur H., *The "Cured" Alcoholic.* John Day, New York, 1964.

Cairns, T. H., *Preparing Your Church for Ministry to Alcoholics and Their Families.* Charles C Thomas, Springfield, IL, 1986.

Cappell, Howard, and C. P. Herman, "Alcohol and Tension Reduction," *QJSA,* 1972, 33:33–64.

Carlen, P. L., et al., "Reversible Cerebral Atrophy in Recently Abstinent Chronic Alcoholics Measured by Computed Tomography Scans," *Science,* June 2, 1978, 200:1076–78.

Carol, Gail, *Alcoholics in Recovery: Spiritual and Cultural Revitalization.* Hazelden, Center City, MN, 1991.

Carroll, J. F., and T. E. Malloy, "Combined Treatment of Alcohol- and Drug-dependent Persons: A Literature Review and Evaluation," *American Journal of Drug and Alcohol Abuse,* 1977, 4:343–64.

Carroll, J. F.; T. E. Malloy; and F. McKendrick, "Alcohol Abuse by Drug-dependent Persons: A Literature Review and Evaluation," *American Journal of Drug and Alcohol Abuse,* 1977a, 4:293–316.

———, "Drug Abuse by Alcoholics and Problem Drinkers: A Literature Review and Evaluation," *American Journal of Drug and Alcohol Abuse,* 1977b, 4:317–42.

Cary, Sylvia, *Jolted Sober: Getting to the Moment of Clarity.* Lowell House, Los Angeles, 1989.

Casement, Mary R., "Editor's Forum: Economic Research and Prevention," *Alcohol Health and Research World,* Fall 1987, 12(1):16–29.

Catanzaro, Ronald J. (ed.), *Alcoholism: The Total Treatment Approach.* Rev. ed. Charles C Thomas, Springfield, IL, 1972.

Cermak, Timmen, *A Primer on Adult Children of Alcoholics.* Health Communications, Deerfield Beach, FL, 1985

———, *Diagnosing and Treating Co-dependency: A Guide for Professionals.* Johnson Institute, Minneapolis, 1986.

———, *A Time to Heal: The Road to Recovery for Adult Children of Alcoholics.* Tarcher, Los Angeles, 1988.

Chalfant, H. Paul, *Social and Behavioral Aspects of Female Alcoholism: An Annotated Bibliography.* Greenwood Press, Westport, CT 1980.

Chasnoff, Ira J., *Drugs, Alcohol, Pregnancy and Parenting.* Kluwer, Boston, 1988.

Chaudron, C. D., and D. A. Wilkinson (eds.), *Theories on Alcoholism.* Addiction Research Foundation, Toronto, 1988.

Chiauzzi, Emil J., *Preventing Relapse in the Addictions: A Biopsychosocial Approach.* Pergamon Press, New York, 1991.

Christmas, June J., "Alcoholism Services for Minorities: Training Issues and Concerns," *Alcohol Health and Research World,* Spring 1978, 2(3):20–27.

Clark, W., and L. Midanik, "Alcohol Use and Alcohol Problems Among U.S. Adults," pp. 3–52 in *NIAAA Alcohol and Health Monograph #1: Alcohol Consumption and Related Problems.* DHHS (ADM) 82-1190, NIAAA, Rockville, MD, 1982.

Clarren, Sterling K., and David W. Smith, "The Fetal Alcohol Syndrome: A Review of the World Literature," *New England Journal of Medicine,* 1978, 298:1063–67.

Clinebell, Howard J., "Philosophical-Religious Factors in the Etiology and Treatment of Alcoholism," *QJSA,* 1963, 24:473–88.

———, *Understanding and Counseling the Alcoholic Through Religion and Psychology.* Rev. ed. Abingdon Press, Nashville, 1968.

———, *Counseling for Spiritually Empowered Wholeness.* Haworth, Binghamton, NY, 1995.

Cloniger, C. R., "Genetic and Environmental Factors in the Development of Alcoholism," *Journal of Psychiatric Treatment and Evaluation.* December 30, 1983, 5:487–96.

Cohen, Sidney, "The Effects of Combined Alcohol-Drug Abuse on Human Behavior: A Review of the Literature," *Drug Abuse and Alcoholism Review,* 1979, 2 (3):1–13.

———, *The Alcoholism Problems.* Haworth, New York, vol. 1, 1983; vol. 2, 1985.

Cohen, Sidney, and J. F. Callahan (eds.), *The Diagnosis and Treatment of Drug and Alcohol Abuse.* Haworth, New York, 1986.

Coleman, J. H., and W. E. Evans, "Drug Interaction with Alcohol." *Alcohol Health and Research World,* Winter 1975–76, pp. 16–19.

Collins, James J. (ed.), *Drinking and Crime.* Guilford, New York, 1981.

Conley, Paul, and Andrew Sorensen, *The Staggering Steeple: The Story of Alcoholism and the Churches.* Pilgrim Press, Philadelphia, 1971.

Cook, P., "The Economics of Alcohol Consumption and Abuse," in J. West (ed.), *Alcoholism and Related Problems: Issues for the American Public.* Prentice-Hall, Englewood Cliffs, NJ, 1984.

Coombs, Robert H., *The Family Context of Adolescent Drug Abuse.* Haworth, New York, 1989.

Corey, Marianne S., and Gerald Corey, *Groups: Process and Practice.* Brooks-Cole, Pacific Grove, CA, 1992.

Cork, R. Margaret, *The Forgotten Children.* Addiction Research Foundation, Toronto, 1969.

————, *Alcoholism and the Family.* Addiction Research Foundation, Toronto, 1971.

Corrigan, Eileen M., *Alcoholic Women in Treatment.* Oxford University Press, New York, 1980.

Costello, C. G., "An Evaluation of Aversion and LSD Therapy in the Treatment of Alcoholism," *Canadian Psychiatric Association Journal,* 1969, 14:31–42.

Courtwright, D. T., *Dark Paradise: Opiate Addiction in America Before 1940.* Harvard University Press, Cambridge, MA, 1982.

Courville, C. H., *The Effects of Alcohol on the Nervous System of Man.* San Lucas Press, Los Angeles, 1955.

Cox, W. Miles (ed.), *Treatment and Prevention of Alcohol Problems: A Resource Manual.* Academic Press, New York, 1986.

Crancer, Alfred, et al., "Comparison of the Effects of Marihuana and Alcohol on Simulated Driving Performance," *Science,* 1969, 164:851–54.

Crandell, John S., *Effective Outpatient Treatment for Alcohol Abusers and Drinking Drivers.* D. C. Heath, Lexington MA, 1988.

Criqui, M. H., and B. L. Ringel, "Does Diet or Alcohol Explain the French Paradox?" *Lancet,* 1994, 344 (8939–40): 1719–23.

Crosby, Linda R., and LeClair Bissell, *To Care Enough: Intervention with Chemically Dependent Colleagues.* Johnson Institute, Minneapolis, 1989.

Cruz-Coke, R. "Genetics and Alcoholism," *Neurobehavioral Toxicology and Teratology,* 1983, 5(2):179–80.

Cruz-Coke, R., and A. Varda, "Genetic Factors in Alcoholism," in R. E. Popham (ed.), *Alcohol and Alcoholism.* University of Toronto Press, Toronto, 1970, pp. 284–89.

Cuomo, M. J.; P. G. Dyment; and V. M. Gammino, "Increasing Use of Ecstasy (MDMA) and Other Hallucinogens on a College Campus," *Journal of American College Health,* 1994, 42(6):271–74.

Curlee-Salisbury, Joan, *When the Woman You Love Is An Alcoholic.* Abbey Press, St. Meinrad, IN, 1978.

Daley, Dennis C., *Relapse Prevention Workbook.* Learning Publications, Inc. Holmes Beach, FL, 1988.

————, *Kicking Addictive Habits Once and For All: A Relapse Prevention Guide.* D. C. Heath, Lexington, MA, 1991.

Daley, Dennis C., et al., *Dual Disorders: Counseling Clients with Chemical Dependency and Mental Illness.* 2d ed. Hazelden, Center City, MN, 1994.

Darrah, Mary C., *Sister Ignatia: Angel of Alcoholics Anonymous.* Loyola University Press, Chicago, 1992.

Davidson, W. S., "Studies of Aversive Conditioning for Alcoholics: A Critical Review of Theory and Research Methodology," *Psychological Bulletin,* 1974, 81:571–81.

Davies, D. L., "Normal Drinking in Recovered Alcohol Addicts," *QJSA,* 1962, 23:94–104.

————, "Notes and Comments—Normal Drinking in Recovered Alcohol Addicts: Comment on the Article by D. L. Davies," *QJSA,* 1963, 24:109–21, 321–32, 727–35.

————, "Normal Drinking in Recovered Alcohol Addicts: Response," *QJSA,* 1963, 24:330–32.

Davis, V. E., et al., "Alcohol, Amines, and Alkaloids: A Possible Biochemical Basis for Alcohol Addiction," *Science,* 1970, 167:1005–7.

Dawkins, M. P., *Alcohol and the Black Community: Exploratory Studies of Selected Issues.* Century Twenty One Publishing, Saratoga, CA, 1980.

Day, Nancy L., and Gale A. Richardson, "Comparative Teratogenicity of Alcohol and Other Drugs," *Alcohol Health and Research World,* 1994, 18(1): 42–48.

DeFoe, J. R., and W. Breed, "Television's Heavy Drinking Problem," *Alcoholism: The National Magazine,* 1983, 3(7): 62–63.

Delbanco, A., and T. Delbanco, "A.A. at the Crossroads," *The New Yorker,* 1995, March 20, pp. 50–63.

Denenberg, Tia S., and R. V. Denenberg, *Alcohol and Other Drugs: Issues in Arbitration.* Bureau of National Affairs, Washington, DC, 1991.

Denzin, Norman K., *The Alcoholic Self.* Sage, New York, 1987a.

———, *The Recovering Alcoholic.* Sage, New York, 1987b.

De Soto, C. B., et al., "Symptomatology in Alcoholics in Various Stages of Abstinence," *Alcoholism: Clinical and Experimental Research,* 1985, 9:505–12.

Ditman, Keith S., "Review and Evaluation of Current Drug Therapies in Alcoholism," *International Journal of Psychiatry,* 1967, 3:248–66.

Doe, Father John (Ralph Pfau), *Sobriety and Beyond.* Guild, New York, 1955. See also his *Sobriety Without End.* Both Hazelden reprints.

Donigan, Robert L., *Chemical Tests and the Law.* Northwestern University Press, Evanston, IL, 1966.

Donohew, Lewis, et al. *Persuasive Communication and Drug Abuse Prevention.* Erlbaum Associates, Hillsdale, NJ, 1991.

Donovan, Dennis M., and G. Alan Marlatt (eds.), *Assessment of Addictive Behaviors.* Guilford, New York, 1988.

Dorn, N., and N. South, *Message in a Bottle: Theoretical Overview and Annotated Bibliography on the Mass Media and Alcohol.* Gower Publishing, Brookfield, VT, 1983.

Dowsling, Janet, and Anne MacLennan (eds.), *The Chemically Dependent Woman.* Addiction Research Foundation, Toronto, 1978.

Drews, Toby R., *Getting Them Sober.* 3 vols. Bridge Publishing, South Plainfield, NJ, 1980–86.

Dunn, Robert B., James W. Smith, et al., "A Comprehensive Intensive Treatment Program for Alcoholism," *Southwestern Medicine,* 1971, 52:102–4.

DuPont, R. L., *Getting Tough on Gateway Drugs: A Guide for the Family.* American Psychiatric Press, Washington, DC, 1984.

——— (ed.), *Stopping Alcohol and Other Drug Use Before It Starts: The Future of Prevention.* OSAP Prevention Monograph No. 1. Rockville, MD, 1989.

DuWors, George, *White Knuckling and Wishful Thinking.* Hogrefe & Huber, Kirkland, WA, 1992.

Dwinell, Lorie, *We Did the Best We Could: Help for Parents of Adult Children.* Health Communications, Deerfield Beach, FL, 1993.

Edelwich, Jerry, and A. Brodsky, *Burn-out: Stages of Disillusionment in the Helping Professions.* Human Sciences Press, New York, 1980.

———, *Group Counseling for the Resistant Client.* Free Press, New York, 1992.

Edlin, B. R., et al., "Intersecting Epidemics: Crack Cocaine Use and HIV Infection Among Inner-city Young Adults," *New England Journal of Medicine,* 1994, 331 (21): 1422–27.

Edwards, Griffith, "Epidemiology Applied to Alcoholism: A Review and Examination of Purposes," *QJSA,* 1973, 34:28–56.

———, *The Treatment of Drinking Problems: A Guide for the Helping Professionals.* McGraw-Hill, New York, 1984.

———, "A Later Follow-up of a Classic Case Series: D. L. Davies' 1962 Report and Its Significance for the Present," *JSA,* 1985, 46:181–90.

———, *The Nature of Drug Dependence.* Oxford University Press, New York, 1990.

———, "D. L. Davies and 'Normal Drinking in Recovered Alcohol Addicts': The Genesis of a Paper," *Drug and Alcohol Dependence,* 1994, 35:249–59.

Edwards, G., et al., (eds.), *Drugs, Alcohol and Tobacco: Making the Science and Policy Connections.* Oxford University Press, New York, 1993.

Edwards, Patricia, et al., "Wives of Alcoholics: A Critical Review and Analysis," *QJSA,* 1973, 34:112–32.

Eiseman, S. (ed.), *Focus on Alcohol.* Baywood Publishing, Los Gatos, CA, 1995.

Elkins, M. *Families Under the Influence.* Norton, New York, 1984.

Emrick, Chad D., "The Rand Report," *JSA,* 1977, 38:152–63.

Engs, Ruth C., *Alcohol and Other Drugs: Self-responsibility.* TIS, Bloomington, IN, 1987.

Eriksson, K., "Behavioral and Physiological Differences Among Rat Strains Specially Selected for Their Alcohol Consumption," *Annals of the New York Academy of Sciences,* 1972, 197:32–41.

Estes, Nada J., and M. Edith Heinemann (eds.), *Alcoholism: Development, Consequences, and Interventions.* 3d ed. C. V. Mosby, St. Louis, 1986.

Evans, David, *A Practitioner's Guide to Alcoholism and the Law.* Hazelden, Center City, MN, 1983.

Everett, Michael W.; Jack O. Waddell; and Dwight B. Heath (eds.), *Cross-Cultural Approaches to the Study of Alcohol: An Interdisciplinary Perspective.* Mouton, The Hague, 1976.

Ewing, John A., *Psychiatric News,* September 17, 1975, 10, no. 18.

Ewing, John A., and Beatrice A. Rouse, "Alcohol Sensitivity and Ethnic Background," *American Journal of Psychiatry,* 1974, 131:206–10.

———, "Failure of an Experimental Treatment Program to Inculcate Controlled Drinking in Alcoholics," *British Journal of Addiction,* 1976, 71:123–34.

——— (eds.), *Drinking: Alcohol in American Society.* Nelson-Hall, Chicago, 1977.

Fagan, Ronald W., and A. L. Mauss, "Social Margin and Social Reentry: An Evaluation of a Rehabilitation Program for Skid Row Alcoholics," *JSA,* 1986, 47(5):413–25.

Falco, Mathea, *The Making of a Drug-free America: Programs That Work.* Times Books, New York, 1992.

Farmer, Rae H., "Functional Changes During Early Weeks of Abstinence, Measured by the Bender-Gestalt," *QJSA,* 1973, 34:786–96.

Favazza, A., and J. Pires, "The Michigan Alcoholism Screening Test: Application in a General Military Hospital," *QJSA,* 1974, 35:925–29.

Fein, Rashi, *Alcohol in America: The Price We Pay.* CompCare Publications, Minneapolis, 1984.

Fichter, Joseph H., "Priests and Alcohol," *Homiletic and Pastoral Review,* August–September 1976, pp. 10–21. Reprinted in *Military Chaplain's Review,* Winter 1977, 39–50 (Department of the Army, PAM 165-112).

———, "Spirituality, Religiosity, and Alcoholism," *America,* 1977a, 136:458–61.

———, "Alcohol and Addiction: Priests and Prelates," *America,* 1977b, 137:258–60.

———, *The Rehabilitation of Clergy Alcoholics: Ardent Spirits Subdued.* Human Sciences Press, New York, 1981.

Fillmore, Kaye M., *Alcohol Use Across the Life Course: A Critical Review of 70 Years of International Longitudinal Research.* Addiction Research Foundation, Toronto, 1988.

Filstead, William; Jean Rossi; and Mark Keller (eds.), *Alcohol and Alcohol Problems: New Thinking and New Directions.* Ballinger, Cambridge, MA, 1976.

Finch, John R., *Psychiatric and Legal Aspects of Automobile Fatalities.* Charles C Thomas, Springfield, IL, 1970.

Fingarette, Herbert, *Heavy Drinking: The Myth of Alcoholism as a Disease.* University of California Press, Berkeley, 1988.

Finn, Peter, *Alcohol: You Can Help Your Kids Cope—A Guide for the Elementary School Teacher.* National Council on Alcoholism, New York, 1975.

Finnegan, Dana, and E. B. McNally, *Dual Identities: Counseling Chemically Dependent Gay Men and Lesbians.* Hazelden, Center City, MN, 1987.

Fitzgerald, Kathleen, *Alcoholism: The Genetic Inheritance.* Doubleday, Garden City, NY, 1988.

Fitzgerald, Robert, *The Soul of Sponsorship: The Friendship of Fr. Ed Dowling, S.J. and Bill Wilson in Letters.* Hazelden, Center City, MN, 1995.

Fleming, Alice, *Alcohol: The Delightful Poison.* Delacorte Press, New York, 1975.

Flores, P. J., *Group Psychotherapy with Addicted Populations.* Haworth, New York, 1988.

Ford, Gene, *Ford's Illustrated Guide to Wines, Brews and Spirits.* Wm. C. Brown, Dubuque, IA, 1983.

Ford, John C., *Depth Psychology, Morality, and Alcoholism.* Weston College, Weston, MA, 1951.

————, "Clerical Attitudes on Alcohol—Most of Them Wrong," *The Priest,* April 1955. NCA reprint.

————, "Chemical Comfort and Christian Virtue," *American Ecclesiastical Review,* 1959, 141:361–79.

Forsander, O., and K. Eriksson (eds.), *Biological Aspects of Alcohol Consumption.* Swets & Zeitlinger, Helsinki, 1972.

Fort, Joel, *Alcohol: Our Biggest Drug Problem.* McGraw-Hill, New York, 1973.

Fox, Ruth, "Antabuse as an Adjunct to Psychotherapy in Alcoholism," *New York State Journal of Medicine,* 1958, 58:1540–44. NCA reprint.

————, "Children in the Alcoholic Family," in W. C. Bier (ed.), *Problems in Addiction: Alcohol and Drug Addiction.* Fordham University Press, New York, 1962, pp. 71–96.

————, "Disulfiram (Antabuse) as an Adjunct in the Treatment of Alcoholism," in Ruth Fox (ed.), *Alcoholism: Behavioral Research, Therapeutic Approaches.* Springer, New York, 1967a, pp. 242–55.

————, "A Multidisciplinary Approach to the Treatment of Alcoholism," *American Journal of Psychiatry,* 1967b, 123:769–78.

————, "Treating the Alcoholic's Family," in R. J. Catanzaro (ed.), *Alcoholism: The Total Treatment Approach.* Charles C Thomas, Springfield, IL, 1968, pp. 105–15.

————, *The Effects of Alcoholism on Children.* National Council on Alcoholism, New York, 1972, Pamphlet.

————, "Disulfiram," in Peter Bourne and Ruth Fox (eds.), *Alcoholism: Progress in Research and Treatment.* Academic Press, New York, 1973, pp. 236–39.

Fox, Vernelle, *Day Hospital as a Treatment Modality for Alcoholism.* National Clearinghouse for Alcohol Information, Rockville, MD, 1974. Pamphlet.

Franks, H. M., et al., "The Interaction of Alcohol and Tetrahydrocannabinol in Man: Effects on Psychomotor Skills Related to Driving," in S. Israelstam and S. Lambert (eds.), *Alcohol, Drugs, and Traffic Safety.* Addiction Research Foundation, Toronto, 1975, pp. 461–66.

Freed, Earl X. (ed.), *Interfaces Between Alcoholism and Mental Health.* Rutgers Center of Alcohol Studies, New Brunswick, NJ, 1982.

Freudenberger, Herbert J., and G. Richelson, *Burn-out: The High Cost of High Achievement.* Anchor Books, Garden City, NY, 1980.

Freund, G., and N. Butler (eds.), "Symposium: Neurological Interaction Between Aging and Alcohol Abuse," *Alcoholism: Clinical and Experimental Research,* 1982, 6(1):1–63.

Friedman, Alfred S., and S. Granick, *Family Therapy for Adolescent Drug Abuse.* D. C. Heath, Lexington, MA, 1990.

Fuad, Margaret, *Alcohol and the Church.* Hope Publishing, Pasadena, CA, 1992.

Fuchs, C. S., M. J. Stampfer, et al., "Alcohol Consumption and Mortality Among Women," *New England Journal of Medicine,* 1995, 332(19):1245–50.

Fuller, Richard K., et al., "Disulfiram Treatment of Alcoholism: A Veterans Administration Cooperative Study" *JAMA,* 1986, 256(11): 1449–55, 1489.

Funkhouser, M. N., "Identifying Alcohol Problems Among Elderly Hospital Patients," *Alcohol Health and Research World,* Winter 1977–78, pp. 27–34.

Galizio, Mark, and S. Maisto (eds.), *Determinants of Substance Abuse: Biological, Psychological, and Environmental Factors.* Plenum, New York, 1985.

Gallant, Donald M., *Alcoholism: A Guide to Diagnosis, Intervention and Treatment.* Norton, New York, 1987.

Gantner, Leslie P., *Alcohol and Pregnancy: A Retrieval Index and Bibliography.* Jen Hse, Reiserstown, MD, 1984.

Gehring, D., and C. Geraci, *Alcohol on Campus: A Compendium of the Law and Guide to Campus Policy.* College Administration Publications, Asheville, NC, 1989.

Gerstein, Dean R. (ed.), *Toward the Prevention of Alcohol Problems: Government, Business, and Community Action.* National Academy Press, Washington, DC, 1984.

Gilbert, M. J., et al. (eds.), *Alcohol-related Issues in the Latino Population: An Annotated Bibliography.* Chicano Studies Library, Berkeley, CA, 1993.

Gitlow, S. E., and H. S. Peyser (eds.), *Alcoholism: A Practical Treatment Guide.* 2d ed. Grune & Stratton, New York, 1988.

Glaser, Frederic B., et al., *A Systems Approach to Alcohol Treatment.* Addiction Research Foundation, Toronto, 1978.

Glass, G. S., and M. B. Bowers, "Chronic Psychosis Associated with Long-term Psychotomimetic Drug Abuse," *Archives of General Psychiatry,* 1970, 23: 97–103.

Glass, Ilana B., *International Handbook of Addiction Behaviour.* Tavistock/Routledge, London, 1991.

Glassner, B., and J. Loughlin, *Drugs in Adolescent Worlds: Burnouts to Straights.* St. Martin's Press, New York, 1986.

Glatt, Max M., "Group Therapy in Alcoholism," *British Journal of Addiction,* 1957–58, 54:133–48.

———, *The Alcoholic and the Help He Needs.* Taplinger, New York, 1974a.

———, *A Guide to Addiction and Its Treatment.* Halstead Press, New York, 1974b.

———, *Alcoholism: A Social Disease.* St. Paul's, London, 1975a.

———, "The Alcoholisms: The Disease Concept—Newer Developments," *Nursing Times,* 1975b, 71:856–58.

———, "Alcoholism Disease Concept and Loss of Control Revisited," *British Journal of Addiction,* 1976, 71:135–44.

———, "Characteristics and Prognoses of Alcoholic Doctors," *British Medical Journal,* 1977, 1:507.

Globetti, Gerald, "Teenage Drinking," in Nada J. Estes and M. Edith Heinemann (eds.), *Alcoholism: Development, Consequences, and Interventions.* Mosby, St. Louis, 1977, pp. 162–73.

Goby, Marshall J., *Alcoholism: Treatment and Recovery.* Catholic Health Association, St. Louis, MO 63134, 1988.

Goedde, Werner H., and D. P. Argoural, *Genetics and Alcoholism.* A. R. Liss, New York, 1987.

Gold, Mark S., *Marijuana.* Plenum Medical Books, New York, 1989.

———, *The Good News About Drugs and Alcohol: Curing, Treating and Preventing Substance Abuse.* Villard Books, Random, New York, 1991.

———, *Cocaine.* Plenum Medical Book Co., New York, 1993.

Gold, Mark S., and A. Slaby, *Dual Diagnosis in Substance Abuse.* Dekker, New York, 1991.

Goldberg, Raymond (ed.), *Taking Sides: Clashing Views on Controversial Issues in Drugs and Society.* Dushkin Publishers, Guilford, CT, 1993.

Goldstein, Avrum, *Addiction: From Biology to Social Policy.* W. H. Freeman, San Francisco, 1993.

Goldstein, Dora, *Pharmacology of Alcohol.* Oxford University Press, New York, 1983.

Gomberg, Edith S., et al. (eds.), "Women with Alcohol Problems," in Nada J. Estes and M. Edith Heinemann (eds.), *Alcoholism: Development, Consequences, and Interventions.* Mosby, St. Louis, 1977, pp. 174–85.

———, *Alcohol, Science and Society Revisited.* University of Michigan Press, Ann Arbor, 1983.

Goode, Erich. *Drugs in American Society.* 2d ed. Knopf, New York, 1984.

Goodwin, D. W., "Is Alcoholism Hereditary? A Review and Critique," *Archives of General Psychiatry,* 1971, 25:545–49.

———, "Drinking Problems in Adopted and Nonadopted Sons of Alcoholics," *Arch. Gen. Psychiat.,* 1974, 31:164–69.

———, *Is Alcoholism Hereditary?* Oxford University Press, New York, 1976.

———, "The Alcoholic Blackout and How to Prevent It," in I. M. Birnbaum and E. S. Parker (eds.), *Alcohol and Memory.* Lawrence Erlbaum Associates, Hillsdale, NJ, 1977, pp. 177–83.

———, "Hereditary Factors in Alcoholism," *Hospital Practice,* 1978a, 13:121–30.

———, "The Genetics of Alcoholism: A State of the Art Review," *Alcohol Health and Research World,* Spring 1978b, 2:2–12.

———, *Alcoholism: The Facts.* 2d ed. Oxford University Press, New York, 1994.

Goodwin, D. W., et al. (eds.), *Longitudinal Research in Alcoholism.* Kluwer-Nijhoff, Boston, 1984.

Gordon, Gary, et al., "Effects of Alcohol Administration on Sex-hormone Metabolism in Normal Men," *New England Journal of Medicine,* 1976, 295:783–97.

Gordon, G., and C. S. Lieber, "Alcohol, Hormones, and Metabolism." In C. S. Lieber (ed.), *Medical and Nutritional Complications of Alcoholism.* Plenum, New York, 1992, pp. 59–90.

Gordon, Nancy P., and Alfred McAlister, *Adolescent Drinking: Issues and Research.* Academic Press, New York, 1992.

Gorski, Terence, and M. Miller, *Counseling for Relapse Prevention.* Herald House, Independence, MO, 1986.

———, *Staying Sober: A Guide for Relapse Prevention.* Herald House, Independence, MO, 1987.

Gossop, Michael (ed.), *Relapse and Addictive Behavior.* Routledge, Chapman & Hall, London, 1989.

Gottheil, E. (ed.), *Combined Problems of Alcoholism, Drug Addiction, and Aging.* Charles C Thomas, Springfield, IL, 1985.

———, *Stress and Addiction.* Bruner/Mazel, New York, 1987.

Gottheil, Edward, et al., *Matching Patient Needs and Treatment Methods in Alcoholism and Drug Abuse.* Charles C Thomas, Springfield, IL, 1981.

———, *Alcohol, Drug Abuse and Aggression.* Charles C Thomas, Springfield, IL, 1983.

Gottheil, Edward, et al. (eds.), *Etiologic Aspects of Alcohol and Drug Abuse.* Charles C Thomas, Springfield, IL, 1983.

Grad, F. P., et al., *Alcoholism and the Law.* Oceana Publications, Dobbs Ferry, NY, 1971.

Graham, Kathryn, et al., *Addictions Treatment for Older Adults.* Haworth, Binghamton, NY, 1995.

Grant, Marcus, and B. Ritson, *Alcohol: The Prevention Debate.* St. Martin's Press, New York, 1983.

Grant, Marcus, et al. (eds.), *Economics and Alcohol.* Gardner Press, New York, 1983.

Gravitz, Herbert L., and Julie Bowden, *Recovery: A Guide for Adult Children of Alcoholics.* Learning Publications, Holmes Beach, FL, 1987.

Green, R. C., et al. (eds.), *The Care and Management of the Sick and Incompetent Physician.* Charles C Thomas, Springfield, IL, 1978.

Greenblatt, M., and M. A. Schuckit (eds.), *Alcoholism Problems in Women and Children.* Grune & Stratton, New York, 1976.

Greenstreet, R. L., *Cost-effective Alternatives in Alcoholism Treatment.* Charles C Thomas, Springfield, IL, 1988.

Gross, Leonard, *How Much Is Too Much? The Effects of Social Drinking*. Random House, New York, 1983.

Gross, M. M., "Psychobiological Contributions to the Alcohol Dependence Syndrome: A Selective Review of Recent Research," in G. Edwards, M. M. Gross, M. Keller, J. Moser, and R. Room (eds.), *Alcohol-Related Disabilities*. World Health Organization, Geneva, 1977, (no. 32) pp. 107–31.

Gross, M. M. (ed.) *Alcohol Intoxication and Withdrawal: Experimental Studies I.* Plenum, New York, 1973. (*Advances in Experimental Medicine and Biology*, vol. 35, 1972.) *Experimental Studies II*, 1975.

Groupé, Vincent (ed.), *Alcoholism Rehabilitation: Methods and Experiences of Private Rehabilitation Centers*. National Institute on Alcohol Abuse and Alcoholism and Rutgers Center of Alcohol Studies, New Brunswick, NJ, 1978.

Grutchfield, Lee, "What AA Meetings Taught a Non-AA Counselor," *Alcohol Health and Research World*, Spring 1979, 3(3):15–17. Reprinted from *AA Grapevine*, December 1977.

Gusfield, Joseph R., "The Prevention of Drinking Problems," in William Filstead, Jean Rossi, and Mark Keller (eds.), *Alcohol and Alcohol Problems: New Thinking and New Directions*. Ballinger, Cambridge, MA, 1976, pp. 267–91.

Haggard, H. W., and E. M. Jellinek, *Alcohol Explored*. Doubleday, New York, 1942.

Hall, P. (ed.), *Alcoholic Liver Disease: Pathobiology, Epidemiology, and Clinical Aspects*. Wiley, New York, 1985.

Hamer, John, and Jack Steinbring, *Alcohol and Native Peoples of the North*. University Press of America, Lanham, MD, 1980.

Hammer, D. D., et al., "A New Definition of Learning Disabilities," *Journal of Learning Disabilities*, 1987, 20: 109–13.

Hanna, Joel M., "Metabolic Responses of Chinese, Japanese and Europeans to Alcohol," *Alcoholism: Clinical and Experimental Research*, 1978, 2:89–92.

Harper, Frederick D., "Alcohol Use Among North American Blacks," in Y. Israel et al. (eds.), *Research Advances in Alcohol and Drug Problems*. Vols. 4–5. Plenum, New York, 1978, vol. 4, pp. 349–64.

Harper, Frederick D. (ed.), *Alcohol Abuse and Black America*. Douglass Publications, Alexandria, VA, 1976.

Hasselbrock, Victor M., et al., *Biological Genetic Factors in Alcoholism*. NIAAA, Rockville, MD, 1983.

Havard, J. D., "Drinking Driver and the Law: Legal Countermeasures in the Prevention of Alcohol-related Road Traffic Accidents," in Robert J. Gibbins and Yedy Israel (eds.), *Research Advances in Alcohol and Drug Problems*. Vol. 2. Wiley, New York, 1975, pp. 123–45.

Heath, Dwight B., "A Critical Review of Ethnographic Studies of Alcohol Use," in M. Douglas (ed.), *The Anthropology of Drink, Hospitality and Competition*. Cambridge University Press, Cambridge, 1982.

———, "Drinking and Drunkenness in Transcultural Perspective," *Transcultural Psychiatric Research Review*, 1986, 23(1):7–41; 23(2):103–26.

Heinemann, Allen (ed.), *Substance Abuse and Physical Disability*. Haworth, New York, 1993.

Helzer, J. E., and G. J. Canino (eds.), *Alcoholism in North America, Europe and Asia*. Oxford, New York, 1992.

Helzer, John, et al., "The Extent of Long-term Moderate Drinking Among Alcoholics Discharged from Medical and Psychiatric Treatment Facilities," *New England Journal of Medicine*, June 25, 1985, 312(26):1678–82.

Henningfield, J. E.; K. Miyasato; and D. R. Jasinki, "Abuse Liability and Pharmacodynamic Characteristics of Intravenous and Inhaled Nicotine," *Journal of Pharmacology and Experimental Therapeutics*, 1985, 234: 1–12.

Heuer, Marti, *Happy Daze*. MAC, Denver, 1985

Hewitt, T. Furman, *A Biblical Perspective on the Use and Abuse of Alcohol and Other Drugs.* North Carolina Council on Alcoholism, Greenville, 1980.

Hill, S. Y., et al., "Association and Linkage Between Alcoholism and Eleven Serological Markers," *JSA*, 1975, 36:981–92.

Hoffmann, A., "Notes and Documents Concerning the Discovery of LSD," *Agents and Actions*, 1994, 43(3–4): 79–81.

Holder, H. D., et al., "Economic Benefits of Alcoholism Treatment: A Summary of Twenty Years of Research," *Journal of Employee Assistance Research*, 1992, 1(1):63–82.

Homiller, Jonica D., *Women and Alcohol: A Guide for State and Local Decision Makers*, Alcohol and Drug Problems Association of North America, Washington, DC, 1977.

Hornik, Edith Lynn, *The Drinking Woman.* Association Press, New York, 1978.

Hubbard, R. L., et al., *Drug Abuse Treatment: A National Study of Effectiveness.* University of North Carolina Press, Chapel Hill, 1989.

Huberty, C., and D. J. Huberty, "Treating the Parents of Adolescent Drug Abusers," *Contemporary Drug Problems*, 1976, 5:573–92.

Hunt, W. A., *Alcohol and Biological Membranes.* Guilford, New York, 1985.

Hunt, W. A., and E. D. Witt, "Behavioral Effects of Alcohol Ingestion: Implications for Drug Testing," *Toxic Substance Abuse Journal*, 1994, 13:41–49.

Hutchison, Ira W., *Screwtape Letters on Alcohol.* Sheed & Ward, Kansas City, MO, 1994.

Hyde, Margaret, *Alcohol: Uses and Abuses.* Enslow, Hillside, NJ, 1988.

Iber, Frank L., "The Effect of Fructose on Alcohol Metabolism," *Archives of Internal Medicine*, 1977, 137:1121.

"Intervention," *Alcoholism and Addiction*, October 1988, 9(1): 18–24.

Institute of Medicine, *Causes and Consequences of Alcohol Problems: An Agenda for Research.* National Academy Press, Washington, DC, 1987.

———, *Broadening the Base of Treatment for Alcohol Problems.* National Academy Press, Washington, DC, 1990a.

———, *Prevention and Treatment of Alcohol Problems.* National Academy Press, Washington, DC, 1990b.

Isaacson, Eileen B. (ed.), *Chemical Dependency: Theoretical Approaches and Strategies Working with Individuals and Families.* Haworth Press, New York, 1991.

Israel, Y., and J. Mardones (eds.), *Biological Basis of Alcoholism.* Wiley, New York, 1971.

Israelstam, S., and S. Lambert (eds.), *Alcohol, Drugs, and Traffic Safety.* Addiction Research Foundation, Toronto, Canada, 1975.

Isralowitz, R. E., and M. Singer (eds.), *Adolescent Substance Abuse.* Haworth, New York, 1983.

Isselbacher, Kurt, "Metabolic and Hepatic Effect of Alcohol," *New England Journal of Medicine*, 1977, 296:612–17.

Jackson, Joan K., "The Adjustment of the Family to the Crisis of Alcoholism," *QJSA*, 1954, 15:562–86. NCA reprint.

———, "Types of Drinking Patterns of Male Alcoholics," *QJSA*, 1958, 19:269–302.

Jackson, Joan K., and Ralph G. Connor, "The Skid-Road Alcoholic," *QJSA*, 1953a, 14:468–86.

———, "The Attitudes of Parents of Alcoholics, Moderate Drinkers, and Nondrinkers Toward Alcohol," *QJSA*, 1953b, 14:569–613.

Jackson, T. R., and J. W. Smith, "A Comparison of Two Aversion Treatment Methods for Alcoholism," *JSA*, 1978, 39:187–91.

Jacobs, James B., *Drunk Driving: An American Dilemma.* University of Chicago Press, Chicago. 1989.

Jacobson, George R., *The Alcoholisms: Detection, Assessment and Diagnosis.* Human Sciences Press, New York, 1976a.

———, "The Mortimer-Filkins Test: Court Procedures for Identifying Problem Drinkers," *Alcohol Health and Research World,* Summer 1976b, pp. 22–26.

Jacobson, Michael, et al., *The Booze Merchants: The Inebriating of America.* Center for Science in the Public Interest, Washington, DC, 1983.

Jaynes, Judith H., and Cheryl Rugg, *Adolescents, Alcohol and Drugs: A Practical Guide for Those Who Work with Young People.* Charles C Thomas, Springfield, IL, 1988.

Jellinek, E. M., "Phases of Alcohol Addiction," *QJSA,* 1952, 13:673–84.

———, "Estimating the Prevalence of Alcoholism: Modified Values in the Jellinek Formula and an Alternative Approach," *QJSA,* 1959, 20:261–69.

———, *The Disease Concept of Alcoholism.* College and University Press, New Haven, CT, 1960.

Jessor, R., and S. Jessor, "Adolescent Development and the Onset of Drinking," *JSA,* 1975, 36:27–51.

———, *Problem Behavior and Psychosocial Development: A Longitudinal Study of Youth.* Academic Press, New York, 1977.

Jilek, W. G., *Indian Healing: Shämanic Ceremonialism in the Pacific Northwest Today.* Hancock House, Surrey, BC, 1982.

John, Harrison W., "Alcohol and the Impaired Physician," *Alcohol Health and Research World,* Winter 1978, pp. 2–8.

Johnson, Vernon, *I'll Quit Tomorrow.* Rev. ed. Harper & Row, New York, 1980.

———, *Intervention: How to Help Someone Who Doesn't Want Help.* Johnson Institute, Minneapolis, 1986.

Johnson Institute, *How to Use Intervention in Your Professional Practice.* Johnson Institute, Minneapolis, 1987.

Johnston, Lloyd D., *Drug Use Among American High School Students, College Students, and Other Young Adults.* Government Printing Office, Washington, DC, 1986.

Jones, K. L.; D. W. Smith; C. N. Ulleland; and A. P. Streissguth, "Pattern of Malformation in Offspring of Chronic Alcoholic Mothers," *Lancet,* 1973, 1:1267–71.

Jones, R. W., and A. R. Helrich, "Treatment of Alcoholism by Physicians in Private Practice: A National Survey," *QJSA,* 1972, 33:117–31.

K., Ernie, *90 Meetings in Ninety Days.* Johnson Institute, Minneapolis, 1984.

Kaa, E., "Impurities, Adulterants, and Diluents of Illicit Heroin," *Forensic Science International,* 1994, 64(2–3): 171–79.

Kaij, H. L. and J. Dock, "Definitions of Alcoholism and Genetic Research," *Annals of the New York Academy of Sciences,* 1972, 97:110–13.

———, "Grandsons of Alcoholics," *Archives of General Psychiatry,* 1975, 32:1379–81.

Kalant, Oriana (ed.), *Alcohol and Drug Problems in Women.* Vol. 5, *Research Advances in Alcohol and Drug Problems.* Plenum, New York, 1978.

Kane, Geoffrey P., *Inner-city Alcoholism: An Ecological Analysis and Cross-cultural Study.* Human Sciences Press, New York, 1981.

Kasl, Charlotte, *Many Roads, One Journey: Moving Beyond the 12 Steps.* Harper-Collins, New York, 1992.

Katzung, B. G., *Basic and Clinical Pharmacology.* 5th ed. Appleton & Lange, Norwalk, CT, 1992.

Kaufman, E., *Power to Change: Family Case Studies in the Treatment of Alcoholism.* Gardner Press, New York, 1984.

———, *Substance Abuse and Family Therapy.* Grune & Stratton, New York, 1985.

Kaufman, E., and P. N. Kaufman (eds.), *Family Therapy of Alcohol and Drug Abuse.* Gardner Press, New York, 1979.

Keehn, J. D., "Neuroticism and Extraversion: Chronic Alcoholic's Report on Effects of Drinking," *Psychological Reports*, 1970, 27:767–70.

Keller, Rev. John E., *Ministering to Alcoholics*. Augsburg Publishing, Minneapolis, 1966.

———, *Let Go, Let God*. Parkside Publishers, Park Ridge, IL, 1988.

Keller, Mark, "Alcohol in Health and Disease: Some Historical Perspectives," *Annals of the New York Academy of Sciences*, 1966, 113:820–27.

———, *Some Views on the Nature of Addiction*. Rutgers Center of Alcohol Studies, New Brunswick, NJ, 1969.

———, "The Great Jewish Drink Mystery," *British Journal of Addiction*, 1970, 64:287–96.

———, "On the Loss-of-Control Phenomenon in Alcoholism," *British Journal of Addiction*, 1972, 67:153–66.

———, "Multidisciplinary Perspectives on Alcoholism and the Need for Integration: An Historical and Prospective Note," *JSA*, 1975a, 36:133–47.

———, "Problems of Epidemiology in Alcohol Problems," *JSA*, 1975b, 36:1442–51.

———, "Problems with Alcohol: An Historical Perspective," in William Filstead, Jean Rossi, and Mark Keller (eds.), *Alcohol and Alcohol Problems: New Thinking and New Directions*. Ballinger, Cambridge, MA, 1976a, pp. 5–28.

———, "Disease Concept of Alcoholism Revisited," *JSA*, 1976b, 37:1694–1717.

———, "A Lexicon of Disablements Related to Alcohol Consumption," in G. Edwards, M. M. Gross, M. Keller, J. Moser, and R. Room (eds.), *Alcohol-Related Disabilities*, World Health Organization, Geneva, 1977 (no. 32), pp. 23–60.

———, "The Patriarch of Alcoholism in America: The Pioneer Work of Doctor Benjamin Rush," *Digest of Addiction Theory and Application*, July 1986, 5(4):5–14.

Keller, Martin H., "Reports of Antabuse Depression Debunked," *The Journal* (ARF), July 1976, 5(7):8.

Kellerman, Rev. Joseph L., *Alcoholism: A Merry-Go-Round Named Denial*. Hazelden, Center City, MN, 1973.

———, "Pastoral Care in Alcoholism," *Annals of the New York Academy of Sciences*, 1974, 233:144–47.

———, *Al-Anon: A Message of Hope*. Hazelden, Center City, MN, 1976.

———, *Grief: A Basic Reaction to Alcoholism*. Hazelden, Center City, MN, 1977.

———, *Alcoholism: A Guide for Ministers and Other Church Leaders*. North Carolina Council on Alcoholism, Greenville, 1980.

Kelly, T. H.; R. W. Foltin; and M. W. Fischman, *Effects of Alcohol on Human Behavior: Effects on the Workplace*. NIDA Research Monograph no. 100, U.S. Department of Health and Human Services, Washington, DC, 1990.

Kelso, Dennis (ed.), *Descriptive Analysis of the Impact of Alcoholism and Alcohol Abuse in Alaska*. 4 vols. State Office of Alcoholism, Juneau, AK, 1977.

Kendis, Joseph B., "The Effect of Attitudes in the Therapy of the Alcoholic," *British Journal of Addiction*, 1967, 62:307–15.

Ketcham, K., and G. Gustafson, *Living on the Edge: A Guide to Intervention for Families with Drug and Alcohol Problems*. Bantam, New York, 1989.

Kilbourne, Jean, "Alcohol Advertising: The Not-So-Hidden Persuader," *Alcoholism and Addiction*, November–December 1985, pp. 49–52.

Kimball, Bonnie-Jean, *The Alcoholic Woman's Mad, Mad World of Denial and Mind Games*. Hazelden, Center City, MN, 1978.

King, Sr. Eleace, and Jim Castelli, *Alcoholism Among Men and Women Religious*. Georgetown University Press, Washington, DC, 1995.

Kirsch, M. M., *Designer Drugs*. CompCare, Minneapolis, 1986.

Kissin, Benjamin, and Henri Begleiter. *The Biology of Alcoholism*. Vol I through VII Plenum Press, New York, 1971–83.

Klaas, Joe, *The Twelve Steps to Happiness*. Ballantine Books, New York, 1990.

Kleiman, Mark A. R., *Marijuana: Costs of Abuse, Costs of Control*. Greenwood Press, Westport, CT, 1989.

Klingemann, H., et al. (eds.), *Cure, Care, or Control*. State University Press, Albany, NY, 1992.

Knott, D. H., *Alcohol Problems: Diagnosis and Treatment*. Pergamon, New York, 1986.

Knott, David H., and James D. Beard, "Acute Withdrawal from Alcohol," *Postgraduate Medicine*, 1967, 42:A109–15.

Kritsberg, Wayne, *Adult Children of Alcoholics Syndrome: From Discovery to Recovery*. Health Communications, Deerfield Beach, FL, 1985.

Krupnick, Louis B., and E. Krupnick, *From Decision to Despair*. CompCare, Minneapolis, MN, 1985.

Krystal, H., and R. A. Moore, "Who Is Qualified to Treat the Alcoholic? A Discussion," *QJSA*, 1963, 24:705–20.

Kurtz, Ernest, *Shame and Guilt*. Hazelden, Center City, MN, 1981.

———, "Why A.A. Works: The Intellectual Significance of Alcoholics Anonymous," *JSA*, 1982, 43:38–80.

———, *Not-God: A History of Alcoholics Anonymous*. Hazelden, Center City, MN, 1979; expanded ed., 1991.

Kurtz, Ernest, and K. Ketcham, *The Spirituality of Imperfection: Modern Wisdom from Classic Stories*. Bantam, New York, 1992.

Kus, Robert J. (ed.), *Spirituality and Chemical Dependency*. Haworth, Binghamton, NY, 1995.

L'Abate, Luciano, et al., *Handbook of Differential Treatments for Addictions*. Prentice-Hall, Englewood Cliffs, NJ, 1991.

Lader, M., "Anxiolytic Drugs: Dependence, Addiction, and Abuse," *European Neuropsychopharmacology*, 1994, 4(2): 85–91.

Lader, M., et al. (eds.) *The Nature of Alcohol and Drug Related Problems*. Oxford University Press, New York. 1992.

Larkins, John R., *Alcohol and the Negro: Explosive Issues*. Record Publishing, Zebulon, NC, 1965.

Laurence, Michael, et al., *Social Control of the Drinking Driver*. University of Chicago Press, Chicago, 1988.

Lawson, Gary W., and Ann Lawson, *Alcoholism and Substance Abuse in Special Populations*. Aspen Publishers, Frederick, MD, 1988.

Lawson, Gary W.; J. S. Peterson; and A. W. Lawson, *Alcoholism and the Family: A Guide to Treatment and Prevention*. Aspen Publishers, Frederick, MD, 1983.

———, *Essentials of Chemical Dependency Counseling*. Aspen Publishers, Frederick, MD, 1984.

Lecca, Peter J., and Thomas D. Watts, *Substance Abuse Strategies and Preschool Children: Prevention and Intervention*. Haworth, New York, 1991.

Ledermann, S., *Alcool, alcoolisme, alcoolization; donnés scientifiques de caractère physiologique, économique et social*, (Institut National d'Etudes Démographiques, Travaux et Documents, Cahier no. 29). Presses Universitaires, Paris, 1956.

Lehman, W. E., and D. D. Simpson, *Patterns of Drug Use in a Large Metropolitan Work Force*. NIDA Research Monograph no. 100 U.S. Department of Health and Human Services, Washington, DC, 1990.

Leland, Joy, *Firewater Myths: North American Indian Drinking and Alcohol Addiction*. Rutgers University, Center of Alcohol Studies (Monograph 11), New Brunswick, NJ, 1976.

Lemere, Frederick, "What Causes Alcoholism?" *Journal of Clinical and Experimental Psychopathology*, 1956, 17:202–6.

———, "Who Is Qualified to Treat the Alcoholic? Comment on the Krystal-Moore Discussion," *QJSA*, 1964, 25:558–60.

Lemere, Frederick, et al., "Motivation in the Treatment of Alcoholism," *QJSA*, 1958, 19:428–31.

Lemere, Frederick, and James W. Smith, "Alcohol-induced Sexual Impotence," *American Journal of Psychiatry*, 1973, 130:212–13.

Lemere, Frederick, and Walter L. Voegtlin, "Heredity as an Etiological Factor in Chronic Alcoholism," *Northwest Medicine*, 1943, 42:110–14.

Lemoine, P.; H. Haraousseau; J.-P. Borteyru; and J.-C. Menuet, "Les enfants de parents alcooliques: Anomalies observées—A propos de 127 cas." *Quest Médical*, 1968, 25:477–82.

Lender, M. E., and J. K. Martin, *Drinking in America: A History*. Free Press, New York, 1982.

Lerner, W. D., and M. Barr (eds.), *Handbook of Hospital Based Substance Abuse Treatment*. Pergamon Press, New York, 1990.

Lester, David, "Self-selection of Alcohol by Animals, Human Variation, and the Etiology of Alcoholism," *QJSA*, 1966, 27:395–438.

Levy, Richard, et al., "Intravenous Fructose Treatment of Acute Alcohol Intoxication," *Archives of Internal Medicine*, 1977, 137:1175–77.

Levy, Stephen J., and Jacqueline Cohen, *The Mentally Ill Chemical Abuser*. Free Press, New York, 1992.

Lewis, Jay S., "Fifteen Years of Alcoholism Report Coverage—1972–1987: The Thick and the Thin," *The Alcoholism Report*, 1987, 16(2):1–8.

Lewis, Judith A., et al., *Substance Abuse Counseling: An Individualized Approach*. Brooks/Cole, Pacific Grove, CA, 1988.

Lewis, Michael J., and Jane C. Lockmuller, "Alcohol Reinforcement: Complex Determinant of Drinking," *Alcohol Health and Research World*, 1990, 14(2): 98–104. See the whole issue, *Alcohol and the Brain*, vol. 14, no. 2, 1990.

Li, Ting-Kai, "Genetic Variability in Response to Ethanol in Humans and Experimental Animals," in *Proceedings: NIAAA-WHO Collaborating Center Designation Meeting and Alcohol Research Seminar*. NIAAA, Washington, DC, 1984, pp. 50–62.

Lieber, Charles S., "Metabolism of Ethanol and Alcoholism: Racial and Acquired Factors," *Annals of Internal Medicine*, 1972, 76:326–27.

———, "The Metabolism of Alcohol," *Scientific American*, 1976, 234:25–33.

———, "Recent Advances in the Biology of Alcoholism," *Advances in Alcohol and Substance Abuse*, Winter 1981, vol. 1, no. 2.

———, "To Drink (Moderately) or Not to Drink?" *New England Journal of Medicine*, 1984, 310:846–48.

———, *Medical and Nutritional Complications of Alcoholism*. Plenum, New York, 1992.

Lieber, Charles S. (ed.), *Metabolic Aspects of Alcoholism*. University Park Press, Baltimore, 1977.

———, *Medical Disorders of Alcoholism: Pathogenesis and Treatment*. W. B. Saunders, Philadelphia, 1992.

Lieberman, Lisa R., and Mario Orlandi, "Alcohol Advertising and Adolescent Drinking," *Alcohol Health and Research World*, Fall 1987, 12(1): 30–33.

Lief, H. I., and C. Schuster, *Alcohol and Sexuality*. Praeger, New York, 1988.

Light, William J., *Neurobiology of Alcohol Abuse*. Charles C Thomas, Springfield, IL, 1986.

Lindbeck, Vera L., "The Woman Alcoholic: A Review of the Literature," *The International Journal of Addictions*, 1972, 7:567–80.

Lindworsky, Johannes, S.J., *The Training of the Will*. Bruce, Milwaukee, 1928.

Lisansky, Ephraim T., "Alcoholism—The Avoided Diagnosis," *Bulletin of the American College of Physicians,* 1974, 15:18–24.

Litman, G. K., et al., "Dependence, Relapse, and Extinction: A Theoretical Critique and a Behavioral Examination," *Journal of Clinical Psychology,* 1979, 35:192–99.

Littlejohn Associates, *Proposed National Standard for Alcoholism Counselors: Final Report.* Roy Littlejohn Associates, Inc., Washington, DC, 1974.

Lowinson, Joyce H., et al., *Comprehensive Textbook of Substance Abuse.* Williams & Wilkins, Baltimore, 1992.

Luce, Bryan R., and Stuart O. Schweitzer, "Smoking and Alcohol Abuse: A Comparison of Their Economic Consequences," *New England Journal of Medicine,* 1978, 298:569–71.

Ludwig, Arnold M., *Sobriety: Strategies for Recovery.* Oxford University Press, New York, 1987a.

———, *Understanding the Alcoholic's Mind: The Nature of Craving and How to Control It.* Oxford University Press, New York, 1987b.

Lundquist, Frank, "Medical Consequences of Alcoholism," *Annals of the New York Academy of Sciences,* 1975, 252:11–20.

Lurie, Nancy O., "The World's Oldest On-going Protest Demonstration: North American Indian Drinking Patterns," *Pacific Historical Review,* 1971, 40:311–32.

MacAndrew, Craig, and Robert Edgerton, *Drunken Comportment: A Social Explanation.* Aldine, Chicago, 1969.

MacDonald, D. Ian, *Drugs, Drinking, and Adolescents.* Year Book Medical Publishers, New York, 1984.

Maddox, G. L., and J. R. Williams, "Drinking Behavior in Negro Collegians: Patterns, Problems and Correlations with Social Factors," *QJSA,* 1968, 29:117–29.

Madsen, William, *The American Alcoholic: The Nature-Nurture Controversy in Alcoholic Research and Therapy.* Charles C Thomas, Springfield, IL, 1973.

———, *Defending the Disease of Alcoholism: From Facts to Fingarette.* Wilson, Brown & Co., Akron, OH, 1988.

Mail, Patricia D., and D. R. McDonald, *Tulapai to Tokay: A Bibliography of Alcohol Use and Abuse Among Native Americans of North America.* HRAF Press, Box 2015, New Haven, CT, 1981.

Maisto, S. A., "The Constructs of Craving for Alcohol and Loss of Control in Drinking: Help or Hindrance to Research," *Addictive Behaviors,* 1977, 2:207–17.

Maltzman, Irving, "Controlled Drinking and the Treatment of Alcoholism," *JAMA,* 1987a, 257(7): 927.

———, "In Reply," *JAMA,* 1987b, 257(23): 3229.

———, "Why Alcoholism Is a Disease," *Journal of Psychoactive Drugs,* 1994, 26(1):13–31.

Mann, Marty, *New Primer on Alcoholism.* Holt, Rinehart & Winston, New York, 1972.

———, "Attitude: Key to Successful Treatment," in George Staub and Leona Kent (eds.), *The Para-Professional in the Treatment of Alcoholism: A New Profession.* Charles C Thomas, Springfield, IL, 1973, pp. 3–8.

Mann, Peggy, *Marijuana Alert.* McGraw-Hill, New York, 1985.

Mannion, Lawrence, "Co-Dependency: A Case of Inflation," *Employee Assistance Quarterly,* 1991, 7(2):67–81.

Manson, S. M. (ed.), *New Directions in Prevention Among American Indians and Alaska Native Communities.* Oregon Health Sciences University, Portland, 1982.

Mantell, Margaret, *Recovery for Women.* Author: 2401 Brooks # 245, Missoula, MT 59801, 1995.

Mardones, J., "Evidence of Genetic Factors in the Appetite for Alcohol and Alcoholism," *Annals of the New York Academy of Sciences,* 1972, 197:138–42.

Markey, Morris, "Alcoholics and God," *Liberty,* September 30, 1939, 16:6–7.

Marlatt, G. Alan, "Alcohol, the Magic Elixir: Stress, Expectancy, and the Transformation of Emotional States," in E. Gottheil et al. (eds.), *Stress and Addiction.* Bruner/Mazel, New York, 1987, or "Alcohol, Expectancy, and Emotional States: How Drinking Patterns May Be Affected by Beliefs About Alcohol's Effects," *Alcohol Health and Research World,* Summer 1987, 11(4): 10–13, 80–81.

Marlatt, G. Alan, and J. R. Gordon, *Relapse Prevention: Maintenance Strategies in the Treatment of Addictive Behaviors.* Guilford, New York, 1985.

Marsh, Jack, *You Can Help the Alcoholic: A Christian Plan for Intervention.* Ave Maria Press, Notre Dame, IN, 1983.

Marshall, Mac (ed.), *Beliefs, Behaviors, and Alcoholic Beverages: A Cross-cultural Survey.* University of Michigan Press, Ann Arbor, 1979.

Martin, Joseph C., *No Laughing Matter: Chalk Talks on Alcoholism.* Harper & Row, San Francisco, 1983.

Maslach, Christina, *Burnout: The Cost of Caring.* Prentice-Hall, Englewood Cliffs, NJ, 1982.

Masserman, Jules, "Experimental Neuroses," *Scientific American,* 1950, 182:38–43.

Matlins, Stuart M., *A Study of the Actual Effects of Alcoholic Beverage Control Laws.* National Institute on Alcohol Abuse and Alcoholism, Rockville, MD, 1976, PB-262-641, 642. (2 vols.)

Maxwell, Milton A., *The A.A. Experience: A Close-up View for Professionals.* McGraw-Hill, New York, 1984.

Maxwell, Ruth, *The Booze Battle,* Praeger, New York, 1976. Ballantine Books paperback, 1977.

———, *Breakthrough.* Ballantine Books, New York, 1986.

May, Gerald G., *Addiction and Grace.* Johnson Institute, Minneapolis, 1989.

———, *The Awakened Heart: Living Beyond Addiction.* Harper, San Francisco, 1991.

McCabe, Thomas R., *Victims No More.* Hazelden, Center City, MN, 1978.

McClelland, David C., et al. (eds.), *The Drinking Man.* Free Press, New York, 1972.

McCrady, Barbara S., and William R. Miller (eds.), *Research on Alcoholics Anonymous: Opportunities and Alternatives.* Rutgers Center of Alcohol Studies, New Brunswick, NJ, 1993.

McGuire, Patricia, *The Liberated Woman.* Hazelden, Center City, MN, 1977.

McLearn, G. E., et al. (eds.), *Development of Animal Models as Pharmacogenetic Tools.* NIAAA Research Monograph No. 6, Government Printing Office, Washington, DC, 1981.

McNichol, R. W., and S. A. Logsdon, "Disulfiram: An Evaluation Research Model," *Alcohol Health and Research World,* 1988, 12(3):203–9.

McSherry, P. J., *Wine as Sacramental Matter and the Use of Mustum.* National Clergy Council on Alcoholism, Washington, DC, 1986.

Medicine in the Public Interest, Inc., *The Effects of Alcohol Beverage Control Laws.* U.S. Government Printing Office, Washington, DC, 1979.

Mello, N. K., "Behavioral Studies in Alcoholism," in B. Kissin and H. Begleiter (eds.), *The Biology of Alcoholism.* Wiley, New York, 1972, vol. 2, pp. 219–91.

———, "A Review of Methods to Induce Alcohol Addiction in Animals," *Pharmacology, Biochemistry and Behavior,* 1973, 1:89–101.

Mellor, Steven, et al., "Comparative Trait Analysis of Long-term Recovering Alcoholics," *Psychological Reports,* 1986, 58:411–18.

Mendelson, Jack H., and Nancy K. Mello, *Alcohol: Use and Abuse in America.* Little, Brown, Boston, 1985.

Meryman, Richard, *Broken Promises, Mended Dreams.* Little, Brown, Boston, 1984.

Metzger, Lawrence, *From Denial to Recovery: Counseling Problem Drinkers, Alcoholics, and Their Families.* Jossey-Bass, San Francisco, 1987.

Meyer, Lewis, *Off the Sauce*. Macmillan, New York, 1976.

Meyer, Roberta, *The Parent Connection: How to Communicate with Your Child about Alcohol and Other Drugs*. Franklin Watts, New York, 1984.

Meyer, Roger E. (ed.), *Psychopathology and Addictive Disorders*. Guilford, New York, 1986.

Middlelton-Moz, Jane, and Lorie Dwinell, *After the Tears: Grief and Alcoholic Family Systems*. Health Communications, Deerfield Beach, FL, 1986.

Milam, James R., *The Emergent Comprehensive Concept of Alcoholism*. Rev. ed. Alcenas, Box 286, Kirkland, WA 98033, 1974.

Milam, James R., and K. Ketcham, *Under the Influence*. Bantam, DesPlaines, IL, 1981.

Miletich, J. J., *Work and Alcohol Abuse*. Greenwood Press, Westport, CT, 1988.

Milgram, Gail G., *Alcohol Education Materials, 1950–1981: An Annotated Bibliography*. Rutgers University, New Brunswick, NJ, 1981.

Milkman, H. B., and H. J. Shaffer (eds.), *The Addictions: Multidisciplinary Perspectives and Treatments*. D. C. Heath Books, Lexington, MA, 1985.

Milkman, H. B., and S. Sunderwirth, *Craving Ecstasy: The Consciousness and Chemistry of Escape*. D. C. Heath, Lexington, MA, 1987.

Milkman, H. B., et al., *Treatment Choices for Alcoholism and Substance Abuse*. D. C. Heath, Lexington, MA, 1990.

Miller, Gary E., and Neil Agnew, "The Ledermann Model of Alcohol Consumption," *QJSA*, 1974, 35:877–98.

Miller, Merlene, et al., *Learning to Live Again*. Herald House, Independence, MO, 1988.

Miller, Norman S., *Treating Coexisting Psychiatric and Addictive Disorders*. Hazelden, Center City, MN, 1994.

Miller, N. S., and Mark S. Gold, "Benzodiazepines: Reconsidered," *Advances in Alcohol and Substance Abuse*, 1990 (3-4):67–84.

———, *Alcohol*. Plenum, New York, 1991.

Miller, W. R., "Alcoholism Scales and Objective Assessment Methods: A Critical Review," *Psychological Bulletin*, 1976, 83:649–74.

———, "Motivation for Treatment: A Review with Special Emphasis on Alcoholism," *Psychological Bulletin*, 1985, 8(1):84–107.

———, "Spirituality: The Silent Dimension in Addiction Research." *Drug and Alcohol Review*, 1990, 9:258–66; or *PIRI Newsletter* (Div. 36, American Psychological Association) 1991–92, pp. 9–15.

Miller, W. R., and R. K. Hester, "Inpatient Alcoholism Treatment: Who Benefits?" *American Psychologist*, July 1986, 41(7):794–805.

Miller, W. R., and E. Kurtz, "Models of Alcoholism Used in Treatment: Contrasting A.A. and Other Perspectives with Which It Is Often Confused," *JSA*, 1994: 159–66.

Miller, W. R., and S. Rollnick. *Motivational Interviewing*. Guilford Press, New York, 1992.

Mishara, B. L., and R. Kastenbaum, *Alcohol and Old Age*. Grune & Stratton, New York, 1980.

Mondanaro, Josette, *Treating Chemically Dependent Women*. D. C. Heath, Lexington, MA, 1989.

Monti, Pete M. *Treating Alcohol Dependence: A Coping Skills Training Guide*. Guilford Press, New York, 1989.

Moore, Mark H., and Dean R. Gerstein (eds.), *Alcohol and Public Policy: Beyond the Shadow of Prohibition*. National Academy Press, Washington, DC, 1981.

Moore, M. M. M., "Codependence Theory: Heuristic or Reductionistic?" *Journal of Ministry in Addiction & Recovery*, 1995, 2(1): 59–77.

Moore, S. R., and T. W. Teal, *Geriatric Drug Use: Clinical and Social Perspectives*. Pergamon Press, New York, 1985.

Moos, Rudolf, C.; J. W. Finney; and R. C. Cronkite, *Alcoholism Treatment: Context, Process, Outcome.* Oxford University Press, New York, 1990.

Morey, L., and R. Blashfield, "Empirical Classification of Alcoholism: A Review," *JSA,* 1981, 42:925–37.

Mueller, C. W., and F. Klajner, "The Effect of Alcohol on Memory for Feelings: Does It Really Help Users to Forget?" *Journal of Nervous and Mental Diseases,* 1984, 172:225–27.

Mulford, H. A., "Drinking and Deviant Drinking, USA, 1963," *QJSA,* 1964, 25: 634–50.

Murphy, G. E., *Suicide in Alcoholism.* Oxford University Press, New York, 1992.

Musto, D. F., "Opium, Cocaine and Marijuana," *Scientific American,* 1991, 265(1): 40–47.

Myers, Judy, *Staying Sober: The Complete Nutrition and Exercise Program for the Recovering Alcoholic.* Congdon & Wood, New York, 1987.

Myers, Robert D., and C. L. Melchior, "Alcohol Drinking: Abnormal Intake Caused by Tetrahydropapaveroline in Brain," *Science,* 1977, 196:554–56.

NAADAC (National Association of Alcoholism and Drug Abuse Counselors), "Code of Ethics," *The Counselor,* 1987, 5(5):13–16 and entire issue; or Arlington, VA: NAADAC, 1987.

———, "National Understanding of the NAADAC Code of Ethics," *The Counselor,* 1990, 8(3):37–38.

Nace, Edgar. *The Treatment of Alcoholism.* Brunner/Mazel, Columbus, OH, 1987.

Nathan, Peter E., "Failures in Prevention, *American Psychologist,* 1983, 38:459–67.

———, "The Addictive Personality Is the Behavior of the Addict," Journal of Consulting and Clinical Psychology, 1988, 56:183–88.

National Clergy Council on Alcoholism (NCCA), *Alcoholism: A Source Book for the Clergy.* NCAA, Washington, DC, 1960.

National Institute on Aging. *Drug Abuse in Nursing Homes.* Government Printing Office, Washington, DC, 1980.

NCA (National Council on Alcoholism) Criteria Committee, "Criteria for the Diagnosis of Alcoholism," *Annals of Internal Medicine,* 1972, 77:249–58; and *The American Journal of Psychiatry,* 1972, 129:127–35; "Definition of Alcoholism," *Annals of Internal Medicine,* 1976, 85:764.

———, *Prevention Policy Handbook.* NCA, New York, 1983.

NCADD/ASAM (National Council on Alcoholism and Drug Dependence and American Society of Addiction Medicine) Joint Committee, "The Definition of Alcoholism," *JAMA,* 1992, 268:1012–14.

Negrete, J. C., "Cultural Influences on Social Performance of Alcoholics: A Comparative Study," *QJSA,* 1973, 34: 905–16.

Nellis, Muriel, *Final Report on Drugs, Alcohol and Women's Health.* National Institute of Drug Abuse, Rockville, MD, 1978.

Newlove, Donald, *Those Drinking Days.* Horizon, New York, 1981.

NIAAA (National Institute on Alcohol Abuse and Alcoholism), *Special Report to the U.S. Congress on Alcohol and Health.* DEW/HHS, Washington, DC, First, 1871 (o.p., reprinted by Scribner's, New York); Second, 1974; Third, 1978; Fourth, 1981; Fifth, 1983; Sixth, 1987; Seventh, 1990; Eighth, 1993.

———, *Alcohol and Nutrition.* NIAAA Research Monograph no. 2. U.S. Government Printing Office, Washington, DC, 1979.

———, "Alcohol and the Brain," *Alcohol Health and Research World,* 1990, vol. 14(2), entire issue.

———, "Definitions and Diagnostic Criteria of Alcoholism," *Alcohol Health and Research World,* 1991, 15(4): 251–302.

———, "Alcohol, Infectious Diseases, and Immunity," *Alcohol Health and Research World,* 1992, 16(1): 1–92.

———, "Alcohol and Hormones," *Alcohol Alert,* 1994, no. 26, PH 352, and references therein.

Nolan, James P., "Intestinal Endotoxins as Mediators of Hepatic Injury: An Idea Whose Time Has Come Again," *Hepatology,* 1989, 10(5): 887–91.

Norris, John L., "What AA Can Offer Professional Schools and What it Cannot," *Annals of the New York Academy of Sciences,* 1971, 178: 61–65.

———, "The Role of A.A. in Rehabilitation," in V. Groupé (ed.), *Alcoholism Rehabilitation.* Rutgers, New Brunswick, NJ, 1978.

Norwood, Robin, *Women Who Love Too Much.* Tarcher, Los Angeles, 1985.

Nowinski, J. *Substance Abuse in Adolescents and Young Adults.* Norton, New York, 1990.

O'Briant, Robert G., and H. L. Lennard, *Recovery from Alcoholism: A Social Treatment Model.* Charles C Thomas, Springfield, IL, 1973.

O'Connell, David F. (ed.), *Managing the Dually Diagnosed Patient.* Haworth Press, New York, 1990.

O'Connell, Kathleen, *Bruised by Life? Turn Life's Wounds into Gifts.* Deaconess Press, Minneapolis, 1994.

O'Farrell, T. J., and C. A. Weyand, *Alcohol and Sexuality: An Annotated Bibliography on Alcohol Use, Alcoholism, and Human Sexual Behavior.* Onyx Press, Phoenix, AZ, 1983.

O'Gorman, Patricia, and Peter Finn, *Teaching About Alcohol: Concepts, Methods, and Classroom Activities.* Allyn & Bacon, Boston, 1981.

Olds, J., "Differentiation of Reward Systems in Brain by Self-stimulation Technics," in E. R. Ramey and D. S. O'Doherty (eds.), *Electrical Studies on Unanesthetized Brain.* Hoebler, New York, 1960, pp. 17–51.

Olson, Steve, and Dean R. Gerstein, *Alcohol in America: Taking Action to Prevent Abuse.* National Academy Press, Washington, DC, 1986.

O'Malley, P. M., and A. C. Wagenaar, "Effects of Minimum Drinking Age Laws on Alcohol Use, Related Behaviors and Traffic Crash Involvement Among American Youth, 1976–1987," *JSA,* 1991, 52(5): 478–91.

Orford, Jim, "Alcoholism and Marriage: The Argument Against Specialization," *JSA,* 1975, 36:1537–63.

———, "The Future of Alcoholism: A Commentary on the Rand Report" (editorial), *Psychological Medicine,* 1978, 8:5–8.

———, *Excessive Appetites: A Psychological View of Addictions.* Wiley, New York, 1985.

Orford, Jim, and J. Harwin (eds.), *Alcohol and the Family.* St. Martin's Press, New York, 1982.

Page, Penny B., *Alcohol Use and Alcoholism: A Guide to the Literature.* Garland, New York, 1986.

Paine, H. S., "Attitudes and Patterns of Alcohol Use Among Mexican Americans: Implications for Service Delivery," *JSA,* 1977, 8:544–53.

Paolino, Thomas J., and Barbara S. McCrady, *The Alcoholic Marriage: Alternative Perspectives.* Grune & Stratton, New York, 1977.

Parakrama, C., and R. Taylor, *Concise Pathology.* Appleton & Lange, Norwalk, CT, 1991.

Parker, R. N., and L.-A. Rebhun, *Alcohol and Homicide: A Deadly Combination of Two American Traditions.* State University of New York Press, Albany, 1995.

Parsons, Oscar A., et al., *Neuropsychology of Alcoholism: Implications for Diagnosis and Treatment.* Guilford Press, New York, 1987.

Partanen, J., "On the Relevance of Twin Studies," *Annals of the New York Academy of Sciences,* 1972, 197:114–16.

Partington, John T., and F. Gordon Johnson, "Personality Types Among Alcoholics," *QJSA,* 1969, 30:21–34.

Parvez, S., et al. (eds.), *Progress in Alcohol Research,* vol. 1: *Alcohol, Nutrition and the Nervous System.* VNU Science Press, Utrecht, The Netherlands, 1985.

Pattison, E. M., "Differential Diagnosis of Alcoholism," *Postgraduate Medicine,* 1967, 41:A127–32.

———, "Population Variation Among Alcoholism Treatment Facilities," *International Journal of the Addictions,* 1973, 8:199–229.

Pattison, E. M.; M. B. Sobell; and L. C. Sobell (eds.), *Emerging Concepts of Alcohol Dependence.* Springer, New York, 1977.

Pendery, M. L., and I. Maltzman, "Controlled Drinking by Alcoholics? New Findings and a Reevaluation of a Major Affirmative Study," *Science,* July 9, 1982, 217:169–75.

Perez, Joseph F., *Counseling the Alcoholic Group.* Gardner Press, New York, 1986.

———, *Counseling the Alcoholic Woman.* Accelerated Development, Inc., Muncie, IN, 1994.

Pernanen, Kai, *Alcohol in Human Violence.* Guilford Press, New York, 1991.

Perrin, Thomas W., *I Am an Adult Who Grew Up in an Alcoholic Family.* Cross-road/Continuum, New York, 1991.

Perrine, M. W. (ed.), *Alcohol, Drugs and Driving.* National Highway Traffic Safety Administration, Washington, DC, 1974. Technical report DOT HS-801-096.

Peteet, John R., "A Closer Look at the Role of a Spiritual Approach in Addictions Treatment," *Journal of Substance Abuse Treatment,* 1993, 10:263–67.

Petrakis, P. L., *Alcoholism: An Inherited Disease.* NIAAA, Rockville, MD, 1985. DHHS Pub. no. ADM 85-1426.

Pfau, Father Ralph, *Prodigal Shepherd.* Lippincott, Philadelphia, 1958. Hazelden reprint.

Pines, A. M., et al., *Burnout: From Tedium to Personal Growth.* Free Press, New York, 1982.

Pita, Dianne D. *Addictions Counseling: A Practical Guide to Counseling People with Chemical and Other Addictions.* Continuum, New York, 1992.

Pittman, Bill, *AA: The Way It All Began.* Glen Abbey Books, Seattle, 1988.

Pittman, David J., and C. W. Gordon, *The Revolving Door: A Study of the Chronic Police Case Inebriate.* Free Press, Glencoe, IL, 1968.

Platt, Jerome L., et al. (eds.), *The Effectiveness of Drug Abuse Treatment.* Robert Krieger, Melbourne, FL, 1990.

Polich, J. M., et al., *The Course of Alcoholism.* Rand Corporation, Santa Monica, CA, 1980.

Pontifical Council for Pastoral Assistance to Health Care Workers, *Drugs and Alcoholism Against Life.* Proceedings of the 6th International Conference. Vatican Press, Rome, 1992.

Popham, Robert E., "The Relevance of Basic Research," *Addictions,* 1968, 15:21–25.

Porjesz, B., and H. Begleiter, "Brain Dysfunction and Alcohol," in B. Kissin and H. Begleiter (eds.), *The Pathogenesis of Alcoholism: Biological Factors.* Plenum, New York, 1983, pp. 415–83.

Postman, N., et al., *Myths, Men, and Beer: An Analysis of Beer Commercials on Broadcast Television, 1987.* AAA Foundation for Traffic Safety, Falls Church, VA, 1988.

Potter-Efron, R. T., *Shame, Guilt, and Alcoholism.* Haworth Press, New York, 1989.

Potter-Efron, R. T., and P. S. Potter-Efron, *Anger, Alcoholism, and Addiction: Treating Individuals, Couples, and Families.* Norton, New York, 1991.

Powell, D. J. (ed.), *Alcoholism and Sexual Dysfunction.* Haworth, New York, 1984.

Propping, P., et al., "An EEG Study of Genetic Disposition to Alcoholism," *Digest of Alcoholism Theory and Application,* October 1982, 2:51–55.

Pursch, J., *Dear Doc.* CompCare Publishers, Minneapolis, 1985.

R.S., "Pill Consciousness: An AA Member-psychiatrist Looks at the Uses of Medication," *AA Grapevine,* September 1981, 37:14–16.

Ray, O., and C. Ksir, *Drugs, Society and Human Behavior.* 6th ed. Mosby, St. Louis, 1993.

Redda, Kinfe, et al., *Cocaine, Marijuana, Designer Drugs: Chemistry, Pharmacology and Behavior.* CRC Press, Boca Raton, FL, 1989.

Reddy, Betty, "Detachment and Recovery from Alcoholism," *Alcohol Health and Research World,* Spring 1978, 2:28–33.

Reed, T. Edward, "Racial Comparisons of Alcohol Metabolism," *Alcoholism: Clinical and Experimental Research,* 1978, 2:83–87.

Research Triangle Institute, *A National Study of Adolescent Drinking Behavior.* Research Triangle Park, NC, 1975, 1984, 1986.

Rinaldi, R. C., et al., "Clarification and Standardization of Substance Abuse Terminology," *JAMA,* January 22–29, 1988, 259(4): 555–57.

Ripley, H. S., and Joan K. Jackson, "Therapeutic Factors in Alcoholics Anonymous," *American Journal of Psychiatry,* 1959, 116:44–50.

Rippey, John N., *Drug Abuse in America: An Historical Perspective.* Behavioral Health Resources Press, Alexandria, VA, 1995.

———. *Treatment of the Pregnant Addict.* Behavioral Health Resources Press, Alexandria, VA, 1995.

Rivers, P. Clayton (ed.), *Alcohol and Addictive Behavior: Theory, Research and Practice.* Prentice-Hall, Englewood Cliffs, NJ, 1994.

Robe, Lucy B., "Rich Alcoholics: How Dollars Buy Denial," *Addictions,* 1977, 24(2):43–57.

———, "Jewish Alcoholics Coming out of the Woodwork," *U.S. Journal of Drug and Alcohol Dependence,* March, 1978.

———, *Just So It's Healthy.* Rev. ed. CompCare, Minneapolis, 1982.

———, *Co-Starring: Famous Women and Alcohol.* CompCare, Minneapolis, 1986.

Robertson, Nan, *Getting Better: Inside Alcoholics Anonymous.* Morrow, New York, 1988.

Robins, Arthur J., *Alcohol Detoxification Manual.* Human Sciences Press, New York, 1988.

Roe, A., "The Adult Adjustment of Children of Alcoholic Parents Raised in Foster Homes," *QJSA,* 1944, 5:378–93.

Rohan, W. P., et al., "MMPI Changes in Alcoholics during Hospitalization," *QJSA,* 1969, 30:389–401.

Roman, Paul M., "The Emphasis on Alcoholism in Employee Assistance Programming," *Labor–Management Alcoholism Journal,* 1979, 8(5):186–91.

——— (ed.), *Alcohol Problem Intervention in the Workplace: Employee Assistance Programs and Strategic Alternatives.* Greenwood, Westport, CT, 1990.

Rose, John D., "Cocaethylene: A Current Understanding of the Active Metabolite of Cocaine and Ethanol," *American Journal of Emergency Medicine,* 1994, 12: 489–90.

Rose, Robert M., and J. C. Barrett (eds.), *Alcoholism: Origins and Outcome.* Raven Press, New York, 1988.

Ross, George R., *Treating Adolescent Substance Abuse.* Allyn & Bacon, Des Moines, IA, 1994.

Ross, H. L., *Confronting Drunk Driving: Social Policy for Saving Lives.* Yale University Press, New Haven, CT, 1992.

Roth, Paula (ed.), *Alcohol and Drugs Are Women's Issues.* 2 vols. Scarecrow Press, Metuchen, NJ, 1991.

Royce, James E., S.J., *Personality and Mental Health.* Rev. ed. Bruce, Benziger & Glencoe, Beverly Hills, CA, 1964.

———, "Inside the Alcoholic," *Voices: The Art and Science of Psychotherapy*, Spring 1984, 20(1): 21–25.

———, "Alcohol and Other Drug Dependencies," in R. J. Wicks, et al. (eds.), *Clinical Handbook of Pastoral Counseling*. Paulist Press, New York, 1985a, pp. 502–9.

———, "Sin or Solace? Religious Views on Alcohol and Alcoholism," *Journal of Drug Issues*, Winter 1985b, 15(1):51–62. Also in Watts, T. D. (ed.), *Social Thought on Alcoholism*. Krieger Publishing, Malabar, FL, 1986, pp. 53–66.

———, "Addiction: A *Spiritual* Illness?" *Proceedings of the 32nd Institute* (Budapest), International Council on Alcohol and Addictions, Lausanne, Switzerland, 1986.

———, "Alcohol and Other Drugs in Spiritual Formation," *Studies in Formative Spirituality*, May 1987, 8(2): 211–22.

———, "Christianity: An Alternative Tradition," *Journal of Ministry in Addiction and Recovery*, 1994, 1(2): 87–90.

———, "The Effects of Alcoholism and Recovery on Spirituality," *Journal of Chemical Dependency Treatment*, 1995, 7(2): 19–37. Also in Robert J. Kus (ed.), *Spirituality and Chemical Dependency*. Haworth, Binghamton, NY, 1995.

Rubin, Emmanuel (ed.), *Alcohol and the Cell*. New York Academy of Sciences, New York, 1987.

Rubington, Earl, *Alcohol Problems and Social Control*. Charles E. Merrill, Columbus, OH, 1973.

Ruprecht, A. L., "Day-care Facilities in the Treatment of Alcoholics," *QJSA*, 1961, 22:461–70.

Russell, Marcia, and Sheila Blume (eds.), *Children of Alcoholics: A Review of the Literature*. Children of Alcoholics Foundation, New York, 1985.

Ryan, Keith, "Alcohol and Blood Sugar Disorders: An Overview," *Alcohol Health and Research World*, Winter 1983–84, 8(2):3–15.

Sandmaier, Marian, *The Invisible Alcoholics: Women and Alcohol Abuse in America*, 2d ed. McGraw-Hill, New York, 1992.

SASSI Institute, *Substance Abuse Subtle Screening Inventory*. P.O. Box 5069, Bloomington IN, 47407-5069, 1988.

Scanlon, Walter F., *Alcoholism and Drug Abuse in the Workplace: Managing Care and Costs Through Employee Assistance Programs*. Praeger, New York, 1991.

Schacter, Stanley, "Studies of the Interaction of Psychological and Pharmacological Determinants of Smoking," *Journal of Experimental Psychology: General*, 1977, 106(1):3–40. See "Behavior," *Time* Magazine, February 21, 1977.

Schneider, Karl A., *Alcoholism and Addiction: A Study Program for Adults and Youth*. Fortress Press, Philadelphia, 1976.

Schuckit, Marc A., "Sexual Disturbance in the Woman Alcoholic," *Medical Aspects of Human Sexuality*, 1971, 6:44–65.

———, "Alcohol and Alcoholism: An Introduction for the Health Care Specialist," *Journal of Emergency Services*, 1976a, 8:26–34.

———, "Family History as a Predictor of Alcoholism in the U.S. Navy," *JSA*, 1976b, 37:1678–85.

———, "Geriatric Alcoholism and Drug Abuse," *Gerontologist*, 1977, 17:168–74.

———, "Alcoholism: A Symposium with CME Credit Quiz," *Postgraduate Medicine*, 1978, 64(6):76–158.

———, "Ethanol Ingestion: Differences in Blood Acetaldehyde Concentrations in Relatives of Alcoholics and Controls," *Science*, January 5, 1979, 203:54–55.

———, "Biological Vulnerability to Alcoholism," *Journal of Clinical and Consulting Psychology*, 1987, 55:301–90.

———, "The Time Course of Development of Alcohol-related Problems in Men and Women," *JSA*, 1995a, 56(2): 218–25.

———, *Drug and Alcohol Abuse: A Clinical Guide to Diagnosis and Treatment*. 4th ed. Plenum, New York, 1995b.

————, "Adult Children of Alcoholics: Is This an Appropriate Diagnostic Label?" *Drug Abuse & Alcoholism Newsletter,* 1995c, Vista Hill Foundation, San Diego, 24(3).

Scott, J. M., *The White Poppy: A History of Opium.* Heinemann, London, 1969.

Seeburger, F. P., *Addiction and Responsibility: An Inquiry into the Addictive Mind.* Crossroad, New York, 1993.

Seixas, Frank A., "Alcohol and Its Drug Interactions," *Annals of Internal Medicine,* 1975, 83:86–92.

————, "The Course of Alcoholism," in Nada J. Estes and M. Edith Heinemann (eds.), *Alcoholism: Development, Consequences, and Interventions.* Mosby, St. Louis, 1977, pp. 59–66.

Seixas, Frank A. (ed)., "Alcoholism and the Central Nervous System," *Annals of the New York Academy of Sciences,* 1973, 215:1–389.

Seixas, Frank A., et al. (eds.), "Work in Progress in Alcoholism," *Annals of the New York Academy of Sciences,* 1970–76. Titles include: "Professional Training in Alcoholism," 1971, n. 178; "Nature and Nurture in Alcoholism," 1972, n. 197; "Alcoholism and the Central Nervous System," 1973, n. 215; "The Person with Alcoholism," 1974, n. 233; "Medical Consequences of Alcoholism," 1974, n. 252.

Seixas, Judith, and Geraldine Youcha, *Children of Alcoholism: A Survivor's Manual.* Crown Publishers, New York, 1985.

Selye, Hans, *The Stress of Life.* McGraw-Hill, New York, 1956.

Selzer, M. L., "Normal Drinking in Recovered Alcohol Addicts: Comment on the Article by D. L. Davies," *QJSA,* 1963, 24:113–14.

————, "The Michigan Alcoholism Screening Test: The Quest for a New Diagnostic Instrument," *American Journal of Psychiatry,* 1971, 127:1653–58.

Shaffer, H. (ed.), *The Addictive Behaviors.* Haworth, New York, 1984.

Shaffer, H., and M. E. Burgess (eds.), *Classic Contributions in the Addictions.* Brunner/Mazel, New York, 1981.

Sharp, Elaine B. *The Dilemma of Drug Policy in the United States.* HarperCollins College Publishers, New York, 1994.

Sherouse, Deborah L., *Professional's Handbook on Geriatric Alcoholism.* Academic Press, New York, 1983.

Siegel, Larry (ed.), *AIDS and Substance Abuse.* vol. 7, no. 2 of *Advances in Alcohol and Substance Abuse,* 1988.

Siegel, Ronald K. *Intoxication: Life in Pursuit of Artificial Paradise.* Dutton, New York, 1989.

Simonson, W., *Medications and the Elderly.* Aspen Publishers, Frederick, MD, 1984.

Single, E., and T. Storm (eds.), *Public Drinking and Public Policy.* Addiction Research Foundation, Toronto, 1985.

Smart, Reginald G., "Future Time Perspectives in Alcoholics and Social Drinkers," *Journal of Abnormal Psychology,* 1968, 73:81–83.

————, "Spontaneous Recovery in Alcoholics: A Review and Analysis of the Available Research," *Drug and Alcohol Dependence,* 1975–76, 1:277–85.

————, "Young Alcoholics in Treatment: Their Characteristics and Recovery Rates at Follow-up," *Alcoholism: Clinical and Experimental Research,* 1979, 3:19–23.

————, *The New Drinkers: Teenage Use and Abuse of Alcohol.* Rev. ed. Addiction Research Foundation, Toronto, 1980.

Smart, Reginald G., et al., "A Controlled Study of Lysergide in the Treatment of Alcoholism: I. The Effects on Drinking Behavior," *QJSA,* 1966, 27:469–82.

————, *Lysergic Acid Diethylamide (LSD) in the Treatment of Alcoholism.* University of Toronto Press, Toronto, 1967.

Smith, Annette R. *Alcoholics Anonymous: A Social World Perspective.* University of California at San Diego, 1991 (University of Michigan Microfilms).

Smith, David E., and G. R. Goy (eds.), *"It's So Good, Don't Even Try It Once":* *Heroin in Perspective.* Prentice-Hall, Englewood Cliffs, NJ, 1972.

Smith, David E., and D. R. Wesson, *Treating the Cocaine Abuser.* Hazelden, Center City, MN, 1985.

Smith, David W., "Fetal Alcohol Syndrome: A Tragic and Preventable Disorder," in Nada J. Estes and M. Edith Heinemann (eds.), *Alcoholism: Development, Consequences and Interventions,* Mosby, St. Louis, 1986.

Smith, James W., "Rehabilitation for Alcoholics," *Postgraduate Medicine,* December 1978, 64(6):143–52.

———, "Abstinence-oriented Alcoholism Treatment Approaches," in J. Ferguson (ed.), *Advances in Behavioral Medicine.* Spectrum Publications, Prentice-Hall, Englewood Cliffs, NJ, 1979.

———, "Aversion Conditioning Hospitals," in E. Kaufman and E. M. Pattison (eds.), *The American Encyclopedic Handbook of Alcoholism.* Gardner Press, New York, 1982.

———, "Alcohol and Disorders of the Heart and Skeletal Muscles," in Nada J. Estes and M. Edith Heinemann (eds.), *Alcoholism: Development, Consequences, and Interventions.* Mosby, St. Louis, 1986a.

———, "Neurological Disorders in Alcoholism," in Nada J. Estes and M. Edith Heinemann (eds.), *Alcoholism: Development, Consequences and Interventions.* Mosby, St. Louis, 1986b.

Smith, James W., and G. A. Brinton, "Color Vision Defects in Alcoholism" *QJSA,* 1971, 32:41–44.

Smith, James W.; F. Lemere; and R. B. Dunn, "Pentothal Interviews in the Treatment of Alcoholism," *Psychosomatics,* 1971, 12:330–31.

———, "Impotence in Alcoholism," *Northwest Medicine,* 1974, 71:523–24.

Smith, James W., and Ruth E. Little, "Alcohol Abuse in Medical Practice," in J. E. Carr and H. A. Dengerink (eds.), *Behavioral Science in the Practice of Medicine,* Elsevier, New York, 1983, pp. 419–41.

Smith, Rev. Susanne, *Working the Steps.* Hazelden, Center City, MN, 1977.

Smith, Wrynn, *Mental Illness and Substance Abuse.* Facts on File, New York, 1989.

Snyder, Charles R., *Alcohol and the Jews: A Cultural Study of Drinking and Sobriety.* Free Press and Yale Center of Alcohol Studies, New Haven, CT, 1958.

Sobell, M., and L. Sobell, *Moderation as a Goal or Outcome of Treatment for Alcohol Problems.* Haworth, New York, 1987.

Sonnenstuhl, W. J., and H. M. Trice, *Strategies for Employee Assistance Programs: The Crucial Balance.* Cornell University, Ithaca, NY, 1986.

Sorensen, Andrew A., *Alcoholic Priests: A Sociological Study.* Seabury, New York, 1976.

Sournia, Jean Charles, *A History of Alcoholism.* Basil Blackwell, Oxford, England, 1990.

Spradley, James P., *You Owe Yourself a Drunk.* Little, Brown, Boston, 1988.

Stanton, M. Duncan, and T. C. Todd, *The Family Therapy of Drug Abuse and Addiction.* Guilford, New York, 1982.

Staub, George, and Leona Kent (eds.), *The Para-Professional in the Treatment of Alcoholism: A New Profession.* Charles C Thomas, Springfield, IL, 1973.

Steindler, E. M., "Help for the Alcoholic Physician: A Seminar," *Alcoholism: Clinical and Experimental Research,* 1977, 1:129–30.

Steiner, Claude M., *Games Alcoholics Play: The Analysis of Life Scripts.* Grove Press, New York, 1972.

Steinglass, Peter, "Family Therapy with Alcoholics: A Review," in E. Kaufman and P. N. Kaufman (eds.), *Family Therapy of Drug and Alcohol Abuse.* Gardner Press, New York, 1979.

————, "The Roles of Alcohol in Family Systems," in J. Orford and J. Harwin (eds.), *Alcohol and the Family.* St. Martin's Press, New York, 1982.

Steinglass, Peter, et al., *The Alcoholic Family.* Harper & Row, New York, 1987.

Stephens, Richard C. *The Street Addict: A Theory of Heroin Addiction.* State University of New York, Albany, 1991.

Sterman, Chilly. *Neuro-Linguistic Programming in Alcoholism Treatment.* Haworth, Binghamton, NY, 1990.

Stewart, David, *Thirst for Freedom.* Hazelden, Center City, MN, 1960.

————, *Addicted and Free at the Same Time: A Study of Addiction and Fellowship.* Empathy Books, Toronto, 1984.

Stimmel, Barry, *Effects of Maternal Alcohol and Drug Abuse on the Newborn.* Haworth, New York, 1982.

————, *Alcohol and Drug Abuse in the Affluent.* Haworth, New York, 1984.

————, *Alcohol and Substance Abuse in Women and Children.* Haworth, New York, 1986.

Stivers, Richard, *A Hair of the Dog: Irish Drinking and American Stereotype.* Pennsylvania State University Press, University Park, 1976.

Strachan, J. George, *Alcoholism: Treatable Illness.* Mitchell Press, Vancouver, BC, 1968.

————, *Practical Alcoholism Programming.* Mitchell Press, Vancouver, BC, 1971.

Strang, John, and G. Stimson, (eds.), *AIDS and Drug Misuse: The Challenge for Policy and Practice in the 1990's.* Routledge, London, 1990.

Streissguth, A. P., "Psychologic Handicaps in Children with Fetal Alcohol Syndrome," *Annals of the New York Academy of Sciences,* 1976a, 273:140–45.

————, "Maternal Alcoholism and the Outcome of Pregnancy," in M. Greenblatt (ed.), *Alcohol Problems in Women and Children.* Grune & Stratton, New York, 1976b, pp. 251–77.

————, "A Long-Term Perspective of FAS," *Alcohol Health and Research World,* 1994, 18(1): 74–81.

Streissguth, A. P.; C. S. Herman; and D. W. Smith; "Intelligence, Behavior, and Dysmorphogenesis in the Fetal Alcohol Syndrome: A Report on 20 Patients," *Journal of Pediatrics,* 1978, 92:363–67.

Streissguth, A. P., and R. LaDue, "Psychological and Behavioral Effects in Children Prenatally Exposed to Alcohol," *Alcohol Health and Research World,* Fall 1985, 10(1):6–12.

Substance Abuse Librarians, *SALIS Directory.* Alcohol Research Group, Berkeley, CA, 1988.

Sudduth, William V., "The Role of Bacteria and Enterotoxemia in Physical Addiction to Alcohol," *Journal of the International Academy of Preventive Medicine,* 1977, 4(2):23–46, or in *Microecology and Therapy,* 1989, 18:77–81.

Sullivan, E. J., LeClair Bissell; and E. Williams, *Chemical Dependency in Nursing: The Deadly Diversion,* Johnson Institute, Minneapolis, 1988.

Surgeon General Report, *The Health Consequences of Smoking: Nicotine Addiction.* DHHS Pub. No. (CDC) 88-8406, U.S. Government Printing Office, Washington, DC, 1988.

Tabakoff, Boris, et al. (eds.), *Medical and Social Aspects of Alcohol Abuse.* Plenum, New York, 1983.

Tabor, Jonathan, "My Trials as a Nondrinking Alcoholic," *Saturday Evening Post,* October 24, 1959, 232:36 ff. Reprinted in *Reader's Digest,* November 1960, 77:78–82.

Tarter, R. E., and A. Sugerman (eds.), *Alcoholism: Interdisciplinary Approaches to an Enduring Problem.* Addison-Wesley, Reading, MA, 1976.

Tarter, R. E., and D. H. Van Thiel, *Alcohol and the Brain: Chronic Effects.* Plenum, New York, 1985.

Tarter, R. E., et al., "Adolescent Sons of Alcoholics: Neuropsychological and Personality Characteristics," *Alcoholism: Clinical and Experimental Research,* 1984, 8:216–21.

Tewari, S., and E. P. Noble, "Ethanol and Brain Protein Synthesis," *Brain Research,* 1971, 26:469–74.

Thompson, Robert, Jr., *Substance Abuse and Employee Rehabilitation.* BNA Books, Washington, DC, 1990.

Thomsen, Robert, *Bill W.* Harper & Row, New York, 1975.

Tiebout, Harry M., *Conversion as a Psychological Phenomenon.* National Council on Alcoholism, New York, 1944. Pamphlet.

———, "Therapeutic Mechanisms of Alcoholics Anonymous," *American Journal of Psychiatry,* 1944, 100:468–73.

———, "The Syndrome of Alcohol Addiction," *QJSA,* 1945, 5:535–46.

———, "The Act of Surrender in the Therapeutic Process with Special Reference to Alcoholism," *QJSA,* 1949, 10:48–58. NCA reprint.

———, "The Role of Psychiatry in the Field of Alcoholism," *QJSA,* 1951, 12:52–57. NCA reprint.

———, "Surrender Versus Compliance in Therapy with Special Reference to Alcoholism," *QJSA,* 1953, 14:58–68. NCA reprint.

———, "The Ego Factors in Surrender in Alcoholism," *QJSA,* 1954, 15:610–21. NCA reprint.

———, "Direct Treatment of a Symptom," in P. H. Hoch and J. Zubin (eds.), *Problems of Addiction and Habituation.* Grune & Stratton, New York, 1958, pp. 17–26. NCA reprint.

———, "Alcoholics Anonymous: An Experiment of Nature," *QJSA,* 1961, 22:52–68. NCA reprint.

———, "Intervention in Psychotherapy," *American Journal of Psychoanalysis,* 1962, 22:74–80. NCA reprint.

———, *Alcoholism: Its Nature and Treatment.* National Council on Alcoholism, New York, n.d.

Tivis, Laura, and Judith Gavalier, "Alcohol, Hormones, and Health in Postmenopausal Women," *Alcohol Health and Research World,* 1994, 18(3):185–88.

Tong, J. E., et al., "Alcohol, Visual Discrimination and Heart Rate," *QJSA,* 1974, 35:1003–22.

Tonigan, J. S., and S. Hiller-Sturmhofel, "Alcoholics Anonymous: Who Benefits?" *Alcohol Health and Research World,* 1994, 18(4): 308–10.

Topel, Helga, "Biochemical Basis of Alcoholism: Statements and Hypotheses of Present Research," *Alcohol,* vol. 2(6), November–December 1985.

Trimble, Joseph E., et al. (eds.), *Ethnic and Multicultural Drug Abuse.* Haworth Press, Binghamton, NY, 1992.

Turner, Carlton E., et al., *Cocaine: An Annotated Bibliography.* 2 vols. University Press of Mississippi, Jackson, MS, 1988.

Tuyns, Albert J., "Alcohol and Cancer," *Alcohol Health and Research World,* Summer 1978, 2(4):20–31.

Twerski, Abraham J., *Caution: "Kindness" Can be Dangerous to the Alcoholic.* Prentice-Hall, Englewood Cliffs, NJ, 1981.

———, *Self-Discovery in Recovery.* Hazelden, Center City, MN, 1984.

———, *It Happens to Doctors, Too.* Hazelden, Center City, MN, 1986.

Tygstrup, Niels, and R. Olsson, *Alcohol and Disease.* Coronet Books, Philadelphia, 1985.

Tyrrell, Bernard J., *Christotherapy: Healing Through Enlightenment,* 1975; *Christotherapy II: A New Horizon for Counselors, Spiritual Directors, and Seekers of Healing and Growth in Christ,* Paulist Press, New York, 1982.

Ullman, A., "The First Drinking Experience of Normal and Addictive Drinkers," *QJSA*, 1953, 14:181–91.

United States Department of Health and Human Services, *Advances in Alcoholism Treatment: Services for Women*. Government Printing Office, Washington, DC, 1983.

———, *Alcohol and Other Drug Thesaurus*. Government Printing Office, Washington, DC, 1993.

United States Department of Justice, *Alcohol, Drug and Substance Abuse Among Juveniles: Topical Bibliography*. National Criminal Justice Resource Center, Rockville, MD, 1985.

United States General Accounting Office (GAO), *Comptroller General's Report to Special Subcommittee on Alcoholism and Narcotics, Committee on Labor and Public Welfare, United States Senate: Substantial Cost Savings from Establishment of Alcoholism Program for Federal Civilian Employees*. U.S. Government Printing Office, Washington, DC, 1970.

United States Indian Health Service, *Alcoholism: A High Priority Health Problem*. U.S. Government Printing Office, DHEW Publ. 73-12002, Washington, DC, 1972.

United States National Commission on Marihuana and Drug Abuse, *Drug Abuse in America: Problem in Perspective*. U.S. Government Printing Office, Washington, DC, 1973.

United States Navy, *Navy Alcohol Safety Action Program (NASAP), Crisis Intervention*. USN Bureau of Navy Personnel, Washington, DC, July 1976.

———, *Navy Alcoholism Prevention Program, The Chaplain's Role*. USN Bureau of Naval Personnel, Washington, DC, n.d.

United States Office of Juvenile Justice and Delinquency Prevention, *Drug Abuse, Mental Health and Delinquency*. U.S. Department of Justice, Washington, DC, 1985.

Vaillant, George, "Alcoholism Not a Symptom of Neurotic or Psychotic Disorders," *Alcoholism and Alcohol Education*, May 1977, 11–12.

———, "Dangers of Psychotherapy in the Treatment of Alcoholism," in M. H. Bean and N. E. Zinberg (eds.), *Dynamic Approaches to the Understanding and Treatment of Alcoholism*. Free Press, New York, 1981, pp. 36–54.

———, *The Natural History of Alcoholism*. Harvard University Press, Cambridge, MA, 1983.

———, *The Natural History of Alcoholism Revisited*. Harvard University Press, Cambridge, MA, 1995.

Vaillant, George, and E. S. Milofsky, "The Etiology of Alcoholism: A Prospective Viewpoint," *American Psychologist*, 1982, 37:494–503.

Valle, Stephen K., *Alcoholism Counseling: Issues for an Emerging Profession*. Charles C Thomas, Springfield, IL, 1979.

Valle, Stephen K. (ed.), *Drunk Driving in America: Strategies and Approaches to Treatment*. Haworth, New York, 1986.

Valles, Jorge, *How to Live with an Alcoholic*. Essendes Special Editions, Simon & Schuster, New York, 1965.

———, *From Social Drinking to Alcoholism*. TANE Press, Dallas, TX, 1969.

Van Thiel, David H., et al., "Alcohol-induced Testicular Atrophy: An Experimental Model for Hypogonadism Occurring in Chronic Alcoholic Men," *Gastroenterology*, 1975, 69:326–32.

———, "Sex and Alcohol: A Second Peek," *New England Journal of Medicine*, 1976, 295:835–36.

Vannicelli, Marsha, *Group Psychotherapy with Adult Children of Alcoholics*. Johnson Institute, Minneapolis, 1989.

Victor, Maurice, et al., *The Wernicke-Korsakoff Syndrome and Related Neurologic Disorders Due to Alcoholism and Malnutrition*. 2d ed. F. A. Davis, Philadelphia, 1989.

"Vietnam," *Alcoholism and Addiction,* October 1988, 9(1):41–45, 60.

Von Wartburg, J. P., "Alcohol Dehydrogenase Distribution in Tissues of Different Species," in R. E. Popham (ed.), *Alcohol and Alcoholism.* University of Toronto Press, Toronto, 1970, pp. 13–21.

———, "Polymorphism of Human Alcohol and Aldehyde Dehydrogenase," *Advances in Alcohol and Substance Abuse,* 1981, 1(2): 7–23.

W., Bill, *The Language of the Heart: Bill W's Grapevine Writings.* AA Grapevine, New York, 1988.

W., Lois, *Lois Remembers.* Al-Anon Family Group Headquarters, New York, 1979.

Wagenaar, A. C., *Alcohol, Young Drivers, and Traffic Accidents.* D. C. Heath, Lexington, MA, 1983.

———, "Research Affects Public Policy: The Case of the Legal Drinking Age in the United States," *Addiction,* 1993, 88 (Supplement): 75S–81S.

Walker, Bill, *AA: The Way It Began.* Glen Abbey Books, Seattle, 1988.

Wallace, Barbara C., *Crack Cocaine: A Practical Treatment Approach for the Chemically Dependent.* Brunner-Mazel, New York, 1991.

Wallace, John, "Alcoholism from the Inside Out: A Phenomenological Analysis," in Nada J. Estes and M. Edith Heinemann (eds.), *Alcoholism: Development, Consequences and Interventions.* Mosby, St. Louis, 1986.

———, *Alcoholism: New Light on the Disease.* Edgehill, Newport, RI, 1990a.

———, "Controlled Drinking, Treatment Effectiveness, and the Disease Model of Addiction: A Commentary on the Ideological Wishes of Stanton Peele," *Journal of Psychoactive Drugs,* 1990b, 22:261–84.

Wallen, Jacqueline, *Addiction in Human Development.* Haworth Press, New York, 1993.

Wallgren, H., and H. Barry, *Actions of Alcohol.* 2 vols. American Elsevier, New York, 1970.

Walsh, D. C., et al., "A Randomized Trial of Treatment Options for Alcohol-abusing Workers," *New England Journal of Medicine,* 1991, 325(11):775–82.

Washton, Arnold. *Willpower's Not Enough: Understanding and Overcoming Addiction and Obsessive Behavior.* Harper/Lippincott, Philadelphia, 1989.

Washton, A. M., and Mark S. Gold. (eds.), *Cocaine: A Clinician's Handbook.* Guilford Press, New York, 1987.

Watts, Thomas D., *Prevention of Black Alcoholism: Issues and Strategies.* Praeger, New York, 1985.

———, *Black Alcohol Abuse and Alcoholism: An Annotated Bibliography.* Praeger, New York, 1986.

———, *Alcoholism in Minority Populations.* Charles C Thomas, Springfield, IL, 1989.

Watts, Thomas D., and R. Wright (eds.), *Black Alcoholism: Toward a Comprehensive Understanding.* Charles C Thomas, Springfield, IL, 1983.

Webb, W. R., and I. U. Degerli, "Ethyl Alcohol and the Cardiovascular System: Effects on Coronary Blood Flow," *JAMA,* March 28, 1965, 191(13):1055–58.

Wechsler, H., et al., "Health and Behavioral Consequences of Binge Drinking in College: A National Survey of Students at 140 Campuses," *JAMA,* 1994, 272(21):1672–77.

Wegscheider, Sharon, *Another Chance.* Science and Behavior Books, Palo Alto, CA, 1980.

Wegscheider-Cruse, Sharon, *Alcoholism and the Family: A Book of Readings.* Caron, Severna Park, MD, 1985.

———, *Choice-Making.* Health Communications, Deerfield Beach, FL, 1985.

———, *Understanding Me.* Health Communications, Deerfield Beach, FL, 1985.

Weil, Andrew, *The Natural Mind.* Houghton Mifflin, Boston, 1972.

———, "Letter from Andes: The New Politics of Coca," *The New Yorker,* May 15, 1995, pp. 70–80.

Weinberg, Jon R., *Sex and Recovery.* Recovery Press, P.O. Box 21215, Minneapolis, MN 55421, 1977, or Compcare reprint.

———, "Counseling the Person with Alcohol Problems," in Nada J. Estes and M. Edith Heinemann (eds.), *Alcoholism: Development, Consequences and Interventions.* Mosby, St. Louis, 1986.

Weisman, Maxwell, and Lucy Barry Robe, *Relapse/Slips.* Johnson Institute, Minneapolis, 1983.

West, James R. (ed.), *Alcohol and Brain Development.* Oxford University Press, New York, 1986.

West, Jolyon (ed.), *Alcoholism and Related Problems: Issues for the American Public.* Prentice-Hall, Englewood Cliffs, NJ, 1984.

Westermeyer, Joseph, "The Drunken Indian: Myths and Realities," *Psychiatric Annals,* 1974, 4(11):29–36.

———, *Primer on Chemical Dependency: A Clinical Guide to Alcohol and Drug Problems.* Williams & Wilkins, Baltimore, 1976.

Whelan, Elizabeth, *Preventing Cancer.* W. W. Norton, New York, 1978, Chapter 5.

White, W. F., "Personality and Cognitive Learning among Alcoholics with Different Intervals of Sobriety," *Psychological Reports,* 1965, 16:1125–40.

White, W. F., and P. T. L. Porter, "Self-concept Reports Among Hospitalized Alcoholics During Early Periods of Sobriety," *Journal of Consulting Psychology,* 1966, 13:352–55.

White, William L., *Critical Incidents: Ethical Issues in Substance Abuse Prevention and Treatment.* Lighthouse Training Institute, Bloomington, IL, 1993.

Whitehead, Paul C., "Effects of Liberalizing Alcohol Control Measures," *Addictive Behaviors,* 1976, 1:197–202.

———, *Alcohol and Young Drivers: Impact and Implications of Lowering the Drinking Age.* Research Bureau, Department of National Health and Welfare, Ottawa, 1977.

Widler, P.; K. Mathys; R. Brenneisen; P. Kalix; and H. U. Fisch, "Pharmacodynamics and Pharmacokinetics of Khat: A Controlled Study," *Clinical Pharmacology and Therapeutics,* 1994, 55(5): 556–62.

Williams, Roger J., *Alcoholism: The Nutritional Approach.* University of Texas Press, Austin, 1959.

———, *Biochemical Individuality: The Basis for the Genetotrophic Concept.* University of Texas Press, Austin, 1969.

Willoughby, Alan, *The Alcohol Troubled Person: Known and Unknown.* Nelson-Hall, Chicago, 1984.

Wilsnack, R., and S. Wilsnack (eds.), *Gender and Alcohol.* Rutgers, New Brunswick, NJ, 1994.

Wilsnack, S. C., "Effects of Social Drinking on Women's Fantasy," *Journal of Personality,* 1974, 42:43–61.

Wilsnack, S. C., and L. J. Beckman (eds.), *Alcohol Problems in Women: Antecedents, Consequences, and Intervention.* Guilford, New York, 1986.

Windle, Michael, and John S. Searles, *Children of Alcoholics: Critical Perspectives.* Guilford Press, New York, 1991.

Wine Institute, *Code of Advertising Standards.* Rev. ed. The Trade Association of California Winegrowers, San Francisco, 1988.

Wing, Nell, *Grateful to Have Been There.* Parkside Publishers, Park Ridge, IL, 1992.

Winokur, G.; T. Reich; J. Rimmer; and F. N. Pitts, "Alcoholism III: Diagnosis and Familial Psychiatric Illness in 259 Alcoholic Probands," *Archives of General Psychiatry,* 1970, 12:104–11.

Wiseman, J. P., *Stations of the Lost: Treatment of Skid Road Alcoholics.* Prentice-Hall, Englewood Cliffs, NJ, 1970.

———, *The Other Half: Wives of Alcoholics and Their Social-Psychological Situation.* Aldine, Chicago, 1992.

Woititz, Janet, *Going Home: A Reentry Guide for the Newly Sober.* CompCare, Minneapolis, 1981.

———, *Adult Children of Alcoholics.* Health Communications, Deerfield Beach, FL, 1983.

———, *Struggle for Intimacy.* Health Communications, Deerfield Beach, FL, 1985.

———, *Guidelines for ACoA Support Groups.* Health Communications, Deerfield Beach, FL, 1986.

Wolf, Irving, and M. E. Chafetz, "Social Factors in the Diagnosis of Alcoholism. II. Attitudes of Physicians," *QJSA,* 1965, 26:72–79.

Women and Cocaine: Personal Stories of Addiction and Recovery. Lowell House, Los Angeles, 1989.

Youcha, Geraldine, *Women and Alcohol: A Dangerous Pleasure.* Hawthorne, New York, 1986.

Zimberg, Sheldon, *The Clinical Management of Alcoholism.* Brunner/Mazel, New York, 1982.

Zimberg, Sheldon; John Wallace; and Sheila Blume (eds.), *Practical Approaches to Alcoholism Psychotherapy.* 2d ed. Plenum, New York, 1985.

Zuska, Joseph J., "Wounds Without Cause," *Bulletin of the American College of Surgeons,* October 1981, pp. 5–10.

Index